# THE GHOSTWRITERS

The European Union is often depicted as a cradle of judicial activism and a polity built by courts. Tommaso Pavone shows how this judge-centric narrative conceals a crucial arena for political action. Beneath the radar, Europe's political development unfolded as a struggle between judges who resisted European law and lawyers who pushed them to embrace change. Under the sheepskin of rights–conscious litigants and activist courts, these "Euro-lawyers" sought clients willing to break state laws conflicting with European law, lobbied national judges to uphold European rules, and propelled them to submit noncompliance cases to the European Union's supreme court – the European Court of Justice – by ghostwriting their referrals. By shadowing lawyers who encourage deliberate law-breaking and mobilize courts against their own governments, *The Ghostwriters* overturns the conventional wisdom regarding the judicial construction of Europe and illuminates how the politics of lawyers can profoundly impact institutional change and transnational governance.

TOMMASO PAVONE is Assistant Professor at the University of Arizona, where he researches how lawyers and courts impact social and political change. His work has been published in leading peer-reviewed journals and has won the LSA and the EUSA best dissertation prizes alongside APSA's Corwin Award. He holds a PhD from Princeton University.

CAMBRIDGE STUDIES IN LAW AND SOCIETY

Founded in 1997, Cambridge Studies in Law and Society is a hub for leading scholarship in socio-legal studies. Located at the intersection of law, the humanities, and the social sciences, it publishes empirically innovative and theoretically sophisticated work on law's manifestations in everyday life: from discourses to practices, and from institutions to cultures. The series editors have long-standing expertise in the interdisciplinary study of law, and welcome contributions that place legal phenomena in national, comparative, or international perspective. Series authors come from a range of disciplines, including anthropology, history, law, literature, political science, and sociology.

*Series Editors*

Mark Fathi Massoud, *University of California, Santa Cruz*

Jens Meierhenrich, *London School of Economics and Political Science*

Rachel E. Stern, *University of California, Berkeley*

*Past Editors*

Chris Arup, Martin Chanock, Sally Engle Merry,
Pat O'Malley, Susan Silbey

*A list of books in the series can be found at the back of this book.*

# THE GHOSTWRITERS

Lawyers and the Politics behind the Judicial
Construction of Europe

Tommaso Pavone
University of Arizona

CAMBRIDGE
UNIVERSITY PRESS

## CAMBRIDGE
### UNIVERSITY PRESS

Shaftesbury Road, Cambridge CB2 8EA, United Kingdom

One Liberty Plaza, 20th Floor, New York, NY 10006, USA

477 Williamstown Road, Port Melbourne, VIC 3207, Australia

314–321, 3rd Floor, Plot 3, Splendor Forum, Jasola District Centre, New Delhi – 110025, India

103 Penang Road, #05–06/07, Visioncrest Commercial, Singapore 238467

Cambridge University Press is part of Cambridge University Press & Assessment, a department of the University of Cambridge.

We share the University's mission to contribute to society through the pursuit of education, learning and research at the highest international levels of excellence.

www.cambridge.org
Information on this title: www.cambridge.org/9781009074988

DOI: 10.1017/9781009076326

First published 2022
First paperback edition 2022

*A catalogue record for this publication is available from the British Library*

*Library of Congress Cataloging-in-Publication data*
Names: Pavone, Tommaso, 1989– author.
Title: The ghostwriters : lawyers and the politics behind the judicial
    construction of Europe / Tommaso Pavone, University of Arizona.
Description: Cambridge, United Kingdom ; New York, NY : Cambridge
    University Press, 2022. | Series: Cambridge studies in law and society |
Based on author's thesis (doctoral - Princeton University, 2019). |
    Includes bibliographical references and index.
Identifiers: LCCN 2021044745 | ISBN 9781316513910 (hardback) |
    ISBN 9781009074988 (paperback) | ISBN 9781009076326 (epub)
Subjects: LCSH: Law–European Union countries–History. |
    European Union–History. | Lawyers–Political activity–European Union countries
Classification: LCC KJE947 .P38 2022 |
    DDC 341.242/2–dc23/eng/20211029
LC record available at https://lccn.loc.gov/2021044745

ISBN    978-1-316-51391-0    Hardback
ISBN    978-1-009-07498-8    Paperback

# CONTENTS

# FIGURES

# TABLE

# ACKNOWLEDGMENTS

This book concerns the politics of ghostwriters and their place in two worlds. First, it shadows lawyers in several national contexts in Europe as they choreograph legal actions and judicial decisions for others, triggering important policy reforms and institutional changes. In probing the influence of these actors in the social world, this book's secondary aim is to rectify their place in the research world. The forging of the world's sole supranational polity in Europe has spurred troves of perceptive scholarship. Therein, you will be hard-pressed to come across even passing references to the protagonists of this book.

And yet, many policymakers and jurists who witnessed firsthand the tortuous construction of the European Union (EU) and its legal order will likely know exactly who and what this book is about. They might even dismiss its findings as obvious. Yet well into the seven years it took to produce this manuscript, the implicit narrative that the following pages make explicit was hardly obvious to me. It took months before its contours became perceptible, years before I felt like I had a grip. In your hands is my imperfect yet best effort to piece this story together for you, in a more mercifully compressed span of time.

I wrote this book aspiring that it sit at the junction of several debates and research streams. Despite my initial worry that by trying to speak to everyone I would convince no one, I have been heartened that early drafts have been recognized by the three research communities that I most desired to engage: EU studies and comparative politics (the EU Studies Association [EUSA] awarded the dissertation prize to this manuscript, which also received an honorable mention for the Ernst B. Haas award of the European Politics section of the American Political Science Association [APSA]); law and society (this manuscript won the dissertation prize from the Law and Society Association [LSA]); and judicial politics (the manuscript received APSA's Edward S. Corwin award). I owe the realization of my dream of becoming a university professor, in no small part, to the members of the foregoing award committees who put my research on the map as I navigated the bloodiest academic job market in recent memory.

In broad brushstrokes, what does this book add? For readers interested in comparative and EU politics, *The Ghostwriters* contributes a revisionist, bottom-up, and less teleological analysis of European integration that places legal practitioners at the heart of the study of institutional change and transnational political development. For the law and society community, this book illuminates in textured detail how lawyers mobilize their boundary position between states, societies, and international organizations to construct the litigation strategies of clients and the behavior of judges when both prove less inclined to change than we might think. And for students of judicial politics, *The Ghostwriters* recenters the presumed policymaking drive of courts by elucidating when and how lawyers fuel processes of judicialization often misattributed to innate judicial activism.

This book began its life as a PhD dissertation at Princeton University and grew into a book at the University of Oslo and the University of Arizona, racking up a number of debts along the way. The Princeton Institute for International and Regional Studies (PIIRS) and the Bobst Center for Peace and Justice funded an initial round of interviews in the summer of 2015. PIIRS became my dissertation-writing home, while the PluriCourts Center at the University of Oslo became my book-revising home, providing the first office I could proudly call my own – at least until the COVID-19 pandemic intervened. In fall of 2020 I presented a draft of the revised manuscript at the School of Government and Public Policy at the University of Arizona. A few weeks later, on the same day that television networks called the 2020 US Presidential election for Joe Biden, I received a call with a job offer from Arizona. With these news, I gained the peace of mind necessary to finish revisions. The primary financial support for the book's fieldwork came from the American taxpayer, in the form of a Dissertation Grant (DDRIG) from the National Science Foundation's (NSF) Law & Social Sciences Program. Conversely, support for completing the book came from the Norwegian taxpayer, via the Research Council of Norway and its Centers of Excellence funding scheme under project number 223274, which financed my postdoctoral fellowship in Oslo.

The argument of this book has not been published before, but some chapters integrate and reproduce select materials from my journal articles. Chapters 2 and 3 build upon my 2018 *Journal of Law & Courts* article, "Revisiting Judicial Empowerment in the European Union," and expand its empirical scope from one country to three; a small selection of the interview evidence in Chapters 4 and 6 appears in my 2019 *European Law Journal* article (with Dan Kelemen), "The Evolving Judicial Politics of European Integration," and my 2020 *European Constitutional Law Review* article, "Putting European Constitutionalism in Its Place"; finally, a draft of the case study in Chapter 7 was published as my 2019 *Law & Society Review* article, "From Marx to Market."

Speaking of publishing, I am immensely appreciative of my acquisition editor, Tom Randall, and the series editors of the Cambridge Studies in Law and Society – Mark Massoud, Jens Meierhenrich, and Rachel Stern – who championed this project from the beginning and granted me more free rein than any first-time author can hope for. To be published in the flagship book series in socio-legal studies by the world's oldest university press is an honor. Along the way, three anonymous reviewers took the time to read the draft manuscript and provide thoughtful and thought-provoking feedback, which served as a guide during the final stretch of revisions in the tumultuous days of the COVID-19 pandemic.

Beyond funders and publishers, a number of individuals deserve special praise for graciously hosting me in their homes across various Italian, French, and German cities and putting up with my frenetic fieldwork schedule: Michele and Bianca in Genoa, Vera in Milan, Andrea and Denise in Trento, Carlo and Mario in Naples, Francesco in Bari, Valeria in Palermo, Anthony in Paris, Dominique in Marseille, Alexander in Berlin, Killy in Munich, and my cousin Tommaso, my aunt Flavia, and my sister Federica in Rome.

Next, all of my 353 interviewees contributed to this manuscript by brokering contacts, taking me out to dinner, and dedicating their precious time to my research. I hope that I have done justice to your generosity and that you will recognize your voices in this book. I was also privileged to gain access to the Historical Archives of the European Court of Justice under the auspices of the European University Institute in Florence. I particularly want to thank Dieter Schlenker, the archives director, as well as Valérie Manthevon and Giuliano Terzuoli for their invaluable assistance in opening select archival files and securing permission to reproduce excerpts. I am similarly grateful to *La Repubblica*, *leccenews24.it*, and Valerio Saracino for permission to reproduce photos in Chapter 8, and to Fondazione Corriere della Sera for granting me permission to reproduce materials from the Historical Archive of *Corriere della Sera* in Chapter 7. Finally,

I am indebted to Karen Alter for sharing archival and interview materials undergirding her first book, which blazed the way for scholars like me.

In the long and winding road to writing *The Ghostwriters*, a few mentors deserve special recognition. If I have been able to channel even a tiny fraction of the unrelenting energy, creativity, and intersdisciplinarity of Kim Scheppele, I would consider myself blessed. A genuine champion for others, Kim is capable of advising one's path in the academy (and in life) in ways that always leave you feeling realistic yet hopeful. She is the scholar, teacher, colleague, and mentor that I aspire to be. Dan Kelemen embraced an apprenticeship model that socialized me within political science. As we began to coauthor together, Dan taught me that intelligence does not derive from expressing the world's complexity but from making its complexity intelligible. With Dan I gained not just a professional role model and intellectual partner but also a true friend. When the conformist pathologies of academic life proved too much, Paul Frymer helped bring me back to the light. In those moments when I felt like a misfit, Paul reminded me that I belong and that there is dignity in not chasing after fads. Finally, I began my PhD drawn to Andy Moravcsik's towering stature in the discipline. I soon came to recognize Andy's pugnaciousness as his form of flattery, a signal that your ideas are serious and worthy of critical engagement. I resurrected this skeptical spirit to keep myself honest, and this book is better for it.

My extended family of intellectual interlocutors – too many to name them all – has contributed indirectly to this project in essential ways. I am especially indebted to Chris Achen, Karen Alter, Amedeo Arena, Lola Avril, Paul Baumgardner, Chantal Berman, Erik Bleich, Fausto Capelli, Marta Cartabia, Pola Cebulak, Siv Cheruvu, Rachel Cichowski, Killian Clarke, Lisa Conant, Bill Davies, Julian Dederke, John DiIulio, Cassie Emmons, Chuck Epp, Federico Fabbrini, Orfeo Fioretos, Andreas Føllesdal, Jennifer Fredette, Bryant Garth, Tom Ginsburg, Laura Goffman, Mark Graber, Peter Hall, Terry Halliday, Silje Hermansen, Ran Hirschl, Mikael Holmgren, Dimitry Kochenov, Jan Komárek, Tomek Koncewicz, Lauren Konken, Jay Krehbiel, Jasper Krommendijk, Jeff Kucik, Paulette Kurzer, Tolya Levshin, Jack Levy, Mikael Madsen, James Mahoney, Dorte Martinsen, Mark Massoud, Roberto Mastroianni, Juan Mayoral, Sophie Meunier, Hans Micklitz, Steve Monroe, Daniel Naurin, Fernanda Nicola, Michal Ovádek, Laurent Pech, Ingolf Pernice, Will Phelan, Mark Pollack, Morten

Rasmussen, Alessandro Rosanò, Urška Šadl, Enrico Salmini Sturli, Scott Siegel, Taylor St. John, Øyvind Stiansen, Dan Tavana, Geir Ulfstein, Antoine Vauchez, Manuel Vogt, Michelle Weitzel, Chad Westerland, Keith Whittington, Jennifer Widner, Deborah Yashar, and Yang-Yang Zhou. Some of these individuals may not remember it, but they shaped my growth as a social scientist by supplying inspiring conversations, thoughtful written feedback, essential contacts, and invaluable friendship when I needed it most.

Finally, I must acknowledge those whose love has warmed my spirit and kept me going. My parents, Gerardo and Fabrizia, took the gamble of leaving Europe for America with the futures of my brother, Alessandro, and me in mind. The United States has not always proven kind to their own aspirations, but of one thing I am certain: never would I have dreamt of becoming the first person in my family to obtain a PhD without my parents' courage and sacrifice. Their unrelenting love has since been bolstered by Jocelyn, Brian, Lorenzo, Klara Jaicel, and my partner, Carlos, an astonishingly beautiful human being who blesses my life daily with his kindness, whimsy, and those handsome black eyes that first struck me on that evening at the Metropolitan Opera in New York.

Dedicating something as abstruse as an academic book to those you hold dear has always struck me as a rather curious way of expressing gratitude. Then again, academics are a decidedly curious bunch. So forgive me, my loves, but this one is for you.

**PART ONE**

# INTRODUCTION

## CHAPTER ONE

# THE POLITICS OF GHOSTWRITING LAWYERS

This is a book about political actors who rarely make the headlines and a political outcome that often does. It is about the concealed politics behind a conspicuous transformation: the growing reliance on law and courts to shape public policy and resolve political struggles. Across many countries, memories of men on horseback past who built states through war[1] have been gradually displaced by jurists in robes who govern through law.

This transformation is often attributed to the political empowerment of courts and the activism of judges themselves. As successive waves of democratization swept the post–World War II (WWII) world, many countries across Europe, Asia, the Americas, and Africa committed to liberal constitutionalism. Two dozen transnational courts with permanent jurisdiction proliferated alongside states' obligations under international law. As judicial supremacy waxed, parliamentary sovereignty and executive power partially waned. Policymakers were increasingly forced to govern alongside an emboldened network of judges at home and abroad. Scholars, journalists, and politicians disagree about whether to celebrate or malign this "judicialization of politics," but few deny this momentous change.[2]

---

[1] See: Finer, Samuel. 1966. *The Man on Horseback*. London: Pall Mall Press; Tilly, Charles. 1993. *Coercion, Capital, and European States, A.D. 990–1992*. New York, NY: Wiley-Blackwell.

[2] For some exemplary contributions to this debate, see: Shapiro, Martin, and Alec Stone Sweet. 2002. *On Law, Politics, and Judicialization*. New York, NY: Oxford University Press; Ginsburg, Tom. 2003. *Judicial Review in New Democracies: Constitutional Courts in Asian Cases*. New York, NY: Cambridge University Press; Hirschl, Ran. 2007. *Towards Juristocracy: The Origins and Consequences of the New Constitutionalism*.

The European Union (EU) is widely regarded as the "model of expansive judicial lawmaking" propelling this "new world order."[3] For it is national judiciaries that enable the EU to govern through law and implement policy across twenty-seven member states without a supranational army, an independent tax system, and a capacious bureaucracy. In this view, audacious national judges mobilized to hold states accountable to their treaty obligations and claim judicial review powers denied by their domestic legal orders. They referred cases of state noncompliance to the EU's supreme court – the European Court of Justice (ECJ) – and refused to apply national laws violating supranational rules. Along the way they Europeanized domestic public policies and supported the ECJ's rise as "the most effective supranational judicial body in the history of the world."[4]

*The Ghostwriters* challenges this judge-centric narrative by showing how it conceals a crucial arena for political action. Without decentering courts as fulcrums of policymaking and governance, it uses the puzzle of how Europe became "nowhere as real as in the field of law"[5] to rethink the origins, agents, and mechanisms behind the judicialization of politics. Contrary to the conventional wisdom, I argue that the promise of uniting Europe through law and exercising judicial review was not sufficient to transform national courts into transnational policymakers. National judges broadly resisted empowering themselves with European law, for they were constrained by onerous workloads, lackluster legal training, and the careerist pressures of their domestic judicial hierarchies. The catalysts of change proved instead to be a group of lesser-known "Euro-lawyers" facing fewer bureaucratic shackles.[6] Under the sheepskin of rights-conscious litigants and activist courts, these World War II survivors pioneered a remarkable

Cambridge, MA: Harvard University Press; Alter, Karen. 2014. *The New Terrain of International Law: Courts, Politics, Rights*. Princeton, NJ: Princeton University Press.

[3] Alter, Karen, and Laurence Helfer. 2017. *Transplanting International Courts*. New York, NY: Oxford University Press, at 4; Slaughter, Anne-Marie. 2004. *A New World Order*. Princeton, NJ: Princeton University Press, at 33–34; 134–135.

[4] Stone Sweet, Alec. 2004. *The Judicial Construction of Europe*. New York, NY: Oxford University Press, at 1.

[5] Vauchez, Antoine. 2015. *Brokering Europe: Euro-Lawyers and the Making of a Transnational Polity*. New York, NY: Cambridge University Press, at 1.

[6] I borrow this term from: Dezelay, Yves, and Bryant Garth. 1995. "Merchants of Law as Moral Entrepreneurs." *Law & Society Review* 29(1): 27–64, at 54; Vauchez, Antoine. 2009. "The Force of a Weak Field: Law and Lawyers in the Government of Europe." *International Political Sociology* 2(2): 128–144, at 132. I explain and distinguish how I use the term "Euro-lawyer" later in this chapter.

repertoire of strategic litigation. They sought clients willing to break national laws conflicting with European law, lobbied judges about the duty and benefits of upholding EU rules, and propelled them to submit cases to the ECJ by ghostwriting their referrals.

Beneath the radar, Europe has to a large extent been built by lawyers who converted state judiciaries into transmission belts linking civil society with supranational institutions. Yet Euro-lawyering was neither limitless in its influence nor static in its form. Over time, burgeoning networks of corporate law firms displaced the more idealistic pioneers of Euro-lawyering, and the politicization of European integration exposed the limits of strategic litigation in the absence of vigorous public advocacy. These evolutions stratified access to transnational justice, catalyzed new risks and opportunities for court-driven change, and continue to refract the EU's capacity to govern through law.

By shadowing lawyers who encourage deliberate law-breaking and mobilize courts against their own governments, this book reworks conventional understandings of judicial policymaking, advances a novel narrative of the judicial construction of Europe, and illuminates how the politics of lawyers can have a profound impact on institutional change and transnational governance.

## 1.1 A THEORY OF LAWYERS, COURTS, AND POLITICAL DEVELOPMENT

This book "starts with individuals to better understand institutions – to show how institutions impose themselves on actors while institutions themselves are also the product of the actors' continuing struggles."[7] Specifically, it uses the European experience as a springboard to tackle three broad questions:

- First, how do political orders forged through multilevel networks of courts emerge and evolve?
- Second, why would judges resist these institutional changes if they would augment their own power?
- Finally, under what conditions can lawyers mobilize as agents of change and overcome resistances to judicialization?

---

[7] Dezelay, Yves, and Bryant Garth. 1996. *Dealing in Virtue: International Commercial Arbitration and the Construction of a Transnational Legal Order*. Chicago, IL: University of Chicago Press, at 16–17.

Answering these queries begets a number of important payoffs. First, it pushes us to critically assess a "long presum[ption]" that courts in Europe are the primary architects of their own empowerment and are uniquely supportive of transnational governance.[8] If European integration has been spearheaded by a spontaneous, self-reinforcing, and jointly empowering partnership between national judges and their counterparts at the ECJ,[9] then the European experience has little in common with other world regions where judiciaries are less independent and courts are reluctant to flex their policymaking muscles. But if European judges have actually borne similar apprehensions and wrestled with their own institutional constraints, then the judicial construction of Europe may be less exceptional and more comparable than we thought. Even in what appears to be a transnational cradle of judicial activism, judicialization may be less of an inevitable process driven by the ambitions of judges and more of a contingent process hinging on how "judicial institutions interact with the nonjudicial world."[10]

Second, this revisionist lens invites us to unpack when lawyers can erode judicial obduracy and become motors of court-driven change. It focuses our gaze on the fact that judges and lawyers do not always work in tandem: though they jointly constitute the heart of a "legal complex" of professionals, surface-level alliances for judicial policymaking may conceal deeper struggles between bar and bench.[11] Identifying when and why lawyers are the first movers pushing for institutional change requires that we take their agency seriously instead of focusing predominantly on structural factors.[12] It also requires that we resist vaporizing lawyers into go-betweens[13] or pawns maneuvered

---

[8] Alter and Helfer, *Transplanting International Courts*, at 7–8, 16.

[9] For a discussion of this view, see: Stone Sweet, *Judicial Construction of Europe*, 20–21; Kelemen, R. Daniel, and Alec Stone Sweet. 2017. "Assessing the Transformation of Europe." In *The Transformation of Europe*, Marlene Wind and Miguel Poiares Maduro, eds. New York: Cambridge University Press, at 204.

[10] Gonzáles-Ocantos, Ezequiel. 2016. *Shifting Legal Visions: Judicial Change and Human Rights Trials in Latin America*. New York, NY: Cambridge University Press, at 289.

[11] See: Halliday, Terence, Lucien, Karpik and Malcolm Feeley. 2007. *Fighting for Political Freedom*. New York, NY: Bloomsbury, at 9–23.

[12] For more on this critique, see: Vanhala, Lisa. 2009. "Anti-discrimination Policy Actors and Their Use of Litigation Strategies." *Journal of European Public Policy* 16(5): 738–754, at 740–741.

[13] For instance, Fligstein and Stone Sweet describe legal mobilization in the EU as a sequence of "lawyers activated by their clients and judges activated by lawyers":

by other actors – such as social movements, interest groups, and resourceful clients[14] – presumed to be the true protagonists of political action. A few perceptive studies have begun trekking this path by demonstrating that the experience, reputation, and size of lawyers' teams condition judicial decisions.[15] But political scientists still need to move beyond probing *attributes* of lawyer capability to portray how their *agency* can shape processes of political development transcending individual wins or losses in court. This is surprising, given that one of the central concerns of political science – the development of the modern state – is intimately tied to the rise of the legal profession.[16] As states bestowed status to lawyers by granting them monopoly rights to legal representation, lawyers labored to legitimate rule-based social order and supplied expertise to fledgling bureaucracies.[17] From

Fligstein, Neil, and Alec Stone Sweet. 2002. "Constructing Polities and Markets." *American Journal of Sociology* 107(5): 1206–1243, at 1222; See also: Shapiro, Martin. 1993. "The Globalization of Law: An Institutionalist Account of European Integration." *Indiana Journal of Global Legal Studies* 1(1): 37–64, at 41–42.

[14] See: Hilson, Chris. 2002. "New Social Movements: The Role of Legal Opportunity." *Journal of European Public Policy* 9(2): 238–255; Smith, Miriam. 2005. "Social Movements and Judicial Empowerment: Courts, Public Policy, and Lesbian and Gay Organizing in Canada." *Politics & Society* 33(2): 327–353; Szmer, John, Donald Songer, and Jennifer Bowie. 2016. "Party Capability and the US Courts of Appeals: Understanding Why the Haves Win." *Journal of Law and Courts* 4(1): 65–102.

[15] See: McGuire, Kevin. 1995. "Repeat Players in the Supreme Court." *Journal of Politics* 57(1): 187–196; Kritzer, Herbert. 1998. *Legal Advocacy: Lawyers and Nonlawyers at Work*. Ann Arbor, MI: University of Michigan Press; Haire, Susan, Roger Brodie, and Stefanie Lindquist. 1999. "Attorney Expertise, Litigant Success, and Judicial Decisionmaking in the US Courts of Appeals." *Law & Society Review* 33(3): 667–686; Szmer, John, Susan Johnson, and Tammy Sarver. 2007. "Does the Lawyer Matter? Influencing outcomes on the Supreme Court of Canada." *Law & Society Review* 41(2): 279–304.

[16] Halliday, Terence, and Lucien Karpik. 1997. *Lawyers and the Rise of Western Political Liberalism*. New York, NY: Oxford University Press; Dezelay, Yves, and Mikael Rask Madsen. 2012. "The Force of Law and Lawyers." *Annual Review of Law & Social Science* 8: 433–452, at 439–440.

[17] Abel, Richard. 1988. "Lawyers in the Civil Law World." In *Lawyers in Society, Volume II: The Civil Law World*, Richard Abel and Philip Lewis, eds. Berkeley and Los Angeles, CA: University of California Press; Bourdieu, Pierre. 1986. "The Force of Law." *Hastings Law Journal* 38: 805–853, at 820, 846.

Hungary to Italy to the United States,[18] lawyers made states and states made lawyers.

To be sure, tracing the constitutive relationship between lawyering and political development can prove remarkably elusive. Lawyers rarely spearhead protests, mount coups, levy taxes, or pass controversial legislation that make the headlines, least of all in their own name. As Alexis de Tocqueville wrote in *Democracy in America*:

> [L]awyers ... form a party which is but little feared and scarcely perceived, which has no badge peculiar to itself, which adapts itself with great flexibility to the exigencies of the time ... it acts upon the country imperceptibly, but it finally fashions it to suit its purposes.[19]

The challenge of intercepting the imperceptible ways that lawyers fashion politics renders polities that govern through courts ideal laboratories for social inquiry. With less of a role for soldiers and bureaucrats, these "law-states"[20] allow us to place the politics of lawyers in starker relief. While there are many examples of such polities – from the nineteenth-century American "state of courts and parties"[21] to present-day "transnational legal orders" like the Andean and Caribbean Communities[22] – none is as exemplary and successful as the EU. Having grown into the world's only quasi-federal, supranational polity, EU officials have nonetheless lacked the resources to

---

[18] Malatesta, Maria. 1995. "The Italian Professions from a Comparative Perspective." In *Society and the Professions in Italy, 1860–1914*, Maria Malatesta, ed. New York, NY: Cambridge University Press, at 23; Olgiati, Vittorio, and Valerio Pocar. 1988. "The Italian Legal Profession: An Institutional Dilemma." In *Lawyers in Society, Volume II*, Richard Abel and Philip Lewis, eds. Berkeley and Los Angeles, CA: University of California Press, at 342–343.

[19] Tocqueville, Alexis de. 2003 [1862]. *Democracy in America, Vols. I & II*. New York, NY: Barnes & Noble Books, at 254–255.

[20] Strayer, Joseph. 1970. *On the Medieval Origins of the Modern State*. Princeton, NJ: Princeton University Press, at 61. See also: Kelemen, R. Daniel, and Tommaso Pavone. 2018. "The Political Geography of Legal Integration: Visualizing Institutional Change in the European Union." *World Politics* 70(3): 358–397, at 358–360.

[21] Skowronek, Stephen. 1992. *Building a New American State: The Expansion of National Administrative Capacities, 1877–1920*. New York, NY: Cambridge University Press, at 29.

[22] Halliday, Terence, and Gregory Shaffer. 2015. *Transnational Legal Orders*. New York, NY: Cambridge University Press; Caserta, Salvatore. 2020. *International Courts in Latin America and the Caribbean: Foundations and Authority*. New York, NY: Oxford University Press; Alter and Helfer, *Transplanting International Courts*.

command compliance[23] and emulate the pathways of traditional state-building.[24] Yet their postwar commitment to building a transnational "community based on the rule of law"[25] opened a political opportunity to invoke the force of law to mobilize judges, reshape state institutions, and compensate for the EU's weak military and administrative capacity.

But why, precisely, was it lawyers that grabbed the baton of change, and what was the extent of their influence? This is the political story that remains untold. In the United States, studies of cause lawyering, elite law firms, and lawyer-politicians[26] have peeled back how "lawyers make the politics and produce the law."[27] Yet these accounts often presume that lawyers' political influence may not travel beyond the uniquely litigious American system of "adversarial legalism."[28] In response, other scholars have started uncovering how lawyers in authoritarian and transitional regimes are often at the

---

[23] The EU's budget relies upon customs duties and semi-voluntary state contributions, and amounts to just 1 percent of Europe's GDP – only 6 percent of which is allocated to administration. The executive body of the EU – the European Commission – is staffed by just 33,000 employees, comparable to the civil service of a medium-sized European city. See: European Commission. 2015a. "Myths and Facts." Available at: http://ec.europa.eu/budget/explained/myths/myths_en.cfm; European Commission. 2015b. "Frequently Asked Questions." Available at: http://ec.europa.eu/budget/explained/faq/faq_en.cfm; European Commission. 2015c. "Who We Are." Available at: http://ec.europa.eu/civil_service/about/who/index_en.htm.

[24] Kelemen, R. Daniel, and Kathleen McNamara. 2021. "State-building and the European Union: Markets, War, and Europe's Uneven Political Development." *Comparative Political Studies* (ahead of print): 1–29.

[25] Case 294/83, *Les Verts v. European Parliament* [1986] ECR 1339, at par. 23; For historical overviews, see: Scheingold, Stuart. 1965. *The Rule of Law in European Integration.* New Haven, CT: Yale University Press.

[26] For instance, see: Sarat, Austin, and Stuart Scheingold, eds. 2006. *Cause Lawyers and Social Movements.* Stanford, CA: Stanford University Press; Halliday, Terence. 1987. *Beyond Monopoly: Lawyers, State Crises, and Professional Empowerment.* Chicago, IL: University of Chicago Press; Hain, Paul, and James Piereson. 1975. "Lawyers and Politics Revisited." *American Journal of Political Science* 19(1): 41–51.

[27] Dezelay, Yves, and Bryant Garth. 1997. "Law, Lawyers, and Social Capital." *Social & Legal Studies* 6(1): 109–141, at 132.

[28] See: Kagan, Robert. 2003. *Adversarial Legalism: The American Way of Law.* Cambridge, MA: Harvard University Press; Kagan, Robert. 1997. "Should Europe Worry About Adversarial Legalism?" *Oxford Journal of Legal Studies* 17: 165–184. For a nuanced retort, see: Kelemen, R. Daniel. 2011. *Eurolegalism: The Transformation of Law and Regulation in the European Union.* Cambridge, MA: Harvard University Press.

forefront of civil rights battles in the name of political liberalism.[29] Yet in the liberal civil law states of post—WWII Europe, the absence of such dramatic political struggles and the specter of "legal science" continues to obscure lawyers' influence "behind a cult of traditions or legal technique."[30] Even the few instances where lawyer activism is acknowledged[31] usually end up being treated as curiosities or exceptions that prove the rule. And the presumed rule is that the judicial construction of Europe has always been "essentially, if not exclusively, a judicial task" wherein courts actively "retain control over such matters."[32] Or, as the French government tersely put it in 1958: "The [European] common market can have nothing to do with lawyers."[33]

Yet there is more to this story than meets the eye. Europe's political development through law is an exemplary story of how lawyers mobilize courts to catalyze institutional change, alongside the limits, mutations, and consequences accompanying these efforts. To make this case, this book combines a geocoded dataset of thousands of lawsuits, hundreds of interviews across three of the EU's founding states, and historical evidence from newspaper and court archives. In so doing, I build a historical institutionalist theory explicating when lawyers – and not other potential change agents – are best placed to advance political development through law, alongside the obstacles they encounter and

---

[29] Halliday, Karpik and Feeley, *Fighting for Political Freedom*; Liu, Sida, and Terence Halliday. 2016. *Criminal Defense in China: The Politics of Lawyers at Work*. New York, NY: Cambridge University Press; González-Ocantos, *Shifting Legal Visions*; Massoud, Mark. 2021. *Shari'a, Inshallah: Finding God in Somali Legal Politics*. New York, NY: Cambridge University Press.

[30] Dezelay and Garth, "Law, Lawyers, and Social Capital," 132; See also: Merryman, John Henry, and Rogelio Perez-Perdomo. 2007. *The Civil Law Tradition*, 3rd ed. Stanford, CA: Stanford University Press, at 61–67.

[31] One well-known example is of Belgian lawyer Éliane Vogel-Polsky's campaign for gender equality in the ECJ's *Defrenne* cases. See: Cichowski, Rachel. 2004. "Women's Rights, the European Court, and Supranational Constitutionalism." *Law & Society Review* 38(3): 489–512.

[32] Schermers, Henry. 1987. "Introduction." In *Article 177 EEC*, Henry Schermers, Christiaan Timmermans, Alfred Kellermann, and J. Stewart Watson, eds. New York, NY: Elsevier, at 12; Koopmans, Thijmen. 1987. "The Technique of the Preliminary Question – A View from the Court of Justice." In *Article 177 EEC: Experiences and Problems*. Henry Schermers, Christiaan Timmermans, Alfred Kellermann, and J. Stewart Watson, eds. New York, NY: Elsevier, at 328.

[33] Quote from a reply to the national bar association president, found in: Laguette, Serge-Pierre. 1987. *Lawyers in the European Community*. Luxembourg: Office for Official Publications of the European Communities, at 269.

the conditions under which their efforts take (and do not take) root. The result recasts judge-centric narratives of European integration and reveals how legal mobilization in Europe takes on a different hue from the better-known American context.

### 1.1.1 Euro-lawyers and a Repertoire for Court-Driven Change

Why have lawyers, rather than judges, tended to be the drivers of the EU's political development through law? What advantages did lawyers have as agents of institutional change? In this prototypical struggle between innovation and inertia, the key is to consider the extent to which prospective change agents are anchored in place by preexisting institutions.

After all, processes of political development do not occur atop a *tabula rasa*: they are reconstructions of previous relations of authority.[34] By the time the European Community was born in 1957, national states initially broken by war boasted reformed judiciaries and increasingly entrenched constitutions. Unwilling to displace these structures and give up the sovereignty necessary to create a European superstate, postwar statesman opted for a more incremental process of integration instead.[35] For example, rather than creating a US-style federal system of European courts, the Treaty founding the European Community provided for a single supreme court: the ECJ in Luxembourg. It then granted national courts the ability to apply European rules in the disputes before them, and to refer interpretive questions or noncompliance cases to the ECJ.[36] As European law was "layered"[37] atop national law, areas of ambiguity and conflict were bound to emerge. And national courts, through their prospective dialogue with the ECJ, became the stage upon which these incongruences would be resisted to maintain the status-quo or exploited to promote European integration.

---

[34] Orren, Karen, and Stephen Skowronek. 2004. *The Search for American Political Development*. New York, NY: Cambridge University Press, at 21.

[35] Boerger-de Smedt, Anne. 2012. "Negotiating the Foundations of European Law, 1950–57." *Contemporary European History* 21(3): 339–356, at 347–348.

[36] This mechanism, the "preliminary reference procedure," is described in detail in Chapter 2.

[37] See: Streeck, Wolfgang, and Kathleen Thelen. 2005. *Beyond Continuity*. New York: Oxford University Press, at 22–30; Mahoney, James, and Kathleen Thelen. 2010. "A Theory of Gradual Institutional Change." In *Explaining Institutional Change: Ambiguity, Agency, and Power*, James Mahoney and Kathleen Thelen, eds. New York, NY: Cambridge University Press, at 16–22.

Upon this stage, the prospect of institutional change is likely to be perceived first by those actors least constrained by preexisting relations of authority. When institutions evolve incrementally, those most embedded in existing institutions will seldom incur the short-term costs of long-run change:[38] everyday habits and forms of consciousness tied to the application of entrenched rules can powerfully obscure the benefits of novelty.[39] In contrast, mediatory actors facing fewer constraints who stand to ideologically or materially benefit from a new institutional environment are more likely to mobilize as innovators. Historically, then, judges anchored in civil service judiciaries have tended toward stasis, whereas lawyers shuttling between states, societies, and nascent international institutions have tended toward change.

This claim flips the conventional wisdom that national judges bore sufficient discretion and institutional incentives to spur their participation in the construction of Europe. In this view, judges in lower national courts in particular became "wide and enthusiastic" "motors"[40] of European integration by referring cases of state noncompliance with EU law to the ECJ.[41] Through this "quiet revolution,"[42] judges empowered themselves to disapply national legislation and rebel against disliked decisions of their own supreme courts.[43] They acquired expansive judicial review powers unavailable under domestic law and

---

[38] Bednar, Jenna, and Scott E. Page. 2018. "When Order Affects Performance: Culture, Behavioral Spillovers, and Institutional Path Dependence." *The American Political Science Review* 112(1): 82–98, at 94.

[39] González-Ocantos, *Shifting Legal Visions*, at 32–36.

[40] See, respectively: Weiler, Joseph. 1991. "The Transformation of Europe." *The Yale Law Journal* 100: 2403–2483, at 2426; Alter, Karen. 1996. "The European Court's Political Power." *West European Politics* 19(3): 458–487, at 467.

[41] This book spans the periods before and after the Treaty of Maastricht subsumed the European Economic Community (EEC) into one of the three pillars of the EU in 1993 and the EU acquired a single legal personality in 2009 via the Treaty of Lisbon. For ease of reading, I use European, Community, and EU law interchangeably, though I try to avoid using "EU" anachronistically.

[42] Weiler, Joseph H. H. 1994. "A Quiet Revolution: The European Court of Justice and Its Interlocutors." *Comparative Political Studies* 26(4): 510–534.

[43] Other works in this tradition include: Burley, Anne-Marie, and Walter Mattli. 1993. "Europe Before the Court." *International Organization* 47(1): 41-76; Alter, Karen. 2001. *Establishing the Supremacy of European Law.* New York, NY: Oxford University Press. For a critical review, see: Pavone, Tommaso. 2018. "Revisiting Judicial Empowerment in the European Union." *Journal of Law & Courts* 6(2): 303–331.

supplied the ECJ with a stream of cases to "federaliz[e] the polity in all but name" via path-breaking judgments,[44] thereby opening the floodgates to subsequent litigation.[45]

By positing that European integration is driven by judicial activism, this "judicial empowerment thesis" became the dominant explanation of Europe's political development through law.[46] While perceptive in many ways, this narrative under-theorizes or dismisses the role of litigants and lawyers[47] while ignoring the enduring constraints on judges in civil service judiciaries. Lower court judges in continental Europe resemble "street-level bureaucrats"[48] more than they do the "culture heroes" animating the history of the common law.[49] Historically undertrained in European law, swamped by piles of case files involving routine national rules, and subject to careerist pressures within their judicial hierarchies that dissuade Europeanizing rebellions, these judges have had plenty of pressing institutional incentives to *resist their own empowerment.* In turn, these incentives cultivated a set of entrenched habits and what I will call an "institutional consciousness" favoring inertia: for judges to break free of it, they would have to be pushed by outside actors intent on minimizing the costs and highlighting the benefits of judicial policymaking.

It was in this light that in the 1960s and 1970s, a small group of Euro-lawyers mobilized to advance the judicial construction of Europe. By "Euro-lawyers," I do not mean jurists within the Brussels bubble or global fields such as international commercial arbitration. While the latter have animated several important studies,[50] the protagonists of this book are a vanguard of lesser-known attorneys who kept their feet

---

[44] Stone Sweet, *Judicial Construction of Europe*, at 1.

[45] Cichowski, Rachel. 2007. *The European Court and Civil Society: Litigation, Mobilization, and Governance.* New York, NY: Cambridge University Press.

[46] Kelemen and Stone Sweet, "Assessing the Transformation of Europe," at 193.

[47] For instance, Weiler claims that "litigants are usually not politically motivated" and act "willy-nilly"; Weiler, "Transformation of Europe," at 2421; Mattli and Slaughter suggest that lawyers and litigants act as a "constraint" on judicial policymaking: Mattli, Walter, and Anne-Marie Slaughter. 1998. "The Role of National Courts in the Process of European Integration." In *The European Court and National Courts,* Alec Stone Sweet Anne-Marie Slaughter, and Joseph Weiler, eds. New York, NY: Hart, at 264.

[48] Lipsky, Michael. 2010. *Street-Level Bureaucracy, 30th ed.* New York, NY: Russell Sage.

[49] Merryman and Perez-Perdomo, *The Civil Law Tradition,* at 34–37.

[50] See: Dezelay and Garth, "Merchants of Law as Moral Entrepreneurs"; Vauchez, *Brokering Europe*; Avril, Lola. 2019. "Le Costume Sous la Robe: Les avocats en

in their home states and sought to change the behavior of local courts. They did not so much labor to construct a supranational legal order to which they could escape as they sought to bring home Europe's "juris touch."[51]

To be sure, some of these entrepreneurs did have stints working at fledgling European institutions, and all were WWII survivors eager to found and participate in lawyers' associations across national borders. While their aspiration to function as a "private army of the [European] Communities"[52] may be overstated, their room for political maneuvering was significant. Unlike domestic judges or EU bureaucrats, lawyers could shuttle between their local community, state judiciaries, and European institutions, mobilizing courts and clients along the way. Yet they were not completely free-floating actors, and this is key. Their embeddedness in society endowed them with the local knowledge to cultivate potential litigants and salient controversies for legal mobilization. Their transnational expertise and institutional access enabled them to translate these controversies into courtroom disputes revealing noncompliance with EU rules or enticing opportunities for Europeanization via judicial policymaking. By working this Janus-faced embeddedness,[53] lawyers moved beyond a passive role as go-betweens without disturbing the appearance that other actors – namely litigants and judges – were doing all the work (see Figure 1.1). Instead of agency flowing through them it radiated out of them:[54] they became *ghostwriters* of change, catalyzing a rights-consciousness in litigants and an activism in judges appearing to be innate.

The evidence suggests that these political entrepreneurs were neither principally driven by "ruthless egoism" nor because "this course appear[ed] profitable," as many existing accounts imply.[55] Few could imagine the importance that the fledgling European Community would

professionnels multicartes de l'État régulateur européen." PhD dissertation, Université Paris 1 Panthéon-Sorbonne.

[51] Kelemen, *Eurolegalism*, at 19.

[52] Vauchez, *Brokering Europe*, at 88.

[53] On conceptualizing this type of "boundary work," see: Liu, Sida. 2013. "The Legal Profession as a Social Process." *Law & Social Inquiry* 38(3): 670–693, at 673.

[54] In my reading, scholars have recognized the "radiating effects of courts," but have paid less attention to the radiating effects of lawyers. See: Galanter, Marc. 1983. "The Radiating Effects of Courts." In *Empirical Theories about Courts*, Keith Boyum and Lynn Mather, eds. New York, NY: Longmans.

[55] This assumption underlies accounts inspired by "neofunctionalist" theory. See: Haas, Ernst. 1958. *The Uniting of Europe: Political, Social, and Economic Forces*,

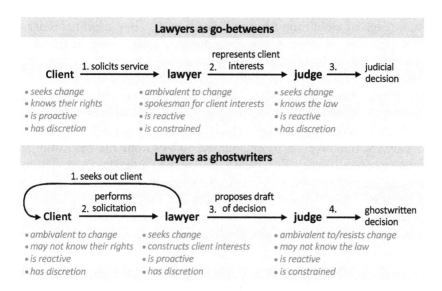

Figure 1.1 The radiating effect of lawyers: from go-betweens to ghostwriters

eventually muster, and it was hardly evident in the 1960s and 1970s that there was money to be made in the construction of what the ECJ hoped would become a "new legal order of international law."[56] More decisive in light of their WWII experience was their idealism (favoring a liberal Europe governed by the rule of law) and their pleasure of exercising their agency (to challenge and reshape state policies); self-interest (to gain a competitive advantage in the legal services market) played a secondary role. Despite being a relatively uncoordinated group, these pioneers encountered shared institutional obstacles and consequently converged upon a common, transposable *repertoire for change* via the construction of test cases. They sought clients willing to break national laws conflicting with EU law, occasionally turning to friends or family if a "real" client was unavailable. In so doing, they began to cultivate a European "legal consciousness" within civil society.[57] Once in court, they pivoted from nurturing local

*1950–1957.* Stanford, CA: Stanford University Press, at xxxiv; Burley and Mattli, "Europe before the Court," at 54; Stone Sweet, *Judicial Construction of Europe,* at 41.

[56] Case 26/62, *Van Gend & Loos* v. *Nederlandse Administratie der Belastingen* [1963] ECR 1, at 12.

[57] Sarat, Austin, and William Felstiner. 1989. "Lawyers and Legal Consciousness." *Yale Law Journal* 98(8) (1989): 1663–1688.

knowledge to mobilizing labor and expertise.[58] They educated judges about the duty and benefits of upholding EU rules – even in the face of contradictory legislation or supreme court decisions – by drafting detailed memos serving as crash courses in European law. And they ghostwrote the referrals to the ECJ that judges were unable or reluctant to write themselves, supplying the European Court with opportunities to deliver pathbreaking judgments.

Lawyers thus worked to emancipate judges from the institutional constraints obstructing Europeanization and to integrate them within a fledgling transnational network of European courts. At the same time, their efforts were most effective when they least upset existing bureaucratic relations of authority: that is, in decentralized judiciaries where lower courts were already habituated to occasionally engage in bottom-up policymaking. Europe's judicial construction does not so much invert or revolutionize domestic judicial politics, as is often claimed.[59] Rather, it tends to channel and build upon these politics.

Finally, this account suggests that it was not only – or primarily – the supranational entrepreneurship of the European Court that "convinced lower national courts to leapfrog the national judicial hierarchy and work directly with the ECJ."[60] The more proximate and decisive pushes came from the bottom-up. By the close of the 1970s, nearly half of all national court referrals to the ECJ from the three largest founding member states of the EU (Italy, France, and Germany) could be retraced to just a handful of enterprising lawyers, who traveled from city to city and courtroom to courtroom soliciting the judicial construction of Europe.

### 1.1.2 The Evolution of Euro-Lawyering and Judicial Policymaking

Legal mobilization and judicial policymaking did not stop with the first Euro-lawyers. Since the 1980s, this process has evolved and become unevenly institutionalized across space and time. While ghostwriting permitted the first Euro-lawyers to cultivate the sense that a "rights revolution" was blossoming,[61] it also produced a repertoire for court-

---

[58] By expertise, I mean both "substantive expertise" concerning European laws and principles and "process expertise" concerning how to solicit the ECJ. On this distinction, see: Kritzer, *Legal Advocacy*, at 203.

[59] Weiler, "Quiet Revolution"; Alter, *Establishing the Supremacy of European Law*, at 20.

[60] Burley and Mattli, "Europe before the Court," at 62, 58, fn.78.

[61] Kelemen, R. Daniel. 2003. "The EU Rights Revolution: Adversarial Legalism and European Integration." In *The State of the European Union 6: Law, Politics, and*

driven change that rising networks of corporate law firms could co-opt and whose limits crystallized with heightened contestation of judicial policymaking. As Euro-lawyering began clustering within corporate law firms, it both regularized and stratified access to the EU's multilevel judicial system. And as compliance with disruptive judicial interventions could no longer be presumed in an increasingly politicized climate, it illuminated the neglected importance of pairing strategic litigation with vigorous public advocacy.

The evolution of Euro-lawyering thus represents a broader passage from idealism to interest and from concealment to contestation. In the first instance, studies of institutional change often begin with individuals with strong normative commitments and participatory drives.[62] That the first European lawsuits were of limited worth hardly dissuaded the first Euro-lawyers. But as the judicial construction of Europe progressed, it could no longer rest on the shoulders of a few idealistic World War II survivors: mobilizing European law had to become perceived as advantageous to later generations of practitioners. This is why Euro-lawyering took root in cities such as Milan, Paris, and Hamburg with burgeoning business clusters ready to reward specialized legal services. Facing this clientele "situated" lawyers' legal consciousness,[63] as some practitioners began treating local practice and European law as an inseparable and professionally lucrative ecology. As lawyers agglomerated into larger "Euro-firms"[64] to navigate this ecology, interactions between businesses, Euro-lawyers, and specialized chambers of local courts regularized hand-in-hand with the judicialized enforcement of EU law. And as Euro-firms displaced the first Euro-lawyers, soliciting the ECJ to further business interests began trumping the ideal of building a political community based on the rule of law.

Yet Euro-lawyering did not corporatize and become entrenched everywhere. Across many subnational communities, the political economy of litigation was (and remains) hostile to Euro-lawyering and judicial policymaking. In cities such as Marseille, Naples, and Palermo, the

*Society*, Tanja Borzel and Rachel Cichowski, eds. New York, NY: Oxford University Press.

[62] Parsons, Craig. 2003. *A Certain Idea of Europe*. Ithaca, NY: Cornell University Press; St. John, Taylor. 2019. *The Rise of Investor-State Arbitration: Politics, Law, and Unintended Consequences*. New York, NY: Oxford University Press.

[63] Nielsen, Laura Beth. 2000. "Situating Legal Consciousness." *Law & Society Review* 34(4): 1055–1090.

[64] Vauchez, Antoine, and Bruno de Witte, eds. 2013. *Lawyering Europe: European Law as a Transnational Social Field*. New York, NY: Hart.

legal profession remains balkanized into generalist solo-practitioners. While a few stubborn lawyers may try to mobilize European law, these efforts are crowded out by streams of more localized and mundane lawsuits. In turn, tending to the variegated demands of a poorer clientele cultivates a place-based identity[65] that dismisses specializing in EU law as a one-way ticket to unemployment instead of a tool to attract clients. Mobilizing European law and the ECJ becomes perceived as something one does in "global cities,"[66] but not in communities at the margins of globalization. And with no lawyers invoking EU law and soliciting referrals to the ECJ, local judges have little incentive to shed entrenched habits and do so themselves.

This argument builds on studies emphasizing that litigation depends on resource mobilization, thus stratifying which social actors take advantage of judicial policymaking.[67] It also integrates a more recent strand of sociological institutionalist scholarship highlighting identity and legal consciousness as drivers of legal mobilization.[68] Yet *The Ghostwriters* adds four distinct contributions.

First, I leverage a bottom-up perspective to illuminate why legal mobilization and judicial policymaking are not destined to generate an expansive litigation cycle. Functionalist scholars argue that as national courts solicit rulings from the ECJ, these rulings set off a "feedback loop" where new areas of noncompliance are exposed, new rights claims are generated, and new litigation opportunities are mobilized.[69] Yet these opportunities do not cascade upon all people and places equally. I will show that a cycle of litigation and judicial policymaking can take hold in fertile terrains where Euro-lawyers and Euro-firms cluster, but it emphatically does not characterize lived experience in communities where the ECJ's on-the-ground authority

---

[65] Altman, Irwin, and Setha Low, eds. 1992. *Place Attachment*. Boston, MA: Springer.

[66] Sassen, Saskia. 2004. "The Global City: Introducing a Concept." *Brown Journal of World Affairs* 11(2): 27–44.

[67] Galanter, Marc. 1974. "Why the 'Haves' Come out Ahead: Speculations on the Limits of Legal Change." *Law & Society Review* 9(1): 95–160.

[68] Vanhala, Lisa. 2011. *Making Rights a Reality?: Disability Rights Activists and Legal Mobilization*. New York, NY: Cambridge University Press; Arrington, Celeste. 2016. *Accidental Activists: Victim Movements and Government Accountability in Japan and South Korea*. Ithaca, NY: Cornell University Press.

[69] Stone Sweet, Alec, and Thomas Brunell. 1998. "The European Court and National Courts." *Journal of European Public Policy* 5(1): 66–97; Stone Sweet, *Judicial Construction of Europe*, at 41; Cichowski, *European Court and Civil Society*, at 16–22.

is hard to perceive and the political economy of litigation obstructs mobilizing EU law. Instead of a uniformly rising tide, Euro-lawyering in national courts generates a patch-worked quilt whose transformative opportunities are increasingly "contained"[70] within resourceful client markets.

Second, although the demands of resource mobilization condition where EU judicial enforcement becomes *entrenched*, they do not explain how this process *emerged* in the first place. These two dimensions are often collapsed in American studies of litigation where the "haves" consistently come out ahead.[71] For instance, the US Supreme Court tends to only hear cases after a broad "litigation support structure" has financed lawsuits across multiple jurisdictions and spurred conflicts among lower federal courts.[72] Yet because the ECJ proved more accessible,[73] the first Euro-lawyers could develop a repertoire for court-driven change before anything like a litigation support structure emerged. Indeed, the institutional environment in Europe retarded such resource mobilization: to resist US-style adversarial legalism, states such as Germany, Italy, and France forbade legal partnerships well into the 1970s,[74] businesses, NGOs, and interest groups were initially reluctant to invoke their EU rights in court, and even law schools resisted integrating European law in their curricula.[75]

Third, existing studies tend to collapse lawyers into proxies of social movements or big business, while neglecting the spatial and professional logics of legal mobilization. On the one hand, some treat lawyers as part and parcel of the advocacy groups they represent.[76] On the other hand, some cast lawyers as a bundle of "resources (person power,

---

[70] Conant, Lisa. 2002. *Justice Contained: Law and Politics in the European Union*. Ithaca, NY: Cornell University Press.

[71] Songer, Donald, Reginald Sheehan, and Susan Haire. 1999. "Do the Haves Come Out Ahead Over Time?" *Law & Society Review* 33(4): 811–832.

[72] See: Epp, Charles. 1998. *The Rights Revolution: Lawyers, Activists, and Supreme Courts in Comparative Perspective*. Chicago, IL: University of Chicago Press; Perry, H. W. 1994. *Deciding to Decide*. Cambridge, MA: Harvard University Press.

[73] If stubborn lawyers could persuade *any* judge, even the humblest local court, to refer a case, the ECJ's mandatory jurisdiction in reference cases would usually require it to answer.

[74] Partnerships of more than five lawyers were permitted in France after 1972; In Italy, partnerships were legalized in 1973; In Germany, as late as 1967 no law firm had more than nine employees. See: Abel, "Lawyers in the Civil Law World," at 19–20.

[75] Kelemen, *Eurolegalism*; Vauchez, *Brokering Europe*, at 77.

[76] Cichowski, *European Court and Civil Society*.

expertise, money)" wielded by "the already powerful."[77] In truth, Euro-lawyering is neither a social movement nor a mere corporate resource. Lawyers have their own interests and identities shaped by the contexts they inhabit, and these play a key role in how lawyers mobilize civil society and businesses dependent on their tactical repertoires. The evolution of Euro-lawyering thus follows its own situated logic: it hinges on how practitioners rework political economy and the demands of their clientele into a place-based consciousness that structures the costs and benefits of mobilizing EU law.

Finally, Euro-lawyering has not only undergone a "big, slow-moving ... and invisible"[78] process of uneven corporatization. Since the 1990s the judicial construction of Europe has also been politicized and subjected to occasionally vigorous contestation,[79] raising questions about the capacity of lawyers to act as brokers of compliance when controversy erupts. Scholars worry that as public scrutiny of European policymaking grows and backlash against disruptive ECJ rulings becomes more frequent, law may no longer serve as a "mask and shield" for political development,[80] foreshadowing a possible "dejudicialization of international politics."[81] While this narrative perceptively highlights that judicialization is not inherently self-reinforcing, it also

---

[77] Börzel, Tanja. 2006. "Participation through Law Enforcement." *Comparative Political Studies* 39(1): 128–152, at 130.

[78] Pierson, Paul. 2003. "Big, Slow-Moving, and ... Invisible: Macrosocial Processes in the Study of Comparative Politics." In *Comparative Historical Analysis in the Social Sciences*, James Mahoney and Dietrich Rueschemeyer, eds. New York, NY: Cambridge University Press.

[79] Hooghe, Liesbet, and Gary Marks. 2009. "A Postfunctionalist Theory of European Integration: From Permissive Consensus to Constraining Dissensus." *British Journal of Political Science* 39(1): 1–23; Zürn, Michael. 2016. "Opening up Europe: Next Steps in Politicisation Research." *West European Politics* 39(1): 164–182.

[80] Blauberger, Michael, and Dorte Martinsen. 2020. "The Court of Justice in times of politicisation: 'Law as a Mask and Shield' Revisited." *Journal of European Public Policy* 27(3): 382–399.

[81] Madsen, Mikael Rask, Pola Cebulak, and Micha Weibusch. 2018. "Backlash against International Courts: Explaining the Forms and Patterns of Resistance to International Courts." *International Journal of Law in Context* 14: 197–220; Voeten, Erik. 2020. "Populism and Backlashes against International Courts." *Perspectives on Politics* 18(2): 407–422; Abebe, Daniel, and Tom Ginsburg. 2019. "The Dejudicialization of International Politics?" *International Studies Quarterly* 63(3): 521–530; Turnbull-Dugarte, Stuart, and Daniel Devine. 2021. "Can EU Judicial Intervention Increase Polity Scepticism?" *Journal of European Public Policy* (online first): 1–26; Conant, Lisa. 2021. "Failing Backward? EU Citizenship, the Court of Justice, and Brexit." *Journal of European Public Policy* 28(10): 1592–1610.

risks trading one teleology for another. Politicization and backlash campaigns are not destined to yield regressive outcomes,[82] and under certain conditions they can actually broaden opportunities for court-driven change.

This counterintuitive outcome hinges on lawyers "creating their own legal opportunities" by supplementing behind-the-scenes ghost-writing with proactive public advocacy.[83] As choreographers of strategic litigation, Euro-lawyers can time when the law is mobilized and the ECJ is solicited to take advantage of favorable shifts in the political climate and to blindsight potentially recalcitrant interest groups. Even when these efforts provoke protest and backlash, the resulting controversies also illuminate the relevance of EU law and generate public demand to "vernacularize" the prospect of socio-legal change.[84] Here, Euro-lawyers' capacity to translate between European legal expertise and local knowledge positions them favorably to act as *interpretive mediators*[85] in the public sphere. By proactively engaging local stakeholders and the press, they can translate EU laws into popular discourse to promote change, preempt backlash, and awaken dormant "compliance constituencies."[86] Conditional on tapping into some diffuse public support, contentious politics can magnify Euro-lawyers' capacity to cultivate people's legal consciousness and make EU law "real" on the ground.[87]

In short, as politicization intermittently punctures a process of European "integration by stealth,"[88] a broader array of stakeholders can be made aware, often for the first time, that European law is relevant to daily life and can serve as a tool for change. Public controversies can be negotiated to amplify "the radiating effects of courts" and law.[89] It is in the absence of mediatory public advocacy that politicization

[82] Alter, Karen, and Michael Zürn. 2020. "Theorising Backlash Politics." *British Journal of Politics and International Relations* 22(4): 739–752, at 740.

[83] Vanhala, Lisa. 2012. "Legal Opportunity Structures and the Paradox of Legal Mobilization by the Environmental Movement in the UK." *Law & Society Review* 46(3): 525.

[84] Merry, Sally Engle. 2009. *Human Rights and Gender Violence: Translating International Law into Local Justice.* Chicago, IL: University of Chicago Press, at 193–194.

[85] Fischer, Frank. 2000. *Citizens, Experts, and the Environment.* Durham, NC: Duke University Press, at 80.

[86] Alter, *New Terrain of International Law*, at 19.

[87] Vanhala, *Making Rights a Reality?*

[88] Majone, Giandomenico. 2005. *Dilemmas of European Integration.* New York, NY: Oxford University Press.

[89] Galanter, "Radiating Effects of Courts."

spikes the risk that EU law is scorned as "descend[ing] on the everyday as an all-powerful outsider,"[90] emboldening backlash and entrenching noncompliance. Lawyers can play a key role in tipping the scales, but only if they shed the ghostwriter's cloak and plunge into the public sphere.

To put the puzzle pieces together, Figure 1.2 breaks down the outline of the foregoing argument into time periods, explanatory variables, mechanisms, outcomes, and scope conditions. I next turn to the research design and data that I use to evaluate this theory, concluding with a road map for the rest of this book.

## 1.2 TRACING THE POLITICS OF LAWYERS

### 1.2.1 Case Selection and Research Design

The contours of this book's argument first emerged in the summer of 2015, when I was conducting a set of preliminary interviews with jurists in Italy. I was interested in what the judicial construction of Europe looked like from the ground-up, and the patchwork of local socio-legal communities in one of the EU's largest founding member states seemed like a fertile place to start. While I brought little theoretical baggage with me, through "soaking and poking"[91] I expected that my fieldwork would primarily focus on the behavior of entrepreneurial judges within national judiciaries and interest groups within civil society.

As conversations with Italian jurists proceeded, it became clear that lawyers had played a pivotal role and I lacked a ready-made theory to make sense of it. As I scouted the existing literature, it felt like much scholarly theorizing echoed Dick the Butcher in Shakespeare's *Henry VI*: "The first thing we do, let's kill all the lawyers."[92] I therefore developed a research design to enable me to trace how Euro-lawyering emerged, evolved, and impacted judicial policymaking. I chose to focus on Italy, France, and Germany for two reasons:

- *Empirical and historical importance:* As the three largest founding member states of the EU, Italy, France, and Germany provide six decades' worth of historical record that can be probed and compared

---

[90] Sarat, Austin, and Thomas Kearns. 1995. *Law in Everyday Life*. Ann Arbor, MI: University of Michigan Press, at 5.

[91] Fenno, Richard. 1978. *Home Style: Congressmen in Their Districts*. New York, NY: Little, Brown, and Company, at 250–252.

[92] Boyarsky, Saul. 1991. "'Let's Kill All the Lawyers'." *Journal of Legal Medicine* 12: 571–574.

| Periodization | Explanatory variables → | | Mechanisms → | Outcomes → | Scope Conditions |
|---|---|---|---|---|---|
| Origins 1960s to early 1980s | Embeddedness in preexisting institutional environment | *Higher:* national judges | Labor and career costs of embracing new practices | Resistance to change | Less careerist judges in decentralized judiciaries more open to change |
| | | *Lower:* national lawyers | Pleasure in agency and discretion to pursue new practices | Openness to change | Most lawyers continue with business as usual |
| Evolutions late 1980s to present | Resourcefulness of local market for legal services | *Higher:* corporate hubs and wealthier cities | Incentives to specialize in EU law and corporatize | Hot spot of litigation and judicialization | Politicization may deepen or erode hot spot |
| | | *Lower:* rural regions and poorer cities | Disincentives to specialize in EU law and corporatize | Cold spot of litigation and judicialization | Politicization may deepen or erode cold spot |

Figure 1.2 Theory road map: lawyers and the judicial construction of Europe

to trace the evolution of Euro-lawyering and its impact on judicial policymaking. Indeed, these states account for about a third of *all* national court referrals to the ECJ from the EU's twenty-seven member states. Furthermore, many of these references enabled the ECJ to deliver pathbreaking decisions advancing the EU's political development, such as those establishing the supremacy of European law, the doctrine of fundamental rights protections, the principle of mutual recognition, and the principle of state liability.[93] Hence in both quantitative and qualitative terms, Italy, France, and Germany account for an important share of lawsuits undergirding the judicial construction of Europe.

- *Theoretical relevance:* Italy, France, and Germany represent the very cases that inspired the prevailing understanding of the judicial construction of Europe as an outcome spurred by the empowerment of courts and the activism of judges. They thus serve as crucial "pathway cases"[94] to retrace the sources of courts' behavior and probe the hitherto neglected role that lawyers may have played. Furthermore, these three countries' judicial hierarchies vary in ways that enable testing this book's argument that bureaucratic pressures constrain judges' willingness to turn to EU law and embrace judicial policymaking. Embedded in a centralized state, the French courts – particularly the administrative courts – are more hierarchically organized than Italy's, which in turn is a more hierarchical judiciary than Germany's. We should thus expect French judges to have been more resistant to Euro-lawyers' efforts than their German counterparts. Finally, these three countries boast diverse subnational political economies ranging from financial centers such as Paris to global port cities such as Hamburg to more economically marginalized cities such as Naples. This subnational tapestry allows us to unpack the variegated corporatization of Euro-lawyering and explain why Euro-lawyers clustered in some communities over others.

Of course, fieldwork is never undertaken in countries as a whole, but in specific field sites. In identifying these sites, I did not seek to

---

[93] Case 6/64, *Flaminio Costa* v. *ENEL* [1964], ECR 1141; Case 11/70, Internationale Handelsgesellschaft [1970], ECR 1126; Case 120/78, *Rewe-Zentral AG* v. *Bundesmonopolverwaltung für Branntwein* ("Cassis de Dijon") [1979], ECR 649; Joined cases C-6/90 and C-9/90, *Andrea Francovich and others* v. *Italian Republic* [1991], ECR I-5357.

[94] Gerring, John. 2007. "Is There a (Viable) Crucial-Case Method?" *Comparative Political Studies* 40(3): 231–253.

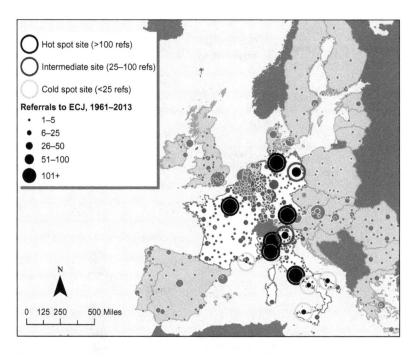

Figure 1.3 Referrals to the ECJ from national courts (1961–2013), with field sites
Note: Map excludes referrals from supreme courts with nation-wide jurisdiction, since including these referrals can generate an inflated picture of the extent to which local judges solicit the ECJ.

approximate a random or representative sample of subnational communities. Rather, I aimed to follow previous field researchers who purposively visited a variety of local contexts and interacted with diverse sets of people.[95] In particular, I selected sites that maximized my capacity to trace the impact of Euro-lawyering on judicial policymaking and to compare how Euro-lawyering evolves and becomes unevenly rooted. I started by geocoding a proxy measure for my outcome variable: the number of cases referred from national courts to the ECJ from 1961 to 2013. Figure 1.3 visualizes the distribution of these referrals, with Italy, France, and Germany in lighter shading. Drawing on these maps to finalize site selection, I balanced what I will call "hot spots" – cities where judges started dialoguing with the ECJ in the 1960s, and local (non-supreme) courts have since referred many (over 100) cases to the ECJ – with "cold spots" – cities where this judicial dialogue struggled

[95] Pachirat, Timothy. 2018. *Among Wolves: Ethnography and the Immersive Study of Power*. New York, NY: Routledge, at 85–88.

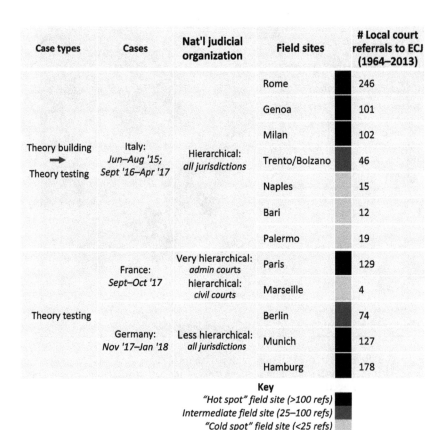

| Case types | Cases | Nat'l judicial organization | Field sites | # Local court referrals to ECJ (1964–2013) |
|---|---|---|---|---|
| Theory building → Theory testing | Italy: Jun–Aug '15; Sept '16–Apr '17 | Hierarchical: *all jurisdictions* | Rome | 246 |
| | | | Genoa | 101 |
| | | | Milan | 102 |
| | | | Trento/Bolzano | 46 |
| | | | Naples | 15 |
| | | | Bari | 12 |
| | | | Palermo | 19 |
| Theory testing | France: Sept–Oct '17 | Very hierarchical: *admin courts* hierarchical: *civil courts* | Paris | 129 |
| | | | Marseille | 4 |
| | Germany: Nov '17–Jan '18 | Less hierarchical: *all jurisdictions* | Berlin | 74 |
| | | | Munich | 127 |
| | | | Hamburg | 178 |

**Key**
*"Hot spot" field site (>100 refs)*
*Intermediate field site (25–100 refs)*
*"Cold spot" field site (<25 refs)*

Figure 1.4 Case selection design and primary field sites
*Note:* Preliminary reference statistics comprise local non-supreme courts in each site.

to take root and less than 25 references originated during the same time period.[96] A mapping of the twelve primary field sites within the overall case selection design is summarized in Figure 1.4. To be sure, I also took side trips when possible to meet with critical interviewees or acquire additional archival materials.

Ultimately, the most extensive fieldwork period (ten months) was undertaken in Italy, for two reasons. First, Italy has received less attention in studies of European integration than France and Germany, yet as we will see, litigation before Italian courts was central to the judicial construction of Europe. Second, I used a comparative-

---

[96] On the promise of studying European integration by looking outward from a variety of cities, see: Mamadouh, Virginie, and Anne van Wegeningen, eds. 2016. *Urban Europe: Fifty Tales of the City.* Amsterdam: Amsterdam University Press.

sequential approach, wherein Italy first served as a "theory-building" case study to generate inductive insights in a preliminary phase of fieldwork. As a native Italian and fluent speaker, Italy was the best context to gain initial access and start soaking and poking. Then in a second fieldwork phase, I returned to Italy and expanded research to France and Germany, which approximated "theory-testing" case studies to corroborate findings, explore generalizability, and identify scope conditions.[97] Since fieldwork in France and Germany was more targeted, it did not need to be as exhaustive or intensive.

### 1.2.2 Original Data

Novel arguments often require novel data. So from 2015 to 2019, I developed a tripartite empirical strategy to gather data impinging on this book's argument (see Figure 1.5). In particular, I combine the satellite view of the transnational using geospatial data, the granular view of the subnational using fieldwork, and the temporal view of the past using oral histories and previously unavailable archival sources.

First, I built upon my efforts with R. Daniel Kelemen to construct the first geocoded dataset of national court referrals to the ECJ from the 1960s to the present.[98] Spatial analyses of these data not only helped me identify and select sites for fieldwork, but they also enabled me to visualize the evolving geography of national court referrals to the European Court. These empirics lie at the heart of my analysis of the origins and evolution Euro-lawyering. Throughout this book, geospatial data anchor, complement, and set the stage for qualitative evidence.

---

[97] On inductive or iterative research designs for comparative analysis, see: Pavone, Tommaso. 2022. "Selecting Cases for Comparative Sequential Analysis: Novel Uses for Old Methods." In *The Case For Case Studies*, Michael Woolcock, Jennifer Widner, and Daniel Ortega-Nieto, eds. New York, NY: Cambridge University Press; Yom, Sean. 2015. "From Methodology to Practice: Inductive Iteration in Comparative Research." *Comparative Political Studies* 48(5): 616–644.

[98] For the first publication using these data, see: Kelemen, R. Daniel, and Tommaso Pavone. 2016. "Mapping European Law." *Journal of European Public Policy* 23(8): 1118–1138. For more recent analyses using geospatial data, see: Dyevre, Arthur, and Nicolas Lampach. 2020. "Subnational Disparities in EU Law Use Exploring the GEOCOURT Dataset." *Journal of European Public Policy* 28(4): 615–631; Pavone, Tommaso. 2020. "Putting European Constitutionalism in Its Place: The Spatial Foundations of the Judicial Construction of Europe." *European Constitutional Law Review* 16: 669–690.

| Type of original data | Functions | Sources |
| --- | --- | --- |
| Geocoded litigation data: preliminary references from national courts to ECJ | Identify field sites and visualize the evolving geography of Euro-lawyering and national courts' engagement with EU law | Online case law database of the European Court of Justice |
| Semi-structured interviews: with 353 lawyers, judges, and law professors | Provide oral histories and testimony of how lawyers mobilize EU law and catalyze judicial policymaking | Fifteen months of field research in Italy, France, and Germany, 2015–2018 |
| Archival data: original dossiers of references to ECJ, newspaper records | Corroborate and complement oral histories, reveal textual evidence of lawyers' litigation and public advocacy strategies | Historical archives of the EU, lawyers' personal archives, newspaper archives |
| Participant observation: in national courts across 12 European cities | Contextualize interviews with judges concerning their habits and behavior under institutional constraints | Fifteen months of field research in Italy, France, and Germany, 2015–2018 |

Figure 1.5 Types, functions, and sources of original data gathered

Second, I conducted 353 semi-structured interviews with lawyers, judges, and law professors (the list of interviewees is included in the Appendix). More than any other data gathered, interviews barraged me with serendipitous insights that prompted revisions and refinements to this book's argument. First, I managed to interview nearly all of the first Euro-lawyers who are still alive, and these conversations provided key oral histories. Second, interviews opened unexpected opportunities to access documents from lawyers' personal archives. Third, interviewees helped me perceive the preliminary work and tacit practices left out of official litigation records. To construct as unbiased a narrative as I could, I repeatedly "triangulate"[99] between conversations with lawyers and judges. Only speaking to lawyers about their efforts would offer no way of evaluating the extent to which they might "exaggerate their roles."[100] In the spirit of the dictum to "trust but verify,"[101] conversations with judges thus proved essential for validating lawyers' claims to agency and influence.

Third, whenever possible I conducted scattershot participant observation in national courts. I asked to meet judges in the places where

---

[99] Arksey, Hilary, and Peter Knight. 1999. *Interviewing for Social Scientists*. Thousand Oaks, CA: SAGE, at 21–32; Gallagher, Mary. 2013. "Capturing Meaning and Confronting Measurement." In *Interview Research in Political Science*, Layna Mosley, ed. Ithaca, NY: Cornell University Press.

[100] Berry, Jeffrey M. 2002. "Validity and Reliability Issues in Elite Interviewing." *PS: Political Science & Politics* 35(4): 679–682, at 680.

[101] Moravcsik, Andrew. 2014. "Trust but Verify." *Security Studies* 23(4): 663–688.

they work and kept a fieldnotes journal[102] of these visits that ultimately spun a couple hundred pages. I depended heavily on these observations and "notes to self" to reconstruct the daily pressures and practices embodied by judges. Visiting national courts alerted me in a way that no phone interview could to the ways that courthouses, as built and resource-scarce spaces, can ensconce habits and institutional identities resistant to change. I left convinced that the value of interview evidence is impoverished if it is not contextualized with an ethnographic sensibility.[103]

Finally, I benefitted immensely from a stroke of luck: "In 2014, the [European] Court of Justice ... began shipping more than 270 boxes of official documents with restricted access to the public to Villa Salviati, home of the Historical Archives of the European Union at the European University Institute (EUI) in Florence."[104] For a notoriously secretive institution that had been denying researchers access to any archival evidence for decades, the ECJ's move was something of an unexpected coup. In the subsequent two years, I requested and obtained access to over 100 of the original dossiers for the first lawsuits punted to the European Court in the 1960s and 1970s, and I received permission to reproduce excerpts of these files in this book. These materials reveal traces and corroborations of the "hidden transcript"[105] of Euro-lawyering that was first relayed to me by interviewees. In particular, they provide granular historical evidence of lawyers ghostwriting national courts' referrals to the ECJ, enabling an initial archival reconstruction of how lawyers educated, cajoled, and partially substituted themselves for national judges. To trace selected lawsuits in greater depth and compensate for the unavailability of

---

[102] I relied heavily upon: Sanjek, Roger. 1990. *Fieldnotes*. Ithaca, NY: Cornell University Press.

[103] On the value of taking institutional and spatial context seriously in interview research, see: Smith, Dorothy. 2005. *Institutional Ethnography: A Sociology for People*. New York, NY: Rowman & Littlefield; Cramer Walsh, Katherine. 2012. "Putting Inequality in Its Place: Rural Consciousness and the Power of Perspective." *American Political Science Review* 106(3): 517–532; Schatz, Edward. 2009. "Ethnographic Immersion and the Study of Politics." In *Political Ethnography*, Edward Schatz, ed. Chicago, IL: University of Chicago Press, at 5.

[104] Nicola, Fernanda, and Bill Davies. 2017. *EU Law Stories: Contextual and Critical Histories of European Jurisprudence*. New York, NY: Cambridge University Press, at 1.

[105] Scott, James C. 1990. *Domination and the Arts of Resistance: Hidden Transcripts*. New Haven, CT: Yale University Press, at 4–5; 183–184.

dossiers, I supplement this evidence with newspaper records, secondary historical accounts, and the personal archives of lawyers.

## 1.3 THE ROAD AHEAD

What can readers expect from the rest of this book, and what are the primary empirical findings and theoretical takeaways of each chapter that follows?

*The Ghostwriters* is organized into three parts, each comprised of two to three chapters, followed by a conclusion that evaluates the overall findings. The logic of this road map is as follows. First, I explain why national judges embedded in civil service judiciaries have, on their own, historically been ill-suited as agents of institutional change, how the EU's political development builds upon domestic judicial politics, and how these findings reconfigure predominant understandings of judicial empowerment (Part II: Chapters 2–4). Second, I reconstruct the origins of Euro-lawyering and trace its impact on judicial behavior, unpacking the repertoire for court-driven change that lawyers developed and how it was gradually co-opted by clustered networks of corporate law firms (Part III: Chapters 5 and 6). Third, I explain how the growing politicization of European integration reshapes Euro-lawyering and opens new risks and opportunities for legal mobilization and judicial policymaking (Part IV: Chapters 7 and 8). Finally, I take stock of this book's findings in light of the mounting challenges plaguing democracy, the rule of law, and judicial policymaking in Europe (Chapter 9). A more detailed mapping of the proposed theory to this book's chapters is provided in Figure 1.6.

More precisely, Chapter 2 sets the descriptive, theoretical, and methodological stage for probing the behavior of national courts in the process of European integration. I describe the central mechanism through which national courts can partner with the ECJ to apply EU law and promote integration: the preliminary reference procedure. I summarize how courts' use of this procedure has been theorized by the prevailing account of Europe's judicial construction: the "judicial empowerment thesis." And I highlight suggestive qualitative and quantitative evidence that this thesis may conceal as much as it reveals. This chapter concludes by outlining the fieldwork strategy deployed to revisit the thesis and probe whether national judges have harbored more diffuse and persistent resistances to EU law, the ECJ, and judicial review than has been acknowledged. Readers familiar with the judicial

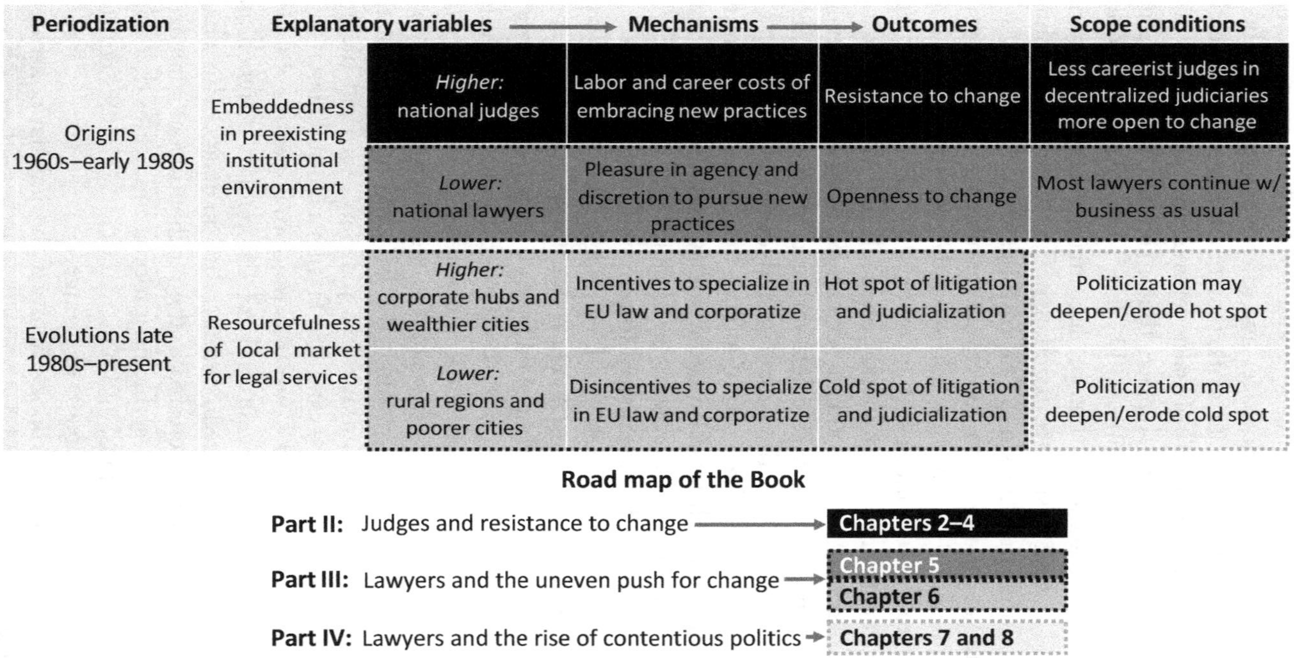

| Periodization | Explanatory variables | | Mechanisms → | Outcomes → | Scope conditions |
|---|---|---|---|---|---|
| Origins 1960s–early 1980s | Embeddedness in preexisting institutional environment | *Higher:* national judges | Labor and career costs of embracing new practices | Resistance to change | Less careerist judges in decentralized judiciaries more open to change |
| | | *Lower:* national lawyers | Pleasure in agency and discretion to pursue new practices | Openness to change | Most lawyers continue w/ business as usual |
| Evolutions late 1980s–present | Resourcefulness of local market for legal services | *Higher:* corporate hubs and wealthier cities | Incentives to specialize in EU law and corporatize | Hot spot of litigation and judicialization | Politicization may deepen/erode hot spot |
| | | *Lower:* rural regions and poorer cities | Disincentives to specialize in EU law and corporatize | Cold spot of litigation and judicialization | Politicization may deepen/erode cold spot |

**Road map of the Book**

Part II: Judges and resistance to change ⟶ Chapters 2–4

Part III: Lawyers and the uneven push for change ⟶ Chapter 5 / Chapter 6

Part IV: Lawyers and the rise of contentious politics ⟶ Chapters 7 and 8

Figure 1.6 Theory: chapter road map

empowerment thesis or agnostic about methodological preliminaries can skip this chapter without losing the narrative thread.

Chapter 3 unpacks why judges broadly eschewed turning to EU law and the ECJ when doing so could bolster their own power. It reveals historically rooted practices and knowledge deficits embodied in the trudge of daily judicial work that entrenched what I call an "institutional consciousness" of path dependence: an accrued social identity tied to institutional place that magnifies the reputational risks and labor costs of mobilizing EU law. This consciousness reifies judges' sense of distance to Europe, legitimating a renouncement of agency and a tacit resistance to change. The core of this chapter revolves around interviews and oral histories with 134 judges across French, Italian, and German courts, contextualized via ethnographic fieldnotes, descriptive statistics, and secondary sources. This chapter will speak to readers interested in a sociological understanding of what path dependence looks, sounds, and feels like in the courthouse, why judges in civil service judiciaries can be likened to street-level bureaucrats, and how immersive fieldwork can illuminate the habitual practices subtly calcifying the behaviors and identities of judges.

Chapter 4 broadens the scope of inquiry from daily judicial routine to the bureaucratic politics of hierarchy within civil service judiciaries. Contra the judicial empowerment thesis' claim that applying EU law and soliciting the ECJ emancipated lower courts from supreme court control, it argues that the few low-level judges who wield EU law to empower themselves are most likely to be positioned within decentralized judiciaries wherein they already enjoy sufficient autonomy and discretion to occasionally promote bottom-up change. European legal integration thus builds upon these preexisting hierarchical politics within national judiciaries. To support these claims, I compare the willingness of lower courts to solicit the ECJ and rebel against their superiors in the French administrative judiciary – a rigid hierarchy under the Council of State – and the French civil judiciary – a less hierarchical order under the Court of Cassation. For external validity, I conclude with a shadow case study of the politics of rebellion in Germany's more decentralized administrative judiciary. This chapter should appeal to readers interested in the mechanisms of bureaucratic domination within judiciaries, the institutional conditions that enable and quash judicial rebellions, and how hierarchical politics constrain judges' capacity to serve as agents of change.

Chapter 5 pivots to this book's heart: if the judicial construction of Europe was not catalyzed by innately activist judges, who were the pioneers of change? Focusing on the 1960s, 1970s, and early 1980s, I introduce the first Euro-lawyers: a vanguard of independent-minded WWII survivors committed to liberal legality and to uniting Europe from the ground up. Less institutionally constrained than their judicial counterparts, they nonetheless had to erode ubiquitous knowledge deficits, entrenched habits, and reticences embodied by courts and clients. This chapter traces how they cultivated local litigants and salient controversies exposing national barriers to European integration; constructed test cases to introduce local judges to European rules they hardly knew; cajoled their interlocutors to solicit the ECJ by subsidizing their labor and ghostwriting their referrals; and in so doing generated opportunities for the ECJ to advance Europe's political development. I support these inferences by combining oral history interviews with the first surviving Euro-lawyers, original dossiers from the ECJ and lawyers' personal archives, secondary historiographies and newspaper records, and geocoded data of the first cases referred to the ECJ. This chapter speaks to readers seeking a new perspective on the origins of European integration, the creativity and mischievousness of strategic litigation, how lawyers choreograph the rights-consciousness of litigants and the activism of judges, and how individuals promote new rules and practices that cut against imagined possibilities.

Chapter 6 tackles the passing of the pioneers and the evolution of Euro-lawyering. The repertoire of strategic litigation and judicial ghostwriting developed by the first Euro-lawyers only took root in those communities where practitioners came to perceive it as professionally advantageous. Beginning at the close of the 1980s, Euro-lawyering has clustered within networks of corporate law firms for whom mobilizing EU law is a tool to tend to a resourceful clientele and charge hefty legal fees. Conversely, in more resource-scarce client markets practitioners continue to perceive mobilizing EU law as impractical at best. Since the only national courts routinely solicited to apply EU law and refer cases to the ECJ are in cities where big law firms cluster, the judicial construction of Europe has evolved as patch-worked ecology hollowed by black holes. I support this argument by complementing geospatial clustering analysis with comparative fieldwork across five cities where Euro-lawyering was corporatized – Rome, Milan, Paris, Hamburg, and Munich – and four cities where Euro-lawyering never took root – Palermo, Naples, Bari, and Marseille. Readers curious about how lawyers rework economic and spatial inequities into place-based identities, how these identities refract citizens' access to courts and contain the opportunities sparked by judicial policymaking, and how repertoires of legal mobilization can be repurposed and corporatized will find this chapter of interest.

Chapters 7 and 8 transition to how the politicization of European integration since the 1990s disrupts Euro-lawyering, and how legal entrepreneurs can shape the legacies of controversial judicial decisions. In moments of protest and breaking news, lawyers intent on sustaining judicial policymaking and compliance with EU law cannot fall back on behind-the-scenes ghostwriting: they must embrace vigorous public advocacy and engage both local stakeholders and the press. I illustrate this argument by comparing two explosive controversies in Italy that generated litigation before the ECJ and subsequent backlash: the 1991 *Port of Genoa* case (Chapter 7), which quashed the control over port labor of a centenarian union of dockworkers, and the 2015 *Xylella* case (Chapter 8), which mandated the eradication of thousands of centenarian olive trees. While equally controversial, *Port of Genoa* produced a legacy of Europeanization and compliance whereas *Xylella* emboldened backlash and noncompliance. Via comparative process tracing, I tie the source of this divergence to how Euro-lawyers in *Port of Genoa* proactively mobilized public support by supplementing strategic litigation with media-saavy public advocacy, whereas lawyers in *Xylella* did not mobilize as intermediaries and reactively bolstered efforts to resist compliance. These chapters speak to readers interested in how contentious politics transform legal mobilization, how lawyers can serve as interpretive mediators in the public sphere, and why similar backlashes against laws and courts produce divergent legacies of compliance.

Finally, Chapter 9 proposes a normative and historical evaluation of the foregoing findings. I first consider how lawyers compare to other ghostwriters of institutional change, suggesting that what distinguishes lawyers is their capacity to wield a mediatory, boundary-blurring agency to seize opportunities for change that may be lost upon actors shackled to single institutional settings. I then address the ethics of lawyers' ghostwriting, submitting that while concealed actions pushing the bounds of the acceptable are often necessary to jump-start institutional change, Euro-lawyering became more normatively problematic as it corporatized. I conclude by taking stock in light of the contemporary challenges plaguing the rule of law in Europe. As a wave of illiberalism and constitutional breakdowns has swept some EU member states, Euro-lawyers have gained a new *raison d'être* in the struggle to reclaim the elusive liberal promise of the judicial construction of Europe.

Ultimately, *The Ghostwriters* reveals but the initial submerged parts of a large iceberg of litigation, judicialization, and political development in one region of the world. My aim is to contribute meaningfully to this iceberg's study, not to settle the debate or to weave a seamless analytic web.[106] While in every empirical chapter I critically engage and sometimes challenge existing arguments, I largely build upon the perceptive scholarship that inspired me to write this book in the first place. And although *The Ghostwriters* revolves around the politics of lawyers, I emphatically do not wish to portray lawyers as herculean, to imply that they single-handedly advanced European integration, or to lose sight of how litigation is "just one potential dimension or phase of a larger, complex, dynamic, multistage process of disputing."[107] This book, then, is not a holistic history. It is rather a selective archeology, an exhumation of some of the under-appreciated ways that lawyers shaped the tortuous development of the world's sole supranational polity.

---

[106] For instance, this book says relatively little about how the ECJ decides cases, illuminating this process indirectly like astronomers who study black holes by observing how they effect surrounding matter. This analogy is a bit misleading, however, for despite the Court's best efforts to evade the gaze of social science, we actually know a lot more about its pro-integration proclivities and about what goes on in its *Palais de Justice* than in countless local communities where the disputes that fuel judicial policymaking originate (or not), and where lawmaking is translated into practice (or not). These are the black holes that preoccupy this book.

[107] McCann, Michael. 2008. "Litigation and Legal Mobilization." In *The Oxford Handbook of Law and Politics*, Gregory Caldeira, R. Daniel Kelemen, and Keith Whittington, eds. New York, NY: Oxford University Press, at 525.

# PART TWO

# JUDGES AND RESISTANCE TO CHANGE

## CHAPTER TWO

# REVISITING JUDICIAL EMPOWERMENT IN EUROPE

## A Prelude

*Everything must change, so that everything can remain the same.*
— Giuseppe Tomasi di Lampedusa, *The Leopard*[1]

## 2.1 LENINISTS AND LEOPARDS

The view of a European Union (EU) forged by activist judges has long captured the imagination of social scientists. But this narrative actually originated with law professors channeling the grumblings of national policymakers. Following his participation in a 1979 conference in Paris organized by French officials, renown law professor Maurice Duverger took to the pages of *Le Monde* to rail against "European judges" whose overt politics recalled "the soviet judges of Leninist times."[2] Five years later Hjalte Rasmussen, a law professor in Copenhagen, channeled the grievances of Danish bureaucrats[3] in a controversial book accusing the European Court of Justice (ECJ) of "judicial activism ... beyond the limits of the acceptable."[4]

While charges of judicial activism initially targeted the European Court, political scientists soon posited that national judges had behaved similarly. More sanguine about judicialization than either Rasmussen or Duverger, they claimed that domestic courts had partnered with the ECJ and embraced European integration to bolster their own power. The roots of the judicial construction of Europe not only lay in the European Court's *Palais de Justice* but also with audacious local judges interspersed throughout the Union.

---

[1] Di Lampedusa, Giuseppe T. 1963. *The Leopard*. London: Fontana, at 29.

[2] Duverger, Maurice. 1980. "Le gouvernement des juges européens." *Le Monde*, September 20; Bernier, Alexandre. 2018. "La France et le Droit Communautaire 1958–1981." PhD dissertation, University of Copenhagen, at 234–35.

[3] Pedersen, Jonas Langeland. 2016. "Constructive Defiance? Denmark and the Effects of European Law, 1973–1993." PhD dissertation, Aarhus University, at 252.

[4] Rasmussen, Hjalte. 1986. *On Law and Policy in the European Court of Justice*. Dordrecht Nijhoff, at 62.

This chapter provides a brief geneology of this *judicial empowerment thesis* and motivates why the next two chapters embark upon the road less taken. Instead of presuming a drive for empowerment in judges, the chapters that follow scrutinize whether the very national courts taken as cradles of activism and Europeanization in theory may well function as the opposite in practice. Instead of the "leninists" of Duverger, these judges may be more akin to the "leopards" of Lampedusa's famous novel, whose resignation perpetuates the status quo.

It might seem counterintuitive to approach the judicial construction of Europe by probing why judges would resist reform. But taking these resistances seriously highlights how the EU has had to grapple with the same challenge facing all processes of political development: the fact that "change confronts political authority already on the scene. By virtue of its historical character, political change is always a reconstruction."[5] Only by studying why change does not happen, or why it proceeds so tortuously, can we then appreciate the struggles of those who work against the grain to remake politics and policy.

To set the stage, Section 2.2 begins with a summary of the development and core claims of the judicial empowerment thesis. In Section 2.3, I then provide suggestive quantitative evidence that this thesis may understate resistances to Europeanization within lower national courts. I conclude in Section 2.4 by describing the qualitative strategy deployed in subsequent chapters to intercept these potential resistances.

## 2.2 THE JUDICIAL EMPOWERMENT THESIS

The judicial empowerment thesis began influencing research on European integration shortly after Joseph Weiler published a seminal 1991 article, wherein he provocatively claimed:

> [T]he most significant change in Europe, justifying appellations such as "transformation" and "metamorphosis," concerns the evolving relationship between the [European] Community and its Member States ... Noble ideas (such as the Rule of Law and European Integration) aside, the legally driven constitutional revolution was a narrative of plain and simple judicial empowerment. The empowerment was not only, or even primarily, of the European Court of Justice, but of the Member State courts, of lower national courts in particular ... Lower courts and their judges were given the facility to engage with the highest jurisdiction in

---

[5] Orren and Skowronek, *Search for American Political Development*, at 21.

the Community and thus to have de facto judicial review of legislation. For many this would be heady stuff.[6]

Weiler's conjecture was but a small afterthought in his eighty-page argument, though one he grew fond of reiterating. When he presented a draft of the article at Harvard's Center for European Studies in 1990, a discussion of national judges' interests was conspicuously missing, prompting political scientist Stanley Hoffmann to quip "with his usual sharp wit ... that Weiler's presentation reminded him of why he switched from international law to international relations and political science: Lawyers think that a judge says something and it becomes a reality."[7] Most political scientists, after all, took "intrajudicial friction ... for granted as the expected state of affairs. The trick then was to explain" why national judges would cooperate with the ECJ.[8] In response, Weiler introduced his empowerment thesis – "has not power been the most intoxicating potion in human affairs?"[9] – even as he encouraged others to deepen "why national judges and politicians accepted the ECJ's bold legal assertions."[10]

Weiler's article "has been taught to a generation of students, driving a quarter-century of academic work."[11] Scholars following in Weiler's footsteps, like Anne-Marie Slaughter, Walter Mattli, and Alec Stone Sweet argued that "judicially-driven integration proved to be self-reinforcing," perhaps even more than Weiler posited.[12] Unlike their American counterparts, ordinary judges in the civil law states of continental Europe historically lacked the power to review the legality of legislation.[13] Therefore, their prospective empowerment by turning

---

[6] Weiler, "Transformation of Europe," at 2406; 2426.

[7] Alter, Karen. 1996. "The Making of a Rule of Law in Europe." PhD dissertation, MIT, at 4.

[8] Stone Sweet, *Judicial Construction of Europe*, at 22.

[9] Weiler, Joseph H. H. 1993. "Journey to an Unknown Destination: A Retrospective and Prospective of the European Court of Justice in the Arena of Political Integration." *Journal of Common Market Studies* 31(4): 417–446, at 425; Weiler, "Quiet Revolution," at 523.

[10] Alter, *Establishing the Supremacy of European Law*, at ix.

[11] Moravcsik, Andrew. 2013. "Did Power Politics Cause European Integration?" *Security Studies* 22(4): 773–790, at 786.

[12] Burley and Mattli, "Europe before the Court"; Mattli and Slaughter, "Role of National Courts in the Process of European Integration"; Kelemen and Stone Sweet, "Assessing the Transformation of Europe," at 204.

[13] See: Volcansek, Mary. 2007. "Appointing Judges the European Way." *Fordham Urban Law Journal* 34(1): 363–385; Merryman and Perez-Perdomo, *The Civil Law Tradition*, at 34–38.

to EU law and acknowledging its supremacy was substantial. No longer would they have to cow to their high courts or parliaments, provided that a "higher" EU law applied and that the ECJ, upon being solicited, confirmed that EU law trumped a conflicting national law. In so doing, lower national courts became the presumed linchpins or motors of European integration in what has been labeled "the most striking example ... of significant unintended consequence in world politics."[14] After all, in European constitutional democracies "under the prevailing legal culture of the postwar decades," government noncompliance with EU law "was clearly frowned upon" when it targeted its "own" national courts rather than a faraway "foreign" court with questionable legitimacy.[15] Even those scholars probing judicial resistances to the ECJ focused on the intermittent defiance of national supreme courts[16] who had less to gain from European integration and predictably proved more protective of their national prerogatives.[17]

This narrative of empowerment seduced my expectations about the motives and behaviors I would encounter once I began visiting national courts. Yet I soon became a little dejected when judges repeatedly hinted that this thesis may mask as much as it reveals. Exemplary of what I heard was my discussion with Roger Grass, a French judge who also served as registrar at the European Court for two decades. Drawing on his panoramic view of European judicial politics, at a certain moment during our interview Grass took a reflective pause, gathered his thoughts, and delivered what I took as a reality check:

> European law, today, constitutes a considerable upheaval of the office of the judge ... from the "voice of the law" he has become something else, he has the possibility to disapply the law to apply a superior law. It's not nothing! ... So imagine, all of a sudden, this situation within which the national judge finds himself! One might have thought that there would

[14] Moravcsik, "Did Power Politics Cause European Integration," at 786.

[15] Lindseth, Peter. 2010. *Power and Legitimacy: Reconciling Europe and the Nation-State*. New York, NY: Oxford University Press, at 134–135; Alter, *Establishing the Supremacy of European Law*.

[16] See: Pollack, Mark. 2013. "The New EU Legal History." *American University International Law Review* 28(5): 1257–1310; Rasmussen, Hjalte. 2007. "Present and Future European Judicial Problems after Enlargement and the Post-2005 Ideological Revolt." *Common Market Law Review* 44(1): 1661–1687; Davies, Bill. 2013. *Resisting the European Court of Justice*. New York, NY: Cambridge University Press; Lindseth, *Power and Legitimacy: Reconciling Europe and the Nation-State*, at 133–187.

[17] Alter, *Establishing the Supremacy of European Law*; Stone Sweet, *Judicial Construction of Europe*, at 81.

be a spirit of enthusiasm, that our frontiers would blow away! And yet
no, no, no ... there wasn't this enthusiasm, and this is rather striking.[18]

Hearing these comments from judges provoked a realization that forced
me to revisit the very thesis that had fostered my interest in European
judicial politics. Much of what we think we know – of what *I* thought *I*
knew – about the judicial construction of Europe stems from a narrative
that was presumed to be true by its authors, but whose "speculations"
received remarkably "scant" empirical scrutiny.[19] Among the thesis'
proponents in the 1990s, only Karen Alter undertook serious fieldwork
in national courts (producing a more nuanced account than her
contemporaries, as we will see). Weiler, Mattli, and Slaughter imputed
motives and behaviors upon judges via backward induction: if the
outcome of soliciting the ECJ and applying EU law was judicial
empowerment, then surely the agents and mechanism driving this
outcome were judges acting to further their own empowerment. But
what if the outcome they described was mostly right, yet the underlying
process they presumed was largely wrong?

## 2.3 SOLICITING THE EUROPEAN COURT OF JUSTICE: QUANTITATIVE PRELIMINARIES

The call for revisiting the judicial empowerment thesis is not limited
to the suggestions of any particular judge; It is also implied by the
available quantitative evidence. In particular, descriptive statistics of
national court referrals to the ECJ from Italy, France, and Germany
seem to cut against the presumption that "lower national courts
in particular" were "wide and enthusiastic" about the prospect of
collaborating with the ECJ to enforce EU law.[20]

In concrete terms, the main observable implication of the judicial
empowerment thesis concerns the behavior of national judges vis-
à-vis a key institutional provision of the EU Treaties known as the
*preliminary reference procedure* (see Figure 2.1). Modeled on the then-
fledgling Italian system of constitutional referral and inserted as Article

---

[18] Interview with Roger Grass, French Court of Cassation and ex-*greffier* at the ECJ,
September 29, 2017 (in-person).

[19] Alter, Karen. 1998. "Explaining National Court Acceptance of European Court
Jurisprudence: A Critical Evaluation of Theories of Legal Integration." In *The Euro-
pean Court and National Courts: Doctrine and Jurisprudence*, Anne-Marie Slaughter,
Alec Stone Sweet, and Joseph Weiler, eds. New York, NY: Hart, at 229, 238–241.

[20] Weiler, "Transformation of Europe," at 2426.

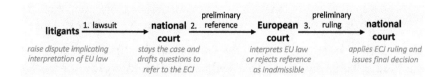

Figure 2.1 The preliminary reference procedure to the European Court of Justice

177 into the Treaty of Rome "without awareness of this innovation's importance,"[21] the procedure empowers any national court to refer a question to the ECJ on the interpretation of EU law or the compatibility of national legislation arising in the disputes before it. Now governed by Article 267 of the Treaty on the Functioning of the European Union (TFEU), the procedure – which has since been transplanted to twelve regional and international court systems[22] – serves as a transmission belt linking national judiciaries and supranational judges to jointly promote integration and domestic policy change. For once the ECJ renders a ruling, its interpretation of European law becomes legally binding on the governments and courts of all member states. The procedure opened the floodgates to a "copernican revolution":[23] even the humblest justice of the peace could wield its dialogue with the ECJ to challenge supreme court jurisprudence and parliamentary legislation via de facto judicial review.

The judicial empowerment thesis, then, intuitively presumes that "lower courts are much more willing to send references to the ECJ."[24] And at first glance, the evidence from Italy, France, and Germany appears supportive. Over sixty years from 1964 through 2013, lower courts in these three states issued almost 2,400 referrals to the ECJ, compared to just under 1,100 referrals by high courts. Yet using such aggregate data to infer individual judicial behavior risks leading us toward a classic ecological fallacy,[25] since in hierarchical judicial

[21] Pescatore, Pierre. 1981. "Les Travaux du 'Groupe Juridique' dans la Negociation des Traités de Rome." *Studia Diplomatica* 34: 159–92, at 159; 173.

[22] Alter, *New Terrain of International Law.*

[23] Interview with Roberto Conti, Italian Court of Cassation, October 12, 2016 (in-person).

[24] Alter, Karen. 2000. "The European Union's Legal System and Domestic Policy: Spillover or Backlash?" *International Organization* 54(3): 489–518, at 504–505; 513.

[25] Freedman, David. 2011. "Ecological Fallacy." In Michael Lewis-Beck, Alan Bryman, and Tim Futing Liao, eds. *The SAGE Encyclopedia of Social Science Research.* Thousand Oaks, CA: SAGE.

systems, courts of first instance far outnumber courts of appeal and last instance. Strikingly, most judicial empowerment arguments have neglected this crucial point:[26] the large number of lower court referrals may merely indicate that these courts are more numerous, rather than greater enthusiasm for European integration and thirst for empowerment by the judges that staff them.

Figure 2.2 provides a better portrait of the propensity of national courts to solicit the ECJ. By disaggregating reference data at the individual court level, it becomes clear that lower courts have a *much lower* propensity to refer than high courts. In all three states, high courts have each submitted dozens or hundreds of referrals to the ECJ, with the German Federal Fiscal Court reaching a peak of 290 references. This translates to several referrals *every year*. By contrast, on average lower courts have only referred a couple of cases each *over sixty years*. This disparity holds even in the pre-1985 era, before the most significant growth in high court referral rates.[27]

In truth, even the low referral rate of lower courts in Figure 2.2 is inflated, because its denominator comprises the subset of all lower courts that have dialogued with the ECJ at least once. As in other member states,[28] lower courts that refer even a single case are fairly rare: out of the thousands of courts of first instance in Italy, France, and Germany,[29] only 220, 196, and 190, respectively, ever dialogued with the ECJ from 1964 to 2013. If the denominator comprised all lower courts, the propensity of the average lower court to solicit the ECJ would approach zero. And given that lower courts are usually

---

[26] See, for example: Stone Sweet and Brunell, "European Court and National Courts," at 89–90; Cichowski, *European Court and Civil Society*, at 80–81.

[27] From 1964 to 1985, the mean number of cases referred to the ECJ from each referring Italian, French, and German high court is 33, 15.5, and 28, respectively, compared to only 2, 1.6, and 5.6 cases on average for each referring Italian, French, and German lower court, respectively. On high courts' steadily growing propensity to solicit the ECJ over time, see: Pavone, Tommaso, and R. Daniel Kelemen. 2019. "The Evolving Judicial Politics of European Integration: The European Court of Justice and National Courts Revisited." *European Law Journal*, 25(3): 352–373.

[28] Wind, Marlene. 2010. "The Nordics, the EU and the Reluctance towards Supranational Judicial Review." *Journal of Common Market Studies* 48(4): 1039–1063; Glavina, Monika. 2020. "To Refer or Not to Refer – That Is the (Preliminary) Question." *Croatian Yearbook of European Law* 16: 25–60.

[29] From 1964 to 2013, the Italian, French, and German judiciaries have respectively comprised as many as 10,011, 2,441, and 1,117 simultaneously operational courts – the vast majority being lower courts. I thank Michal Ovádek and the EUTHORITY project for these statistics.

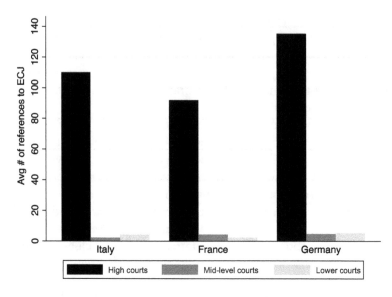

| | | Total # references | # referring courts | Average # references per referring court |
|---|---|---|---|---|
| **Italy** | High courts | 220 | 2 | 110 |
| | Mid-level courts | 64 | 28 | 2.3 |
| | Lower courts | 924 | 220 | 4.2 |
| **France** | High courts | 184 | 2 | 92 |
| | Mid-level courts | 136 | 31 | 4.4 |
| | Lower courts | 457 | 196 | 2.3 |
| **Germany** | High courts | 677 | 5 | 135.4 |
| | Mid-level courts | 298 | 62 | 4.8 |
| | Lower courts | 1,015 | 190 | 5.3 |

Figure 2.2 National courts' propensity to solicit the ECJ by court level, 1964–2013
Note: Statistics comprise courts in a judicial hierarchy, excluding standalone tribunals.

comprised of multiple judges, it becomes clear that any one low-level judge is very unlikely to dialogue with the ECJ over the course of their career. Of course, these statistics do not imply that no judges behave consistent with the judicial empowerment thesis: we will meet some of them in this book. But they do suggest that such behavior may be less innate and more exceptional than we think. Clearly "understanding why most judges, to this day, choose not to empower themselves via EU law is just as important as understanding why a few of them do."[30]

[30] Pavone, "Revisiting Judicial Empowerment," at 326.

To be sure, preliminary references are not always necessary to apply EU law,[31] and "since all it takes is one court referral to allow the ECJ to expand its jurisdictional authority, the possibilities for legal expansion presented by the preliminary ruling system [are] abundant."[32] Yet "laws on paper [may be] widely circumvented and ignored,"[33] particularly in polities like the EU that lack in administrative and enforcement capacity. As Weiler himself acknowledges, only the "growing involvement of the national judiciary in the administration of Community law [can] transfor[m] doctrinal acceptance into procedural and social reality" by fomenting an essential "habit of obedience" among courts interspersed throughout the Union.[34] In this light, national judges' propensity to solicit the ECJ "indicates where litigants' EU legal rights are most likely to be judicially enforced, and where evidence of local noncompliance is most likely to percolate upwards to the ECJ ... In historical institutionalist terms, preliminary references signal where the 'layering' of EU law atop national law has successfully 'converted' national judges into Union judges."[35] Yet to unpack the foregoing claims, there is no substitute for visiting courts and talking to judges.

## 2.4 TALKING TO NATIONAL JUDGES: QUALITATIVE PRELIMINARIES

Over the course of three years from June 2015 through January 2018, I conducted fifteen months of field research in Italy, France, and Germany. The core of this fieldwork comprised semi-structured interviews with hundreds of judges, lawyers, and law professors, usually in the places where they work. Since this research in European courts

---

[31] Lower courts have the *discretion* to refer questions to the ECJ (only supreme courts usually have an *obligation* to refer). Under the ECJ's *acte clair* doctrine, national courts can also apply EU law on their own if there is no interpretative doubt. See: Case 106/77, *Amministrazione delle Finanze dello Stato* v. *Simmenthal SpA*, [1978], ECR 629; Case 283/81, *Srl CILFIT and Lanificio di Gavardo SpA* v. *Ministry of Health*, [1982], ECR 3417. Of course, uncertainty can preclude invoking the *acte clair* doctrine, and even if EU law is clear, a superior court (or government) might still not to comply, which could motivate a lower court to refer to the ECJ.

[32] Alter, "European Court's Political Power," at 468.

[33] Helmke, Gretchen, and Steven Levitsky. 2004. "Informal Institutions and Comparative Politics." *Perspectives on Politics* 2(4): 725–740, at 727.

[34] Weiler, "Quiet Revolution," at 518–519.

[35] Kelemen and Pavone, "Political Geography of Legal Integration."

has rarely been undertaken[36] and undergirds Chapters 3 and 4, it is worthwhile to briefly describe how I pursued it.

In inviting legal professionals to speak with me, I wanted to speak with those individuals with comparatively greater levels of knowledge and experience concerning the way EU law is incorporated in domestic judicial practice. Although I ended up speaking with many individuals, my purpose was not to "increase the number of [interview] observations,"[37] but rather to increase their *quality*. When tracing a social process via qualitative fieldwork, "the most appropriate sampling procedures are ... those that identify the key political actors that have had most involvement with the processes of interest ... the goal will ultimately be to reduce randomness as much as possible."[38] Of course, speaking *only* with those judges who have mastered EU law and behave the way the judicial empowerment thesis predicts would be a mistake. For we are also interested in how these judges are perceived by their many colleagues who trek along a different path. Nevertheless, when a social process under study is complex or concealed, it is helpful to oversample those who are comparatively more knowledgeable and engaged.

Unfortunately, identifying these key judicial interlocutors can be a real challenge. Judiciaries are many things; "transparent" is not one of them. First, the ECJ fails to publish the names of the specific judges (or the court chambers) that submit referrals to it. According to one of its staffers, the Court never thought such information could be of interest to researchers.[39] Second, judges do not advertise their activities and specializations: they are usually busy enough without overzealous researchers bothering them! Finally, the numeric rarity of judges who have referred cases to the ECJ renders this search even more difficult.

So how to proceed? My primary strategy was to tap judges' institutional knowledge via snowball sampling. Person-to-person referrals (or snowballs) have been praised for producing findings that are both

[36] For an exception, see: Nowak, Tobias. 2019. "Using Mixed Methods to Explore the Legal Consciousness of Judges." *SAGE Research Methods Cases*, 1–11, https://methods.sagepub.com/case/using-mixed-methods-explore-the-legal-consciousness-of-judges.

[37] See: King, Gary, Robert Keohane, and Sidney Verba. 1994. *Designing Social Inquiry*. Princeton, NJ: Princeton University Press, at 208–228.

[38] Tansey, Oisin. 2007. "Process Tracing and Elite Interviewing: A Case for Nonprobability Sampling." *PS: Political Science and Politics* 40(4): 765–73, at 766.

[39] Interview with a librarian at the European Court of Justice, February 10, 2017 (via phone).

"emergent" and "interactional" through flexible face-to-face engagement.[40] Snowballing not only forced me to meet a greater diversity of judges than I might have otherwise contacted, but it improved my sense of how judges network, how they perceive one another, and how they associate themselves with the ways most judges act and think.

Despite these benefits, snowball sampling runs the risk of excluding key informants by getting stuck in a closed network. If interview-intensive fieldwork is not meant to certify generalizations,[41] neither is it meant to promote the voice of individuals without any sense of where they fit in a broader social context. I adopted two strategies to attenuate this risk. First, I initiated multiple snowballs from different starting positions. For example, when soliciting interviews with judges in Italy and France, whose judiciaries are comprised of administrative and civil court judges, I started "snowballs" within each of these jurisdictions. Second, I adopted a multi-sited fieldwork agenda, spending at least a month in twelve cities where I invited myself into their networks of legal professionals. This approach minimized the risk of getting stuck in a closed network and opened opportunities to have conversations speak to (and contextualize) one another. For example, I found that some of the most informative exchanges arose when I asked lawyers and judges to compare their experience to what their colleagues in other cities or countries told me. I was thus able to probe interviewees about themes that had emerged in prior interviews without cornering them into having to agree or disagree with members of their immediate community. This approach revealed whether specific logics were context-bound or common across a variety of sites.

In total, I spoke with 353 individuals in 320 separate conversations, including 134 judges (see Figures 2.3 and 2.4).[42] The nonrepresentativeness of this sample, if anything, introduces a slight bias in favor

---

[40] Gray, Paul, John B. Williamson, David A. Karp, and John R. Dalphin. 2007. *The Research Imagination*. New York, NY: Cambridge University Press, at 151–178; Noy, Chaim. 2008. "Sampling Knowledge." *International Research of Social Research Methodology* 11(4): 327–344.

[41] See: Cramer, *The Politics of Resentment* at 214, Schwartz-Shea, Peregrine, and Dvora Yanow. 2012. *Interpretive Research Design: Concepts and Processes*. New York, NY: Routledge, at 47.

[42] Forty-two of these were group interviews comprised of 2–6 interviewees. Conversations with 22 interviewees extended across multiple (2–3) interviews. Interviews in Italy and France were conducted in Italian and French, whereas in Germany they were conducted in English.

| | Judges | Lawyers | Law professors | Other | Total # |
|---|---|---|---|---|---|
| Italy | 76 | 121 | 71 | 16 | 223 |
| France | 27 | 20 | 6 | 9 | 51 |
| Germany | 31 | 38 | 26 | 3 | 75 |
| Other | 0 | 0 | 1 | 4 | 4 |
| Total # | 134 | 179 | 104 | 32 | 353 |

Figure 2.3 Descriptive statistics of interview sample, by interviewee type

| | Field Site | # Interviewees |
|---|---|---|
| | Rome | 42 |
| | Genoa | 29 |
| | Milan | 36 |
| Italy | Trento/Bolzano | 28 |
| | Naples | 20 |
| | Bari | 29 |
| | Palermo | 26 |
| | Other | 13 |
| | Paris | 33 |
| France | Marseille/Aix-en-Provence | 16 |
| | Other | 2 |
| | Berlin | 24 |
| Germany | Munich | 15 |
| | Hamburg | 18 |
| | Other | 18 |
| Other | Luxembourg | 4 |
| | Total #: | 353 |

Figure 2.4 Descriptive statistics of interview sample, by fieldsite

of confirming the judicial empowerment thesis. Judges who felt they would not be able to reference personal experiences applying EU law or soliciting the ECJ were more reticent to speak with me, replying along similar lines to a first instance judge in Germany: "[M]y limited knowledge of this subject will not be of much help to you. Personally, I never in my judicial career made use of the preliminary reference procedure to the ECJ and – asking my colleagues, if they had any likewise experiences – I also know of no one else here … I have the impression that this procedure is being followed only very rarely ..."[43] I was often able to persuade these judges to speak with me by stressing interest in their daily work, but clearly those who approximate the behavior presumed by the judicial empowerment thesis were more likely to self-select into my interview sample. Despite this fact, as I began speaking with judges, I often felt that I had unwittingly opened Pandora's box.

---

[43] Interview with judge in a lower German civil court, December, 2017 (via email; name/date redacted).

## CHAPTER THREE

# RENOUNCING POWER AND RESISTING CHANGE

## Daily Work and Institutional Consciousness

**Paola**: "It happened to us as soon as we arrived [at the Court of] Appeal: A problem of conflict between our supreme court [the Court of Cassation] – its plenary session – and the Court of Justice of Strasbourg, which told us the exact opposite."

**Tommaso Pavone (TP)**: "You mean the European Court of Human Rights?"

**Paola**: "No, the ... of Luxembourg! Apologies – the [European] Court of Justice, in a preliminary ruling, said something different, it went beyond interpretation and entered into the merits using the facts of the case, and so it bound us since it basically said: 'You have to resolve it in this way'. So we found ourselves with two opposing judgments ..."

**Marta**: "And, furthermore, the plenary session for us is the maximum for interpretation ..."

**Paola**: "They're binding ... just imagine that I was the judge charged with writing the judgment! And I asked my [chamber] president ... [turning to Marta], I'm recounting how we decided to decide by using the filter in that case."

**Marta**: "Yes, yes."

**Paola**: "... so I told my president: 'We'll decide this one using 348 *bis*' – a filter. We almost never use it ..."

**TP**: "What does that mean?"

**Paola**: "That is, an admissibility filter. We sift through the paperwork and decide if it's manifestly inadmissible ..."

**TP**: "Ah, so you declared it inadmissible ..."

**Paola**: "And thus, there are no reasonable possibilities in law to welcome the appeal ..."

**Marta**: "... so in this way we got rid of the case, using a civil procedure, because we would have had to decide which of the two rulings – we would have had to write a treatise on EU law ..."

**TP**: "... political scientists who sometimes study this type of problematic ... posited that, in fact, perhaps lower court judges ... would oftentimes be happy to welcome this sort of situation because it means they're no longer bound by superior judges, and they could even disapply a national law, so a sort of – I don't know – cultural transformation for a judge that acquires new powers ... "

**Paola:** "But that makes some sense only up to a point."

**Marta:** "Mmh, that doesn't characterize us."

**Paola:** "Plus, the principles [of European law] don't belong to us ... "[1]

If you are not an aficionado of Italian civil procedure, you might have missed how these judges renounced an opportunity to serve as agents of change.

Paola and Marta are two Italian judges who were confronted with a conflict between national and European law shortly after being promoted to the Court of Appeal of a large Italian city. Their national "boss" (the Court of Cassation) told them the answer to the dispute was X. By contrast, their European "boss" (the European Court of Justice [ECJ]) maintained that the legal solution was Y. A space of ambiguity emerged, a classic opportunity to exercise agency and reshape policy.[2] After all, they could have referred the case to the ECJ to determine whether the Court of Cassation was correctly interpreting European Union (EU) law. By turning to a "second parent" in Luxembourg,[3] they could have proposed how the case should be decided. If successful in persuading the ECJ, the latter's judgment would have been legally binding upon the Court of Cassation. Paola and Marta thus had an opportunity to tell their superiors what to do while Europeanizing domestic policy along the way.

Instead, they found a procedural means to get rid of the case and preserve the status quo. But why? After all, this behavior runs counter to the expectations of the judicial empowerment thesis described in the previous chapter. Why were Paola and Marta so unenthusiastic about this opportunity to empower themselves and promote change?

---

[1] Interview with two judges, Court of Appeal of Bari, March 2017 (in-person; date/names redacted).

[2] Historical institutionalists emphasize that "the ambiguities [rules] embody provide critical openings for creativity and agency; Individuals exploit their inherent openness to establish new precedents." See: Mahoney and Thelen, "Theory of Gradual Institutional Change," at 12. On how this type of argument has been applied to explain innovative judicial decision-making, see: Stern, Rachel. 2013. *Environmental Litigation in China: A Study in Political Ambivalence*. New York, NY: Cambridge University Press, at 123–149.

[3] Alter, "European Court's Political Power," at 466–467.

This chapter's epigraph is ripe with clues that resurfaced repeatedly in conversations with 134 judges across Italy, France, and Germany: from confusing the ECJ and the European Court of Human Rights; to the fear of expending days "to write a treatise on EU law"; to the belief that EU laws "don't belong to us." These might seem like the opinions of a couple of lethargic or Euroskeptic judges. Both inferences are wrong. What Paola and Marta *are* conveying is how the trudge of daily work within civil service judiciaries can ossify habits and collective identities in ways that calcify judicial behavior. They are speaking to what social scientists call "path dependence": the fact that institutions can entrench mindsets and practices highly resistant to change.

To unpack these claims, in Section 3.1 I adapt the concept of path dependence to study the behavior of judges – particularly within lower courts – as they confront the prospect of institutional change, and I explain why it is useful to conceive path dependence as a form of consciousness. I then leverage fieldwork across Italian, French, and German courts to trace how a history of insufficient training (Section 3.2) combined with the enduring pressures of daily work (Section 3.3) entrenched mindsets and habits renouncing judicial empowerment and resisting Europeanizing change. Finally, I illustrate these dynamics in greater depth via a group conversation with six judges in a lower French court (Section 3.4).

## 3.1 PATH DEPENDENCE AND JUDICIAL PRACTICE

The concept of path dependence is central to each of the three "new institutionalisms" in the social sciences.[4] Most existing accounts draw on economic scholarship[5] and stress how contingent events can generate "increasing returns"[6] from adopting a new institutional practice and augment the costs of deviating from said practice. Institutions

---

[4] That is, rational choice or economic institutionalism, historical institutionalism, and sociological institutionalism. See: Hall, Peter, and Rosemary Taylor. 1996. "Political Science and the Three New Institutionalisms." *Political Studies* 44(5): 936–957; Mahoney, James. 2000. "Path Dependence in Historical Sociology." *Theory and Society* 29: 507–538.

[5] See, in particular: Arthur, Brian. 1994. *Increasing Returns and Path Dependence in the Economy.* Ann Arbor, MI: University of Michigan Press.

[6] Pierson, Paul. 2000. "Increasing Returns, Path Dependence, and the Study of Politics." *American Political Science Review* 94(2): 251–267; Pierson, Paul. 2004. *Politics in Time: History, Institutions, and Social Analysis.* Princeton, NJ, Princeton University Press, at 17–53.

thus become resistant to change even if they prove inefficient. These approaches tend to adopt a "punctuated equilibrium" model, wherein new institutions created during "critical junctures"[7] render collective action for change difficult, particularly when multiple actors can veto reform[8] or constituencies of beneficiaries mobilize to keep new rules in place.[9]

This approach to path dependence seeks to explain why new institutions endure. But when institutional change unfolds as a process of layering – as when EU law gradually percolates into national legal orders – asking how new rules get locked-in puts the cart before the horse. The first order of business should be to probe whether institutions that are already up and running resist the prospective reconstructions wrought by newly layered rules.[10] To intercept how this dynamic unfolds inside national judiciaries, I adopt a sociological approach to path dependence: I want to unpack what resistance to Europeanizing change looks and sounds like from the granular perspective of "street-level" judges,[11] who should have the most to gain by turning to EU law and the ECJ.

My starting premise is that civil service judiciaries are rule-governed communities staffed by individuals whose behavior is shaped by memories of past action[12] and the patterned demands of present labor. Particularly at their lower rungs, inherited routines and quotidian demands

---

[7] Mahoney and Thelen, "Theory of Gradual Institutional Change," at 3; Capoccia, Giovanni, and R. Daniel Kelemen. 2007. "The Study of Critical Junctures: Theory, Narrative, and Counterfactuals in Historical Institutionalism." *World Politics* 59(3): 341–367.

[8] Tsebelis, George. 2002. *Veto Players: How Political Institutions Work*. Princeton, NJ: Princeton University Press.

[9] Pierson, Paul. 1996. *Dismantling the Welfare State?* New York, NY: Cambridge University Press; Pierson, Paul. 1996. "The Path to European Integration." *Comparative Political Studies* 29(2): 123–163.

[10] Path dependence is thus central to gradual institutional change, contra some arguments: Mahoney and Thelen, "Theory of Gradual Institutional Change," at 3.

[11] As we will see, the lower we descend national judiciaries, the more the constraints upon judges resemble those upon "street-level bureaucrats." See: Lipsky, *Street-Level Bureaucracy*, at 29–30; On why civil law judges resemble street-level bureaucrats more than common law judges, see: Biland, Émilie, and Hélène Steinmetz. 2017. "Are Judges Street-Level Bureaucrats? Evidence from French and Canadian Family Courts." *Law & Social Inquiry* 42(2): 298–324.

[12] Abbott, Andrew. 2016. *Processual Sociology*. Chicago, IL: University of Chicago Press, at 1–32.

favor the emergence of what practice theorists[13] call "habitus": an "embodied history" and taken-for-granted mindsets rejecting new stimuli that call accrued ways of doing into question.[14] Building on these notions, I suggest that we can fruitfully conceive path dependence in contexts like national courts as a type of *institutional consciousness*: an accrued social identity tied to institutional place that structures how actors make sense of lived experience. By "consciousness," I mean "the way people conceive of the 'natural' and normal way of doing things, their habitual patterns of talk and action."[15] That is, consciousness is "not only the realm of deliberate, intentional action," but also about habitual matters that "people do not think about."[16] While consciousness can be a catalyst for change,[17] its entanglement with bureaucratic routine can turn it into a cognitive shackle, "becom[ing] part of the material and discursive systems that limit and constrain future meaning making."[18]

Over the course of fieldwork, it became clear that the puzzling resistances to EU law that I kept encountering in national judges exemplify a long-standing consciousness of path dependence that can be traced to the historical interaction of two mechanisms. First, lackluster training in and knowledge of European law – universal in the past and still diffuse today – entails that judges broadly lack a reflex probing whether national laws conform with EU law. Lower court judges in particular are habituated to apply well-known rules as conventionally interpreted, and they usually avoid confrontations

---

[13] Pouliot, Vincent, and Jérémie Cornut. 2015. "Practice Theory and the Study of Diplomacy: A Research Agenda." *Cooperation and Conflict* 50(3): 297–315; Pouliot, Vincent. 2015. "Practice Tracing." In *Process Tracing: From Metaphor to Analytic Tool*, Andrew Bennett and Jeffrey Checkel, eds. New York, NY: Cambridge University Press; Dunoff, Jeffrey, and Mark Pollack. 2018. "A Typology of International Judicial Practices." In *The Judicialization of International Law*, Andreas Follesdal and Geir Ulfstein, eds. New York, NY: Oxford University Press.

[14] See: Bourdieu, Pierre. 1990. *The Logic of Practice*. Stanford, CA: Stanford University Press, at 53–54; 60–61.

[15] Merry, Sally Engle. 1990. *Getting Justice and Getting Even: Legal Consciousness among Working-Class Americans*. Chicago, IL: University of Chicago Press, at 5.

[16] Ibid.; Nielsen, "Situating Legal Consciousness," at 1059.

[17] McCann, Michael. 1994. *Rights at Work: Pay Equity Reform and the Politics of Legal Mobilization*. Chicago, IL: University of Chicago Press.

[18] Silbey, Susan. 2005. "After Legal Consciousness." *Annual Review of Law & Social Science* 1: 323–368, at 334; Smith, *Institutional Ethnography*, at 68.

with new and lesser-known laws and courts, where the risk of error is high. Knowledge deficits also impinge on street-level bureaucrats, but they are especially consequential for judges who wish to safeguard their professional reputation as custodians of legal expertise.[19]

Second, work pressures that are most acute in the lower rungs of civil service judiciaries "thicken" how judges experience temporality in constraining ways. Temporality is thickened because physical objects, like case files processed in built and resource-scarce spaces, imbue daily routine with a weighty materiality. Speedily processing documents and getting rid of files in cramped office spaces disciplines the rhythm of daily life.[20] As a result, seeking out legal training, invoking complex EU rules, and drafting referrals to the ECJ become perceived as counterproductive or burdensome ruptures of routine to be avoided if possible.

The resulting institutional consciousness magnifies the reputational risks and labor costs that judges associate with Europeanization, reifying their sense of distance and lack of ownership over EU law. In so doing, this consciousness legitimates judges' renouncement of power and resistance to change. It explicates why judges have been broadly disinclined to claim the opportunities for judicial review and expansive policymaking bestowed by European integration. More generally, it illustrates that "when institutions evolve incrementally, existing behaviors become reinforced, preventing new behaviors from emerging ... [since] breaking from tradition requires strong carrots and weak sticks."[21] The judicial empowerment thesis presumes an emancipatory activism in judges because it focuses on the one-shot "carrots" and neglects the everyday "sticks." Its proponents argue that "lower courts found few costs and numerous benefits in making their own referrals to the ECJ and in applying EC law."[22] At least, they would "save themselves the work of deciding the case themselves."[23] As we will see, these plausible claims often fail to map onto the patterned realities of judicial practice.

---

[19] Garoupa, Nunu, and Tom Ginsburg. 2015. *Judicial Reputation*. Chicago, IL: University of Chicago Press.

[20] Here too, judiciaries can develop "patterns of practice" similar to those that bureaucrats develop under resource scarcity: Lipsky, *Street-Level Bureaucracy*, at 81–158.

[21] Bednar and Page, "When Order Affects Performance," at 94.

[22] Alter, "European Court's Political Power," at 466.

[23] Burley and Mattli, "Europe before the Court," at 62–63.

## 3.2 MANAGING KNOWLEDGE AND JUDICIAL REPUTATION

### 3.2.1 The Problem of *Lacunae*

In September 1993, some thirty-six years after the Treaty of Rome established the European Community, the governing council of the Italian judiciary inaugurated its first training course on European law. Delivering the seminar's opening remarks, professor Giovanni Conso concluded: "The judge perceives the Community law as extraneous ... [he] tends, therefore, to reject, almost instinctively, the Community rules," revealing a "resistance towards the communitarian phenomenon" and a "sort of judicial chauvinism" linked to a "lack of education in EU law."[24]

To the judges in attendance, these remarks from the recently retired President of the Italian Constitutional Court probably felt like a personal rebuke. My approach is to instead take seriously how well-meaning, hardworking, and otherwise ambitious judges faced – and continue to face – daily institutional incentives to turn their backs on EU law and the ECJ. First and foremost, if European integration is to induce domestic courts into serving the interests of an emergent transnational polity, then newly lawyered EU rules must come to be *known*. A novel body of transnational legal knowledge must be integrated within local judicial practice and foster some sense of identification with the new political order. Yet nothing about this process is intuitive, costless, or risk free.

To unpack this claim, we must take history seriously, even though we are not explaining an outcome that has come to pass. After all, surprisingly little has changed in the state of affairs that Italian Constitutional Court President Conso decried almost thirty years ago. The signs – both quantitative and qualitative – are everywhere for those who wish to look. In a 2011 survey of over 6,000 national judges conducted by the European Parliament, three-fifths admitted that they did not know how to refer a case to the ECJ if the occasion required

---

[24] Bartolini, Antonio, and Angela Guerrieri. 2017. "The Pyrrhic Victory of Mr. Francovich and the Principle of State Liability in the Italian Context." In *EU Law Stories: Contextual and Critical Histories of European Jurisprudence*. Fernanda Nicola and Bill Davies, eds. New York, NY: Cambridge University Press, at 341.

it.[25] Fast-forward to 2016 and consider the remarks of Roberto Conti, a leading Italian civil judge, whose tone suggested the confiding of an open secret:

> Let me tell you, quite sincerely ... that the dialogue with the European Court of Justice has been lacking over the years for one primary reason that is often unstated: that EU law has not been well known in our legal order ... even I, as part of a cohort of fairly young judges, in 1997 had no knowledge of EU law. So think of a judiciary – we are about 9,000 – where the majority are older than me![26]

As with other judges in Italy, France, and Germany, discussing knowledge gaps provokes unease. Judges in civil service judiciaries may not be the "culture heroes" and "bevy of platonic guardians"[27] that they are in common law countries, but none will deny that they, too, ought to know the law. Just as Hamilton justified the judicial power as "neither Force nor Will, but merely Judgement,"[28] so did the most prominent civil law figure – Montesquieu – argue that courts are *bouche de la loi*, "the mouth that pronounces the words of the law."[29] A latin maxim – *iura novit curia*, or "courts know the law" – captures this same spirit. Judges may lack the purse or sword, but at least they have expert knowledge.

Except when they do not. In discussing EU law, national judges usually referenced *iura novit curia* in opposition to the realities of everyday practice. "[I]t's a theoretical principle," confides an Italian judge, for "the reality is that no judge can master in a deep way all the universe of administrative law" derived from EU legislation.[30] "Many colleagues have found themselves in the situation ... of not being prepared" to apply EU law, echoes a lower court colleague. Yet – she adds sardonically – *iura novit curia*! We must know the laws,

---

[25] European Parliament. 2011. "Judicial Training in the European Union Member States." Directorate General for Internal Policies. Available at: www.europarl .europa.eu/RegData/etudes/etudes/join/2011/453198/IPOL-JURI_ET(2011)45319 8_EN.pdf.

[26] Interview with Roberto Conti, October 12, 2016.

[27] See: Merryman and Perez-Perdomo, *The Civil Law Tradition*, at 34–37; Hand, Learned. 1958. *The Bill of Rights*. Cambridge, MA: Harvard University Press, at 73–74.

[28] Hamilton, Alexander. 1961 [1788]. "The Federalist No. 78." In *The Federalist*, Jacob E. Cooke ed., Middletown, CT: Wesleyan University Press, at 523.

[29] Montesquieu. 1951. *De l'ésprit des lois*, Chapitre VI, Livre XI, Paris: Gallimard.

[30] Interview with Claudio Zucchelli, Council of State and Council of Administrative Justice for Sicily, April 12, 2017 (in-person).

even if nobody has taught us or explained how they work!"[31] When sharing these remarks at a German law school in 2017, one attendee wondered aloud whether I was really questioning *iura novit curia*. The student's query conveys how the maxim remains part of the imaginary of civil law education, while the judges' comments indicate how it can evaporate in the lived reality of judicial practice.

Of course, the judge as master of the laws is an unrealizable ideal. But tending to this ideal serves an important social function. As with all professionals, the ability to apply abstract knowledge (legal principles) to concrete facts (cases) lies at the heart of judges' claims to authority.[32] Expertise enhances their individual and collective reputation for quality, which legitimates the judicial power, attracts social esteem, and insulates courts from outside encroachment.[33] All of the judges that I met instinctively want to know the laws they apply (and have others know that they know the laws they apply).

It is in this vein that a new and complex field of transnational rules may be perceived as threatening. Although Italy, France, and Germany are founding members of the EU, European law was not integrated in most of their law schools' curricula until the 1990s and early 2000s. To this day, judges and lawyers in all three states are not required to undergo continuing training in EU law (see Figure 3.1). These deficits are particularly glaring given that up to 40 percent of state legislation is partially or fully regulated by European law.[34]

To counteract these shortfalls in national judicial training,[35] in 1967 the ECJ obtained funding from the European Commission to

---

[31] Interview with Monica Velletti, Tribunal of Rome October 7, 2016 (in-person).

[32] Abbott, Andrew. 1988. *The System of Professions: An Essay on the Division of Expert Labor.* Chicago, IL: University of Chicago Press, at 8.

[33] Garoupa and Ginsburg, *Judicial Reputation.*

[34] Toeller, Annette E. 2010. "Measuring and Comparing the Europeanization of National Legislation: A Research Note." *Journal of Common Market Studies* 48(2): 417–444.

[35] For France, the figure is based on: Décret No. 91-1197 du 27 Novembre 1991; Arrête du 7 décembre 2005; European Commission. 2011. "Judicial Training Structures in the EU: France." Available at: https://e-justice.europa.eu/fileDownload.do?id=d607ab8c-3fbb-44d1-86e5-69da430ae370. For Germany, the figure is based on: The German Judiciary Act, as last amended by Article 1 of the Law of 11 July 2002 (Bundesgesetzblatt, Part 1 p. 2592); European Commission. 2014. "Judicial Training Structures in the EU: Germany." Available at: https://e-justice.europa.eu/fileDownload.do?id=c5d9bc8b-e31f-442b-87d2-ecdf023e3b4b; European Parliament. 2017. "The Training of judges and Legal Practitioners." Directorate General for Internal Policies, PE 583.134-March 2017,

| | France | Germany | Italy |
|---|---|---|---|
| **EU Law mandatory in law schools?** | **No:** EU law is not considered part of basic legal training under national law, but law school curricula increasingly integrate EU law | **Yes (since 2002):** Federal reforms to university legal education in 2002 require integrating "links to European law" in all subject matters | **Yes (since 2000):** EU law was incorporated as a mandatory subject in all law schools between 1995 and 2000 |
| **EU Law a subject of the bar exam?** | **Yes (since 2005):** The candidate can further select EU law as a subject for their oral exam | **Yes (since 2002):** The basics of EU law are part of the first and second state exams in all Länder | **No:** But the candidate can select EU law as a subject for their oral exam |
| **Continuing training in EU Law required for lawyers?** | **No:** Continuous training is mandatory for all lawyers since 1971, but EU law is not a required subject | **No:** Continuing training is only required for specialized lawyers, and EU law is not a required subject | **No:** Continuous training is mandatory for all lawyers since 2015, but EU law is not a required subject |
| **Continuing training in EU Law required for judges?** | **No:** five days of continuing training per year are required since 2008, but EU law is not a required subject | **No:** At the regional level, continuing training is required only for some Länder, and EU law is not a required subject. At the federal level continuing training at the German Judicial Academy is voluntary, including in EU law | **No:** EU law became a mandatory component of the judicial entrance exam in 1997, but mandatory continuous training (one course every four years, required since 2007) does not require EU law |

Figure 3.1 Overview of legal training in EU law in France, Germany, and Italy

"launc[h] a generous information campaign"[36] centered on inviting national judges to funded seminars and dinners in Luxembourg. Much has been made of these initiatives, but they mostly targeted recalcitrant supreme courts[37] rather than humbler judges of first instance. The first systemic effort to integrate lower courts in EU judicial training occurred with the establishment in 2000 of the European Judicial Training Network (EJTN).[38] Yet as late as 2011 only 10 percent of national judges surveyed had participated in such training, and half of lower court judges reported never taking any coursework on EU law (see Figure 3.2).

Historically, then, those few lower courts who turned to EU law and the ECJ tended to shoot in the dark, and the results were not always pretty. Consider the following historical examples from Italy, Germany, and France:

1. *Dispatch from Italy*: In the famous 1991 *Francovich* case,[39] the ECJ first proclaimed that states can be held liable for damages if they violate European law. But few are aware that the case should have never made it to Luxembourg. The *pretore* (small claims judge) of Vicenza had mailed the *dossier* to the wrong court in the wrong city: the European Court of Human Rights in Strasbourg. It was only "thanks to the initiative of an astute postman" – who had presumably grown accustomed to judges making this error – that the reference was "redirected to the correct recipient" in Luxembourg.[40]

at 32; Richards, Diana. 2016. "Current Models of Judicial Training." *Judicial Education and Training* 6: 41–52, at 44; Deutsche Richter Akademie. 2017. "Chronik." Available at: www.deutsche-richterakademie.de/icc/drade/nav/87c/87c060c6-20f5-0318-e457-6456350fd4c2. For Italy, the figure is based on: Bartolini and Guerrieri, "Pyrrhic Victory of Mr. Francovich," at 341; European Commission. 2014. "Judicial Training Structures in the EU: Italy." Available at: e-justice.europa.eu/fileDownload.do?id=e453a343-4b04-431d-933c-c8f9b8f43d2c.

[36] Rasmussen, *On Law and Policy in the European Court of Justice*, at 247; See also: Burley and Mattli, "Europe before the Court," at 63.

[37] See: Slaughter, Anne-Marie. 1997. "The Real New World Order." *Foreign Affairs* 76(5): 183–197; Slaughter, *New World Order*, at 65–66.

[38] European Judicial Training Network. 2017. "The European Judicial Training Network." Available at: www.ejtn.eu/PageFiles/9572/EJTN_Corp_Presentation_Official_Sept2017_FINAL.pdf.

[39] Joined cases C-6/90 and C-9/90, *Francovich*, ECR I-5357.

[40] Bartolini and Guerrieri, "Pyrrhic Victory of Mr. Francovich," at 341. In an interview with a lawyer involved in the case, I confirmed this fact: Interview with Alberto Dal Ferro, lawyer at Studio Legale Morresi, March 6, 2017 (via Skype).

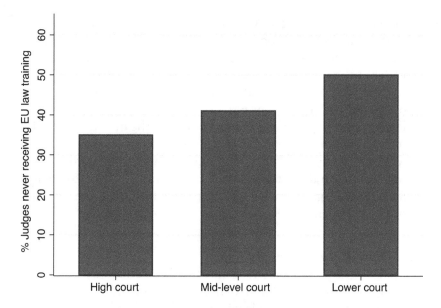

Figure 3.2 Percentage of judges having never received EU law training, by court level
*Notes:* Adapted from European Parliament (2011: 36). Results are based on a 2011 survey of 6,087 judges across 27 member states of the European Union.

2. *Dispatch from Germany*: In 1988, the regional civil court in Munich requested an expert opinion from the Max Planck Institute for Comparative and International Law to certify the applicability of foreign law in a case. It turns out that the judges did not realize that the "foreign" laws at hand comprised European rules that they could directly apply, and that it was the ECJ's task – not that of a local research institute – to interpret them. Some jurists published scathing mockeries of these clueless judges: "It's difficult to resist satirizing," wrote professor Gert Nicolaysen.[41] Apparently, the judges and the Bavarian Ministry of Justice were so embarrassed by Nicolaysen's commentary that they publicly suggested that he should forget about ever applying for a professorship in Munich.[42]

3. *Dispatch from France*: In 1990, Eric Morgan de Rivery – a French competition lawyer – cited European law before a large court of appeal in a case concerning the deregulation of the electricity

[41] Nicolaysen, Gert. 1988. "Difficile Est Satiram Non Scribere." *Europarecht* 23: 409–412.

[42] Interview with Thomas Bruha and Peter Behrens, Europa-Kolleg of Hamburg, January 25, 2018 (in-person).

market. The opposing lawyer resorted to ridicule: "'Listen to my colleague, who invokes a foreign law … that he calls Community law!' Instead of retorting, 'look, stop this, it's not correct, your colleague is right', the presiding judges approvingly burst out laughing … I was shocked! That shocked me," Morgan de Rivery recalls. Perhaps he should not have been: just two years prior, after persuading a lower civil court to refer a case to the ECJ,[43] the investigative judge seemed unaware of what they had gotten themselves into: "Alright, we'll see you at the Hague," they said, convinced they would soon be traveling to the International Court of Justice. "No, excuse me, it's not the Hague," the lawyer corrected. The judge's retort did not inspire confidence: "Oh, right, sorry, I meant Strasbourg!"[44]

### 3.2.2 Burden, Insecurity, and Fear

No judge wishes to publicly confuse one international court for another, to expose their limited grasp of EU law before lawyers and parties, and to be mocked in law journals. So file by file and glance by glance, the incentive is to look the other way. A retired member of the European Commission Legal Service recalls learning as much when in the 1980s he met with 120 German administrative judges in Karlsruhe:

> I was told that, in fact, 90–95% of the judges try to avoid that because they do not feel comfortable with European law. It's not Euroskepti[cism] – they like Europe – but to apply European law [one] needs some skills, and if you don't have [them] … they said: "There are [only a] very few percentage of judges [who] dare to go to Luxembourg" … they may ignore the attitude of the ECJ, to do everything to understand what the judge really wants … If you don't know even this … [then] if you can walk around it, you will.[45]

This legacy of insufficient training suffuses conversations with German lower court judges to this day. Representative is the lament of a social court judge:

> The gaps of knowledge … We had a congress, six weeks ago, where we discussed this … you have almost sixty years of tradition of European law

---

[43] C-369/88, *Criminal proceedings against Jean-Marie Delattre* [1991], ECR I-01487.

[44] Interview with Eric Morgan de Rivery, lawyer at Jones Day in Paris, September 12, 2017 (in-person).

[45] Interview with Ingolf Pernice, ex-Professor at Humboldt University of Berlin, November 3, 2017 (in-person).

in social security.[46] But it's not often recognized. So if you ask judges at the social security court: "Is your work much influenced by the European Union?" 95% would say: "No, I don't have cases." But that's wrong! There's a lack of consciousness in this area.[47]

Neither is this state of affairs unique to German lower courts. Well into the early 2000s, an Italian civil judge in Milan confessed that she did not "recall any judges in particular who confronted themselves" with European law, since "no judge knew how to conduct the research ... you needed the lawyers to cite the ruling [of the ECJ] for you."[48] And when in 2013 a judge at the first instance court of Milan in charge of EU judicial training surveyed her colleagues, she was left stunned: "Judges had no idea what the potential value was of an EU directive rather than an EU regulation, and how to apply it. The responses were fairly stupefying. In the sense that, we indeed found ourselves having to set up meetings on the As, Bs, and Cs of EU law."[49] The general reach of these knowledge deficits was confirmed by the European Parliament's 2011 survey, where only 35 percent and 66 percent of first instance judges admitted at least "some extent" of knowledge of how to refer a case to the ECJ and how to directly apply an EU law, respectively (compared to 70 percent and 80 percent of high court judges – see Figure 3.3).[50]

But what does it *feel like* to be a judge faced with the frailty of your own legal knowledge? In conversations, the problem of *lacunae* was associated with three perceptions: (1) a sense of *burden* or difficulty, (2) a sense of *insecurity* or risk, and (3) a sense of *fear* or exposure.

First, as a result of steep knowledge deficits, becoming familiar with European law can be perceived as a weighty uphill climb. "Lacking training," a member of the civil court of Bari admits, "we find it tiring to confront ourselves with European law."[51] "EU law today is

---

[46] See: Regulation No. 3 of the Council of the EEC of 25 September 1958 concerning social security for migrant workers, *Official Journal* No. 30 of 16 December 1958, at 561.

[47] Interview with Frank Schreiber, Hesse social court, December 4, 2017 (in-person).

[48] Interview with Francesca Fiecconi, Court of Appeal of Milan, December 2, 2016 (in-person).

[49] Interview with Giulia Turri, Tribunal of Milan, November 25, 2016 (in-person).

[50] These results are not driven by recently acceding member states: 67% of judges in pre-2004 accession states reported having at least "some extent" of knowledge of when to apply EU law, compared to 72 percent of judges in newly acceding states. See: European Parliament, "Judicial Training in the European Union," at 113.

[51] Interview with Ernesta Tarantino, Tribunal of Bari, March 20, 2017 (in-person).

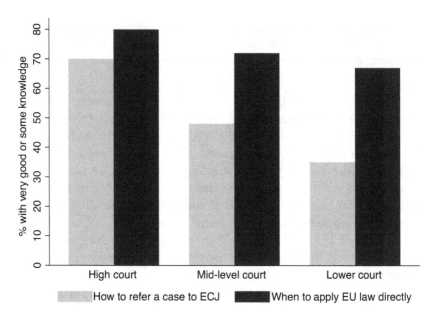

Figure 3.3 Percentage of national judges with "very good" or "some extent" of knowledge of how to refer a case to the ECJ and when to directly apply EU law, by court level
*Notes:* Adapted from European Parliament (2011: 114–115).

something complex," acknowledges a French judge while describing the concerns of his lower court colleagues; "And since we perceive it to be complicated, we oftentimes treat it in a complicated way ... 'Oh là là, this 2001 regulation, what is it? Oof! Nothing's understandable, I don't know!'"[52] A German administrative judge adds that "it is quite hard to follow the judgments of the European Court of Justice. It's quite a lot of decisions that you obviously have to have in mind, and sometimes they're not easy to understand."[53] We will shortly address how this burdensome feeling is joined at the hip with judges' working routines.

Frequently highlighted alongside a sense of burden is a perception of insecurity and risk. Nowhere is the principle of *iura novit curia* so vulnerable to disenchantment as when judges are confronted with a body of rules they hardly know. One concern raised by multiple inter-

[52] Interview with Roger Grass, September 29, 2017.
[53] Interview with Klaus Dienelt, Administrative Court of Darmstadt, January 11, 2018 (via phone).

viewees is the risk of being manipulated by a crafty lawyer – a particular concern in civil law countries, where judges' fears of ceding ground to lawyer-driven "adversarial legalism" have been deeply rooted.[54] Some judges confirmed and decried such manipulation attempts firsthand.[55] One judge in Hesse notes that "some judges may be afraid, not knowing enough about EU law, they may feel tricked, or manipulated."[56] An Italian civil judge confirms how "every judge's concern" is that "the lawyer exploits this knowledge of his and tries to manipulate the judge, and make him pose a question [to the ECJ] that is not founded."[57] Indeed, judges' insecurity is exponentially magnified when faced with the prospect of soliciting the ECJ. "If I just have a look around, in the offices next to me," confides a German judge in Darmstadt, "most of my colleagues would never make a preliminary [reference] because they feel not quite sure about the standard and the status-quo of the judgments of the European Court."[58] In fact, several judges who spoke to me conceded that they would not know how to initiate a dialogue with the ECJ in the first place. The words of a French judge are representative of what others told me off-the-record:

> I'm not sure if this should be off [the record] or not, but I would not even know who to address myself to, at the European Court of Justice, to know what I can ask ... we aren't offered training that could help us ... we have the fear of referring for nothing. To refer a question that was already posed, or a question which has already been settled in one way or another, because we're not specialists in EU law. We don't know enough.[59]

Tellingly, even judges possessing "process expertise" of how the preliminary reference procedure works are adamant that it is a risky tool for change given that judges lack "substantive expertise" in EU law.[60] Some cited widespread concerns about looking "stupid": a civil law judge in Paris remarks that since "you won't necessarily have the reflex

---

[54] Kagan. "Should Europe Worry about Adversarial Legalism?"; Kelemen, *Eurolegalism*.
[55] Interview with Matthias Zigann, judge at the Landgericht in Munich (specialized patent chamber), December 19, 2017 (in-person).
[56] Interview with Frank Schreiber, December 4, 2017.
[57] Interview with Michele Marchesiello, ex-judge at the Tribunal of Genoa, November 10, 2016 (in-person).
[58] Interview with Klaus Dienelt, January 11, 2018.
[59] Interview with a judge at a French administrative court of first instance, October 2017 (in-person; name/date redacted).
[60] On substantive and process expertise, see: Kritzer, *Legal Advocacy*, at 203.

and the knowledge ... a lower court judge might say to himself, 'Well, maybe the question has already been posed and I don't know it, so I'll ask a worthless question ... I'll look a bit stupid'."[61] After all, "it's never pleasant to be told that you didn't do your homework in drafting a question before seizing another court," a colleague confirms.[62] This concern is not unfounded: the ECJ is four times more likely to declare a referral inadmissible when it is submitted by a lower court than a court of last instance.[63]

Sometimes this insecurity can even boil over into a sense of "reverential fear."[64] Applying EU law or turning to the ECJ "scares you, of course!" acknowledges an otherwise Euroenthusiastic judge in Naples, since if you make a mistake "someone can challenge you, [and] you can be afraid of ending up in the newspapers."[65] Consider how Giuseppe Buffone and Philippe Florès, an Italian and a French lower court judge, respectively, describe feeling exposed when they first solicited the ECJ:

> Our judgments are the name of the Italian people, we represent the Italian Republic, we bear the weight of this responsibility, which you perceive only if you do this work. Only if you have a sense of being a judge. You don't just refer like that, in a week or two ... because it's a reference that circulates at the European level ... vis-à-vis EU law you're more insecure, so it's not easy ... if it also comes back as inadmissible, well![66]

> [We] could make a mistake, voilà, it's a complex field of law, that upsets the habits we might have ... You have a lower court judge who is afflicted by his daily case files, by his preoccupations. To launch himself into a preliminary reference which will expose him, expose him vis-à-vis a law he has not mastered well ... Might he see a problem that doesn't exist? And does he pose the question correctly? ... [the ECJ could reply] we've answered this 50,000 times already, or it's a question of purely

---

61 Interview with Sophie Canas, Court of Cassation and ex-judge at the Tribunal de Grande Instance of Paris, September 22, 2017 (in-person).

62 Interview with Lise Leroy-Gissinger, Court of Appeal of Aix-en-Provence, October 24, 2017 (in-person).

63 See: Pavone and Kelemen, "The Evolving Judicial Politics of European Integration."

64 Interview with Margherita Leone, Tribunal of Rome, September 29, 2016 (in-person).

65 Interview with Paolo Coppola, Tribunal of Naples, February 13, 2017 (in-person).

66 Interview with Giuseppe Buffone, Tribunal of Milan, December 14, 2016 (in-person).

national law that doesn't concern EU law, and there the judge will feel completely ridiculous.[67]

Both judges here interpret their colleagues' reluctance to solicit the ECJ as an understandable response to knowledge deficits, a reflex they partly share themselves. But Florès also touches upon something crucial: that "a lower court judge who is afflicted by his daily case files" may perceive EU law as something that "upsets the habits we might have." For these remarks reveal the confluence of another embodied constraint: the discipline required to manage one's time and daily work as a judge in a civil service judiciary.

## 3.3 MANAGING WORKLOAD AND THICKENED TIME

If knowledge deficits in EU law foment fears of making a mistake, why do judges not tend to these *lacunae*? This is a key question, since a recent survey analysis of German, Dutch, Polish, and Spanish judges finds that attending judicial training and participating in exchanges with foreign judges bolsters their sense of competence in EU law.[68] Taking seriously the bureaucratic constraints encoded in judges' daily work provides an answer. Judges' burdensome attempts to maintain some semblance of control over their workload in the built, resource-scarce spaces of lower courts proved the most recurrent leitmotif in our conversations. While these pressures are most acute in Italian lower courts, most interviewees in France and Germany stressed them as well.[69]

Consider a revealing conversation I had with three German judges. Berta is a judge at a small claims court (*Amstgericht*), whereas Hendrik and Christa work at a lower regional court (*Landgericht*) and court of appeal (*Oberlandesgericht*), respectively. Take note of how they describe daily work and how it shapes the choices they make about enrolling in EU law coursework or soliciting the ECJ:

---

[67] Interview with Philippe Florès, Court of Appeal of Versailles, October 4, 2017 (in-person).

[68] Mayoral, Juan, Jaremba, Urszula, & Tobias Nowak. 2014. "Creating EU Law Judges: The Role of Generational Differences, Legal Education and Judicial Career Paths in National Judges' Assessment Regarding EU Law Knowledge." *Journal of European Public Policy* 21(8): 1120–1141.

[69] Survey evidence from Slovenia and Croatia suggests that the following inferences travel to newer member states as well: Glavina, "To Refer or Not to Refer."

**Christa**: "It's exactly the same [as with French and Italian judges ...] The three of us everyday [work] two hours more than are paid."

**Hendrik**: "It's very average [to do] this."

**Berta**: "I come from the *Amstgericht*, the first instance ... and we have a lot of work to do, and in our court, all people, all judges are complaining. Here I have the idea that people are more content – at the *Oberlandesgericht*."

**Christa**: "It's much fewer cases that you have to decide in a single month here ... at the *Amstgericht*, if you're a judge in private law cases, you have to decide about 50 cases a month. At the *Landgericht*, the next higher court, it's between 15 and 17, and we have about 8, 9."

**TP**: "Right, so if you're at the *Amstgericht*, that's a lot, you'd have to ... "

**Berta**: "Chop, chop, chop, chop!"

... [...] ...

**Berta**: "Once I referred to [the ECJ], but it was really, really complicated ... it takes me a lot of time, yeah ... one month."

**Christa**: "Which means another twenty cases are not solved, in that time! So she has to do that."

**Berta**: "The other colleague ... he was burned out, and he was depressive ... no, he wasn't able to help me. But it was a lot of work, so I did it because I thought [national law] was so ... unjust ... "

**Christa**: "You can't really afford to refer a case ... if there's a need to do it, you do it ... "

**Hendrik**: "If it's totally clear! Totally clear! You would do it, of course."

**Christa**: "... [and] the courses on EU law don't help us with our daily work ... the only thing you learn there is you discuss cases decided by the European Court. And this wouldn't enable you to predict the next decision! ... it takes a long time to prepare a referral to Brussels, and while you wait, the case is in your register, it becomes two years old! Everybody asks you: 'Why has the case been there two years?' ... "

**Hendrik**: "I would put it slightly different[ly]. I think this education would probably help a little. But it would not help as much as I will lose time in taking this education ... judges will be evaluated by their boss, if you want, by the president of each court ... and one of the main things they can do is compare the numbers."

**Christa**: "And the age of the pending cases!"

**Hendrik**: "And I think that even among the judges, they think too much: 'This is very important'. ... so there is this spirit: 'I have to [close] many cases per year to get a good evaluation!' It still counts a lot, because it's the only objective thing that we have ... "

**Christa**: "Nevertheless, every judge would refer the case to Brussels if there is no way out ... but if there's any way you could [avoid] that ... "[70]

---

[70] Interview w/ 3 judges in a populous German Länder, December 15, 2017 (in-person; names redacted).

Notice how the problem of *lacunae* is interwoven in this conversation – as when Christa twice speaks of "referring to Brussels" (it is the European Commission, not the ECJ, that is located in Brussels). But these judges are also painting a picture of enclosure and routinized discipline contradicting the presumptions of emancipation and spontaneous creativity central to the existing scholarship on the judicial construction of Europe. It is a picture depicting a fast, regularized temporality: "Chop, chop, chop, chop!" It is a sense of being entrapped in routine: "Every judge," notes Christa, would only collaborate with the ECJ "if there is no way out." It is an environment requiring utilitarian calculations: attending a course on EU law "would not help as much as I will lose time," Hendrik assumes. And it is exhaustion, as when Berta poignantly mentions her colleague who "was burned out, and he was depressive," such that "he wasn't able to help me."

What I would like to evoke is a sense of the *thickness of time* in the everyday life of lower court judges. Not unlike the notion of a "chronotope" developed by Mariana Valverde, here there is an "intrinsic connectedness of spatial and temporal relationships ... Time, as it were, thickens, takes on flesh."[71] For judges, time is thickened and "takes on flesh" not only because it is compressed into little chunks, but also because these chunks take on the form of material objects – case files – tied to built and often overcrowded places – courtrooms and offices that may be shared. This makes the pace of everyday work sticky, limiting breakups of routine and disciplining judicial practice in ways not unlike trying to run through quicksand. In their own words, lower court judges repeatedly evoked this sense of spatiotemporal compression, like a German first instance judge:

> We still have a felt heavy workload, [it's] very stress[ful]. When judges describe their work, it will always be: "It's stress." So you won't get a very relaxed judge! In the media or in fairytales I was told "judges at 1PM are at the golf course or at the tennis court!" But that isn't real ... there's a heavy density of work. It's always getting more dense, and dense, and dense![72]

### 3.3.1 The Demands of the File

Nowhere is the thickening of time as evident as in Italian lower courts. That high litigation rates can overwhelm Italian judges is well

---

[71] Valverde, Mariana. 2015. *Chronotopes of Law*. New York, NY: Routledge, at 9–10.

[72] Interview with Frank Schreiber, December 4, 2017.

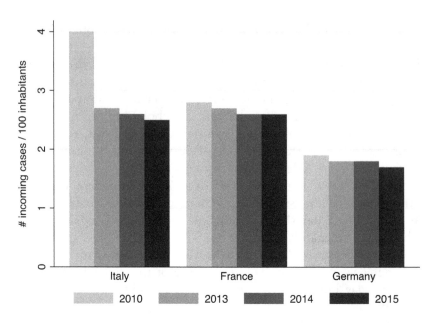

Figure 3.4 Civil and commercial disputes per 100 people at first instance, 2010–2015

known:[73] according to two measures of judicial workload in Figures 3.4 and 3.5,[74] the Italian judiciary is under comparatively greater stress. But it is one thing to cite aggregate statistics and another to witness their daily incarnation as they obstruct Europeanization.

The first thing that captures one's eye when entering an Italian city's courthouse is the ubiquity of stacks of *fascicoli* (case files). The importance of files as material objects of judicial practice has already been evidenced by sociologists:[75] for our purposes, files are a physical reminder of the daily duties that both distract and remove the gloss from an encounter with European law. One first instance judge in Bari confessed that when she was first appointed, her docket comprised

[73] See, for example: International Monetary Fund (IMF). 2014. "Italy: Selected Issues." Washington, DC: IMF. Available at: www.imf.org/external/pubs/ft/scr/2014/cr14284.

[74] Data is adapted from: European Commission. 2017. "The 2017 EU Justice Scoreboard: Quantitative Data." Available at: www.euroskop.cz/gallery/91/27594-quantitativedatafromthe2017eujusticescoreboard.

[75] Latour, Bruno. 2010. *The Making of Law: An Ethnography of the Conseil d'État.* Malden, MA: Polity Press, at 70–106; Zan, Stefano. 2003. *Fascicoli e Tribunali.* Bologna: Il Mulino.

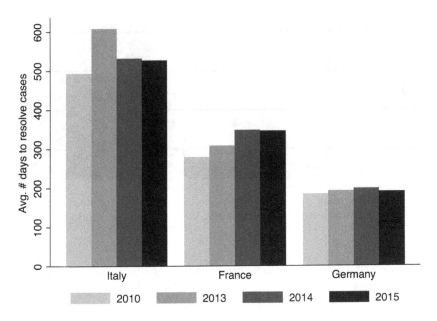

Figure 3.5 Time to resolve civil and commercial disputes at first instance, 2010–2015

some 13,000 *fascicoli*.[76] I did not doubt her, for I routinely witnessed case files being stuffed into suitcases to facilitate transportation, stacked atop carts, or lined into barricades separating judges from lawyers during oral arguments. And because courts of last instance only have to decide points of law whereas lower courts *also* have to adjudicate questions of fact, the latter's files are not only more numerous – often they are also thicker.[77]

Consider three fieldwork dispatches from Italian lower courts. In December 2016, while a civil judge was relaying how the digitalization of paperwork is modernizing judicial practice, a clerk knocked on the office door. He proceeded to push in a cart stacked with five heavy piles of files destined for my interlocutor, the tallest stack at least a couple of feet tall and perilously leaning over the cart's side (see Figure 3.6a).[78] Many judges told me that they dislike reading memos off a screen, so like their colleagues past they continue to request physical paperwork from the lawyers. Second, when conducting participant observation at the lower and appeal courts of Bari, a lawyer led me into a courtroom so

76 Interview with Ernesta Tarantino, March 20, 2017.
77 Interview with Roberto Conti, October 12, 2016.
78 Interview with Francesca Fiecconi, December 2, 2016.

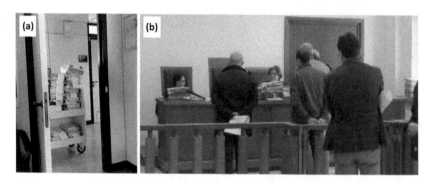

Figure 3.6 Files being carted into a judge's office, Court of Appeal of Milan (a); files partially conceal judges during oral arguments, Court of Appeal of Bari (b)
*Source:* Author photos (2017).

crowded that I assumed a ceremony was taking place. No – the dozens of lawyers impatiently encircling the judges with paperwork in hand were all scheduled for the day's proceedings. The judges at this labor chamber, on the other hand, were hidden behind a barricade of files laying atop the bench. I was granted permission to snap a photo once the courtroom had begun to empty, but thankfully a few seconds before the judges dismantled the file barricade (Figure 3.6b).

Witnessing the ritual frenzy of oral arguments helped me perceive how the materiality and pace of judicial practice intersect. At the Tribunal of Naples – where, in 2014, the criminal chambers alone decided some 232,692 cases and faced a backlog of 122,321 proceedings[79] – oral arguments constitute a stream of lawyers and clients simultaneously attempting to solicit the judge's attention, as chronicled in the following fieldnotes:

**9:38AM:** "There are eight people (some of these are probably the lawyers' clients) in the room involved in two separate disputes … it's only been 15 minutes since we arrived."

**10:02AM:** "A set of files from the bookshelf behind the desk falls to the ground – I pick it and put it back up."

**10:10AM:** "It's clear that it's impossible for an observer to keep up with all the lawyers who have entered. There are cases being discussed, and paperwork for each being signed and consulted, simultaneously."

**11:00AM:** "[The judge] explains … [that] on busy days oral arguments continue through 1:30PM. Then [he] writes the judgments. At 8PM the

[79] Tribunale di Napoli. 2014. Bilancio Sociale 2014. Available at: www.tribunale .napoli.it/allegatinews/A_7223.

building automatically shuts off the lights. But when [he] arrived in Naples, he often would take up to 10:30PM to finish writing judgments (he had a huge docket; now, because he's very efficient, his docket is reduced) ... So he would call the electricians and ask them to keep the lights on for him.'"[80]

As time thickens and takes on a weighty materiality, it shortens judges' time horizons and truncates their openness to encountering novel fields of law. This inference contradicts a core tenet of the judicial empowerment thesis: namely, that judges' long-term vision enabled them to play off the shorter time horizons of politicians to advance European integration.[81] In reality, the default mindset of the lower court judges I encountered aims for the speedy processing of lawsuits, rather than a prolonged search for the points of contact between facts, national law, and EU law. As one Genoese judge emphasizes, "given the quantitative aspect of the workload, this can distract from the evaluation of additional" realms of law.[82] Judges speak of being "frustrated,"[83] "overwhelmed,"[84] and "crushed"[85] by a "massacre-like"[86] stream of lawsuits, which obstructs efforts to "deepen" EU law by "thinking higher."[87] A binary opposition arises, contrasting an immediate daily workload with an abstract body of EU law floating higher, waiting to perhaps be deepened someday – but not today.

While this perception is most evident in Italian lower courts, French and German judges are not immune to the demands of thickened time.[88] This becomes clear by tracing how interviewees describe the economy of everyday judging.

### 3.3.2 The Economy of Everyday Judging

Across conversations with lower court judges, there was clear agreement that workload pressures dissuade participation in EU legal

---

[80] Fieldnotes, Tribunal of Naples, Labor division (judge Paolo Coppola), February 21, 2017.
[81] Alter, *European Court's Political Power*, at 118–121, 133–134.
[82] Interview with Maria Teresa Bonavia, Court of Appeal of Genoa, November 8, 2016 (in-person).
[83] Interview with Giuseppe Buffone, December 14, 2016.
[84] Interview with Margherita Leone, September 29, 2016.
[85] Interview with Monica Velletti, October 7, 2016.
[86] Interview with Francesca Fiecconi, December 2, 2016.
[87] Interview with Giulia Turri, November 25, 2016.
[88] In the case of France, see: Bell, John. 2006. *Judiciaries within Europe*. New York, NY: Cambridge University Press, at 103.

training and encourage a *cost-benefit analysis* that tips the scales against soliciting the ECJ.

Recall how one German judge – Hendrik – believed that coursework on EU law "would probably help a little. But it would not help as much as I will lose time."[89] The judges surveyed by the European Parliament in 2011 sent a similar message in their open-ended responses: judicial training is "perceived as a burden," hence judges "will be less willing to attend judicial training seminars on more remote fields like European law"; a French judge shared how after taking part in EJTN training, "I was asked by my court then to catch up with two weeks' work … This is prohibitive for anyone who is not especially crazy about European cooperation."[90]

This logic was repeatedly invoked by my interlocutors to explain why they do not seek out opportunities to gain a better grasp of European rules. In Paris, a long-standing civil judge confesses that his colleagues "at first instance and in the courts of appeal are content to rid themselves, as much as possible, of case files they have to deal with," for in order to enroll in an EU law course "you need time!"[91] A colleague at the Administrative Court of Marseille adds that "we're within a flow of cases and case files and work which doesn't permit us the time" to attend "continuing training in this domain."[92] A few hundred kilometers away at the first instance court of Milan, judges paint similarly constraining picture:

> The workload is something that completely frustrates the judge … so many judges don't come [to EU training sessions] because on Monday, Tuesday, Wednesday, Thursday, and Friday they hold hearings, on the afternoons they must write the judgments, they must attend section conferences, they have administrative duties to tend, and in this bureaucratic silence EU law dies.[93]

A second impact concerns the attractiveness of soliciting the ECJ. Workload pressures incentivize a short-term instrumental rationality, where the opportunity cost of a referral is weighed as the number of days spent deciding an estimated number of quotidian lawsuits. Usually,

[89] Interview w/ 3 judges in a populous German Länder, December 15, 2017.
[90] European Parliament, "Judicial Training in the European Union," at 34.
[91] Interview with Alain Lacabarats, French Court of Cassation, October 3, 2017 (in-person).
[92] Interview with Hélène Rouland-Boyer, Administrative Tribunal of Marseille, October 23, 2017.
[93] Interview with Giuseppe Buffone, December 14, 2016.

the scales are tipped in favor of addressing immediate needs, thus breeding a *habitus* of non-referral. A judge of first instance in Trento puts it this way: "It's evident that if one is under a lot of pressure, one says: 'Alright, those ten days, I'll dedicate to writing those judgements that impact my docket.'"[94]

Understandably, overburdened judges in Italy are particularly emphatic about the need to adopt a utilitarian logic. "Every week that I put everything down I don't write five judgments," highlights a judge of first instance in Rome, adding that to refer a case to the ECJ "you'd definitely need a week's worth of work."[95] Similarly, for an administrative judge in Milan, one only solicits the European Court when "the question jumps before your eyes" since work-wise, a reference "is like writing ten judgments."[96] "Over that period where you're writing the reference," confirms another colleague, "you could lose three, four, five working days. And so, inevitably, if you're suffocated by the docket ... you'll never refer at all."[97]

Even in slightly less burdened French and German Courts, conversations with judges surfaced echoes. One regional court judge recalls how his former president actively dissuaded dialoguing with the ECJ: "We have a lot to do, we do not have to refer the case ... let the Federal Court of Justice do it. They have fewer cases so they can do it more diligently than we."[98] Most judges who feel pressure to "be efficient, and get things done" hardly need to be told this, for they already embody this spirit in their daily routine.[99] A judge who drafted a few references while on secondment at the Federal Court of Justice confesses stopping upon returning to a lower court: "The problem is time. For a reference you need time ... you have a lot of cases to deal with ... you're doing day by day business – chop, chop, chop! – you have to decide quickly ... I am reluctant to do it."[100]

Judges sketch the contours of this *habitus* presuming that it is common to colleagues in comparable judicial settings. This suggests

---

[94] Interview with Giorgio Flaim, Tribunal of Trento, January 26, 2017 (in-person).

[95] Interview with Lilia Papoff, Tribunal of Rome, October 13, 2016 (in-person).

[96] Interview with Elena Quadri, Regional Administrative Court of Lombardy, December 13, 2016 (in-person, written interview notes).

[97] Interview with Giuseppe Buffone, December 14, 2016.

[98] Interview Ralf Neugebauer, judge at the Higher Regional Court of Duesseldorf, January 8, 2018 (via phone).

[99] Interview with Andreas Middeke and Svenja Kreft, Administrative Court of Muenster, December 19, 2017 (via Skype).

[100] Interview with Jan Tolkmitt, Landgericht Hamburg, January 25, 2018 (in-person).

that it is part of an institutional – rather than an individual – identity. For example, consider the parallel remarks of a German administrative judge and a French civil judge. The German judge notes how "most of the colleagues do not have the time to sit [on] a file over weeks just to decide if this question has to be decided by the European Court of Justice … I think most of my colleagues would never say this. Of course not. But … the normal reaction is 'ok, I'm not sure that I will have the time for such kind of work'."[101] Similarly, the French judge highlights how

> it's not something you can do when you're at the Court of Appeal or a first instance court … Here it's impossible … to refine a preliminary reference, to review all the jurisprudence of the ECJ *et cetera*, for all of that, there would be 10 or 15 case files that will have accumulated in the meantime … you'd have to work for a month to catch up, that's for sure. Already we often have to work on weekends, so it's difficult to find the space, except if it happens just before the holidays, where you work during vacation.[102]

What bolsters the persuasiveness of the foregoing remarks is that even the few judges I encountered who referred cases to the ECJ to challenge national laws or supreme court decisions lament the substantial labor costs. Giovanni Tulumello – an administrative judge in Palermo – shares how for his first referral, "for two weeks I didn't do anything else … because this was a new domain for me, I had to study … everything that was piling up at the regional administrative court and the tax court, I had to make it up by working evenings and weekends."[103] Other speak of having to undertake research after working hours, "to think about it for six months"[104] and even a couple of years,[105] so as to quell any lingering uncertainties or trepidations. When all else fails, some are forced to take time off work and labor through vacation days.[106] The most memorable experience relayed to me is that of Marianne Grabrucker, a retired German patent judge, as she described how soliciting the ECJ disrupted and monopolized her life:

[101] Interview with Klaus Dienelt, January 11, 2018.
[102] Interview with Lise Leroy-Gissinger, October 24, 2017.
[103] Interview with Giovanni Tulumello, Regional Administrative Court of Sicily, April 5, 2017 (in-person).
[104] Interview with Giuseppe Buffone, December 14, 2016.
[105] Interview with Philippe Florès, October 4, 2017.
[106] Interview with Giorgio Flaim, January 26, 2017.

[For] four months, I never went out, walking the dog, or whatever! Just having your potatoes and your muesli, and that's all! And I was sitting sometimes [for] 12 to 14 hours … Four months – no life! … At the courthouse we have guardmen, and they [check], in the evening every two hours, all the rooms. And one of these guardmen said one evening – around 12AM – "Oh, Mrs. Grabrucker, you need to sleep! Please go! Leave the house! I can't stand to see you sitting here! And if I would have been married to you, I would never believe that you are working, I would think you have a lover!" [laughter] "Trademark law is my lover," I said.[107]

Grabrucker's language of being in love with a legal field that is harmonized by EU law suggests that deeply intrinsic motives are necessary to overcome the instrumental rationality that pushes judges to turn away from EU law and the ECJ. "Ruthless egoism" does not "do the trick by itself," as the judicial empowerment thesis assumes.[108] In fact, self-interest often works the other way around: "If I have an escape, I'll take it, and I'll take it gladly," admits an Italian civil judge, "for my own behalf. Because referring means, well, not writing four judgments, you see?"[109]

This cost-benefit logic is not applied case by case like a one-shot game. As an embodied history, it incrementally ossifies: to this day, lower court judges are *not habituated* to solicit the ECJ and to invoke EU law. And "if you don't apply these things … it's clear that your mastery of these problems erodes."[110] As a result, unless judges serve on a small set of specialized chambers where lawyers regularly cite European law, its relevance can be perceived as negligible or indirect. "Those cases [where] EU law is applied," explains a German social court judge, "you get one or two times per year. So there's a problem – the normal judge forgets about it."[111] One Italian judge of first instance depicts the psychological reaction that accompanies the rupture of routine that EU law represents: "There were some oral arguments were I brought along 500 files. You can understand that if in one of those files someone questioned the constitutional legitimacy of an Italian law, I

---

[107] Interview with Marianne Grabrucker, ex-judge at the Munich Administrative Court, the Federal Administrative Court, and the Federal Patent Court, December 15, 2017 (in-person).

[108] Burley and Mattli, "Europe before the Court," at 54; 62; Weiler, "Quiet Revolution," at 523.

[109] Interview with Monica Velletti, Tribunal of Rome, October 7, 2016 (in-person).

[110] Interview with Tania Hmeljak, Tribunal of Palermo, April 21, 2017 (in-person).

[111] Interview with Frank Schreiber, December 4, 2017.

would already get the shivers ... so let's not even talk about a question linking national law to international law!"[112]

Taking the pull of habitual practice seriously problematizes a core tenet of the judicial empowerment thesis. For example, Alter claims that "a court that virtually never hears European law cases might be happy to refer the odd case that comes up to the ECJ."[113] My conversations suggest that the reverse is usually true. For instance, in 2016 Michael Schoenauer, a judge at the first instance court of Munich, became the court's first criminal law judge to refer a case to the ECJ in over thirty years.[114] Initially, "everyone was interested ... and everyone was waiting for someone to do the work." Yet after the ECJ returned its ruling[115] judges relapsed to their ingrained practices, and the ECJ's judgment "completely got forgotten ... many colleagues at the *Landgericht* wouldn't know it or apply it."[116]

## 3.4 PATH DEPENDENCE AS CONSCIOUSNESS

### 3.4.1 Contours: Distance and Lack of Ownership

When we combine the long-standing problem of knowledge deficits of EU law with the enduring demands of workload management in civil service judiciaries, we get a context that is highly favorable to the emergence of an institutional consciousness of path dependence. As an accrued social identity through which judges interpret their world, this consciousness favors a relapse to entrenched habits and the enclosure of judicial practice within preexisting national law.

The contours of this institutional consciousness became vivid throughout my conversations with German lower court judges. One judge describes its inward-looking reflex via the metaphor of the "closed bench": "In the closed bench, they prepare their case, and they have their opinion, they work seriously, but along [the same path]. And they don't want to be argued during the oral hearings ... ok, closed session, we decide in our little room ... you're not allowed to have

---

[112] Interview with Ernesta Tarantino, March 20, 2017.

[113] Alter, *Establishing the Supremacy of European Law*, at 50.

[114] The previous criminal case referred by the Landgericht of Munich was: Case 16/83, *Criminal proceedings against Karl Prantl* [1984], ECR 1299.

[115] Joined cases C-124/16, C-188/16 and C-213/16, *Criminal proceedings against Ianos Tranca and Others* [2017], ECLI:EU:C:2016:563.

[116] Interview with Michael Schoenauer, First Instance Court of Munich, December 19, 2017 (in-person, written interview notes).

your own ideas."[117] Alongside this reflex of closure is a partitioning of national judicial practice from EU law.[118] "You see EC law as something foreign," admits a colleague in Darmstadt, "as an isolate[d] thing that you've put over national law, on the top. This thinking you hear often."[119] Another argues that "we don't have enough time to really take care of European law as a plus."[120] This can exacerbate the sense that "the ECJ is a foreign court … There's a lot of colleagues who read decisions by the Federal Court of Justice every day, but it's not a lot of us that refer to the ECJ's rulings."[121]

These themes also crystallized in interviews with French and Italian judges. Consider the stark words of a French civil judge:

> It no doubt creates a mistrust [of the ECJ] that is unspoken … Well, you might hear it sometimes in a lower court, where the words flow … But it's in the mind! It's certainly in the mind … if you say, "There's a [European] directive that says that in these cases we should reach this result," in [this] case the reflex will be one of closure. Of people saying: "No, we have what we need! Why do we need to go searching for supranational law?" So the battle is not yet won … the mass isn't ready to change completely.[122]

These same elements surfaced in interviews with Italian judges, especially those tasked with promoting training in EU law. One judge in Milan explains that lower courts make "tons of references to the Constitutional Court, which they interpret as their own court. Vis-à-vis the ECJ … there isn't this culture that EU law is something that concerns you."[123] In Rome, a colleague confides that "in our jurisdiction EU law and international law generally were marginalized … the value of EU law didn't permeate our conscience."[124] This institutional consciousness is brought to life by Eugenia – an civil judge of first instance – as she self-consciously describes her and her colleagues' aversion to EU law:

[117] Interview with Marianne Grabrucker, December 15, 2017.
[118] In Chapter 6, we will see how this logic of partition can arise in the bar as well as the bench.
[119] Interview with Frank Schreiber, December 4, 2017.
[120] Interview with three judges in a populous German Länder, December 15, 2017.
[121] Interview with Michael Schoenauer, December 19, 2017.
[122] Interview with Thierry Fossier, French Court of Cassation, October 3, 2017 (in-person).
[123] Interview with Giuseppe Buffone, Tribunal of Milan, December 14, 2016 (in-person).
[124] Interview with Roberto Conti, October 12, 2016.

> If one has the sensibility, the mental openness, perhaps they'll ask to attend these [EU law] courses that look farther, but if one lacks this, ha ha! He stays ancient ... plus, oftentimes ... these European laws are different from ours. And so also because of this the confrontation, due to our more antique mindset, I repeat, can become difficult ... we already have our own laws, lots of them, some of them are also really beautiful ... so we maybe don't even feel a need to search elsewhere for points of reference for our decisions.[125]

Notice how Eugenia references an "antique mindset" in a way that is not altogether pejorative. In fact, she associates herself with this mentality when she juxtaposes "our own laws" that are "really beautiful" with "these European rules [that] are different from ours." In its most extreme (and rare) manifestation, this consciousness can motivate judges to abandon tacit resistance for outright rebellion against a perceived foreign invasion. During a conversation with two lower court judges, one was particularly emphatic about rejecting EU law, for "it seems to me that I'd have to renege on all of the culture upon which I was educated."[126] And when I was conducting fieldwork in Palermo, a lawyer handed me a decision by a lower court judge who rejected his appeal to apply EU law and solicit the ECJ[127] in fiery terms: "The laws stemming from the European Union do not have any legal direct effect in the domestic order," and "the judgments" of the "European Court of Justice ... cannot bind the Italian judge," for only in this way can "the Italian people exercise their sovereignty."[128]

### 3.4.2 An Annotated Transcript

In tracing an institutional consciousness of path dependence permeating national courts, I relied on the neat analytic categories of knowledge deficits and workload pressures. While this approach helps to organize evidence and avoid "conceptual stretching,"[129] it also obscures how, for judges, lived experience is *constituted* holistically by a

---

[125] Interview with a judge at a lower civil court in a large Italian city, March 2017 (in-person; name/date redacted).

[126] Interview with judges at a civil court in a large Italian city, March 2017 (in-person, names/date redacted).

[127] Interview with Giuseppe di Rosa, KEIS Law Studio Legale and Pegaso Università Telematica, April 18, 2017 (in-person).

[128] See: Sentenza No. 847/2013, Tribunale di Termini Imerese (Rel. Razzonico), at 9–11.

[129] Sartori, Giovanni. 1970. "Concept Misformation in Comparative Politics." *The American Political Science Review* 64(4): 1033–1053, at 1034.

conjunction of factors. This, in turn, risks obfuscating how I imposed my own interpretations upon those of my interlocutors.

To attenuate these concerns and promote "analytic transparency,"[130] I conclude this chapter with an annotated transcript of a group conversation with judges working in a lower court.[131] In this way, I invite the reader to listen to judges discuss their work, their views about institutional change, and their opinions of EU law. What will hopefully be clear is the degree to which the themes discussed in this chapter are interwoven, and how judicial resistance to Europeanizing change is both richly textured and anchored in everyday practice.

But why select *this* conversation over more than a hundred others? Consider the serendipitous opportunity I had: a dialogue with six judges at the *Tribunal de Grande Instance* (first instance court) of Marseille, France's second-largest city. I had invited one of the court's judges for an interview, expecting a one-on-one discussion. But as occurred several times during my field research, the judge invited other colleagues to join. This, I was told, is a logic of "safety in numbers" – in a group, hopefully someone would be able to answer this eager researcher's queries about EU law! In no other conversation was I able to observe the confluence of so many prospective points of view while renouncing as much control over discussion. Approximating the methodological *esprit* of Katherine Cramer's studies of informal political talk,[132] I tried to listen "in context" – here, a conference room in the court's top floor – and to nudge the conversation back to the research at hand should it stray too far afield.

The group comprised four women and two men, from approximately forty to sixty years of age, residing in at least four separate chambers, and ranging in seniority. Despite this individual diversity, judges expressed a shared institutional consciousness structuring how they related EU law to their daily life as lower court judges. We jump into the conversation as the judges discuss the reasons for their scarce knowledge of EU law (and show some conceptual slippage between the EU legal order and the European Convention of Human Rights):

**Camille:** "... we find ourselves with European law which has finally become French law, so we don't perceive it. Conversely, where we meet European

---

[130] See: Moravcsik, Andrew. 2014. "Transparency: The Revolution in Qualitative Research." *PS: Political Science & Politics* 47(1): 48–53.

[131] Interview with six judges, Tribunal de Grande Instance de Marseille, October 25, 2017 (in-person, names redacted).

[132] Cramer, *Politics of Resentment.*

law – I see it in air transport, because there there's a European directive that is directly applicable – is when they [the lawyers] don't know what to tell us, they speak to us about Article 6 of the European Convention ..."

**Felicia:** "But you know, I'm thinking back to a field where we don't apply it, but the lawyers would like us to: that's nationality, for example. That's a field where we say that each state does what it wants with its own rules, but the lawyers keep fighting this, which isn't in vain, by the way. Perhaps someday we'll get to a point where these rules ..."

**Fabrice:** "That will, no doubt, be the final domain."

**Ivonne:** "... what's interesting in what they say is that, in the end, it's more so the European Convention and the jurisprudence of the European Court of Human Rights which are fairly well integrated by judges ... [agreement from the group] ... than all the EU regulations, which we apply little, because there's little litigation, I think, here in Marseille."

In these remarks, judges make clear that they see themselves as conduits – not agents – of institutional change. It is up to lawyers to persuade them to Europeanize national rules, not for them to do so by their own motion. The conversation turns to the problem of legal training: why do these judges not simply attend a course on European law at the *École Nationale de la Magistrature?*

**Ivonne:** "Clearly I think there's a deficit of knowledge, of competence, and of practice of European law in French courts, with a few exceptions, besides some very particular litigation ..."

**TP:** "... right, so perhaps in this area it's easier to say: 'Well, I'll take a week to go enroll in a course on ...'"

**Felicia:** "No!"

**TP:** "No?"

**Victor:** "We have five days of continuing training per year, you know ..."

... [...] ...

**TP:** "But the majority of your training, you're the ones that have to do it ..."

**Felicia:** "All on our own."

**TP:** "On your own."

**Ivonne:** "And we only do it out of necessity."

**Camille:** "... we research the problem when it comes before us [broad agreement] ... we're not going to undertake a theoretical study on big questions ... Little by little, we manage to train ourselves in this way. But each time we start from specific cases, because independent of our days of training we don't have much time to study, or else we'd need 48 hours in a day!"

**Felicia:** "On the other hand, I – who now reads many ECJ judgments – we are in difficulty because it's not our culture ... an ECJ judgment is not at all the same as a Court of Cassation judgment ... we'd need to be trained to read. I think it's the EU that ought to take charge of proposing coursework ..."

**Victor**: "They might also rethink their methods. To draft judgments that are more a tad more intelligible ..."
**Fabrice**: "We'll never succeed in that."
**Felicia**: "It's their way of doing things. I think French authorities don't think it's their problem ..."

Just as in many Italian and German courts that I visited, these judges turn to legal training as a burdensome last resort when faced with a recurrent, nagging problem. Nestled within the discussion is also a clear sense of *distance* to the EU, alongside stern criticisms borne out of perceived neglect: why does the EU not propose feasible coursework for us? Why does the ECJ not write in a manner that is more legible for us? This sense of distance becomes ever-more palpable as the conversation proceeds, legitimating a renouncement of agency:

**Ivonne**: "At the Court of Cassation, on extremely sensitive affairs ... they have three or four months to prepare ... but us, we're in a different world, right? We're in a world where we go much faster, and, voilà, we lack the vocation to create law, despite everything ...'"
**TP**: "So in effect it's about resolving the cases in a rapid way, to provide rapid justice ..."
**Victor**: "Yes, to respect the principle of reasonable delay, of course." [broad agreement]
**Ivonne**: "Yes, and we're not forcibly dealing with questions of principle. In any case, we can cut out questions of principle ... If a question of principle presents itself, voilà, it's true we can submit a preliminary reference [to the ECJ], but it's not in our DNA to solicit an interpretation of the Court of Justice [broad agreement]. We don't – I think we don't even know how to do it!"
**Felicia**: "That's right, we don't even know how to do it!"

In these remarks, my interlocutors acknowledge the elephant in the room, that they would not know how to solicit the ECJ in the first place. Victor and Fabrice proceed to query how the EU legal system works: notice how underlying the questions is a search for reasons *not to participate*:

**Victor**: "Once we seize the Court, to get an answer, how long does it take?"
**TP**: "That depends. There's an expedited procedure ... but that still takes five or six months. For the other questions, it takes 16 to 19 months to receive an answer of the Court of Justice."
**Victor**: "Because we have laws, you know. Lower courts are supposed to take nine months. So if we take six months – that puts us to fifteen!"

**Ivonne**: "Yeah, but it's not like we're soliciting the European Court of Justice, voilà. Who, amongst us, in their career, will have seized the Court of Justice?"

**Fabrice**: "Is it up to lower courts to do it?"

**TP**: "You think that, perhaps, it's better if it's the supreme – that it be a dialogue between Cassation and the Court of Justice?'"

**Fabrice**: "Yes."

**TP**: "Why do you think this would be preferable?"

**Fabrice**: "Because I think the first instance judge, his true work is to provide a concrete answer – in conformity with the text, to be sure, but mostly to answer the problem brought by the parties. And it matters little if this answer isn't exactly in conformance with the wishes of a European text ..."

... [...] ...

**Ivonne**: "This perhaps demonstrates that in the end European law is ... scarcely applicable in the quotidianity of the judge ... I think we live the jurisprudence of the EC ... CJ ..."

**Felicia**: "ECJ."

**Ivonne**: "... ECJ! Right, we must even start with the Court! The Court of the European Union as, in the end, a law of principles ... But for the judge, in his everyday, that remains very far away. I also think that it's because of this that we don't apply it. That we lack that culture. It concerns more the supreme courts, which have more proximity ... it's your colleagues who are over there, and they return to the Court of Cassation. Because they don't know where they could possibly work after their years at the Court of Justice. Whew! They've forgotten ... that they have to divorce people!"
[Laughter]

Ivonne's laughter conveys a perception that it would be beneath the ECJ to dialogue with lower court judges dealing with quotidian divorce cases. In theory EU law can be directly invoked by the humblest of national judges, but Ivonne and her colleagues are adamant that in practice it "remains very far away."

To conclude our conversation, I probe how Ivonne and her colleagues react when faced with a counterfactual scenario. I share some of my field research in Genoa, a nearby city with a similar port economy where national judges and lawyers have come to regularly solicit the ECJ (the key role that entrepreneurial lawyers played in the Genoese case is discussed in Chapter 7). Might this prompt the judges to question an institutional consciousness of path dependence?

**TP**: "I wanted to speak to you a little bit about the case of Genoa, in Italy. Because, in essence, it a city near Marseille, with a port of comparable size ..."

**Ivonne**: "Brilliant! Voilà! We will found – we will found a law firm!"

**TP**: "Are there reasons that you can think of why ... this dynamic did not happen in Marseille?"

**Ivonne**: "Well, I think Marseille has an extremely difficult economic life ... there's certainly business lawyers in Marseille but we don't see them in court ..."

**Felicia**: "And in your example, it's really the initiative of individuals which matters ..."

**Ivonne**: "But it's extremely interesting!"

**Felicia**: "One needs – it's almost accidental, as you recounted it ..."

**Ivonne**: "Well, strategic ..." [broad chatter and discussion]

**Françoise**: "But why these judicial affairs in Italy? Because it's true that – I imagine that it could happen, law firms that have this drive. We would hear them, but would we – we should ask ourselves this question: would we reply: 'Ugh, we don't have time!'"

**Felicia**: "Absolutely, yes." [broad agreement]

The end of this conversation showcases the stickiness of an institutional consciousness that encourages habit and discourages change. The initial reaction to an alternative reality just a few hundred kilometers away is one of great interest and excitement. Ivonne even indulges in daydreaming about everyone around the table opening up a law firm so as to mobilize European law! But quickly, reality sinks in. Françoise, the youngest colleague who has been quietly listening for the entire conversation, finally intervenes and asks the crucial question: suppose law firms in Marseille *did* specialize in European law and asked lower court judges to solicit the ECJ. Would we break out of our habits and participate?

No. It would require too much time. The daydream ends.

## CHAPTER FOUR

# THE LIMITS OF REBELLION
## Judges and the Politics of Hierarchy

> *Étienne has discovered the crucial move that will change the tide of battle. It's always delightful when a petty boss bullies you, saying, that's the way it is, tough luck, I don't have to account to anyone, and then you discover that above him is a bigger boss, and this big boss says, you win. Not only does the ECJ contradict the Court of cassation, it outranks it, since European Union law takes precedence over national law. Étienne knows nothing about EU law, but already he finds it wonderful.*
>
> — Emmanuel Carrère, *Lives Other Than My Own*[1]

As arguably the most astute scholar of comparative judicial politics of his generation, it takes a lot for Martin Shapiro to be surprised. Yet as he gazed over the European landscape in 1991, Shapiro admitted that "it has come as something of a surprise that lower-court judges have so frequently invoked [referrals to the European Court of Justice (ECJ)], thus enhancing the power of the Court of Justice and detracting from that of their own national high courts, given that such judges must attend to their career prospects within hierarchically organized national judicial systems."[2] Proponents of the judicial empowerment thesis retorted that there was little to be surprised about:[3] the stricter the national judicial hierarchy, the greater the emancipation from sidestepping it via European Union (EU) law and the ECJ. European integration had transformed domestic judicial politics, and there was no turning back.

In this chapter, I demonstrate that Shapiro's intuition was sounder than he realized.[4] Not only is rebelling against one's judicial

---

[1] Carrère, Emmanuel. 2011. *Lives Other Than My Own: A Memoir.* New York, NY: Metropolitan Books, at 180.

[2] Shapiro, Martin. 1991. "The European Court of Justice." In *Euro-Politics: Institutions and Policymaking in the New European Community*, Alberta Sbragia, ed. Washington, DC: Brookings Institution, at 127.

[3] Burley and Mattli, "Europe before the Court," at 63.

[4] As Stone cautioned in 1995, under the judicial empowerment thesis, "the bureaucratic pressures individual judges may be under to conform to national rather than

hierarchy costly, but under certain conditions, European integration reifies national judiciaries in ways that may counterintuitively solidify the authority of supreme court judges. It turns out that the few low-level judges who turn to EU law to empower themselves are most likely to be positioned within decentralized judiciaries where they already enjoy the autonomy and discretion to occasionally promote bottom-up change. Conversely, those embedded in a strict hierarchy are more likely to let their superiors control the dialogue with the European Court. Therefore, rather than revolutionizing or overturning domestic judicial politics, European integration tends to *build upon* these politics. And rather than propelling the judicial construction of Europe, hierarchical politics within civil service judiciaries more often constrain judges' capacity to serve as agents of institutional change.

This argument adds an important layer atop Chapter 3's focus on how knowledge deficits and daily work pressures entrench path-dependent habits and mindsets in national judges that resist Europeanization. It does so by broadening the scope of inquiry from judicial routine to the bureaucratic politics of hierarchy. In so doing, I show that the more sophisticated narratives of judicial empowerment in Europe were onto something exciting: there *are* a few lower court judges who turn to a "second parent" in Luxembourg[5] to challenge domestic policies and mount judicial rebellions. You probably gathered from the epigraph of this chapter that Étienne is one of these judges, and we will return to him shortly. But we must also take seriously that these judges can incur reputational and career costs that are very real. Thus only in more permissive institutional contexts – namely, decentralized judicial orders – are these costs sufficiently low that a contained dynamic of lower court empowerment can arise.

The story that emerges illuminates how entrenched relations of bureaucratic authority quell the activism of low-level judges and limit the emancipatory promise of European integration. Yet to trace this process, we must embrace a nuanced understanding of the "sticks"[6] undergirding the influence of high courts in civil service judiciaries. Sanction and direct management – the "brute force" tools of

supranational norms of judging ... are surprisingly low or non-existent," yet little evidence was provided to back these claims: Stone, Alec. 1995. "Constitutional Dialogues in the European Community." EUI Working Paper Series No. 95/38, at 25.
[5] Alter, "European Court's Political Power," at 466–467.
[6] Bednar and Page, "When Order Affects Performance," at 94.

hierarchical control – can certainly matter, as studies of judicial behavior in politically centralized states have shown.[7] But following Max Weber, there is more to bureaucratic domination than just the top-down application of sanctioning power. Hierarchy is also an ideology – or what I have preferred to call an institutional consciousness – that *legitimates* subordination and discipline.[8] This is particularly true for judges (compared to bureaucrats[9]) in liberal democracies such as Italy, France, and Germany: it would be quite controversial for supreme court judges in these countries to try to fire or transfer a rebellious lower court judge, let alone to disband their court. In these contexts, hierarchical control operates in the shadow of brute force and in the light of institutional consciousness: lower court judges need not be cowed into obeisance if they are socialized into believing that it is their duty to conform.[10]

The rest of this chapter is organized into four sections. In Section 4.1, I explain why the judicial empowerment thesis overstates the capacity of judges to unshackle themselves from the entrenched authority relations of their judicial hierarchies. In Sections 4.2, 4.3, and 4.4, I compare the willingness of lower court judges to launch Europeanizing rebellions in the French administrative judiciary (a rigid hierarchy), the French civil judiciary (a less hierarchical order), and the German administrative judiciary (a decentralized, regional court system). Finally, Section 4.5 takes stock of this chapter and of Chapters 2 and 3 to motivate a pivot from judges on the bench to lawyers in the bar.

---

[7] See: Rosenbluth, Frances, and J. Mark Ramseyer. 1993. *Japan's Political Marketplace.* Cambridge, MA: Harvard University Press; Ramseyer, J. Mark. 1994. "The Puzzling (In)Dependence of Courts." *The Journal of Legal Studies* 23(2): 721–747.

[8] Weber, Max. 2013. *Economy and Society*, Vol. II. Berkeley and Los Angeles, CA: University of California Press, at 947, 953.

[9] In particular, "compliance with superiors' directives" tends to be an explicit employment requirement in bureaucracies but seldom in judiciaries: Biland and Steinmetz, "Are Judges Street-Level Bureaucrats," at 300–301.

[10] My approach thus differs from Rosenbluth and Ramseyer's account by focusing on how supreme courts condition lower court rebellions rather than how a dominant national party infringes on the separation of powers. Their narrative also fails to evidence how judges experience careerist pressures, how disciplinary acts foment conformism, or how subtler mechanisms of top-down influence temper judicial rebellions. See: Rosenbluth and Ramseyer, *Japan's Political Marketplace*, at 142–181, 179.

## 4.1 REBELLION AND CONFORMITY IN INSTITUTIONAL CONTEXT

This book is not the first to probe judicial empowerment in Europe through the lens of bureaucratic politics. In the most refined analysis of the judicialization process undergirding European integration, Karen Alter nuanced the judicial empowerment thesis by modeling it as a bureaucratic politics of inter-court competitions. She argued that not all courts gain power by turning to EU law and the ECJ but that some "national judges use the EC legal system to escape national hierarchies and the constraints of national law."[11] More precisely, opportunistic low-level judges turned to the ECJ to achieve policy outcomes foreclosed domestically. And while scholars such as Joseph Weiler implied with little evidence that lower courts made "wide and enthusiastic" use of their dialogue with the ECJ,[12] Alter's field research in France and Germany qualified this claim by noting that initially, "this was done not by entire national judiciaries, but by a few judges sending provocative references."[13] With time, however, "national judges have relinquished their historical practices" by realizing that the ECJ is "a rival authority to high courts. Since lower courts can use references to the ECJ to challenge high court jurisprudence ... references to the ECJ have become a convenient means to circumvent higher courts."[14] Given that supreme courts "wanting to limit or hinder European law from entering the national realm cannot really keep it from doing so," they were ultimately "compelled to accept ... EC law supremacy."[15]

Alter thus qualified her predecessors' claims that an unbridled tide of judicial activism swept throughout the national courts of Europe, provoking some exponents of the judicial empowerment thesis to admit that those initial claims were "too crude."[16] Yet my own fieldwork suggests that three points are worth revisiting in Alter's account. First, Alter overemphasized the extent to which "national judges have relinquished their historical practices" and embraced EU law as a tool for rebellion. Second, she interpreted bureaucratic domination over

---

[11] Alter, *Establishing the Supremacy of European Law*, at 3; Alter, "National Court Acceptance of European Court Jurisprudence," at 241–246.

[12] Weiler, "Transformation of Europe," at 2426.

[13] Alter, *Establishing the Supremacy of European Law*, at 17.

[14] Ibid., at 49.

[15] Ibid., at 55–56, 59.

[16] Mattli and Slaughter, "Role of National Courts in the Process of European Integration," at 258.

lower courts too narrowly as the (in)ability of high courts to "quash a referral to the ECJ."[17] Finally, she did not specify how variation in bureaucratic domination impinged upon her argument, although it implies that the stricter the hierarchy, the greater the emancipatory incentive for lower courts to turn to the ECJ.[18]

These limitations began crystallizing as several judges I spoke to underscored that rebellions and provocative references to the ECJ beget reputational and career costs. For even if lower courts win the one-shot battle over their superiors, in the long term they remain embedded in a judicial hierarchy where rebellious partnerships with an "outside" court are perceived with skepticism. Consider the experience of two Italian judges who embody Alter's inter-court competition model: both availed themselves of EU law to sidestep decisions by their superiors, and both faced stern criticism by their colleagues, attenuated career aspirations, and – in one case – a threat of disciplinary sanction.

As a fiercely independent Milanese administrative judge, in the 1990s Francesco Mariuzzo began to refer questions to the ECJ when he disagreed with the Council of State.[19] "[E]very time we encountered these judgments ... we began to send, with some frequency, our orders to the Luxembourg Court ... We tried to jump over the Alps ... and we proceeded ahead like a war ship, forward out at sea, taking hits, a little here, a little there." Mariuzzo admits that these rebellions require judges to be "a little courageous ... and some don't want this responsibility ... I didn't enjoy much sympathy at the Council of State, but I don't care at all!"[20] In truth, Mariuzzo's non-promotion to last instance did cause frustration, according to a former colleague. Furthermore, Mariuzzo's reputation suffered even among lower court judges, who perceived him as "too egocentric ... in the end [supreme court judges] got angry, and annulled everything he did. He wanted

---

[17] Alter, *Establishing the Supremacy of European Law* at 55.

[18] Wind, "Nordics, the EU and the Reluctance towards Supranational Judicial Review," at 1048.

[19] This portrait comes from conversations with multiple interviewees: Interview with Diana Urania-Galetta, University of Milan, December 17, 2016 (in-person); Interview with Antonio Papi-Rossi, Studio Legale Amministrativisti Associati in Milan, November 22, 2016 (in-person); Interview with Alma Chiettini, ex-judge at the Regional Administrative Court of Trento, January 18, 2017 (in-person); Interview with Giuseppe Franco Ferrari, Bocconi University, November 24, 2016 (in-person).

[20] Interview with Francesco Mariuzzo, Regional Administrative Court of Lombardy (retired), December 6, 2016 (in-person).

to jump over the Council of State. But you can't always have the last word ... it's true that European law prevails, but you must be objective about it."[21]

Another rare, pugnacious judge I encountered is Paolo Coppola at the civil court of Naples. Coppola has personally submitted most of the few references originating from the city, largely when he disagreed with the Court of Cassation on labor matters and thought that the ECJ would afford Italian workers better employment protections.[22] While convinced that this was the right thing to do, Coppola became intimately aware that "certainly [my references] bothered many people ... certainly there is a big block ... of diffidence against those who apply EU law in this manner." His repeated referrals even prompted the *avvocatura dello stato* (state legal service) to threaten disciplinary sanction, a claim other interviewees confirmed.[23] His references also sparked backlash within the Italian Constitutional Court, where some judges deemed that his behavior "isn't customary amongst respectable families."[24] And just as Mariuzzo shed careerist aspirations, Coppola notes that he has no intention or illusion of being promoted.[25]

The costs of rocking the boat were emphatically noted by other judges in Italy, France, and Germany, who explained that because judges in civil service judiciaries are also "state employees ... this precludes that liberty, independence, that affirms itself very, very slowly."[26] One civil judge in Genoa who referred several cases to the ECJ confides that many colleagues dismissed him as an attention seeker with a penchant for "journalistic" judgments.[27] In France, a civil judge

---

[21] Interview with judge, Regional Administrative Court of Lombardy (in-person, date/name redacted).

[22] In addition to Coppola himself, this portrait comes from the following: Interview with Amos Andreoni, University of Rome, February 22, 2017 (in-person); Interview with Vincenzo De Michele, University of Foggia and Studio Legale De Michele Cammarino, March 25, 2017 (in-person). The most renown reference he submitted is the *Mascolo* case: Case C-22/13, *Raffaella Mascolo and Others v. Ministero dell'Istruzione, dell'Università e della Ricerca and Comune di Napoli* [2014], ECLI:EU:C:2014:2401.

[23] Interview with lawyer and law professor, University of Rome (in-person, date/name redacted).

[24] Interview with Giuseppe Tesauro, ex-Advocate General at the ECJ and ex-President of the Italian Constitutional Court, and Paolo Coppola, Tribunal of Naples, February 25, 2017 (in-person).

[25] Interview with Paolo Coppola, February 13, 2017.

[26] Interview with Michele Marchesiello, November 10, 2016.

[27] Ibid.

who turned to the ECJ to challenge French law confesses that "you could receive a reputation for being an ideologue, that [you are] motivated by personal reasons, which is the risk in these situations."[28] In Germany, three judges admit that one of their reticences to submitting preliminary references is the fact that their colleagues would interpret their efforts as egocentric: "He thinks he's more important than any other!"[29] Consider the experience of Marianne Grabrucker, a retired judge in Munich who challenged national law by turning to the ECJ:

> The reputation in court was: ... "She's going beyond the border. Oh my god, again! She's again – No, no! Forget it, we won't talk to her anymore!" ... I knew it harmed [me] ... I didn't get promoted in a certain way, because everybody knows: "We never know how Grabrucker will decide."[30]

What seems to distinguish these few judges is how much intrinsic value they place on their own independence and policy preferences and how little they place on career advancement and fitting in. Consider how one novelist describes Étienne, the French judge of this chapter's epigraph: "If someone as brilliant as Étienne chooses the court of first instance, the provinces, petty cases, I think it's because he prefers to be top in his small arena rather than risk winding up even in second place in Paris."[31] We may reasonably admire this spirit, but we should not delude ourselves that it reflects the professional norms of civil service judiciaries.

If, to this day, bureaucratic politics within national court systems are not easily dislodged in the name of Europe, and if hierarchy calcifies a history of conformity and institutionalizes the costs of rebellion, then lower court judges should be less likely to solicit the ECJ precisely where they are under greater bureaucratic domination. As a prime example of how state institutions can prove "obstinate" to European integration, more stringent judicial hierarchies should significantly constrain national courts' dialogue with the ECJ.[32] Conversely, Europeanizing judicial rebellions should be more common where they least upset established relations of authority: in decentralized judiciaries

---

[28] Interview with Philippe Florès, October 4, 2017.

[29] Interview with three judges in a populous German Länder, December 15, 2017.

[30] Interview with Marianne Grabrucker, December 15, 2017.

[31] Carrère, *Lives Other Than My Own*, at 175–176.

[32] Hoffmann, Stanley. 1966. "Obstinate or Obsolete? The Fate of the Nation-State and the Case of Western Europe." *Daedalus* 95(3): 862–915; Kelemen and Pavone, "Political Geography of Legal Integration."

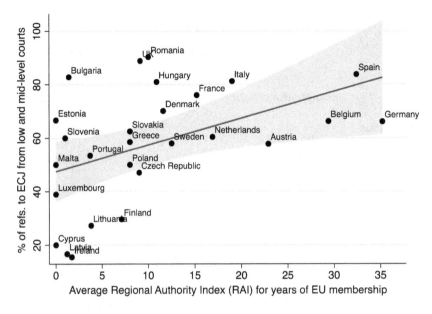

Figure 4.1 Bivariate relationship between the degree of state decentralization (RAI score) and percentage of referrals to the ECJ originating from lower courts, 1964–2013 *Source:* Data is from Kelemen and Pavone (2019), and comprises all EU member states. Correlation coefficient $(R^2) = 0.213$, and the *p*-value = 0.005.

where low-level judges already perceive themselves as occasional agents of bottom-up policy change.

Figure 4.1 provides suggestive evidence in support of this argument by visualizing the correlation between the share of referrals to the ECJ by lower courts across EU member states from 1964 through 2013 and one leading measure of state decentralization: the Regional Authority Index (RAI).[33] The RAI is a composite measure capturing the "self-rule" capacity of subnational jurisdictions as well as their ability to influence national policymaking (a higher score indicates more decentralization). While the RAI is an imperfect proxy for judicial decentralization, the results suggest a positive, statistically significant correlation between the degree of decentralization (along the *x* axis) and the share of references to the ECJ by lower courts (along the *y* axis). On average, low- and mid-level courts in the most centralized member states account for less than half of all preliminary

[33] Hooghe, Liesbet, Gary Marks, Arjan H. Schakel, Sandra Chapman Osterkatz, Sara Niedzwiecki, and Sarah Shair-Rosenfield. 2016. *Measuring Regional Authority*. New York, NY: Oxford University Press.

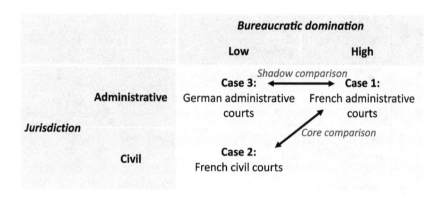

Figure 4.2 Overview of the comparative case study design

references. Conversely, for the most decentralized member states, this percentage rises to 80 percent. This relationship remains strong even when controlling for potential covariates.[34]

To unpack this correlation and surface plausible causal mechanisms, I compare how European law percolates down the rungs of state judiciaries and shapes their bureaucratic politics. Specifically, I compare the administrative and civil judiciaries in France and complement this analysis with a shadow case study of German administrative courts. This comparative case study design (see Figure 4.2) is fertile for multiple reasons. First, it enables me to move beyond descriptive inferences through within-case process tracing,[35] reconstructing how the willingness of lower courts to launch Europeanizing rebellions is shaped by the degree of bureaucratic domination that they experience.[36] Second, case studies permit me to develop a thicker conception of bureaucratic domination than the standardized indicators required for cross-sectional analyses. In particular, fieldwork-intensive case studies help me unpack how hierarchy is experienced by judges and how their behavior embodies and legitimates bureaucratic domination. In this way, we can intercept how hierarchical politics shape the practice-based institutional consciousness traced in Chapter 3.

[34] See: Pavone and Kelemen, "Evolving Judicial Politics of European Integration."
[35] Bennett and Checkel, *Process Tracing*.
[36] On the value of combining within-case process tracing with cross-case comparison, see: Falleti, Tulia, and James Mahoney. 2015. "The Comparative Sequential Method." In *Advances in Comparative-Historical Analysis*, James Mahoney and Kathleen Thelen, eds. New York, NY: Cambridge University Press, at 211–239.

To this end, comparing the French administrative (Section 4.2) and civil judiciaries (Section 4.3) proved surprisingly productive, for two reasons. First, cross-case comparisons always run the risk that so many factors vary between cases that it becomes impossible to determine what is driving the divergent outcomes.[37] Yet by comparing the civil and administrative judiciaries in the same country, I can control for all country-level factors that might influence national courts' dialogue with the ECJ, such as national constitutional tradition or legal culture, national legislative and executive politics, the organization of the legal bar, and the presence of a monist or dualist orientation vis-à-vis international law.[38] Second, although France is often treated as the prototype of a unitary centralized state, in truth the bureaucratic organization of its administrative and civil judiciaries is remarkably different.[39] While both judicial orders are organized into courts of first instance, appeal, and final instance, the administrative courts mimic the vertical centralization of the French state much more closely. Not only does the administrative supreme court – the Council of State – directly manage the ways resources are allocated and careers are advanced among lower courts, but historically it has always forged the legal ideology in which administrative judges are socialized. Conversely, the civil supreme court – the Court of Cassation – not only lacks the power to directly manage lower court resources and careers, but historically its authority has always been in tension with the lower courts. French civil judges should thus be more willing to send provocative references to the ECJ than their administrative counterparts. Figure 4.3 provides initially supportive evidence, and the rest of this chapter provides a textured account of the underlying reasons.

Finally, to confirm that the French case is surfacing the impact of bureaucratic domination rather than legal differences between administrative and civil law, I conclude with a "shadow case study"[40] (Section 4.4). Specifically, I compare the experience of French administrative

---

[37] See: Pavone, "Selecting Cases for Comparative Sequential Analysis"; George, Alexander L., and Andrew Bennett. 2005. *Case Studies and Theory Development in the Social Sciences*. Cambridge, MA: MIT Press, at 151–180.

[38] See: Snyder, Richard. 2001. "Scaling Down: The Subnational Comparative Method." *Studies in Comparative International Development* 36(1): 93–110, at 94.

[39] See: Bell, John. 2001. *French Legal Cultures*. New York, NY: Cambridge University Press; Pavone, Tommaso. 2020. "Lawyers, Judges, and the Obstinate State: The French Case and an Agenda for Comparative Politics." *French Politics* 18: 416–432.

[40] See: Soifer, Hillel. 2015. "Shadow Cases in Comparative Research." Paper for the IQMR Author's Workshop, June 2015, Syracuse, NY.

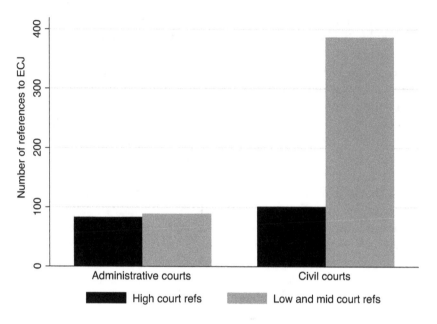

Figure 4.3 Number of preliminary references to ECJ by French civil and administrative courts, 1964–2013

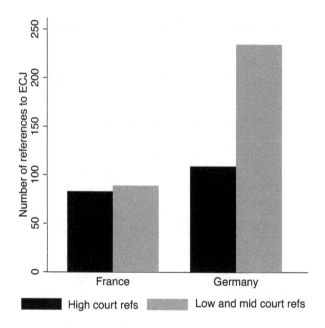

Figure 4.4 Number of preliminary references to ECJ by French and German administrative courts, 1964–2013

judges to that of their German colleagues embedded in a far more decentralized administrative judiciary. If German administrative judges feel that it is more legitimate and possible to rebel against their superiors by soliciting the ECJ than their French counterparts, it bolsters confidence that bureaucratic domination is driving variation in the outcome of interest. Figure 4.4 provides supportive evidence that the rest of this chapter corroborates qualitatively.

## 4.2 DISCIPLINE AND DIRECTION IN FRENCH ADMINISTRATIVE COURTS

### 4.2.1 A Vatican in Paris

In the history-steeped offices and marbled hallways of the Palais Royal in Paris, members of the Council of State (*Conseil d'Etat*) speak of change. It has been over fifty years since President Charles de Gaulle "threatened to do away with the [Council] altogether" if it did not embrace the General's expansive view of executive power.[41] It has been nearly thirty years since Patrick Frydman, then *Commissaire du Gouvernement*, persuaded his colleagues to relax their Gaullist jurisprudence by accepting the supremacy and direct effect of EU law in the *Nicolo* judgment.[42] And it has been nearly fifteen years since sociologist Bruno Latour demystified the Council's self-conception as a "neoclassical temple mysteriously hovering above an astounded citizenry."[43] In on- and off-the-record conversations, the councillors are adamant that they are taking these changes in stride: they are a younger and more Europeanist bunch than their Gaullist forebears. No longer looking backward to "the shadow of Bonaparte" and de

---

[41] See: Alter, *Establishing the Supremacy of European Law*, at 138; Moeschel, Mathias. 2019. "How 'Liberal' Democracies Attack(ed) Judicial Independence." In *Judicial Power in a Globalized World*, Paulo Pinto de Albuquerque and Krzysztof Wojtyczek, eds. Cham: Springer, at 291–300.

[42] Conseil d'État, Assemblée, du 20 Octobre 1989, 108243, recueil Lebon, p. 190. The Vice-President of the Council, Marceau Long, had similarly been pushing for a shift in the Council's jurisprudence, but according to one commentator, "the oracle is clarified by the Frydman conclusions." See Pellet, Alain, and Alina Miron. 2015. *Les Grandes Décisions de la Jurisprudence Française de Droit International Public*. Paris: Dalloz, at 169–171.

[43] Latour, *Making of Law*, at 3–5.

Gaulle,[44] the administrative judiciary seems to be embracing the light of the ECJ.

But such talk of transformation conceals a deeper story of institutional obstinance. It is true that post-*Nicolo*, French administrative law – which is substantially judge-made by the Council – has been greatly Europeanized. There is no doubt that the Council has become the most prolific referrer of cases to the ECJ since the 1990s.[45] Yet it is also certain that the Council continues to place itself at the center of the juridical cosmos: it is for the Council of State to adjudicate the scope and legitimacy of state actions under European law, and it is for lower administrative courts to get in line and follow the Council's lead.

In short, what has not changed is the profound influence – or, in judges' own words, *discipline* – that the Council exercises over lower – nay, *subordinated* – courts. Napoleon's shadow may have receded, but not the Council's. What else is one to conclude when during a conversation, a councillor matter-of-factly affirms that "administrative law is the Council of State, it's always been the Council of State, and it will always remain the Council of State"?[46] The temporal faith evoked by this statement mirrors the religious symbology invoked by many administrative jurists. One administrative judge of first instance told me that "the Council of State's word is something like the gospel."[47] And an administrative lawyer shared how for his judicial counterparts, "the Council of State is the Vatican! The Vatican of administrative justice."[48]

From this state of affairs germinated an open secret at the Council and at the ECJ: that lower administrative courts in France "hesitate, perhaps too much" to solicit the ECJ, their number of referrals being "excessively limited."[49] In a recent exchange between the Council and the European Court, one councillor recalls that the Luxembourg judges inquired with concern, "why aren't there many referrals from the Tribunals and the Courts of Appeal?" "We have a problem in France,"

---

[44] Ibid., at 3.

[45] Pavone and Kelemen, "Evolving Judicial Politics of European Integration."

[46] Interview with Mattias Guyomar, Council of State in Paris, October 5, 2017 (in-person).

[47] Interview with Hélène Rouland-Boyer, October 23, 2017.

[48] Interview with Philippe Guibert, De Pardieu Brocas Maffei, September 21, 2017 (in-person).

[49] Interview with Bernard Stirn, Council of State in Paris, September 20, 2017 (in-person).

the councillor confesses, "the Council of State refers a lot, but the other administrative jurisdictions no, or very little anyway."[50] Demystifying this open secret requires first tracing the origins of discipline among the French administrative courts.

### 4.2.2 History as Hierarchy

History itself is a powerful fulcrum of institutional consciousness. And for administrative judges, history begins with the Council, specifically Napoleon's decision to convert the *Conseil du Roi* (the King's Council) into the Council of State via Article 52 of the Constitution of December 13, 1799. In addition to its inherited role as advisor to the executive, in 1806 a litigation commission (renamed "litigation section" in 1852) was added to adjudicate the legality of state actions, creating what would be recognized today as France's first administrative court. It would take near 150 years for the administrative courts of first instance (*tribunaux administratifs*) to be created in 1953, by delegating competences from the Council itself, followed by the installment of the courts of appeal (*cours administratifs d'appel*) in 1987.[51]

The stylized historical narrative that emerges is of a Council that restructures and extends itself, like an octopus, into an administrative court system. French judges interviewed repeatedly invoked the weight of this history. This is nothing new: Latour's ethnography underscored the "fascinating figures of speech" that allow administrative judges at the Council in particular to "address themselves [to ...] 200 years of phantom councillors" as if to reify "what it has always said."[52] Latour was focusing in particular on history as jurisprudential continuity, to which we will return; but for administrative judges, history is also hierarchy. Invoking his interactions with administrative judges, one Cassation judge remarks how history remains

> anchored within [their] working habits, and the mentalities ... The Council of State is the creator of the administrative courts of appeal and of the administrative tribunals. They are partitions of itself ... the Council of State is the creator, one might even say the owner, of the lower courts ... which it holds by the neck, without any possibility of emancipation.[53]

[50] Interview with Patrick Frydman, Council of State and Paris Administrative Court of Appeal, September 25, 2017 (in-person).
[51] Neville-Brown, Lionel, John Bell, and Jean-Michel Galabert. 1998. *French Administrative Law*, 5th ed. Oxford, UK: Clarendon Press, at 62.
[52] Latour, *Making of Law*, at 15.
[53] Interview with Thierry Fossier, October 3, 2017.

The Council's own judges frequently invoke these origins. A recurrent explication for the *vertical* authority of the Council is to recast it as *temporal* authority, akin to the parent who half-jokingly tells their child, "I brought you into this world, and I can take you out." "Administrative justice in France began with the Council of State," remarks Bernard Stirn, the longstanding President of the Council's litigation section; "It's from the Council of State that we re-allocated judges to the tribunals ... [and] to the courts of appeal. So all of these reforms began from the Council of State, were established from the Council of State, and the jurisprudence of the Council ... is in the culture of administrative judges to respect."[54] Other councillors mirrored these remarks almost verbatim: in the words of the president of one of the litigation chambers, "it was the Council of State that existed first, then the administrative tribunals, and then the administrative appeal courts. So the Council of State remains perceived as the heart of the system, and so what the Council decides in its superior formation is respected."[55]

History is hierarchy in subtler ways as well. Jurisprudential continuity matters greatly to a system of judge-made rules, and administrative judges emphasize their commitment to safeguarding legal certainty from the vicissitudes of inter-court competitions. The Council's "jurisprudence is very stable," observes a civil judge, differentiating the administrative justice system from his own; "For them, a case law should not be touched for ten years! For them, it's an absolute rule! ... What prevails is stability and predictability. So when you're judge in an administrative tribunal or administrative court of appeal, you absolutely cannot dare to detach yourself from the jurisprudence [of the Council]."[56]

The administrative judges I spoke to confirm how they feel the weight of the Council's decisions and value them as binding precedents in practice. Tellingly, they repeatedly use the terminology of "jurisprudential discipline," which highlights how revering legal certainty reifies hierarchy and order. "There's a tradition of jurisprudential discipline amongst administrative courts," remarks a member of the Council, "which means that we have very few rebellions. So very little need to instrumentalize the preliminary reference [to the ECJ] as a lever of

[54] Interview with Bernard Stirn, September 20, 2017.
[55] Interview with Fabien Raynaud, Council of State in Paris, September 29, 2017 (in-person).
[56] Interview with Thierry Fossier, October 3, 2017.

rebellion."[57] Administrative judges of first instance agree: "There exists an evident jurisprudential discipline," notes one judge in Marseille, and "it's a guarantee for the litigants, for the certainty of law. When they come before us, and there's a case law of the Council of State that regulates and settles that point, he knows that the first instance judge whom he's addressing will apply that jurisprudence."[58] Administrative lawyers confirm that persuading judges to rebel against the Council's jurisprudence and solicit the ECJ is nearly impossible: "When the Council of State has taken a position, it's really complicated to get them to change their mind ... you'll never have a lower administrative judge that will detach himself."[59]

A history of hierarchy combined with reverence for legal certainty means that most major judicial evolutions are charted by the Council from the top-down and not the reverse. This certainly applies to EU law, and administrative courts who expose themselves by soliciting the ECJ do so at their own risk.

Exemplary is the infamous 1978 *Cohn-Bendit* case. The case concerned France's expulsion of a student leader of the May 1968 protests that had forced de Gaulle's sudden resignation from the Presidency. Upon being denied reentry in 1975 by the Ministry of the Interior, the activist – Daniel Cohn-Bendit – brought suit before the Administrative Court of Paris alleging that the Ministry's act violated a European directive (Council Directive 64/221/EEC) concerning the limitations that can be legitimately imposed upon free movement of persons on grounds of public security. The Paris judges tried to submit the case to the ECJ, but its reference never made it: the Ministry blocked transmission and appealed to the Council.[60] Not only did the Council quash the reference altogether, but it denied that European directives could have any direct effect in complaints filed against a single administrative act: a veritable "declaration of war" against the ECJ's settled case law.[61]

---

[57] Interview with Mattias Guyomar, October 5th, 2017.
[58] Interview with Christophe Cirefice, Administrative Court of Marseille, October 19, 2017 (in-person).
[59] Interview with Philippe Guibert, September 21, 2017.
[60] Conseil d'État, Assemblée, December 12, 1978, ministre de l'intérieur c/ Cohn-Bendit, recueil Lebon, at 524.
[61] See: case-41/74, *Van Duyn v. Home Office* [1974], ECR 01337; Case 36/75, *Roland Rutili v. Ministre de l'intérieur* [1975], ECR 01219; Alter, *Establishing the Supremacy of European Law*, at 155.

The Council's war declaration in *Cohn-Bendit* – which was not definitively overturned until 2009 – did not just resonate in Luxembourg: it was also heard loud and clear by lower administrative courts. As a former administrative judge explains, the decision "was, in effect, a censure. That's what I wanted to get to – there was truly a censure. Don't have fun referring questions, it's not worth it."[62] Even Patrick Frydman, who now presides Paris' Administrative Court of Appeal, euphemistically acknowledges that "there had been some preliminary references to the ECJ submitted by lower courts which had displeased the Council ... so it's true, when you refer something, that it's not certain that the Council of State will appreciate it."[63] Indeed, the Court of Appeal only referred its first case to the ECJ in 2015, nearly thirty years after being established.[64]

One can thus understand why administrative judges are reticent to use a dialogue with the ECJ to challenge domestic policies and Council decisions. This, in turn, effectively cedes ground to the Council. For example, "after *Nicolo*," a councillor explains, "we played the game [of applying EU law and soliciting the ECJ], but more or less graciously ... we needed to settle some questions that could have been dealt with at lower levels, but because of this reticence, it was necessary for the path to be traced at the highest level."[65] An administrative judge of first instance similarly emphasizes that most EU law referrals comprise "questions that we let the Council of State pose."[66] Indeed, in differentiating the dynamics of legal change in administrative courts from civil courts, a Cassation judge explains that "there's much more quote-in-quote direction [in the administrative judiciary], much more links and rapports and discussions from the top-down, whereas for us it's more from the bottom-up."[67]

Crucially, the combination of (i) lower court reticence and (ii) the opportunity to use the reference procedure to influence the development of EU law magnifies the great authority that the Council already has accrued, particularly compared to its days of subservience to de

---

[62] Interview with ex-administrative judge, September, 2017 (in-person; date and name redacted).
[63] Interview with Patrick Frydman, September 25, 2017.
[64] See: Case C-319/15, *Overseas Financial and Oaktree Finance* [2016], ECLI:EU:C:2016:268.
[65] Interview with Fabien Raynaud, September 29, 2017.
[66] Interview with Ghislaine Markarian, Administrative Court of Marseille, October 23, 2017 (in-person).
[67] Interview with Sophie Canas, September 22, 2017.

Gaulle's imperial presidency. By the 2000s, the Council's annual reports acknowledged their new strategy: to convert the influence of the ECJ "into an opportunity" via an "aggressive" dialogue to "diffuse their legal thought."[68] As one councillor highlighted, the Council increasingly refers cases to the ECJ "to ask the Court to precise its jurisprudence, to complete it ... [or] because we disagree with its case law, and we want to make it evolve ... we make it clear we would like for it to move."[69] And as a former lower court administrative judge corroborates: "It's rather a more intelligent approach, an approach of influence rather than confrontation ... 'We will dialogue with you, and we will try to influence you. We'll listen to you, but you listen to us as well'."[70]

### 4.2.3 Socialization and Management

Where does an institutional consciousness that treats history as hierarchy come from, and how is it enforced? For French administrative judges, it comes from the ENA – the *École Nationale d'Administration* (National School of Administration) – and it is enforced by – surprise! – the Council of State itself.

The ENA was established in 1945 by de Gaulle as a prestigious *grande école* charged with forging the political elite of the postwar French state.[71] Among its graduates – nicknamed *énarques* – are eight of the past thirteen prime ministers of France.[72] The Council has historically played a central role in shaping the ENA's curriculum and selecting its cohort of eighty or so individuals, many of whom then enter the rungs of the administrative courts.[73] This "inculturation" and "socialization" is then reinforced by the Council's *Bureau de*

---

[68] Biland, Émilie, and Rachel Vanneuville. 2012. "Government Lawyers and the Training of Senior Civil Servants." *International Journal of the Legal Profession* 9(1): 29–54, at 46–47.

[69] Interview with Mattias Guyomar, October 5, 2017.

[70] Interview with ex-administrative judge, September 2017 (in-person; date and name redacted).

[71] In April 2021, French President Emmanuel Macron announced that the ENA would be replaced by a new *Institut du Service Public* (ISP). It is unclear whether the ISP will ultimately comprise a major reform of the ENA or a mere cosmetic name change.

[72] "Old School Ties," *The Economist*, March 10, 2012; Neville Brown et al., *French Administrative Law*, at 83, 86; Vauchez, Antoine, and Pierre France. 2021. *The Neoliberal Republic: Corporate Lawyers, Statecraft, and the Making of Public-Private France*. Ithaca, NY: Cornell University Press, at 22–25 at 167–172.

[73] Biland and Vanneuville, "Government Lawyers and the Training of Senior Civil Servants."

*formation*,[74] often following a pit stop within the public administration itself. Indeed, administrative judges are "practitioners who, in some periods, are subject to judicial review and, in others, *exercise* judicial review."[75]

While the *énarques'* grip on the judiciary has been fading over the years,[76] ENA graduates are dispersed throughout the comparatively small number of administrative courts, and interviewees echo scholars of French administrative justice by underscoring their strong "ésprit de corps."[77] This matters, because the *énarques* are trained in the Weberian principles of bureaucratic governance, which inculcates a form of "institutional isomorphism" between the administrative judiciary and the public administration.[78] Through the late 1980s, this dynamic was bolstered by the fact that administrative judges were salaried members of the Ministry of the Interior.[79] As one former judge underscores, "there is, in truth, an ésprit de corps ... the recruitment of administrative judges was, for a long time, at the ENA ... [then] our colleagues work in the administration – [there] the principle of hierarchy ... is one of the fundamental principles, so this idea of subordination, of submission to hierarchy is rather strong."[80]

And just as with civil servants within a bureaucracy, several interviewees described working habits meant to cultivate directions from their superiors. The Council incentivizes this ethos by selecting the judgments it publishes, promoting a "cult of the 'leading case'" signaling that lower courts should fall in line.[81] Councillors bolster this strategy by teaching future judges at the ENA that deferring to the Council is the only way to make sense of European law: one recent ethnography chronicles how "another councillor of state compares

[74] Bell, *Judiciaries within Europe*, at 61–62.
[75] Latour, *Making of Law*, at 29.
[76] Interview with Mattias Guyomar, October 5, 2017; Bell, *Judiciaries within Europe*, at 60.
[77] Bell, *Judiciaries within Europe*, at 105; Neville Brown et al., *French Administrative Law*, at 63; Interview with Hélène Farge, Ordre des Avocats au Conseil d'État et à la Cour de Cassation, September 21, 2017 (in-person); Interview with Philippe Guibert, September 21, 2017.
[78] DiMaggio, Paul, and Walter Powell. 1983. "The Iron Cage Revisited: Institutional Isomorphism and Collective Rationality in Organizational Fields." *American Sociological Review* 48(2): 147–160.
[79] Neville Brown et al., *French Administrative Law*, at 87.
[80] Interview with Jean-Sebastien Pilczer, Cabinet JSP, September 26, 2017 (in-person).
[81] Bell, *Judiciaries within Europe*, at 71.

the Council of State decisions with the European Court of Justice ones during his class. He recalled the difficulty of identifying what is essential in the European Court of Justice's decisions ... while the Council's decisions are said to be clear and easy to understand."[82] My conversations with administrative judges testify to the success of this strategy. "If we know that an [EU] law exists, it's because we know a decision by the Council," one judge of first instance admits; "it will be under the prism – as a subordinated jurisdiction of first instance of the Council of State."[83] If it is striking to hear judges refer to themselves as subordinated, it is also notable that others interpret disagreement with the Council as a breach of ethics: "For us, it would be an error to detach ourselves from the jurisprudence of the Council of State and to address ourselves directly to the ECJ. I'd perceive it almost as professional negligence."[84]

Thus the fact that most administrative judges are recruited from the public administration or from the ENA reshapes what it means to be "independent" as a judge. In the words of the President of the legal bar before Council of State and the Court of Cassation, "administrative judges conceive their independence as an independence of the corps, and to be independent you must remain close-knit, coherent, and very hierarchically organized vis-à-vis the Council of State. Whereas civil judges conceive judicial independence as their individual independence."[85]

Should socialization fail, direct management can intervene. Until 1986, the Council could remove or transfer lower administrative judges without their consent. While this is no longer the case,[86] the gatekeeper of promotions to the Council remains the Council itself, and the career of lower court judges is determined by the High Council of Administrative Tribunals and Administrative Courts of Appeal, which is chaired by the Vice President of the Council, "managed from within the" Council, and wherein lower court judges account for only five of the thirteen members.[87] The Council also appoints its own to

---

[82] Biland and Vanneuville, "Government Lawyers and the Training of Senior Civil Servants," at 47.

[83] Interview with Christophe Cirefice, October 19, 2017.

[84] Interview with judge at an administrative court of first instance, October 2017 (in-person; name/date redacted).

[85] Interview with Hélène Farge, September 21, 2017.

[86] Neville Brown et al., French Administrative Law, at 87.

[87] See: Massot, Jean. 2016. "The Powers and Duties of the French Administrative Judge." Lecture delivered in Split, Croatia, at the Troisièmes journées juridiques et

preside the administrative courts of appeal (before returning to the Council), to ensure that they do not go rogue.[88] Even more importantly, part of the Council recreates the structure of a public ministry or "executive agency,"[89] namely its General Secretariat, which since 1987 has appropriated the competences of the Ministry of the Interior to administer the administrative courts. *Everything* – the lower courts' budget, the organization of their registries, judicial salaries, and the provision of training – is meticulously controlled by this body.[90] As Patrick Frydman describes,

> We don't depend on the Ministry of Justice [as with the civil courts], the Council is like a little ministry for administrative law. It's the Council that administers, that allocates the budget, the resources, that handles judges' careers, et cetera. So there's more influence, if you will, on judges, because everything, everything depends upon the Council of State.[91]

While disciplinary sanctions are rare and can be challenged in court, this is hardly an escape from the Council's influence. For as lower court judges know, "the Council of State as an adjudicator of lawsuits will judge the Council of State as a manager of the administrative judiciary, since if we contest a disciplinary measure that concerns us, at a certain point, it could come before the litigation section of the Council."[92] That judges at the Council routinely switch between the litigation and administrative sections blurs the already-frail separation.[93]

I mention the "brute force" tools of hierarchy last to underscore why it is largely unnecessary that they actually be used. Even within one of the most hierarchical judicial orders in Europe, hierarchy among French administrative judges cannot be understood primarily as a matter of force. Rather, it is better understood as a historically rooted consciousness in which judges are socialized, and which they reproduce daily through their reverence for legal certainty and their treatment of Council decisions as a binding prism for their own work.

The surprising outcome is that the Council is often the body that has to nudge lower administrative courts to refer (uncontroversial)

---

administratives franco-croates," October 26–27, 2009. Translated by Peter Lindseth; Bell, *Judiciaries within Europe*, at 51.
[88] Interview with Thierry Fossier, October 3, 2017.
[89] Bell, *Judiciaries within Europe*, at 50–51.
[90] Neville Brown et al., *French Administrative Law*, at 88.
[91] Interview with Patrick Frydman, September 25, 2017.
[92] Interview with Christophe Cirefice, October 19, 2017.
[93] See: Calon, Jean-Paul. 1978. "La Cour de Cassation et le Conseil d'État: Une comparaison." *Revue internationale de droit comparé* 1: 229–245, at 235.

cases to the ECJ. At the Palais Royal, Bernard Stirn underscores that in conferences with lower administrative courts, he often tells them, "don't hesitate! It's not worth that you wait for the affair to make it to the Council of State to pose a preliminary reference."[94] Stirn's encouragements are well known among administrative judges,[95] but what is usually necessary is not encouragement, but *direction*.

Take, for example, a lower court that appeared to have empowered itself via a dialogue with the ECJ. In April 2011, the administrative court of Montreuil – a small town in Paris' periphery – referred no less than ten closely related taxation cases to the ECJ.[96] What is striking is that the administrative court of Montreuil had been established only one year prior in December 2009. Was this a case of a new set of young, ambitious, rebellious judges seeking to make a name for themselves? Not at all. The administrative judges had solicited the advice of the Council in the case through an advisory mechanism,[97] and it was the Council itself that directed the lower court to refer the case to the ECJ. As an administrative judge involved in the case reveals:

> What's interesting is that before [referring], there was a back and forth with the Council of State. That is ... the Tribunal had asked the Council of State what they thought about it, and the Council ... it's a way to ... authorize ... the Council replied to some questions pertaining to French law, and for the rest it said: "These are questions of EU law. You will refer to the ECJ."[98]

This example demonstrates the degree to which the Council remains firmly in control of the administrative judiciary's dialogue with the ECJ even when, at first glance, it would appear that a lower court circumvented Paris for Luxembourg. It demonstrates how the Council contains and controls the Europeanization of judicial practice from the apex of an institutional hierarchy. And it evidences the inversion of the judicial empowerment thesis: instead of referring frequently to emancipate themselves, administrative judges refer infrequently, and when they do it is often in *response to* – not in rebellion against – their superiors' preferences.

---

[94] Interview with Bernard Stirn, September 20, 2017.
[95] Interview with Patrick Frydman, September 25, 2017.
[96] Joined cases C-338/11 to C-347/11, *Santander Asset Management* [2012], ECLI:EU:C:2012:286.
[97] On advisory procedure, see: Bell, *Judiciaries within Europe*, at 48.
[98] Interview with ex-administrative judge, September 2017 (in-person; date and name redacted).

## 4.3 REBELLION AND REFORM IN FRENCH CIVIL COURTS

### 4.3.1 Traces of 1789

If all roads lead to the Council of State for administrative judges, the historical origins of the civil judiciary are messier and more bifurcated. The civil courts of appeal were first instituted in 1800 by converting the disbanded provincial parliaments – the counterpowers to the monarchy in the lead-up to the French revolution – into fully judicial appeal bodies.[99] By contrast, the Court of Cassation can be traced to the Privy Council (*Conseil des Parties*), a constitutive body of the King's Council that met in a bedroom within the King's palace, and whose decisions were considered to be royal acts.[100] In prerevolutionary France, the Privy Council had the authority to overturn (or *casser*, which means "to break," via *la cassation*) decisions made by the provincial parliaments. In postrevolutionary France, the Court of Cassation assumed this authority over the courts of appeal and first instance.[101]

In short, the origin of the civil courts lies in the struggle between royal center and the parliamentary periphery.[102] The civil judges I spoke to seemed attuned to this history and how it shapes their own identity. As one judge explains:

> The Court of Cassation is the descendant of the royal power ... the courts of appeal are descendants of parliament. So this rebellion is not the pre but the post-figuration of the French revolution itself! ... it's a professional culture, the pit at the center of the fruit, something you cannot destroy from one day to the next ... 230 years after the French revolution, we are still there.[103]

Of course, we are not literally "still there" in revolutionary times, but rather in the realm of more tempered leitmotifs. Yet these echoes are telling nonetheless. For example, while not a single lower administrative court dared to refer a case to the ECJ before the Council did so first

---

[99] Loi du 18 mars 1800, du 27 Ventose an 8 Sur L'Organisation des Tribunaux, recueil Duvergier, at 166.

[100] Barbiche, Bernard. 2010. "Les attributions judiciaires du Conseil du roi." *Histoire, Economie, & Société* 29(3): 9–17.

[101] Ibid.

[102] The civil courts of first instance – the *Tribunaux de Grande Instance* – also date to revolutionary times. Specifically, they were created in 1790 by converting the prerevolutionary *tribunaux de district* (Loi du 16 août 1790 sur l'organisation judiciaire, receuil Duvergier, at 361).

[103] Interview with Thierry Fossier, October 3, 2017.

(in 1970),[104] three civil courts of appeal solicited the ECJ[105] before the Court of Cassation did the same (in 1967).[106] This anticipated the Cassation's recognition of the supremacy and direct effect of European law in the 1975 *Jacques Vabre* case – nearly two decades before the Council.[107] If the Council of State charts the path of policy change from the top-down, the Court of Cassation is sometimes faced with a push to change from the bottom-up.

This is not to say that there is no hierarchy between the Court of Cassation and the lower courts. While "organized rebellions"[108] are acknowledged by civil judges, those involved can face reputational costs. In interviews, some colleagues pejoratively refer to participants as "very militant."[109] Their friends may half-jokingly concede that rebels "will never make it to the Court of Cassation."[110] Half-jokes have serious undertones, since being "crowned" Cassation judge is a validation that many aspire to but few will achieve. That historically a

---

[104] See: Case 34/70, *Syndicat national du commerce extérieur des céréales and Others* v. *ONIC* [1970], ECR 1233.

[105] These are the Court of Appeal of Colmar (in case 44/65), the Court of Appeal of Paris (in case 56/65 and case 9/67), and the Court of Appeal of Orleans (in case 1/67). See: 44/65, *Hessische Knappschaft* v. *Singer and Fils* [1965], ECR 965; 56/65, *Sociéte Technique Minière* v. *Maschinenbau Ulm* [1966], ECR 235; 1/67, *Ciechelsky* v. *Caisse regionale de securite sociale du Centre* [1967], ECR 181; 9/67, *Colditz* v. *Caisse d'assurance vieillesse des travailleurs salariés* [1967], ECR 229.

[106] See: Case 22/67, *Caisse regionale de securite sociale du Nord* v. *Goffart* [1967], ECR 321.

[107] See: Cour de Cassation, Chambre mixte, 24 mai 1975, Société "Cafés Jacques Vabre." In this pivotal case, the role of Adolphe Touffait – future president of the Court of Cassation – is recognized as key in persuading his colleagues to embrace the primacy and direct effect of EU law. Touffait had been cabinet chief for Pierre-Henri Teitgen, one of the most influential Eurofederalists in postwar France. He would later also become judge at the ECJ. See: Alter, Karen. 2016. "Jurist Advocacy Movements in Europe and the Andes." *iCourts Working Paper Series* 65: 1–30, at 20. Crucially, Mr. Touffait was previously President of the Court of Appeal of Paris when it made its first referral to the ECJ (in case 56/65), two years before the Cassation did so for the first time. To get a sense of Mr. Touffait's Europeanism, see: Touffait, Adolphe. 1983. "Réflexions d'un magistrat français sur son expérience à la Cour de justice des Communautés européènnes." *Revue internationale de droit comparé* 2: 283–299.

[108] Interview with Guy Canivet, ex-President of the Court of Cassation in Paris, October 2, 2017 (in-person).

[109] Interview with judge at the Tribunal de Grande Instance of Marseille, October 2017 (in-person; name redacted).

[110] Interview with Thierry Fossier, October 3, 2017.

large majority of these betrothed are of Parisian origin only reinforces a culture of centrality and prestige within the Cassation.[111]

But insofar as the Cassation sits atop a hierarchy, its authority is much less acute than the Council of State's Vatican-esque discipline. Rather than being recruited alongside civil servants from the ENA and socialized to respect hierarchy, any university graduate from any law school in France can become a member of the large and diverse corps of civil judges upon passing the national judicial entrance exam.[112] Their subsequent training occurs at the *École Nationale de la Magistrature* (ENM, the National Judicial Training School) where fellow trainees are judges rather than bureaucrats. Instead of transitioning back and forth between the public administration and the judiciary, most civil judges remain in their posts for the entirety of their professional life. Their career advancement hardly depends upon the Cassation's preferences, given that it requires a nomination by the Ministry of Justice and the consent of the *Conseil Supérieur de la Magistrature* (CSM, the Judicial High Council), wherein supreme court judges comprise less than one-third of the membership.[113] Rebellious judges might risk developing a poor reputation, but there is little that the Court of Cassation can do to discipline such a judge.

And lower court judges know it: "This exasperates the First President of the Court of Cassation, who dreams of a perfect pyramid … but this absolutely doesn't work, doesn't work! The courts of appeal regularly get together to say, 'the Court of Cassation is poisoning us, they do whatever they want, and we'll do whatever we want'."[114] Administrative judges know it too, and in informal meetings with Cassation judges they sometimes cannot resist the occasional tease: "The colleagues at the Council mock us, they tell us: 'But you accept this? You tolerate this?'"[115] Sometimes, passing teases can boil over into ridicule: "'I'm independent, I'm a judge, I decide as I want!'" acts out an administrative judge in interview, "'it's not the Court of

[111] Calon, "Cour de Cassation et le Conseil d'État," at 234.
[112] See: McKee, J. Y. 2007. "Le recruitement et l'avancement des juges français." Tribunal de Grande Instance de Rennes, Rennes, March Paper delivered in Rennes, 6 March 2007, at i–ii. Available at: www.courdecassation.fr/IMG/File/pdf_2007/10-05-2007/10-05-2007_mcKee_fr.
[113] Ibid., at v–vi; Bell, *Judiciaries within Europe*, at 50–51. As Bell (p. 67) notes, unlike administrative judges, civil judges have never been transferred against their will by the CSM or the Ministry of Justice.
[114] Interview with Thierry Fossier, October 3, 2017 (in-person).
[115] Ibid.

Cassation that will teach me the law! Or the Court of Appeal!' Fine! And the litigants? . . . it weakens legal certainty."[116]

In truth, many civil judges are proud to disavow the obedience of their administrative counterparts. As former Cassation president Guy Canivet explains:

> Lower courts have sometimes used the preliminary reference procedure to side-step the jurisprudence of the Court of Cassation. It's their role! It's in the system . . . [the Cassation's] control has nothing to do with force, it's not hierarchical. It's jurisdictional, and there's a tradition of contestation . . . the rapport is not the same [for administrative courts], where the Council of State imposes a ferocious discipline.[117]

The less strict civil court hierarchy thus foments a different kind of institutional consciousness. Instead of privileging legal certainty and loyalty to the gospel of supreme court judges, civil judges privilege their individual independence and link this to the postrevolutionary ideals of democratic liberty. "It's not in our culture to call upon the Court of Cassation to tell it, 'we're going to pose a preliminary reference'," explains the president of the Paris Court of Appeal; "what's very present in civil courts is the independence of courts, and it's the heart of democracy. And that's why when the judge applies the law, he does it based on his soul and conscience."[118] "[If] to side-step the jurisprudence of the Court of Cassation one must pose a preliminary reference, I think neither of us would have the faintest worry," agrees a colleague, "we're very admiring of their decisions, but don't have a particular reverence in their regard."[119]

Lawyers who practice before both administrative and civil courts appear well-attuned to this difference. If they regularly complain that "lower administrative courts never refer,"[120] they also note that "for civil judges . . . if they don't like the path of the Court of Cassation, and the lawyers say there is a preliminary reference to be made, it'll be

---

[116] Interview with Christophe Cirefice, October 19, 2017.
[117] Interview with Guy Canivet, October 2, 2017.
[118] Interview with Chantal Arens [quoted], Marie-Caroline Celeyron-Bouillot and N. Boureois De-Ryck, judges at the Cour d'Appel de Paris, October 4, 2017 (in-person).
[119] Ibid. [quoting Celeyron-Bouillot].
[120] Interview with Philippe Derouin, SCP Philippe Derouin, September 12, 2017 (in-person).

| | Administrative courts | Civil courts |
|---|---|---|
| *Bureaucratic discipline a part of judicial education and training?* | **Yes** – Judges are trained alongside bureaucrats the National School of Administration (ENA) and usually also serve in the public administration | **No** – Judges are trained at the National Judicial School (ENM) and rarely serve in the public administration |
| *Degree of supreme court influence over judicial careers* | **High** – Lower court judges are promoted by a Council [CSTACAA] presided by the head of the Council of State, and the Council of State fully controls recruitment into the Council | **Low** – Lower court judges are promoted following nomination by the Ministry of Justice and approval of the Judicial High Council (CSM), wherein Cassation judges comprise a minority of members |
| *Degree of supreme court influence over judicial salaries and lower court budgets* | **High** – Salaries and lower court resources are managed by the Council of State's General Secretariat | **None** – Salaries and lower court resources are managed by the Ministry of Justice |
| *Procedure for lower courts to challenge supreme court decisions under national law?* | **No** – No procedural means to organize a lower court rebellion against a Council of State decision | **Yes** – Rebellion against a Court of Cassation decision by two courts of Appeal is possible, and is then adjudicated by the Cassation's plenary session |

Figure 4.5 Degree of hierarchy among French administrative and civil courts

easier."[121] By being more attached to their "individual independence," rebellion is "more frequent amongst civil courts."[122]

In fact, unlike French administrative procedure, civil procedure institutionalizes "legitimate resistance"[123] to a Cassation decision (an institutional comparison of the administrative and civil judicial hierarchies is provided in Figure 4.5). A court of appeal in disagreement with a Cassation decision can forward the affair to another court of appeal; if the second court agrees that the Court of Cassation made a mistake, it can resubmit the case to the Court of Cassation (via a second *pourvoi en cassation*), where the disagreement will be adjudicated by the Cassation's plenary session. In this forum, lower court judges feel that they have a real shot at promoting change, since the plenary session tends to side with lower courts one time out of three.[124] Indeed, during a 1994 conference organized at the Cassation,

---

[121] Interview with Philippe Guibert, September 21, 2017.
[122] Interview with Hélène Farge, September 21, 2017.
[123] Bell, *Judiciaries within Europe*, at 70–71.
[124] Interview with Philippe Florès, October 4, 2017.

"judges at all levels acknowledged that the role of lower court judges is to be a rebel, but not too often."[125] In conversations, civil judges confirmed that because rebellion is "integrated in the system of civil justice"[126] and "established institutionally," the idea of turning to the ECJ in order to contest a jurisprudence of their superiors is "marginal" but not unfamiliar.[127] And where institutionalized rebellion fails, lower courts have even occasionally resorted to noncompliance with Cassation rulings.[128] While very rare, any such effort would be totally unimaginable for their administrative colleagues.

### 4.3.2 "The Bigger Boss"

To get a sense of how soliciting the ECJ channels a preexisting institutional consciousness permitting the occasional rebellion, we turn to an audacious civil judge we already encountered in Chapter 3: Philippe Florès.

The first time I heard of Florès was not in France, but in a moment of serendipity in Italy. A civil judge had stumbled upon a memoir by Emmanuel Carrère entitled *Lives Other Than My Own*.[129] In it, Carrère chronicles a social justice crusade led by two French civil judges of first instance – including Florès – to protect consumers. The Italian judge became the first of several interviewees to recommend the book.[130] A year later, I met Florès in Versailles.

All begins in the 1990s as wages stagnated in several European countries including France. A growing number of borrowers found themselves unable to repay loans to credit companies. So the latter began to bleed borrowers to death in court. At the front lines of these efforts were civil judges of first instance, who were "confronted with a brutal reality" of the growing "inequality of resources amongst

---

[125] Bell, *Judiciaries within Europe*, at 70–71.

[126] Interview with Guy Canivet, October 2, 2017.

[127] Interview with Lise Leroy-Gissinger, October 24, 2017.

[128] Bell cites three examples related to civil liability of children (in the mid-1980s), liability for things (in 1930), and dismissal of teachers in religious schools (in the late 1970s). See: Bell, *Judiciaries within Europe*, at 71; See also: Steiner, Eva. 2010. *French Law: A Comparative Approach*. New York, NY: Oxford University Press, at 96–97.

[129] Carrère, *Lives Other Than My Own*.

[130] Interview with Roberto Conti, October 12, 2016. Others who recommended the book were the President of the bar before the Court of Cassation and Council of State, Hélène Farge, and a judge at the Court of Cassation, Sophie Canas.

litigants":[131] credit industry professionals (the prototypical economic "repeat players") on the one hand, and working class consumers (the prototypical "one-shotters") on the other hand.[132] In contract after contract, credit companies embedded terms in the fine print that seemed innocuous to the untrained eye, but which were unfair in practice. For example, contracts might stipulate that only the courts located where a credit company is incorporated could adjudicate an eventual dispute, such that consumers would have to bear travel expenses just to defend themselves in court.[133]

Exacerbating the situation was the case law of the Court of Cassation, which held that judges could not screen a contract for unfair terms by their own motion.[134] In the Cassation's view, consumer protections constituted "public policy rules designed to protect specific interests" rather than "public policy rules designed to order society"; only the latter could be invoked by judges *ex officio*.[135] Now, "all this is fine in theory, but in reality the consumer doesn't complain, because he doesn't know the law, he's not the one who filed the lawsuit, and nine times out of ten he has no lawyer."[136]

Then in 2000, one of Florès' colleagues at the first instance court of Vienne – Étienne Rigal, of this chapter's epigraph – happened upon an ECJ judgment while leafing through newspapers and law reviews. In the judgment, the ECJ noted that under EU law, "the consumer is in a weak position vis-à-vis the seller or supplier ... It follows that effective protection of the consumer may be attained only if the national court acknowledges that it has the power to evaluate [contractual] terms of this kind of its own motion."[137] Rigal was captivated, and "there is something comical in the contrast between [the ECJ's] indigestible prose and the joy it unleashed" as he quickly contacted Florès, then president of the national association of first instance judges.[138]

---

[131] "Comment deux "petits juges" ont mis à terre les sociétés de credit." *Le Monde,* August 2, 2016.

[132] The language of 'repeat players' versus "one shotters" borrows from: Galanter, "Why the "Haves" Come out Ahead."

[133] See, for instance: Joined Cases C-240/98 to C-244/98, *Océano Grupo Editorial* SA [2000], ECLI:EU:C:2000:346.

[134] Court of Cassation, Chambre Civile, July 10, 2002, Bull. I, No. 195, at 149.

[135] Case C-429/05, *Rampion and Godard* [2007], ECLI:EU:C:2007:575, at para. 58.

[136] Carrère, *Lives Other Than My Own,* at 179.

[137] Joined cases C-240/98 to C-244/98, *Océano Grupo,* at paras. 24–26.

[138] Ibid., at 179–180; Interview with Philippe Florès, October 4, 2017.

At night and on weekends for the following year, Rigal, Florès, and a few like-minded judges embarked on the complex quest of researching all aspects of EU consumer law.[139] These were "feverish days of telephone calls and e-mails."[140] Carrère's account – which Florès confirmed – underscores their dual sense of thrill and peril upon discovering that they could solicit the ECJ:

> Étienne gets excited, his eyes start to shine … [but] appealing to European Union law to counter national jurisprudence and engage the Court de Cassation, well, you can always say it won't cost a thing, but that's not true … it's like a presidential pardon in the days of the death penalty: double or nothing, the last card they can play. In the end, they decide to try. Who will make the trip? Who'll write the *jugement provocateur*? … Étienne is the one who most loves going to the front lines.[141]

It took several years, however, before Rigal and then Florès could both submit references to the ECJ. This was not only because it took much effort to master the relevant provisions of EU law to mount their rebellion. It was also because creditors were nearly always the plaintiffs doing the suing, and when they caught a whiff of Rigal and Florès' intentions, they would withdraw their suit.[142]

Eventually, Rigal had the first opportunity to solicit the ECJ in a dispute between a consumer and a credit company. Mr. Fredout had opened a line of credit with Cofidis SA, which took him to court when he failed to make some payments. Rigal noted, however, that Mr. Fredout had responded to "a leaflet printed on both sides, with the words 'Free application for money reserve' in large letters on the front, while the references to the contractual interest rate and a penalty clause were in small print on the reverse."[143] This was exactly the dispute Rigal was waiting for, so he made sure to hide his intention to launch a "little bomb" – a preliminary reference to the ECJ – when interacting with the credit company's veteran lawyer.[144] For the next two months, he meticulously refined the technical details of the reference with Florès, his "co-conspirator": the question was whether

---

[139] In particular, research began to focus on Council Directive 93/13/EEC of April 5, 1993 on unfair terms in consumer contracts, *Official Journal* 1993 L 95, at 29.

[140] Carrère, *Lives Other Than My Own*, at 182.

[141] Ibid.

[142] Interview with Philippe Florès, October 4, 2017.

[143] Case C-473/00, *Cofidis SA* [2002], ECLI:EU:C:2002:705, at para. 13.

[144] Carrère, *Lives Other Than My Own*, at 183.

under EU law national courts can be denied the ability to evaluate the fairness of a consumer contract by their own motion. By the time the "disconcerted" Cofidis lawyer found out, the paperwork had long reached Luxembourg.[145]

Almost two years later, the ECJ handed Rigal a victory, confirming that EU law "precludes a national provision which ... prohibits the national court ... from finding, of its own motion ... that a term of the contract is unfair."[146] This ruling was the exact opposite of what the Cassation had consistently held. But the latter initially resisted the broad implications that the ECJ ruling could comport. In a 2004 judgment, the Cassation narrowed the scope of the ECJ's ruling to the domain of unfair contract terms, denying judges the ability to raise points of law by their own motion in consumer litigation generally.[147]

This is when Florès openly joined Rigal's rebellion as first instance judge in Saintes. After waiting a year for the perfect case, a rare dispute arrived on his desk where it was the consumers who lawyered up to do the suing instead of a resource-rich credit company. Florès seized this opportunity to ask the ECJ whether EU consumer law has "an objective which extends beyond consumer protection alone to the organisation of the market and allows courts to apply of their own motion the provisions which flow from it." Another reference, another victory: in 2007 the ECJ definitively proclaimed that EU law must be interpreted as "allowing national courts to apply of their own motion the provisions transposing" all consumer protection directives.[148] The Court of Cassation was forced to acquiesce, and in January 2008 the French Consumer Code was revised to note that "the judge can invoke all of the dispositions of the present code by his own motion."[149] In turn, Rigal and Florès' actions made headlines: their "Austerlitz"-like rebellion[150] was likened "to the 'bon juge Maganaud' who in a celebrated judgment of 1898 refused to convict a young woman who out of necessity had stolen bread to feed her child."[151]

[145] Ibid., at 183–184.
[146] C-473/00, *Cofidis*, at operative part.
[147] Court of Cassation, Chambre Civile 1, 16 mars 2004, No. 99-17.755.
[148] See: C-429/05, *Rampion and Godard*, at para. 58; operative part, para. 2.
[149] See: Article 34 of Loi No. 2008-3 du 3 janvier 2008 pour le développement de la concurrence au service des consommateurs.
[150] *Le Monde*, "petits juges."
[151] Ramsay, Iain. 2017. *Personal Insolvency in the 21st Century: A Comparative Analysis of the US and Europe*. Oxford, UK: Hart, at 128.

While remarkable, Rigal and Florès' battle occurred within an institutional context that had permitted rebellions before. Their discovery of EU law did not transform them into rebels – they were rebels already – but it did reinforce their hand. As Florès acknowledges, unlike the administrative judiciary, "the civil court culture [includes] the possibility to rebel" given a sufficient *ratio legis*.[152] And in this instance, the *ratio legis* was supplied by the ECJ. A flicker of 1789 thus persists, prolonged by those few *petits juges* who turn to their "bigger boss."

## 4.4 THE SHADOW OF GERMAN ADMINISTRATIVE COURTS

One concern with the foregoing comparative case study is that it may be revealing differences between administrative and civil law instead of differences in bureaucratic domination. Perhaps the fact that civil courts adjudicate disputes between private parties whereas administrative courts address conflicts between citizens and the state accounts for the differences in behavior that we saw.[153] For instance, some scholars have argued that administrative law tends to be more proximate to (and protective of) the sovereignty of the state, which renders administrative judges reticent to refer noncompliance cases to the ECJ.[154]

While the distinctions between civil and administrative law are of great consequence to doctrinal studies, there are three reasons to tie this chapter's findings primarily to the influence of bureaucratic domination. First, jurisdictional distinctions are more relevant for understanding differences in the overall propensity of judges to solicit the ECJ than they are in accounting for variation in their openness to rebel against their superiors. Second, French judges stressed that *the* primary difference between the administrative and civil judiciaries impacting their openness to Europeanizing rebellions is the degree of hierarchy. Finally, across the Rhine river lies an administrative

---

[152] Interview with Philippe Florès, October 4, 2017.

[153] Alter, "European Court's Political Power," at 468–469; Alter, "European Union's Legal System and Domestic Policy," at 503; Stone, "Constitutional Dialogues in the European Community," at 26.

[154] Contant, Lisa. 2001. "Europeanization and the Courts: Variable Patterns of Adaptation among National Judiciaries." In *Transforming Europe*, Maria Green Cowles, James Caporaso, and Thomas Risse, eds. Ithaca, NY: Cornell University Press, at 108–109.

judiciary wherein the bureaucratic politics of ECJ referrals play out quite differently, precisely because it functions as a more decentralized institutional order.

Indeed, if we inverted the French administrative judiciary's top-down origins, we would be left with a decent approximation for the birth of the German administrative courts. Germany's piecemeal unification spearheaded by Prussia in the 1860s was a pacted process that preserved substantial autonomy for the German states.[155] The birth of its administrative court system proved even more bottom-up and uneven. The Grand Duchy of Baden established the first administrative court in 1863, followed by Prussia in 1875.[156] It was not until the postwar era that a national system of administrative courts was established (by the Code of Administrative Procedure of 1960), comprised of courts of first instance and appeal at the state level, and a new Federal Court (established in 1952) at the national level.[157] If the French Council of State can legitimate its authority via temporal precedence, Germany's Federal Administrative Court must instead contend with the fact that some state judiciaries precede it by almost a century.

And if the history of the German administrative courts begins with the states, the adoption of the federal constitution (the Basic Law) in 1949[158] ensured that their postwar organization would remain "predominantly a *Land* [subnational state] matter." It is the subnational Ministries of Justice that salary administrative judges and fund their courts.[159] In most states judicial promotions follow a nomination by the *Land* Minister of Justice and the agreement of a committee comprised of state legislators, judges, and lawyers.[160] This means that the Federal Court has little influence over the professional trajectories

---

[155] Ziblatt, Daniel. 2006. *Structuring the State: The Formation of Italy and Germany and the Puzzle of Federalism.* Princeton, NJ: Princeton University Press, at 7.

[156] Szente, Zoltan and Konrad Lachmayer. 2017. *The Principle of Effective Legal Protection in Administrative Law: A European Comparison.* New York, NY: Routledge, at 123.

[157] Initially situated in Berlin, in 2002 the Court moved to Leipzig to occupy the building of the prewar Imperial Court of Justice.

[158] Burkhart, Simone. 2008. "Reforming Federalism in Germany." *Publius: The Journal of Federalism* 39(2): 341–365.

[159] In Bavaria, it is the *Land* Ministry of the Interior that performs this task; Interview with Ingo Kraft, Federal Administrative Court, January 12, 2018 (in-person).

[160] In five others, promotions are under the *Land* Ministry's exclusive purview; Foster, Nigel, and Satish Sule. 2010. *German Legal System and Laws,* 4th ed. New York, NY: Oxford University Press, at 104; Bell, *Judiciaries within Europe,* at 121.

of lower court judges, who will usually spend their entire career at the state level.[161] Even if they should ascend to last instance, judges must be nominated by their state ministry and approved by a committee comprised of an equal number of *Land* ministers and members of the Federal Parliament (the *Bundestag*).[162] All the Federal Court can do is express a nonbinding opinion on nominated candidates.[163]

The socialization of judges also lies almost exclusively at the state level. Rather than being trained at a national school of administration such as the French ENA, German administrative judges attend one of the country's law schools alongside all future lawyers.[164] They take their first and second law exams in their particular state and are recruited within the state judiciary on the basis of their performance. And besides the occasional traineeship at the Federal Court, their continuing training takes place within the state courts themselves.[165]

The result is that the Federal Administrative Court's decisions tend to be treated as "general directions"[166] rather than oracles of a Vatican-esque authority. Indeed, conversations with German judges revealed their awareness of the occasional lower court rebellions. "[M]ost of the judges are more independent, more critical [vis-à-vis] the Federal Court" than French judges are of their superiors.[167] A lower court judge confirms that Germany is "quite different" from the French adminis-trative hierarchy: "The Federal Administrative Court, of course, we respect [its] judgments but just when they are well-founded ... if we are not convinced ... we don't have any problems deciding in a different way."[168] Even judges at the Federal Court acknowledge this reality: "It's absolutely different [from France]," for lower courts may "try to deviate for sure! ... [if] we made a decision, they put the parallel decision up to [the ECJ in] Luxembourg."[169] Consider the frank words of the Federal Court's former president:

[161] Bell, *Judiciaries within Europe*, at 111.
[162] Günther, Carsten. "Administrative Justice in Europe: Report for Germany." Accessed March 15, 2018, at: www.aca-europe.eu/en/eurtour/i/countries/germany/germany_en, at 6.
[163] Interview with Ingo Kraft, January 12, 2018.
[164] Bell, *Judiciaries within Europe*, at 114, 120.
[165] Günther, "Report for Germany," at 19.
[166] Bell, *Judiciaries within Europe*, at 132.
[167] Interview with Michael Funke-Kaiser, Regional Administrative Court in Mannheim, November 30, 2017 (in-person).
[168] Interview with Klaus Dienelt, January 11, 2018.
[169] Interview with Ingo Kraft, January 12, 2018.

There are quite a lot of "rebels" in German courts ... of course there are some "black sheep" like everywhere. I don't think ... speaking of "overturning the decisions of their judicial superiors" is correct for the Germ[an] court system ... the higher courts have to be open to new and better arguments of the lower courts ... they might have to change their former case law. Wh[ich] happens sometimes! The German court system is at its best a discussion process between the courts of all instances – the better argument should win![170]

As these comments convey, repeated referrals to the ECJ risk tarnishing one's reputation: one can become a "black sheep." Interviewees recount that colleagues sometimes interpret these as unsavory attempts to "[make] the news."[171] But these reputational costs are less tied to the act of breaking from supreme court jurisprudence and more so linked to the sense that they harm a reciprocal inter-court comity that usually eschews the need for rebellious escapades to Luxembourg. As a Federal Court judge explains, "we are not the Vatican. And we speak and we telephone ... it's not that I say, 'as a supreme court, I want that they obey!' Absolutely not. It's only that [informal dialogue] works."[172]

Yet the degree to which the scales are tipped in favor of comity or rebellion depends on individual personalities. Unlike in France, where the Council of State's bureaucratic domination quashes such behavioral diversity, the German administrative judges I spoke to often disagreed about the legitimacy of occasionally circumventing their superiors to engage the ECJ.[173] The dialogue between the president of one Administrative Court and a younger colleague is a case in point:

**Andreas:** "[The choice to rebel] depends from judge to judge ... "
**Svenja:** "If I was really convinced that the Federal Court was wrong, and I wouldn't want to apply the law that way, I would maybe do it ... "
**Andreas:** "We don't rebel against the Federal Court, because in my opinion ... they get a bad reputation, because the judges on the court of appeal or Federal Court, they don't like such judges."
**Svenja:** "I mean ... if you have someone who is really specialized in European law who does it because of the subject itself, and because it's necessary for the case, don't you think that it would be ok? I mean, I would hope

---

[170] Interview with Marion Eckertz-Höfer, ex-President of the Federal Administrative Court, January 12, 2018 (via email).
[171] Interview with Michael Funke-Kaiser, November 30, 2017.
[172] Interview with Ingo Kraft, January 12, 2018. See also: Interview with Alexander Jannasch, Federal Administrative Court, November 22, 2017 (in-person).
[173] Interview with Joachim Tepperwien, Sebastian Baer, and Anna Miria Fuerst, Lower Saxony Administrative Court, January 19, 2018 (in-person).

that I wouldn't be docked forever, you know! ... I don't think anyone would think you're rebellious if you do it once. Maybe if you made it your mission ... "

**Andreas:** "[But] think of a chamber of judges in the court of appeal who decided not to follow the opinion of [federal judges], so they get a reputation of rebels! ... [such as] the court of appeal in Muenster ... or in Baden-Württemberg, or in Bavaria, or in Niedersachsen ..."[174]

Clearly, the costs of breaking with the Federal Administrative Court's jurisprudence have little to do with disciplinary sanction: they are diffuse, reputational risks. Consequently, they are sufficiently low to render rebellions conceivable: even though Andreas disapproves of them, he acknowledges that lower courts in various states are known to sometimes launch these campaigns.

This contained dynamic sprung into action in the early 2000s as German administrative courts were swarmed with "high voltage"[175] cases involving immigration and asylum. As a result, a few judges I met – like Michael Funke-Kaiser[176] and Jan Bergmann in Baden-Wüerttemberg, and Klaus Dienelt in Hessen – referred cases to the ECJ to challenge Federal Court decisions with which they disagreed. "Even my colleagues at the senate of the Federal Administrative Court have no problem with this kind of situation," suggests Dienelt, perhaps a tad optimistically; "Because they say: 'Ok, now we were wrong, we thought it was different, but we are willing to follow the judgment of the European Court of Justice'."[177] Jan Bergmann is less diplomatic in recalling his first rebellion as a judge in the Administrative Court of Stuttgart in the 2001 *Oliveri*[178] case:

> Since years and years ... the Supreme Court in Leipzig's normal decisions [held] that Italian you[th] that are criminals can be expelled if the criminality is important enough ... all that [happens] later on, life goes on, is not important, because the government didn't know that at the time ... [so] I waited for a good case in Stuttgart. We had a case of a young Italian, born in Stuttgart, raised in Stuttgart, criminal in Stuttgart! ... And then, the expulsion, but then he got AIDS, and

---

[174] Interview with Andreas Middeke and Svenja Kreft, December 19, 2017.
[175] Interview with Ingo Kraft, January 12, 2018.
[176] Interview with Michael Funke-Kaiser, November 30, 2017.
[177] Interview with Klaus Dienelt, January 11, 2018.
[178] See: Joined Cases C-482/01 and C-493/01, *Georgios Orfanopoulos and Others and Raffaele Oliveri v. Land Baden-Wüerttemberg* [2004], ECR I-5257, at operative part, para. 3.

almost died. And I asked [the ECJ in] Luxembourg: "Have I to expel him ... is that against EU law, that I'm not allowed to see that he's now ill, because my supreme court says that since 20 years?" ... They answered, "of course not! If he's ill, of course he has to stay." So the dogma of my supreme court was cut. I did it!

One could imagine the Council of State's ire cascading upon Bergmann if he were a French judge! What is more, Bergmann soon began diffusing a newsletter to his colleagues – now boasting some 600 subscribers – detailing new developments in EU law and encouraging referrals to the ECJ. He has assisted dozens of colleagues who doubted how to draft referrals. And he even helped commission a permanent exhibit within the Regional Administrative Court in Mannheim to cajole reluctant passersby about the benefits of referring cases to the ECJ. Yet as I sat in Bergmann's office, I could not help but think of his French colleagues and wonder aloud: was he not concerned about how his superiors at the Federal Court would react to these efforts? His retort was sharp: "I'm a judge of the *Land*. They have no influence at all here, or nearly none."[179]

## 4.5 FROM THE DISENCHANTED BENCH TO THE UNEXPLORED BAR

The judicial construction of Europe is often depicted as a crescendo of self-emancipation. Ordinary judges, hungry for policymaking power and eager to unshackle themselves from their judicial hierarchies, secured the fruits of judicial review and transnational policymaking by turning to EU law and the ECJ. In so doing, they became bottom-up motors of Europe's political development.

In this chapter and in Chapters 2 and 3, I have pushed back against this judge-centric narrative – the judicial empowerment thesis – to make sense of the mostly dissonant reality that I encountered across Italian, French, and German courts. Even in these founding EU member states, civil service judiciaries have proven surprisingly fertile terroirs for diffuse resistances to the reconstructions wrought by European law and the ECJ. Within these institutional contexts, the behavior and collective identities of judges have been calcified by long-standing deficits in training and legal knowledge, the pressing trudge

---

[179] Interview with Jan Bergmann, Regional Administrative Court of Mannheim, November 28, 2017 (in-person).

of daily work, and the internalized discipline and career incentives fomented by subtle forms of bureaucratic domination. While decentralized judiciaries are more permissive of judge-driven campaigns for change, judges have had plenty of enduring reasons to renounce their own empowerment and participation in European integration.

If national courts have, on their own, been bureaucratically constrained as agents of Europeanization, and if the seeds of the judicial construction of Europe are not innate in most national judges, then these seeds had to be planted by others. But who were these cultivators of judicial policymaking and transnational political development? To answer, we must redirect our gaze from the disenchanted bench to the unexplored bar.

# PART THREE

# LAWYERS AND THE UNEVEN PUSH FOR CHANGE

CHAPTER FIVE

# THE FIRST EURO-LAWYERS AND THE INVENTION OF A REPERTOIRE

> In the first cases, the lawyer's role was fundamental ... [look at] the history of the construction of the key decisions of [the European Court of Justice in] Luxembourg. Where, a certain number of lawyers whom you could count on the fingers of one hand, in each member state ... These were not the best lawyers of the bar, those active in the secretariat of the bar association, et cetera. No, these were insiders ... this was the band, all the way into the beginning of the 1980s.
> — Jean-Pierre Spitzer, lawyer & ex-clerk at the European Court[1]

## 5.1 EXTRATERRESTRIALS IN HISTORICAL CONTEXT

"Weird." "Storytellers." "Extraterrestrials."[2] As lawyers and political entrepreneurs, this is how this chapter's protagonists recall being first perceived.

It is not easy to peek behind the "messianism of European integration"[3] and travel back to "a moment in time when there was precisely no common sense about what Europe's polity was about and what its connection with the law ought to be."[4] But by tackling this challenge, we can retrace the birth of a politics of lawyers that fueled the judicial construction of Europe.

Let us set the stage in all its initial idleness. At the dawn of the 1960s in France, as in Italy and Germany, "it was sufficient

---

[1] Interview with Jean-Pierre Spitzer, Cabinet Saint Yves Avocats and ex-référendaire at the ECJ, September 20, 2017 (in-person).

[2] Interview with Paolo De Caterini, lawyer at Studio Cappelli-De Caterini, law professor at LUISS Guido Carli University, and ex-Commission civil servant, December 27, 2017 (in-person); Historical Archives of the European Union (HAEU). 2004. Histoire interne de la Commission europeenne 1958–1973, "Entretien avec Wilma VISCARDINI (25.02.2004)," at 6; Interview with Jean-Pierre Spitzer, September 20, 2017.

[3] Weiler, Joseph. 2012. "In the Face of Crisis: Input Legitimacy, Output Legitimacy and the Political Messianism of European Integration." *Journal of European Integration* 34(7): 825–841.

[4] Vauchez, *Brokering Europe*, at 6.

to push open the doors of the law schools to take measure" of European law's hollow reach within the member states: "No courses or working groups dedicated to Community law existed, no research or documentation centers, nor chairs, and even less so degree tracks in Community law."[5] Law professors invoking the supremacy and direct applicability of European law were "dismissed" by colleagues for "what they widely considered fictitious legal analyses."[6] In Germany, Hans-Peter Ipsen's Hamburg School first advocated for the supremacy of European law, but even its most prominent graduates (like Gert Nicolaysen) were so marginalized that they struggled to find academic appointments outside of Hamburg.[7] In Italy, former European Court of Justice (ECJ) judge Nicola Catalano's efforts to promote a federalist vision of European law became a "victim of [the] professors" whose vigorous opposition "isolated [it] in the public debate."[8] And in France, when ex-government minister Pierre-Henri Teitgen opened the first research center dedicated to European law at the University of Paris in 1963, faculty scorned the move, confidently teaching students that "Community law does not exist."[9] It was not just national governments and supreme courts that tended to resist a Eurofederalist agenda: even the law schools were "zealous guardians of national and international State sovereignty."[10]

This state of affairs meant that "practitioners held a *de facto* monopoly over the interpretation of Community law."[11] Lawyers founded transnational associations like AJE (Association des Juristes Européens) in 1954 and FIDE (Fédération International pour le Droit Européen) in 1961, cultivating financial support from the European Commission.[12] Lawyers founded the first European law journals, like

[5] Bailleux, Julie. 2012. "Penser l'Europe par le droit." PhD dissertation, Université Paris 1 Panthéon-Sorbonne, at 422.

[6] Boerger, Anne, and Morten Rasmussen. 2014. "Transforming European Law." *European Constitutional Law Review* 10(2): 199–225, at 208.

[7] Interview with Ernst-Joachim Mestmäcker, former director of the Max Planck Institute for International and Comparative law, January 26, 2018 (in-person).

[8] Vauchez, *Brokering Europe*, at 78; Boerger and Rasmussen, "Transforming European Law," at 208.

[9] Bailleux, "Penser l'Europe par le droit," at 462.

[10] Vauchez, *Brokering Europe*, at 77.

[11] Ibid.

[12] Rasmussen, Morten. 2012. "Rewriting the History of European Public Law." *American University International Law Review* 28: 1187–1222, at 1207; Byberg, Rebekka. 2017. "A Miscellaneous Network: The History of FIDE 1961–94." *American Journal of Legal History* 2017(57): 142–165.

the *Rivista di Diritto Europeo* in Italy (1961), the *Cahiers de droit européen* in France (1965), and *Europarecht* in Germany (1966).[13] As early as the late 1950s, law firms like Baker & McKenzie and Cleary Gottlieb opened offices in Brussels, with an eye to influencing policymaking at the European Commission.[14] In the words of one of the first Euro-lawyers, "we weren't trying to be protagonists – we just happened to be the only actors on the stage!"[15]

These political initiatives featuring academics, lawyers' associations, and incipient lobbying efforts certainly contributed to the creation of a transnational legal field.[16] But recent studies have also surfaced that these efforts had limited direct impact on the ground.[17] At best they constituted an inchoate patchwork of initiatives rather than a full-fledged transnational "legal complex," "jurist advocacy movement," or "litigation support structure."[18] On their own, they could not have spurred bureaucratically constrained judges interspersed throughout national judiciaries to hold states accountable to their treaty obligations and to partner with the ECJ to advance European law. Lawyers thus stood to matter most if they could weaponize lawsuits to make newly imagined possibilities concrete, to mobilize courts against their own governments. Doing so would mean not being "passive actors simply responding to externally imposed legal opportunities but instead play[ing] a role in creating their own legal opportunities."[19] To make the unthinkable thinkable and the exceptional less exceptional, they would have to dismantle walls: not physical barriers reified by border patrol, but ubiquitous knowledge deficits and habits embodied by courts and clients.[20]

---

[13] Boerger and Rasmussen, "Transforming European Law," at 213–214.

[14] Vauchez, *Brokering Europe*, at 63.

[15] Interview with Paolo De Caterini, December 27, 2017.

[16] Vauchez, *Brokering Europe*; Rasmussen, Morten. 2013. "Establishing a Constitutional Practice." In *Societal Actors in European Integration*, Jan-Henrik Meyer and W. Kaiser, eds. Basingstoke: Palgrave Macmillan; Bailleux, "Penser l'Europe par le droit"; Avril, "Costume Sous la Robe."

[17] Bernier, Alexandre. 2012. "Constructing and Legitimating: Transnational Jurist Networks and the Making of a Constitutional Practice of European Law, 1950–70." *Contemporary European History* 21(3): 399–415; Byberg, "Miscellaneous Network"; Bernier, "France et le Droit Communautaire."

[18] On these three concepts, see, respectively: Halliday, et al. *Fighting for Political Freedom*; Alter, "Jurist Advocacy Movements"; Epp, *Rights Revolution*.

[19] Vanhala, "Legal Opportunity Structures," at 525.

[20] The struggle against these institutional obstacles is not unique to postwar Europe. For an exemplar from Latin America, see: González-Ocantos, *Shifting Legal Visions*.

In this chapter we meet the political entrepreneurs who tackled these resistances to court-driven change, cloaked in the sheepskin of rights-conscious clients and activist judges. "Keep hitting the wall, until it crumbles down" became a favorite motto of one of these Euro-lawyers in Hamburg.[21] Those who knew Italy's first Euro-lawyer similarly describe him as no "ordinary lawyer ... [for] there was a wall initially, a reticence."[22] Part members of their local community and part insiders of an emergent network of European courts, the first Euro-lawyers worked this boundary position to their advantage. Relatively uncoordinated yet facing shared institutional obstacles, they invented a repertoire of strategic litigation that was transposable from place to place. By brokering connections with local import-export and agricultural associations, they sought out clients willing to deliberately break national laws violating European law, occasionally turning to friends and family if a "real" client was unavailable. By mobilizing their access to courts and expertise as insiders, they educated national judges via detailed memos serving as crash courses in European law. And they ghostwrote the referrals to the ECJ that judges were unable or reluctant to write themselves, enabling the European Court to deliver transformative judgments that could serve as cornerstones for future litigation. These pioneers thus mobilized what are often described as mere *attributes* of lawyering – social and institutional embeddedness; substantive and process expertise[23] – to proactively exercise their *agency*. They cultivated the seeds of a transnational legal consciousness, linking civil society and international institutions via national courts.

To substantiate these claims, I draw upon oral history interviews with first-generation Euro-lawyers alongside the younger colleagues who knew them and appropriated their repertoire for court-driven change. I complement these testimonies with novel secondary historical research and newspaper records, a geocoded dataset of the first national court cases referred to the ECJ, and dozens of previously restricted dossiers concerning these lawsuits. I begin in Sections 5.2 and 5.3 by reconstructing the identities and motives animating the first Euro-lawyers. In Sections 5.4 and 5.5, I then trace the litigation repertoire they

---

[21] Interview with Tobias Bender and Corina Kögel, Finanzgericht Hamburg, January 17, 2018 (in-person), referring to Klaus Landry.

[22] Interview with Luigi Daniele, University of Rome-Tor Vergata and ex-référendaire at the ECJ, September 27, 2016 (in-person), referring to Nicola Catalano.

[23] McGuire, "Repeat Players in the Supreme Court"; Kritzer, *Legal Advocacy.*

invented and the concealed ways it cajoled some national courts to turn to the ECJ and explore a more active policymaking role. Finally, in Section 5.6 I begin to identify the scope conditions of Euro-lawyering as a repertoire of institutional change. But first, we need to get a better sense of who these entrepreneurs were, and what they did. So we begin by traveling to a humble local court in the early 1970s.

## 5.2 "BRINGING KNOWLEDGE OF EUROPE TO THE PERIPHERY"

### 5.2.1 The Public Transcript

If the paper trail[24] of court documents is all you had to go by, you would have good reason to think that Mr. Mantero was out of his mind, and that Mr. Donà was the pettiest man in the world. For the official record before the *giudice conciliatore* (justice of the peace) of the northern Italian town of Rovigo on February 7, 1976 curiously reads as follows.

Mario Mantero was the ex-president of the Rovigo football club. In this capacity, he tasked Gaetano Donà – a frequent traveler who lived abroad in Belgium – with recruiting foreign football players. Mr. Donà did so by spending 31,000 lire (approximately $37) to publish an ad in a Belgian sports magazine (see Figure 5.1).[25]

Inquiries started rolling in, and one would think Mr. Mantero would have been delighted. Instead, the court records show that he refused to consider any applicants and to reimburse the expenses Mr. Donà had incurred to publish the ad. Had there been a misunderstanding? Not at all: Mr. Mantero did not deny that he had entrusted Mr. Donà to do exactly as he did. Instead, he argued that Mr. Donà had "acted prematurely," given that the Italian Football Federation's regulations "blocked" the hiring of foreign football players.[26]

It would seem that Mr. Donà had been sent down a rabbit hole. A bad joke or a careless oversight, perhaps, but in the end $37 was all that he had materially incurred. Life goes on. Not so, according

---

[24] Here, I borrow James Scott's distinction between official political action (what he terms the "public transcript") and that which remains concealed, subversive, or private – what he terms the "hidden transcript." See: Scott, *Domination and the Arts of Resistance*, at 4–5, 183–184.

[25] CJUE-1807, *dossier de procedure originale, affaire 13/76*, Gaetano Donà contro Mario Mantero. Historical Archives of the European Union (HAEU), at 5.

[26] Ibid., at 7.

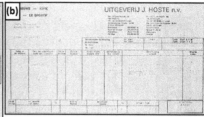

(a) A recruitment ad for football players published in the Belgian magazine *Le Sportif*, dated April 13, 1975

(b) A receipt for the publication of the ad (approx. $37)

Figure 5.1 Two puzzle pieces from the *Donà v. Mantero* case
*Source:* Historical Archives of the European Union (HAEU) CJUE 1807, affaire 13/76, Gaetano Donà contro Mario Mantero, at 22–24.

to the court records: Mr. Donà, in a melodramatic act of righteous indignation, sued. Before Rovigo's justice of the peace, he argued that this was not about the money: Mr. Donà had provided "useless hope to the interested Belgian players," thereby "compromising his personal credibility and prestige."[27]

But there was more: supposedly this was not just a dispute about national law. To Mr. Mantero's claims that he had acted "prematurely," Mr. Donà countered that the regulations of the Italian Football Federation banning foreign players were contrary to Articles 7, 48, and 59 of the Treaty of Rome. These articles, Mr. Donà noted, promote the free movement of workers within the European Community and guarantee nondiscrimination in employment on the basis of nationality.[28] Mr. Donà "regretted that [these] principles, in which he firmly believes, are held to be of so little value by the Italian Football Federation." In short, $37 were $37 too many for an expense derived from a repugnant law.

Unconvinced? Perhaps, Mr. Donà conceded; if so, Mr. Justice, why not ask a faraway court in Luxembourg to interpret the provisions of European law?[29]

[27] Ibid., at 12.
[28] Ibid., at 11–12.
[29] Ibid., at 11.

At this point, one would think that Mr. Mantero would have begun waving his hands about to hold his ground: this is a domestic dispute, he could have argued, and Mr. Donà is merely trying to distract the honorable judge with foreign laws that do not apply. But in yet another curious act, Mr. Mantero did the opposite: he joined Mr. Donà in requesting a referral to the European Court. One can imagine the befuddled look on the judge's face upon receiving the parallel requests to solicit an international court over a $37 dispute.

And so the judge did, but this raises yet another curiosity: faced with soliciting a little-known court over a little-known set of rules, this part-time, local judge referred four syllogistically ordered and carefully crafted questions:

1. Do Articles 48 and 59 and perhaps Article 7 confer upon all nationals of any Member State of the Community the right to engage in their occupations anywhere in the Community either as employed persons or as independent persons providing services?
2. Do football players also enjoy the same right since their services are in the nature of a gainful occupation?
3. If so, does such a right prevail also with regard to rules issued by a national association which is competent to control the game of football on the territory of one Member State when such rules render the participation of players in matches dependent on their membership of the association itself, but reserve membership exclusively to players who are nationals of the State to which the association belongs?
4. If so, may such a right be directly invoked in the national courts and are the latter bound to protect it?[30]

This was a model referral from the European Court's perspective. Rather than vaguely citing "European Community law," the referring judge noted the precise legal provisions relevant to the dispute. He clearly identified the interpretive crux of the case, and he even helpfully suggested the path to take: "Since [football players'] services are in the nature of a gainful occupation," the clear implication was that European protections for the free movement of workers should apply.

The ECJ agreed. Within five months, it released a pathbreaking judgment applicable in all member states: "Rules or a national practice, even adopted by a sporting organization, which limit the right to take part in football matches as professional or semi-professional players

---

[30] Case 13/76, *Gaetano Donà and Mario Mantero* [1976], ECR 1333, at 1335.

solely to the nationals of the State in question, are incompatible" with the Treaty of Rome, unless said matches are purely recreational. Furthermore, Articles 48 and 59 "seek to abolish any discrimination against a person providing a service by reason of his nationality or the fact that he resides in a Member State other than that in which the service is to be provided," and they "have a direct effect in the legal orders of the Member States and confer on individuals rights which national courts must protect."[31]

And so it was that a $37 dispute created a legal opportunity to liberalize Europe's football market, catalyzing a lengthy political battle and series of regulatory reforms. These would culminate with the ECJ's 1995 *Bosman* judgment, which banned any national restrictions on the number of foreign players and enabled transfers without the payment of a fee.[32] From the early 1980s to the present day, the percentage of foreign players in the "big-5" European leagues rose steadily from 9.1 percent to 46.7 percent.[33]

But let us not get ahead of ourselves: what of all those curiosities that produced this pathbreaking outcome in the first place? We might be left to marvel or malign how the most inconsequential of disputes could serve as fodder for activist judges. For instance, few scholars of EU law can resist citing how the ECJ's 1964 *Costa v. ENEL* judgment proclaiming the supremacy of European law originated from a $3 dispute over an unpaid electric bill.[34] Yet insofar as these cases fueled the judicial construction of Europe, judicial activism and rights-conscious litigants hardly deserve all the credit. The hidden story behind *Donà v. Mantero* suggests why.

### 5.2.2 The Hidden Transcript

The story begins with the affair's hitherto unmentioned choreographer: Wilma Viscardini. Viscardini was a trailblazer in more ways than one. In the mid-1950s, she was the first woman admitted to the Rovigo bar: "It almost became an event!" she remembers.[35] After meeting a university graduate with ties to the European Federalist Movement –

---

[31] Ibid., at 1342.

[32] Case C-415/93, *Union Royale Belge des Sociétés de Football Association ASBL v. Jean-Marc Bosman* [1995], ECLI:EU:C:1995:463.

[33] Poli, Raffaele, Loïc Ravanel, and Roger Besson. 2016. "Foreign Players in Football Teams." *CIES Football Observatory Monthly Report* 12: 1–9, at 1.

[34] Or, precisely, 1925 lire; see: 6/64, *Costa v. ENEL*, ECR 587.

[35] HAEU, "Entretien avec Wilma VISCARDINI," at 3.

Gaetano Donà – Viscardini became impassioned by an obscure new treaty that had never been discussed in law school. She successfully applied to research the Treaty of Rome and the ECJ's fledgling case law at the Centre Universitaire du Droit Européen in Strasbourg, while Donà joined the Secretariat of the newly established European Commission.

It did not take long for Viscardini to set her sights on the Commission's Legal Service. After all, under Michel Gaudet's leadership, the service was developing the principles of direct effect and supremacy of European law later recognized by the ECJ in *Van Gend en Loos* and *Costa*.[36] "Mademoiselle, we have no need for secretaries," was Gaudet's initial reply to Viscardini.[37] Her persistence eventually paid off, and in the 1960s and early 1970s she represented the Commission in a number of foundational cases before the ECJ.[38] And it was while they were working at the Commission that Viscardini and Donà got married.

With time, however, the limits of their work inside the Brussels bubble became clear. "From the point of view of our Europeanist convictions," Viscardini recalls, "we had the feeling, at a certain moment, that our work would have been much more useful in Italy rather than in Europe within the Community ... that European integration was a step that signaled the importance of bringing knowledge of Europe to the periphery, that it couldn't be bottled up at the vertices."[39] So in 1974, they returned to Italy to "demonstrate in the reality of things that European integration was not a mere project, that it already had a concrete impact in various sectors ... that it didn't just concern States and institutions, but also individual citizens and their businesses."[40]

This was not going to be an easy task. Well into the 1970s and 1980s, "judges, lawyers, and law professors did not have, for the most part, the faintest idea what [European law] was about." On the flip side, clients involved in litigation usually "brought their problem to lawyers trained exclusively in national law, such that the possibility

---

[36] 26/62, *Van Gend & Loos*, ECR 1; 6/64, *Costa v. ENEL*, ECR 587. See: Bailleux, Julie. 2013. "Michel Gaudet, a Law Entrepreneur." *Common Market Law Review* 50: 359–368.

[37] HAEU, "Entretien avec Wilma VISCARDINI," at 4.

[38] Most prominently *International Fruit Company*: Joined Cases 51/71 to 54/71, *International Fruit Company NV and others v. Produktschap voor groenten en fruit* [1971], ECR 1107.

[39] HAEU, "Entretien avec Wilma VISCARDINI," at 6.

[40] Interview with Wilma Viscardini, Donà Viscardini Studio Legale and ex-lawyer at the Commission Legal Service, September 29, 2017 (via e-mail).

of invoking European law is not even under consideration."[41] Simply telling anyone who would listen about Europe seemed insufficient: as Viscardini and Donà embarked on a multiyear speaking tour "in schools, universities, clubs ... they looked at us a bit like we were recounting fairytales."[42] It would take a sustained and proactive effort to transform this state of affairs.

Which brings us to football. Well before Silvio Berlusconi became the most renown Italian to harness football as a springboard for politics,[43] Viscardini and Donà recognized that football's mobilizational potential extended beyond the domain of athletics: "Our intent was to make people aware ... that the principles of European law impacted the lives of all citizens no matter their area of work and well beyond what they could expect. Football seemed like an important sector to affirm the principle of the free movement of workers given that it was a very salient sector in public opinion." After speaking with the managers of various football clubs who "complained of the "autarchy" imposed by the Italian Football Federation," the "idea of 'constructing' a leading case to liberalize the football market" was born. There was just one problem: when Donà would share their idea with club managers, "nobody believed him."[44]

Yet what strangers lack in vision, friends and family can make up in trust. In many ways, *Donà v. Mantero* was a test lawsuit *costruita a tavolino* – "constructed tableside," as the Italian phrase goes. The lead role of plaintiff would be played by Donà himself. Since he would bear the risk of failure, it was important not to get carried away: a cheap ad buy in a Belgian magazine would be sufficient to trigger the dispute before a friendly local judge, yet minimal as a sunk cost should their efforts fail. As for the defendant, "we consulted and came to an agreement with our friend Mantero," who was himself a lawyer. Mantero would task Donà to do something prohibited by national law, get sued, and support Donà's request to solicit the ECJ. Finally, Viscardini conferred with the prospective referring judge, himself a trusting colleague, to test the waters:

> We set up the preconditions for a preliminary reference to the European Court. We spoke about it to the Justice who signaled that he was

[41] Ibid.

[42] HAEU, "Entretien avec Wilma VISCARDINI," at 6.

[43] Markovits, Andrei, and Lars Rensmann. 2013. *Gaming the World*. Princeton, NJ: Princeton University Press, at 9.

[44] Interview with Wilma Viscardini, September 29, 2017.

Figure 5.2 Three signatures, one author: the defendant's **(a)** & plaintiff's **(b)** briefs and judge's referral to the ECJ **(c)** in *Donà v. Mantero*
*Source:* HAEU CJUE 1807, affaire 13/76, Gaetano Donà contro Mario Mantero, at 8, 16, 21.

willing to send a reference, and so it was. Obviously, given my specific competences and experience, I had to prepare everything myself, both the [parties'] briefs for the lawsuit before the Justice as well as the preliminary reference itself. This was all possible because Mantero and the Justice were both lawyers who knew me and my husband personally as Rovigo natives, and they placed their maximum trust in us.[45]

Once we reconstruct the hidden transcript of the lawsuit that would spark the gradual liberalization of Europe's football market, all curiosities disappear. And it becomes clear how a humble, semiprofessional judge with no training in European law managed to submit a pathbreaking reference to the ECJ: the lawsuit had been ghostwritten by a seasoned Euro-lawyer instead (Figure 5.2).

### 5.2.3 A Modular Repertoire

*Donà v. Mantero* demonstrates that intercepting the concealed politics animating the judicial construction of Europe requires an archeology, that we do not take court decisions or official summaries of litigation at face value. But there is a postscript to this story: the case also exemplifies the invention of a repertoire of Euro-lawyering. It evidences a toolkit for court-driven change that is "modular:" transposable, reconfigurable, and diffusable from place to place.[46] Take Viscardini

---

[45] Ibid.

[46] On the concept of "modular" repertoires of social action, see: Tarrow, Sidney. 1993. "Modular Collective Action and the Rise of the Social Movement." *Politics & Society* 21: 647–670; Tilly, Charles. 1995. *Popular Contention in Great Britain 1758–1834.* Cambridge, MA: Harvard University Press; Wada, Takeshi. 2012. "Modularity and Transferability of Repertoires of Contention." *Social Problems* 59(4): 544–571.

and Donà's son – Gabriele Donà, who is now one of Italy's leading Euro-lawyers and president of the European Lawyer's Union (UAE). He emphasizes that *Donà v. Mantero* represents "a classic lawsuit constructed tableside ... no case serves as a better example" of how "everything rests upon the lawyer and his knowledge of EU law."

According to Donà, the lawyer's role is essential at two stages. First, there is the dispute's origin and the construction of the "facts of the case." Here, to "'construct' could mean to have the idea ... but it could also mean to truly construct it ... in my EU law casebook that I studied at the university ... it would have been called a *procès bidon* – literally a vehicle, fabricated." Second, there is the art of cajoling the national judge into soliciting the ECJ. Here, lawyers "systematically provide the judge with a preliminary reference in brackets ... we're not sure what type of a judge is before us. We don't know if the judge is EU oriented or not. We don't know if they've understood ... we advise all our colleagues with whom we discuss preliminary references to do likewise. It's absolutely fundamental."[47]

Like mother, like son: in his own EU lawsuits, Donà leverages the same repertoire used by Viscardini in *Donà v. Mantero*. Consider a different lawsuit in a different issue area lodged in a different country some four decades later. In 1997, the Council of the European Union (EU) passed Regulation No. 894/97, banning the use of drift nets for catching bluefin tuna.[48] The goal was to protect dolphins from becoming tangled and killed in the nets. But some fishermen's associations thought that the ban was disproportionate: dolphins could be kept away with sonar devices without imposing a blanket ban on drift nets. One of these associations in France turned to Donà and Viscardini, and they got to work constructing a case. The strategy was simple: fisherman X (Mr. Bourgault) would use the banned drift net to catch tuna, and fisherman Y (Mr. Pilato) would sue him "for the loss that he suffered on account of the unfair competitive practice employed."[49] Donà recounts the affair's mischievous choreography thusly:

---

[47] Interview with Gabriele Donà, Donà Viscardini Studio Legale in Padova and President of the UAE, August 26, 2017 (via Skype).

[48] Council Regulation (EC) No. 894/97 of April 29, 1997, "laying down certain technical measures for the conservation of fishery resources," *Official Journal* 1997 L 132, at 1, as amended by Council Regulation (EC) No. 1239/98 of June 8, 1998, *Official Journal* 1998 L 171, at 1.

[49] Case C-109/07, *Pilato v. Bourgault* [2008], ECLI:EU:C:2008:274, at para. 16.

But we asked ourselves: how can we construct the case? We did it in the same way we discussed [for *Donà v. Mantero*]: that is, to literally construct [it, such that] a professional fisherman would return to port with his fishing line and publicly display the fact that he had fished tuna! [laughter] And that it be evident that he had fished the tuna with the net that had been banned. One of his competitors, on the same dock, saw this and sued him for unfair competition ... Obviously, all of this was constructed tableside. We did it on purpose – even the fisherman who sued was in on it! ... The other defended himself saying: "Yes, I fished the tuna with the banned net, but I think the ban is illegitimate." And obviously we defended this fisherman and asked the court to refer the case to the ECJ.

Comparing the litigation strategies in *Pilato* v. *Bourgault* in 2008 to *Donà* v. *Mantero* in 1976, only two differences stand out. First, whereas Viscardini orchestrated the breaking of *national* law to validate a "higher" *European* law, Donà orchestrated the violation of EU *secondary* law (a regulation) to validate a "higher" principle of EU *primary* law (proportionality). Second, Donà's efforts failed on technical grounds: the ECJ ruled that the fishing tribunal did not constitute an independent "court" capable of submitting a reference. "Suing for Europe"[50] is "a lot of hard work,"[51] Donà admits. Two steps forward, one step back.

## 5.3 IDENTITIES AND MOTIVES

Wilma Viscardini was not alone. She is part of a small cohort of first-generation Euro-lawyers who blazed the way for subsequent practitioners. But who were they, and what motivated their political entrepreneurship?

Following scholars of European integration known as the "neofunctionalists," it can seem intuitive to attribute the instrumentalism of the now dominant European business lawyers to pioneers past. Yet, this would be historically inaccurate. A practitioner who "met many of the people who worked at that time" describes the 1960s and 1970s as "the age of the pioneers, an admirable age of people who believed in Europe, who were passionate."[52] But what did it mean to "believe in

[50] Kelemen, R. Daniel. 2006. "Suing for Europe." *Comparative Political Studies* 39(1): 101–127.
[51] Interview with Gabriele Donà, August 26, 2017.
[52] Interview with Charles-Henri Leger, Gide Loyrette Nouel in Paris, September 12, 2017 (in-person).

Europe?" Undoubtedly, the first Euro-lawyers perceived that they might eventually reap the economic benefits of their craft. But they cannot be characterized as "ruthless egoists" or crude utilitarians.[53] Surviving World War II (WWII) had inculcated in them a staunch commitment to fighting nationalist policies and moderating state power.[54] Therein lay the promise of building a transnational community forged through courts and law, a vision that burned most vigorously in those who began their careers at fledgling European institutions and then returned home. And all these lawyers embodied various forms of pleasure in agency: a drive to participate, an attraction to novelty, a mischievous rebelliousness.

In the shadow of the World War II, a vanguard of surviving lawyers saw the then-uncertain project of European integration as a deeply personal calling. All of the first-generation Euro-lawyers who became the most prolific solicitors of national court referrals to the ECJ were old enough to remember the War (see Figure 5.3 for the full list). Peter-Christian Müller-Graff, a law professor at the University of Heidelberg, was friends with several of these pioneers in Germany, and recalls their motives thusly:

> When you are a practicing lawyer, you always have to make your living, so you come to certain economic mandates ... But when you ask me now, looking into the intrinsic motivations of these pioneers, to look into their soul ... they all had the experience of WWII. They knew, that it was essential and necessary to have a new form of order in Europe ... Those who experienced WWII all knew why you should never have war again. They were all imprinted by this experience.[55]

This conclusion echoes the memories of the surviving first-generation Euro-lawyers themselves. Robert Saint-Esteben, who became one of France's first European competition lawyers, "explain[s] why today, at a very old age vis-à-vis 1964, I've never abandoned EU law": before meeting Pierre-Henri Teitgen as a student at the University of Paris and joining the Commission in mid-1960s, Saint-Esteben grew up in

---

[53] Burley and Mattli, "Europe before the Court," at 54; Haas, *Uniting of Europe*, at xxxiv.

[54] On how this fits a broader pattern of "political lawyering," see: Halliday and Karpik, *Lawyers and the Rise of Western Political Liberalism*. Halliday et al., *Fighting for Political Freedom*, at 3–4.

[55] Interview with Peter-Christian Müller-Graff, professor at the University of Heidelberg and ex-intern at the Commission, November 28, 2017 (in-person, rough written transcript). Müller-Graff was speaking about Dietrich Ehle, Arved Deringer, Hans-Jürgen Rabe, Gert Meier, and Fritz Modest.

| Country | Euro-lawyers | Born before WWII? | Worked at European Institution? | Member of European lawyers' association? | # Refs. to ECJ (Total) | # Refs. Pre-1980 | # Cases argued before ECJ | Time span |
|---|---|---|---|---|---|---|---|---|
| Italy | Fausto Capelli and Giovanni Maria Ubertazzi (Milan) | Yes (both) | No | Yes (AIGE) | 78 | 42 | 97 | 1970–2018 |
| | Emilio Cappelli and Paolo De Caterini (Rome) | Yes (both) | Yes (Commission) | Yes (FIDE, AIGE) | 25 | 9 | 35 | 1971–2014 |
| | Wilma Viscardini (Padova) | Yes | Yes (Commission) | Yes (UAE) | 19 | 3 | 35 | 1975–2015 |
| | Nicola Catalano (Rome) | Yes | Yes (ECSC, ECJ) | Yes (FIDE, AIGE) | 16 | 15 | 27 | 1968–1982 |
| | Lise and Roland Funck-Brentano (Paris) | Yes (both) | No | Yes (AJE, UAE) | 15 | 4 | 26 | 1977–1997 |
| France | Marcel Véroone (Lille) | Yes | No | Yes (CCBE) | 9 | 6 | 16 | 1974–1988 |
| | Paul François Ryziger (Paris) | Yes | Yes (ESCS) | Yes (FIDE) | 6 | 1 | 12 | 1962–1992 |
| | Robert Collin (Paris) | Yes | No | Yes (AJE) | 8 | 5 | 11 | 1964–1993 |
| Germany | Fritz Modest, Jürgen Gündisch, Klaus Landry, Barbara Festge, Gabriele Rauschning (Hamburg) | Yes (all) | No | Yes (FIDE, UAE, DNRV) | 140 | 65 | 163 | 1967–2014 |
| | Dietrich Ehle (Cologne) | Yes | No | ? | 90 | 36 | 143 | 1962–2019 |
| | Peter Wendt (Hamburg) | Yes | No | ? | 22 | 18 | 26 | 1965–1985 |
| | Gert Meier (Cologne) | Yes | No | Yes (FIDE) | 17 | 6 | 21 | 1973–2001 |

Figure 5.3 The leading first-generation Euro-lawyers in Italy, France, and Germany

*Note:* Beyond FIDE and AJE, association names are: AIGE, Associazione Italiana Giuristi Europei; DNRV, Deutsch-Niederländische Rechtsanwaltsvereinigung; UAE, Union des Avocats Européens; CCBE, Conseil des Barreaux Européens.

143

the Basque country. There, the wartime disruption of hospital services nearly cost him his life: "The Basque country has been divided for centuries by a state border ... [so] the choice of overcoming borders was very profound for me ... I was also born during the War, and in my infancy I lived the consequences of the War, its hardships. My own health failed, and my parents told me later that I was in grave danger during the occupation."[56] The "euphoric moment of the birth of EU law and the construction of Europe" has thus never left him,[57] just like a fellow Parisian pioneer, Lise Funck-Brentano, who "never ceased to dedicate her life for European integration" and to constructing "emblematic lawsuits" before the ECJ. Born in Germany in 1929 to a Jewish family, her commitment to uniting Europe through law was shaped by a childhood on the run between "exodus and exile, escaping deportation by one day before seeking refuge in Switzerland ... from her Jewish roots and lived History she drew the courage to defend her resolutely European convictions such that the horror would never recur."[58]

In Hamburg, Fritz Modest survived not just World War II, but World War I as well.[59] The impact of these traumas was personified by a towering colleague at Modest's law firm: Jürgen Gündisch. Born in Dresden and raised in Budapest, Gündisch's brothers were both killed during the War. In December 1944, he escaped the Red Army's invasion of Hungary by fleeing to his grandmother's residence in Dresden, where they survived the Allies' air raids.[60] This experience clearly shaped his identity: Gündisch's family remembers how "with heart and soul he was a lawyer and a convinced European." Indeed, Gündisch closed his second book on European law by arguing that transnational "shared values" could broker unity as democratically legitimate as that of nation states.[61] This portrait is corroborated by

---

[56] Interview with Robert Saint-Esteben, Bredin Prat in Paris and former intern at the European Commission, November 13, 2017 (in-person).

[57] Ibid.

[58] Pantade, Philippe. 2020. "Lise Funck-Brentano, avocate spécialiste du droit européen, est morte." *Le Monde*, December 9.

[59] Interview with Klaus Landry, Graf Von Westphalen in Hamburg, January 9, 2018 (in-person).

[60] Gündisch, Konrad. 2009. "Dr. Jürgen Gündisch: Top-Jurist und engagierter Hamburger Bürger." *Seiebenbuerger.de*, March 16.

[61] Gündisch, Konrad. 2018. "Mit Leib und Seele Rechtsanwalt und überzeugter Europäer, im Herzen ein Siebenbürger Sachse: Nachruf auf Dr. Jürgen Gündisch." *Seiebenbuerger.de*, April 5. Gündisch's two books on European law are *Rechtsschutz in der Europäischen Gemeinschaft: ein Leitfaden für die Praxis* (Boorberg, 1994) and

Klaus Landry, one of Modest's mentees who would become the iconic figure of the successor firm, Graf Von Westphalen. "I remember the Second World War. And I remember bombing nights, so we have a different approach to Europe. When I am asked 'what are you?' I tend to say 'I'm European, and not German.' "[62] Landry's father had his textile factory expropriated during the War.[63] Hence he and his colleagues "are grateful for Europe, but I must be careful, because some people might say: 'Grandfather speaks always about the war!' But it's a fact that for us Europe was – it was a gift ... Fritz Modest, who survived two world wars, was quite aware of that gift."[64]

Regardless of the degree to which surviving the War underlay their commitment to European integration, these first-generation Euro-lawyers were convinced Europeanists. A majority were active in FIDE or its national affiliate associations. Nicola Catalano drafted memos brainstorming FIDE's very creation with the head of the Commission Legal Service, Michel Gaudet.[65] Others, such as Giovanni Maria Ubertazzi, Paul-François Ryziger, Paolo De Caterini, and Lise Funck-Brentano co-founded or become presidents of FIDE's national branches.[66] In Germany, alongside the likes of Modest, Gündisch, and Landry we find Barbara Festge, a lifetime "fan of Europe"[67] and FIDE member who also served on the executive committee of the UAE;[68] Gert Meier, similarly active in FIDE and a self-described "liberal lawyer who brings cases for the expressed purpose of developing EC law";[69] and Dietrich Ehle, who was "of course [interested in] developing the law" given that he "had friends at the European Commission [with whom] we discussed this."[70] In Italy, we discover a "convinced European" in Wilma Viscardini,[71] we learn that Fausto Capelli

---

*Rechtsetzung und Interessenvertretung in der Europäischen Union* (Stuttgart, 1999), the latter co-authored with Petrus Mathijsen, himself a World War II veteran, Euro-lawyer in Brussels, and former Commission civil servant.

[62] Interview with Klaus Landry, January 9, 2018.

[63] Interview with Tobias Bender [cited] and Corina Kögel, January 17, 2018; Bender is an ex-lawyer at Graf Von Westphalen.

[64] Interview with Klaus Landry, January 9, 2018.

[65] Bailleux, "Penser l'Europe par le droit," at 347.

[66] Ibid., at 353; Karen Alter interview with Lise Funck-Brentano, May 26, 1994.

[67] Interview with Klaus Landry, January 9, 2018.

[68] See: "Barbara Festge." Prabook, accessed July 12, 2018, at: https://prabook.com/web/barbara.festge/1349109.

[69] Karen Alter interview with Gert Meier, April 26, 1993.

[70] Interview with Dietrich Ehle, lawyer in Cologne, December 13, 2017 (via phone).

[71] HAEU, "Entretien avec Wilma VISCARDINI," at 5.

believed that the "Europeanist ideal"[72] was "capable of vindicating
in the most effective way the general interest of citizens,"[73] and
we find that Paolo De Caterini felt called to EU law "for the idea,
for its beauty," and for his "enthusiasm and interest in Europe."[74]
In France, Funck-Brentano was "convinced in Europe, and in the
fundamental role that law plays in uniting Europe,"[75] and Ryziger
proved a "militant European" who corresponded regularly with Gaudet
and hosted private dinners for ECJ and national judges to help smooth
out their differences.[76]

The subset of Euro-lawyers who worked in Brussels or Luxembourg – like Catalano and Ryziger at the European Coal and Steel
Community (ECSC) High Authority, and Cappelli, De Caterini,
Viscardini, and Saint-Esteben at the Commission – held particularly intense Eurofederalist convictions. As Viscardini recalls, the
nascent European institutions boasted "excellent jurists from diverse
nationalities, and together we forged a new legal system: Community law!"[77] Two anecdotes illustrate the impact of their Brussels
experience:

> One time, I was commuting to Paris ... my work partner was French,
> and he and his wife needed to get back to France that night. So we left
> by car. At a certain point [on our return] we stopped to grab breakfast
> and we realized: he was married to a German since his days as part
> of the French occupation. So here was an Italian, a Frenchman, and
> a German, together in a car, traveling from Paris to Brussels, all civil
> servants at a European authority. We were like: "My goodness!" There
> was this atmosphere.[78]

> [Berthold] Goldman basically sent me to the European Commission for
> an internship [in the mid 1960s] ... My internship director, I'm fond of
> recalling ... Winfried Hauschild, had a prosthetic hand covered with a
> black glove. And when I drafted and presented the memos he requested
> ... I thought to myself – I was 22 years old – ... "This is incredible!

---

72 Interview with Paolo Gori, professor and ex-référendaire at the ECJ, April 6, 2017
(via e-mail).
73 Interview with Fausto Capelli, lawyer and Professor at the University of Parma,
November 23, 2016 (in-person).
74 Interview with Paolo De Caterini, December 27, 2017.
75 Alter interview with Funck-Brentano, May 26, 1994.
76 Bernier, "France et le Droit Communautaire," at 131, 148–149, 230.
77 Interview with Wilma Viscardini, September 29, 2017.
78 Interview with Paolo De Caterini, December 27, 2017.

Here he is, in front of me, disabled during the War's eastern front. And the two us are now in the middle of constructing Europe."[79]

But nobody embodied a Eurofederalist spirit more intensely than Nicola Catalano. A "convinced Europeanist [who] fought for his ideas … [with] a very combative spirit," Catalano is usually noted as one of the ECJ's first judges, yet he did far more to advance European integration before his judicial tenure as a negotiator and after his tenure as a practicing lawyer.[80] Having served as legal advisor to the High Authority of the ECSC – sometimes defending it against his own government – in 1957 he was summoned by Paul-Henri Spaak to join a committee of jurists to draft the Treaty of Rome.[81] Besides his allegiance to the committee's faction that "championed supranationalism," Catalano spearheaded an incalculably consequential proposal. When the option of a US-style Supreme Court was rejected as a political nonstarter, Catalano drafted the plan for an analogue to the Italian Constitutional referral system: the preliminary reference procedure![82] It follows that upon returning to Rome in 1962 following four years as ECJ judge (when the Court hardly heard any cases), Catalano became a lawyer with a "missionary zeal"[83] for pushing national judges to begin availing themselves of this procedure to solicit the ECJ. He "openly disagreed" with members of the ECJ who recommended "that national courts avoi[d] using the [reference] system too much."[84] He expressed feeling "responsible for the institutional system of the Rome Treaty."[85] And he told colleagues that he was "possessed by the European idea, an idea that has shone like a flame through all his activity."[86]

One way to appreciate the convictions of those Euro-lawyers who have passed away is to read the combative editorials they published. When politicians, judges, or professors attacked the European Commu-

---

[79] Interview with Robert Saint-Esteben, November 13, 2017; See also: Avril, "Costume Sous la Robe," at 146–147.

[80] Interview with Paolo Gori, April 6, 2017.

[81] Boerger-De Smedt, "Negotiating the Foundations of European Law, 1950–57," at 350.

[82] Ibid., at 351–352.

[83] Vauchez, *Brokering Europe*, at 109.

[84] Rasmussen, Morten. 2014. "Revolutionizing European Law." *International Journal of Constitutional Law* 12: 136–163, at 146.

[85] Catalano, Nicola. 1965. *Zehn Jahre Rechtsprechung des Gerichtshofs der Europaischen Gemeinschaften*. Cologne: Institut für das Recht europaischen Gemeinschaften, at 42.

[86] Vauchez, *Brokering Europe*, at 55.

nity or the ECJ, some of them pushed back. For instance, in 1964 the Italian Constitutional Court refused to acknowledge the direct effect and supremacy of European law.[87] In turn, Catalano took to the newly minted *Common Market Law Review* and the prestigious *Il Foro Italiano* to convey "respectful but definitive disapproval." European integration was "a real and fundamental turning point in the history of our times ... whether one wishes it or not," giving rise to a polity with "all the aspects of a structure of a federal nature."[88] Catalano then addressed the judges directly:

> It is time to conclude. The conclusions are rather bitter ones. It suffices to [note] the impressive brevity of the [Constitutional Court] judgment under discussion ... to realise, once again, how much a limited knowledge of the relevant texts, and a lack of interest in them, risks transforming our widely proclaimed but vague enthusiasm for Europe into a mere verbal demonstration ... Could the Constitutional Court change its attitude? This would be particularly desirable.[89]

Catalano's admonishments of Italian judges echo those directed at politicians and academics by his foreign counterparts. When in July 1965 French President Charles De Gaulle recalled France's permanent representative from the Council of Ministers (sparking the so-called empty chair crisis[90]), Paul-François Ryziger immediately published a seething editorial in *Le Monde*:

> Does French grandeur mean splendid isolation for our Head of State? ... Those wishing upon the young people of France a destiny on the steps of the world, these people, who are the immense majority of Frenchmen, want the creation of a great European ensemble, which they already consider to be their homeland. This is why they cannot but stand up against the monstrous counter-truths accumulating today.[91]

Similarly, when influential French law professor Maurice Duverger published a *Le Monde* editorial in 1980 charging the ECJ with political activism (see Chapter 2), Lise Funck-Brentano rebuked the allegations in a pointed letter to the editor:

[87] *Costa v. Ente Nazionale per l'Energia Elettrica*, Italian Constitutional Court judgment No. 14/1964.

[88] Catalano, Nicola. 1964. "Annotation by M. Nicola Catalano." *Common Market Law Review* 2: 225–235, at 225, 228, 234.

[89] Ibid., at 234.

[90] See: Dinan, Desmond. 2005. *Ever Closer Union: An Introduction to European Integration*, 3rd ed. Boulder, CO: Lynne Rienner, at 50.

[91] Ryziger, Paul-François. 1965. "Europe et Grandeur Française." *Le Monde*, July 7.

Isn't accusing the Court of being "biased" without citing any case illustrating this critique a sign of the very same "bias" for which the author charges the Court? … The Luxembourg Court's mission is to respect the rule of law as it interprets and applies the Treaty. When the Court is seized with a request for interpretation it cannot refuse to provide it, lest it commit a denial of justice.[92]

Funck-Brentano's rebuttal was not a one-shot. Rather, it was part of a tireless campaign to "defend [the EU's] institutions" and "diffuse [European] Community law amongst practitioners often disinclined to leave their national contexts."[93]

To be sure, some of Funck-Brentano's pioneering contemporaries did support limits on European integration (like Ehle[94]), although most remained unapologetically Eurofederalist (like Catalano). Yet all perceived European integration as an opportunity to exercise their agency. They tended to be curious of legal novelties and to be eager to challenge established rules. After all, in the 1960s it took "a very curious and adventurous spirit to take the time to read the Treaty of Rome"; this was the very "pioneer" spirit embodied by Robert Collin in Paris, a "great debater [and] a man of conviction who loved to persuade," and whose enduring interest in European law spilled beyond his clients' immediate concerns.[95] Collin's colleague, Ryziger, was likewise described by the French public administration as someone who "knew the inclinations of the ECJ very well and never ceased to push' national judges to exploit them."[96] As Saint-Esteben recalls, "we really had to fight! You see, us lawyers. That's why the role of lawyers was determinative … there was th[is] period of construction."[97]

In Germany, the portrait is no different. While Germany is today renown for its high levels of EU law litigation,[98] it initially proved a

---

[92] Funck-Brentano, Lise. 1980. "La prétendue 'partialité' de la Cour de Luxembourg." *Le Monde*, October 20.

[93] Pantade, Philippe. 2020. "Lise Funck-Brentano, avocate spécialiste du droit européen, est morte." *Le Monde*, December 9.

[94] See: Ehle, Dietrich. 1964. "Comment on *Costa v. ENEL*." *New Juristiche Wochenschrif*, December 10: 2331–2333.

[95] Mitchell, Mary-Claude. 2017. "Hommage à Maître Robert Collin." *Association Française d'Etude de la Concurrence*, May 4; Avril, "Costume Sous la Robe," at 143.

[96] Bernier, "France et le Droit Communautaire," at 201.

[97] Interview with Robert Saint-Esteben, November 13, 2017.

[98] Börzel, "Participation through Law Enforcement," at 138–141.

hostile context for European legal mobilization.[99] The burden thus fell upon entrepreneurial lawyers eager to spearhead institutional change. Dietrich Ehle recalls how "it was interesting from the beginning to participate in developing the European law," for this "legal system was very new" and thus a few "lawyers specializing in EC law decided to raise cases to test the system."[100] Hamburg's Peter Wendt systematically "observed which law the Commission develops [to] then raise private cases reflecting similar legal concerns," and Fritz Modest was "a fighting man" who "started to fight against the State" by invoking Community law.[101] The comparable "activism [and] aggressiveness" of Gert Meier made him a "spearhead in tearing down these barriers [to a European common market]. Sometimes he couldn't convince the administration, and when he lost, he went to court!"[102] Meier's activism went so far as to prompt supreme court judges to "blackball him."[103]

Italy's pioneers were similarly motivated by innate participatory drives. Giovanni Maria Ubertazzi's "spontaneous intellectual curiosity always brought him to nurture new interests," enabling him to be "ahead of his time."[104] His partner in practice, Fausto Capelli, was equally drawn to EU law "because of its novelty" and was admired by colleagues for his "ruthlessness" and "spirit of initiative."[105] Having flirted with a political career, Capelli was repulsed by the electoral preoccupations of party politicians, and he concluded that he could better impact politics "with other means and objectives" as a lawyer.[106] He confides that "we engaged in legislative activity, if you will, because we forced the state to adapt its laws to European law ... The lawsuits, let's say, were part of these initiatives."[107] A Milanese colleague, Bruno Nascimbene, expresses a similar sentiment: "In looking back [to

[99] Byberg, "Miscellaneous Network," at 148.

[100] Interview with Dietrich Ehle, December 13, 2017; Karen Alter interview with Dietrich Ehle, January 10, 1994.

[101] Alter interview with Meier, November 8, 1993; Interview with Klaus Landry, January 9, 2018.

[102] Alter interview with Meier, November 8, 1993; Interview with Peter-Christian Müller-Graff, November 28, 2017.

[103] Alter interview with Meier, November 8, 1993.

[104] Capelli, Fausto. 2005. "Giovanni Maria Ubertazzi (1919–2005)." *Diritto Comunitario e degli Scambi Internazionali* 4: 623–624.

[105] Interview with Fausto Capelli, November 23, 2016; Interview with Paolo De Caterini, December 27, 2017; Interview with Paolo Gori, April 6, 2017.

[106] Capelli, Fausto. 2020. *Un Percorso tra Etica e Trasparenza per Riformare la Democrazia in Italia.* Soveria Mannelli: Rubettino, at 30–32.

[107] Interview with Fausto Capelli, November 23, 2016.

the 1970s], there were a few [lawsuits] that were very ambitious and pretentious ... I had posed [the reference requests] so as to be sure that if the judge made them his own, the ECJ would have been able ... to propose those laws that were missing."[108] This pleasure in agency is confirmed by De Caterini:

> It was a magical moment ... there were juridical problems where you basically had to invent everything! ... You set the fuse, and it exploded, with big booms well into the 1980s! There was a sense that we could do the unthinkable! ... We were captured by our interests, by the beauty of things, the beauty of novelty! That by doing this, we could sometimes bring down the whole closet! It wasn't about omnipotence, but about participating.[109]

To be sure, these individuals did not ignore self-interest altogether. They were also betting that EU law would become "an interesting field of activities for the future,"[110] and their reputation as specialists would literally pay off.

While at Modest's law firm Landry emphasizes that his "enthusiasm for Europe" was "always in the back of my mind, and it still is ... of course on the other side, it was a business chance ... it was clear that there would be a development of more European law."[111] Viscardini echoes this sentiment: "I've always been driven by idealist motives. It is nonetheless obvious that once I decided to open a law firm, I also perceived the opportunity of valorizing my experience in a field of law where there were very few competitors at the time."[112] One of the first Genoese Euro-lawyers similarly recalls "a cultural passion for European law ... nevertheless having some business sense, I perceived that the effects of this body of law would come, and could also have some important consequences work-wise."[113] An evident example is the aftermath of the 1965 *Lütticke* case, where Peter Wendt successfully challenged the German turnover equalization tax on imported products. After failing to persuade the Commission to launch an infringement against the German customs authorities,

---

[108] Interview with Bruno Nascimbene, lawyer and professor at the University of Milan, November 22, 2016 (in-person).

[109] Interview with Paolo De Caterini, December 27, 2017.

[110] Interview with Dietrich Ehle, December 13, 2017.

[111] Interview with Klaus Landry, January 9, 2018.

[112] Interview with Wilma Viscardini, September 29, 2017.

[113] Interview with Giuseppe Giacomini, lawyer at Conte & Giacomini Studio Legale in Genoa, October 24, 2016 (in-person).

Wendt cajoled a lower fiscal court to refer the case to the ECJ.[114] As claims for reimbursements overwhelmed customs officials in the month following the ruling, "Wendt saw his victory as a chance to make a lot of money, and he very aggressively pursued more cases."[115]

The point is that these lawyers had convergent reasons to become first movers. But while "they discovered there was a new field of profitable law ... at the same time, these people were quite convinced that it's a wonderful idea to integrate Europe."[116] For instance, in Italy Emilio Cappelli made it a point to convey that he could not be bought. Following his first successful solicitations of national court referrals to the ECJ, an agricultural association began sending him a yearly check for five or six million lire. Every year, Cappelli sent it back.[117] These were independent-minded and iconoclastic practitioners, after all, with deeply held commitments and sometimes difficult personalities.[118] They were not the types of people willing to passively conform as spokespersons for moneyed interests.

## 5.4 THE GHOSTWRITER'S REPERTOIRE

It is one thing to be among the first jurists to take the promise of European law seriously. It is quite another to put these commitments into practice. The first Euro-lawyers were not satisfied publishing articles or attending conferences. So they creatively repurposed their repertoire as practicing attorneys to become prolific catalysts of national court referrals to the ECJ.

As Chapter 2 outlined, to this day I was hard-pressed to locate national judges that had referred a single case to the ECJ over their career. In interviewing 134 judges, the most active of all had referred

---

[114] See: Case 57/65, *Lütticke v. Hauptzollamt Saarlouis* [1966], ECR 205; Schermers, Henry. 1974. "The Law as It Stands against Treaty Violations by States." In *Legal Issues of European Integration*, D. Gijlstra, Henry Schermers, and E. Völker, eds. Dordrecht: Springer, at 130–131.

[115] Alter interview with Meier, November 8, 1993.

[116] Interview with Peter Behrens and Thomas Bruha, January 25, 2018.

[117] Interview with Paolo De Caterini, December 27, 2017.

[118] Notorious for their inability to play well with others were Wendt, Catalano, and Cappelli, but in any case all the lawyers in Figure 5.3 (with the exception of Modest et al.) worked as solo-practitioners or in boutiques throughout their careers. On Catalano and Cappelli's difficult personalities, see: Interview with Paolo De Caterini, December 27, 2017; On Wendt, see: Alter interview with Meier, November 8, 1993; Interview with Klaus Landry, lawyer at Graf Von Westphalen in Hamburg, January 9, 2018 (in-person).

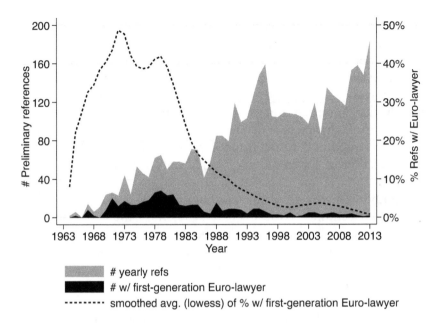

Figure 5.4 Referrals to the ECJ solicited by first-generation Euro-lawyers, 1964–2013
*Notes:* See Figure 5.3 for list of lawyers; smoothed avg. uses a lowess function
(bandwidth = 0.2).

up to 10 cases to the ECJ.[119] By contrast, some of the political
entrepreneurs we have just met were involved in dozens of preliminary
references through 1981 alone. Those 12 teams of lawyers were behind
at least 435 preliminary references to the ECJ (206 of which were
lodged before 1981) and argued at least 598 cases in Luxembourg.[120]
Figure 5.4 denotes that their maximal influence was through the 1970s,
when they participated in at least 41.5 percent of cases punted to the
ECJ by Italian, French, and German courts. I say "at least" because,
despite my best efforts, I could not identify lawyers participating in a
small share of cases, so these statistics almost certainly understate the
pioneers' involvement. For instance, the first Euro-lawyers were behind
51 percent of the 407 cases from 1964 to 1980 containing lawyer
information. And beyond the leading pioneers, "repeat-lawyers"[121]

[119] Interview with Michael Funke-Kaiser, November 30, 2017.
[120] The latter includes direct actions and infringements. These totals through 2020
are slightly lower than the column totals in Figure 5.3 because the Euro-lawyers
overlapped in a few cases.
[121] McGuire, "Repeat Players in the Supreme Court."

participated in soliciting 70 percent ($n = 286$) of referrals to the ECJ through 1980 with lawyer information.

It is not just the total number of references involving these Euro-lawyers that belies their influence. The first Euro-lawyers overwhelmingly exploited the preliminary reference procedure to advance European integration rather than to defend national sovereignty. Eighty percent of references to the ECJ where the plaintiff was represented by a first-generation Euro-lawyer solicited the ECJ's interpretation of European rules, while only 20% challenged their validity.

Another telltale sign of the first Euro-lawyers' impact is that they were often behind a critical subset of referrals: the first cases that national courts sent to Luxembourg. At least eighty-eight courts located in seventy-four French, Italian, and German cities dialogued with the ECJ for the first time when one of these pioneers showed up. If we graph the yearly share of these first-time referrals solicited by the first Euro-lawyers – as in Figure 5.5 – we can paint a familiar picture: the first Euro-lawyers were most influential in initiating a judicial dialogue with the ECJ in the 1960s and 1970s, when they were involved in soliciting 38 percent of all first-time referrals. Figure 5.6

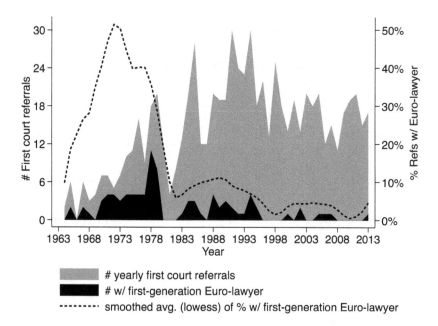

Figure 5.5 First time court referrals by first-generation Euro-lawyers, 1964–2013

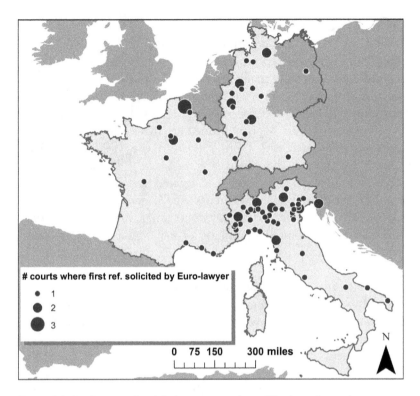

Figure 5.6 Sparking a judicial dialogue: courts ($n = 88$) whose first preliminary reference originated from a dispute lodged by a first-generation Euro-lawyer

maps the locations of these eighty-eight courts to visualize where the first Euro-lawyers were likely decisive catalysts of a process of transnational judicialization. What is more, almost half ($n = 41$) of these courts only referred a case again when one of these Euro-lawyers showed up again![122]

How were these lawyers repeatedly in the right place at the right time? The short answer is they made their own luck. In Section 5.2, we began to reveal the modular litigation repertoire they forged. Aimed at catalyzing preliminary references that would bulldoze national barriers to European integration, this repertoire consists of two elements: (1) the construction of lawsuits, and (2) the ghostwriting of judicial orders. Let us unpack each in turn.

[122] Of the ninety-seven cases these courts referred to the ECJ, several led to pathbreaking judgments: *Lütticke*, *Donà*, *Simmenthal*, and *Foglia*, among others discussed in this chapter.

### 5.4.1 Step 1: Constructing Lawsuits

"The lawsuit would be constructed as much as possible. That's obvious."[123] These words from one of Italy's first Euro-lawyers were euphemistically echoed in many interviews with veteran practitioners. To be sure, a few scholars have noted that some of the ECJ's most pathbreaking judgments began as "test cases."[124] Those working at the European Court appear attuned to this open secret: in the words of Roger Grass, the ECJ's *greffier* in the 1990s and 2000s: "It's no doubt true … the *grands arrêts* – *Costa v. ENEL, Van Gend en Loos* – they're all … a bit constructed … but of course, of course!"[125] Yet these vague statements usually concern a few renown cases, generating the misleading impression that they are exceptional occurrences rather than symptomatic of a modular repertoire. And the question remains: what exactly does it mean to "construct" a lawsuit?

That the word "construction" evokes some trepidation – prompting the generous use of qualifiers, ambiguity, and euphemisms – should come as no surprise. The practice muddies the legitimating narrative of lawyers merely representing rights-conscious clients fighting for their legal entitlements. Certain constructions may conflict with the ethical codes of state bar associations or the Council of Bars and Law Societies of Europe (CCBE). For instance, publicizing one's legal services was forbidden in most EU member states until the late 1980s,[126] and some advertising remains prohibited by the German,[127] Italian,[128] and

---

[123] Interview with Paolo De Caterini, December 27, 2017.

[124] vis-à-vis the Dutch *Van Gend en Loos* case and the Belgian *Defrenne* cases, see: Alter, "Jurist Advocacy Movements"; Vauchez, Antoine. 2014. "Communities of International Litigators." In *The Oxford Handbook of International Adjudication*, Romano, Alter and Shany, eds. New York, NY: Oxford University Press.

[125] Interview with Roger Grass, September 29, 2017.

[126] Hill, Louise L. 1995. "Lawyer Publicity in the European Union." *The George Washington Journal of International law and Economics* 29(2): 381–451.

[127] See Section II, subsection 6 of CCBE Rules of Professional Practice, Available at: www.ccbe.eu/fileadmin/speciality_distribution/public/documents/National_Regul ations/DEON_National_CoC/EN_Germany_BORA_Rules_of_Professional_Prac tice.eps.

[128] See Articles 17 and 18 of Italian National Bar Council Code of Conduct, available at: www.ccbe.eu/fileadmin/speciality_distribution/public/documents/ National_Regulations/DEON_National_CoC/EN_Italy_Code_of_Conduct_for_ Italian_Lawyers.eps.

French[129] bars. The same holds for conflicts of interest arising from assisting multiple clients in the same affair.[130] Italian lawyers are also subject to a blanket prohibition against the solicitation of clients. To ask a lawyer whether they constructed suits can thus be interpreted as querying if they committed a breach of ethics.

Consider the case of Lise Funck-Brentano who, as we have seen, was one of France's first Euro-lawyers. After earning her doctorate in Frankfurt,[131] she completed her traineeship in none other than Fritz Modest's law firm in Hamburg, where she witnessed its lawyers soliciting the first referrals to the ECJ. Upon opening her own office in Paris she maintained ties with her Hamburg colleagues to construct test cases. According to Christian Roth, the ex-president of the UAE and mentee of Funck-Brentano:

> This was our practice, in collaboration with a German law firm with which we were very close ... Lise Funck-Brentano knew and completed her training ... with this firm in Hamburg, it was the Modest, Gündisch, and Landry firm ... [they] also developed European law. And we constructed free movement cases between our two firms, where we believed they would be blocked by customs barriers, by import quotas, and like this, we could eventually go before a court with a real case ... where one of the parties would seek a substantial repayment from the other for a contract that could not be executed ... and before the court we'd formulate a preliminary reference: "Why couldn't this contract be honored? Well, because of an administrative obstacle in turn contrary to the relevant [European] provisions on free movement." And like this we brought some cases together ... such as the commercialization of margarine in Belgium! [in the *Walter Rau*[132] case].[133]

Indeed, the famous *Walter Rau* case was a deliberate effort to expand the ECJ's principle of mutual recognition enshrined in the 1979 *Cassis de Dijon* case (itself based on a test case constructed by Gert

---

[129] See Title II, Article 10 of the Conseil National des Barreaux's "Décision à caractère normatif No. 2005-003 portant adoption du règlement intérieur national (RIN) de la profession d'avocat," available at: www.ccbe.eu/fileadmin/speciality_distribution/public/documents/National_Regulations/DEON_National_CoC/FR_France_CNB_RIN.eps.

[130] German code of conduct, Part II, Section I, subsection 3; French code of conduct, Title I, Article 4; Italian code of conduct, Article 24, section 5.

[131] See: "Lise Funck-Brentano." *Prabook*, accessed July 12, 2018, at: https://prabook.com/web/lise.funck-brentano/1137364.

[132] Case 261/81, *Walter Rau Lebensmittelwerke v. De Smedt PVBA* [1982], ECR 3961.

[133] Interview with Christian Roth, Roth Partners in Paris, September 25, 2017.

Meier – it is test cases all the way down!).[134] Belgium protected its agricultural industry in part via a 1935 law mandating that margarine be packaged in *cubes* (the manifest reason? to distinguish it from butter).[135] Believing that this practice violated the *Cassis* principle that a good legally produced and sold in one member state could only be excluded from another state's market for public health reasons, Jürgen Gündish counseled a German undertaking (Walter Rau) as it struck up a contract with a Belgian importer (De Smedt) for the shipment of margarine packaged in *cones*. The contract stated that the import would be honored so long as the margarine could be lawfully marketed in Belgium. When the Belgian Ministry made clear that it could not be, De Smedt revoked the import, Rau sued before the Hamburg lower regional court,[136] and Gündisch argued that the contract (and the Belgian law upon which it was based) violated Article 30 of the Rome Treaty and the *Cassis* decision. Unsurprisingly, the ECJ agreed.[137]

When I relayed this portrait to Klaus Landry, he confirmed that "for many years, there was a very close cooperation between Funck-Brentano and us. We were even personal friends." But he was reluctant to invoke the word "construction," illustrating the word's polyvalence and how the process worked in practice:

**Klaus Landry:** "I don't think there were so many constructed [cases]. There were a few, very few … I think we had more discussions about constructed cases than [were] realized."

**Tommaso Pavone (TP):** "… obviously the word 'constructed' can mean many things. One of the ways I noticed this happening in Italy … was [lawyers] would nurture connections with particular associations, especially agricultural associations … there would be discussions with a couple of lawyers who were very specialized, and they would collaborate with the agricultural association to find the client. And that is how the case would then make it to court …"

**KL:** "But that's not really constructed. What we did is: we asked agricultural organizations, state organizations, for their opinion. We said: 'We want, our

---

134 120/78 "Cassis de Dijon," ECR 649. For a political science analysis, see: Alter, Karen, and Sophie Meunier-Aitsahalia. 1994. "Judicial Politics in the European Community." *Comparative Political Studies* 26(4): 535–561.

135 Law of 8 July 1935, Article 15.

136 261/81, *Walter Rau*, at 3963.

137 The ECJ held that the Belgian law "hinder[s] the free movement of goods" and "constitutes a measure having an effect equivalent to a quantitative restriction": Ibid., at 3965–3966, 3975.

clients want, to do this or that. And we think that this is legal' ... and when they said: 'Well, we think it's illegal,' then it gave us the chance to go to court."

TP: "So ... you would initiate an export or something and then it would get blocked ... "

KL: "Yeah. So they said, 'Well, you can't, you are not allowed to do this.' So this gave us the chance to attack this, to go to court. And that could give us the chance to go to the European Court of Justice. That's not 'constructed'."

TP: "It's still interesting because ... there was a kind of intentional lawbreaking in one level because there was a higher level of law that sanctioned [it] ... "

KL: "Yeah. Show the differences between the national law, and get the solution that the European law prevail ... [and] if you want to have a decision on customs law, for instance, you can of course: where the import of the goods takes place, you have the competence of the [court]. If you want to have the Düsseldorf fiscal court, then you should import in the west of Germany..."

TP: " ... so, actually, since the word 'constructed' is ambiguous, how would you define a constructed case?"

KL: "Constructed would be artificial ... there's not really a case behind it."[138]

When Euro-lawyers brokered cases to serve as vehicles for referrals to the ECJ, they usually tried to ensure that real disputes would underlay them as much as possible. But to surface "real" disputes, Euro-lawyers often counseled clients to deliberately undertake actions forbidden under national law that, in their view, were permitted by EU law. By "construction," then, I mean *the lawyer's proactive involvement in triggering a conflict between national and European law, or converting a dispute seemingly governed only by national law into one also implicating European law.* Figure 5.7 places this form of agency along a spectrum, distinguishing it from passive representation and the fabrication of fictitious cases.

That many of the first test cases the ECJ hinged on triggering real disputes is corroborated by the experience of Robert Saint-Esteben in Paris:

---

[138] Interview with Klaus Landry, January 9, 2018. Constructing cases to facilitate forum-shopping was raised by other practitioners: "If that set of facts could happen either in northern or southern Germany, then you'd probably pick the situation – I mean, you wouldn't invent the situation, [rather] a case with real facts – but you would pick the dispute to go to a court that is known to be more interested in these European matters." See: Interview with Thomas Luebbig, Freshfields in Berlin, November 1, 2017 (in-person).

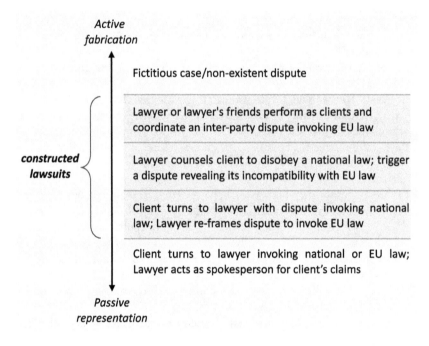

Figure 5.7 Conceptualizing "constructed" lawsuits and lawyers' role in disputes

> It's something that happened, but perhaps more subtly ... for instance, to refuse to transact a deal so as to raise a question which will then be proposed ... It's a way to tailor a dispute, I'd say. Not artificially, because there's a real dispute ... to create a preliminary reference that may not have been posed. I know that it has happened to me, to be consulted and asked, "how could we seize the ECJ?" by labor unions, businesses ... you'd then say, "we can only seize the ECJ if there is a dispute. So go and create the dispute!"[139]

Unlike the lawyer-as-spokesperson or go-between, lawyers-as-constructors and ghostwriters tend to become involved *before* a dispute emerges. One works backward: a problem is identified in theory (like the incompatibility of national and EU law), and then the "perfect" lawsuit is constructed to illuminate it. The messy or poorly documented disputes that tend to emerge organically are poor vehicles for strategic litigation: one needs an incontrovertible paper trail to induce national judges to invoke a set of laws they would otherwise ignore. Jean-Paul

[139] Interview with Robert Saint-Esteben, November 13, 2017.

Montenot, a second-generation Euro-lawyer, highlights this with a personal anecdote:

> A client who had heard of [a previous EU suit] came to see me ... [He] thought he knew it all ... "I should have been allowed to import these phytosanitary products, here's what I would have been able to sell, voilà!" I told him, "we're going to lose, because it's hypothetical! ... you constructed this dossier poorly! ... if you had come to see me first ... you would have requested an official authorization that would have been rejected" ... you'd say, "'Mr. Judge, this product can be purchased in France for 150 euros/liter." And I ask my client, "give me the receipt." "Mr Judge, this same product should be able to be purchased [for less] in Spain or Italy." So I tell my client, "strike up a contract with a Spanish or Italian distributor." But since these products require official authorization, I tell my clients, "submit a request for authorization." And there the dossier is constructed ... that's how you advance EU law.[140]

The foregoing strategy underlay many of the 140 preliminary references pioneered by Modest and partners in Hamburg and the 15 referrals by the Funck-Brentanos in Paris. And in Milan, Fausto Capelli and Giovanni Maria Ubertazzi constructed many of their combined seventy-eight references in the same way.

Following his university studies in the early 1960s, Capelli completed a traineeship in Germany and witnessed how the first Euro-lawyers were triggering European lawsuits before national judges. Crucially, he and Ubertazzi were also friends with Gian Galeazzo Stendardi,[141] a pugnacious law professor in Milan[142] who collaborated with another lawyer, Flaminio Costa, to broker the first (and most pathbreaking) Italian preliminary reference: *Costa v. ENEL* (1964).[143] They thus knew firsthand that *Costa* had been constructed: at Stendardi's suggestion, Costa protested the nationalization of *ENEL* – an energy company – by refusing to pay his electric bill, got sued, and Stendardi defended him by arguing that the nationalization

---

[140] Interview with Jean-Paul Montenot, DS Avocats in Paris, September 13, 2017 (in-person).

[141] Interview with Fausto Capelli, November 23, 2016.

[142] Like Capelli and Ubertazzi, Stendardi was also an ardent Europeanist. In the public hearing before the ECJ in *Costa*, he saluted the "supreme judiciary of the Community, our new great motherland." See: Arena, Amedeo. 2019. "From an Unpaid Electricity Bill to the Primacy of EU Law: Gian Galeazzo Stendardi and the Making of *Costa v. ENEL*." *European Journal of International Law* 30(3): 1017–1037, at 1028.

[143] 6/64, *Costa v. ENEL*, ECR 587.

contravened a supreme body of Community law. Even the choice to protest a tiny $3 bill was deliberate: the small claim allowed Stendardi to represent Costa before a fellow member of the Milan bar – a justice of the peace – rather than one of the city tribunal's professional judges. And "since there was no right to appeal under Italian law for claims worth less than 2000 lire," Stendardi could argue that the justice was "required to refer the case to the ECJ."[144] Capelli and Ubertazzi had a blueprint, and they used it.

They began to study and to network. On the one hand, Ubertazzi's connections within Italian academia and FIDE enabled him to organize numerous seminars and roundtables, to found Italy's second journal dedicated to European law in 1962 to publicize instances of national noncompliance,[145] and to serve on the board (and later as president) of a research center on European law in Milan that was cofounded by the likes of Walter Hallstein, the President of the European Commission, and Pierre Pescatore, one of the ECJ's most influential early judges.[146] On the other hand, Capelli tirelessly forged ties with industrial associations that could serve as reservoirs of prospective clients, particularly the national employer's association (Confindustria). When their research revealed a conflict between national and European law, "we spoke with the national association, and the national association identified the corporation that was open to lodging the proceedings ... [the lawsuits] were all like this."

Scouting for a suitable client was essential to the lawsuit's construction: after all, persuading sectoral associations to sue their own state was not easy, for "the association feared exposing itself, because politically it could incur risks."[147] During oral arguments before the ECJ in the 1975 *Bresciani* case, Capelli justified what might be misconstrued as his "disproportionate aggressiveness" and "excessive lawyerly stubbornness" by emphasizing that "national associations ... never sue their State with a light heart, for obvious reasons, given that they are in a permanent working relationship" with the public administration, so they only do so when they come to see "no other possibility

[144] Arena, "From an Unpaid Electricity Bill," at 1022.
[145] The journal is *Diritto Comunitario e degli Scambi Internazionali*. See: Interview with Fausto Capelli, November 23, 2016.
[146] The research center was known as the CISDCE – Centro Internazionale di Studi e Documentazione sulle Comunità Europee. See: Capelli, *Un Percorso tra Etica e Trasparenza*, at 46–49.
[147] Interview with Fausto Capelli, November 23, 2016.

to safeguard their rights."[148] This legitimated constructed lawsuits bordering on the "fictitious" to illuminate noncompliance and catalyze referrals to the ECJ:

> [T]he objective difficulties to be overcome in obtaining a reference to the Court of Justice ... favored the creation of the proper conditions for the presentation of so-called "fictitious" proceedings (from the procedural standpoint) aimed at obtaining relatively quick reference to the Court of Justice through the introduction of a debate between private parties in an ordinary case in which the compatibility of a State law or an administrative measure by reference to Community law was generally put up for discussion.[149]

Capelli justified proactive legal mobilization as a fail-safe, a compensatory motor of European integration in the absence of government will.[150] One concrete example of this is the 1971 *Eunomia di Porro* case. Mussolini's fascist regime had passed a law in 1939 levying a progressive tax on the export of objects "of an artistic, historical, archeological or ethnographic interest."[151] In 1968 the European Commission had lodged an infringement proceeding against Italy for failing to rescind the law, given that it violated Article 30 of the Treaty of Rome.[152] But like a leitmotif in the history of European integration in Italy, the authorities had dragged their feet. So Capelli and Ubertazzi decided to hold their feet to the fire.

Having networked with an association of artists, Capelli recalls how they "had to apply this ... tax for artistic products in order to export them to other EU member states ... so the association [comes to us] and says: 'What can we do about it?' 'Well, first thing we do is we undertake an export, we await the application of the sanction, and we ask for a refund of the sanction. And then we go to the ECJ.' In the *Eunomia* case that's exactly what happened."[153] They found an art dealer – Casimiro Porro of Turin – willing to

---

[148] Capelli, Fausto. 1979. *Scritti di Diritto Comunitario Vol. II*. Broni: Tipolito Fraschini di G. Pironi, at 444; Case 87/75, *Conceria Daniele Bresciani v. Amministrazione Italiana delle Finanze* [1976], ECR 129.

[149] Capelli, Fausto. 1987. "The Experiences of the Parties in Italy." In *Article 177 EEC: Experiences and Problems*, Henry Schermers, Christiaan Timmermans, Alfred Kellermann, and J. Stewart Watson, eds. New York, NY: Elsevier, at 144.

[150] Capelli, *Scritti di Diritto Comunitario Vol. II*, at 444.

[151] Case 18/71, *Eunomia di Porro e. C. v. Ministry of Education of the Italian Republic* [1971], ECR 811, at 812.

[152] Case 7/68, *Commission v. Italy* [1968], ECR 424.

[153] Interview with Fausto Capelli, November 23, 2016.

serve as plaintiff. Mr. Porro shipped a nineteenth-century Austrian painting to Silvano Lodi, an Italian art collector residing in Munich. At the customhouse of Domodossola, the painting was charged a tax of 108,750 lire ($176). In turn, Mr. Porro sued the Ministry of Public Education for a reimbursement. As we will see, this provided Capelli and Ubertazzi with an opportunity to ghostwrite the Tribunal of Turin's first preliminary reference to the ECJ (and to win the case in Luxembourg).

This repertoire of lawsuit construction was deployed by other Euro-lawyers as well. In France, Ryziger and Funck-Brentano did not wait for clients to come to them, but rather "they mobilized a clientele ... openly letting people know that they were capable" so they could launch lawsuits serving as a "motor" for national court referrals to the ECJ.[154] A leading practitioner who knew Collin, Funck-Brentano, and Ryziger confirms that it was thanks to their "legal imagination" that they "tried to bring cases before a judge which nobody ... believe[ed] at the moment," spurring "the construction of the *grands arrêts* of Luxembourg ... I [likewise] set up some cases, so I can't talk about them, where I set it all up."[155]

In Germany, Ehle regularly met with sectoral associations "to decide which cases [should] be sorted out as a test case, and then it may be that Mr. Landry [was] the leading lawyer for the test case, or it may be another lawyer, including myself ... then we exchange our submissions and discuss these." Most proactive was Meier, who had access to a wide network of import–export companies and agricultural producers as in-house counsel for Rewe supermarkets. His construction of the famous 1978 *Cassis de Dijon* case - for which he consulted Ehle, a personal friend – is part of a modular pattern of strategic litigation:[156] Meier "follow[ed] the lead of the Commission," seeing "which area the Commission develop[ed]" and, particularly, which cases the Commission dropped. Meier then "search[ed] out the cases himself" by working with the food industry.[157] Specifically, *Cassis* originated when a member of the Commission leaked to Meier that they had just "settled a case involving the French liqueur Anisette ... [Meier] simply changed the type of liqueur to Cassis de Dijon and

---

[154] Interview with Guy Canivet, October 2, 2017.
[155] Interview with French lawyer, 2017 (in-person; date and time redacted).
[156] Interview with Dietrich Ehle, December 13, 2017.
[157] Alter interview with Meier, November 8, 1993.

brought his own test case."[158] Meier sometimes constructed cases to overturn supreme court decisions[159] and forge relationships with the few FIDE-affiliated judges, who began asking him "to find cases to address certain issues."[160]

Meier's efforts mimicked those of other Euro-lawyers, particularly Wendt's litigation strategy in the 1965 *Lütticke* case after he failed to persuade the Commission to launch an infringement against Germany. Wendt went so far as to send letters to his clients urging them to participate in his litigation campaigns, extending his outreach efforts in local magazines.[161] Cultivating clients enabled Euro-lawyers to legitimate their aggressive litigation efforts as they became familiar faces in Luxembourg: "If the Commission is not capable of imposing the observance of [European law] on behalf of member States," Capelli and Ubertazzi argued before the ECJ in 1975, then "it's logical that operators will perceive themselves free to defend themselves as best they can, first and foremost, by soliciting the Court of Justice."[162]

We thus see how a repertoire for strategic litigation diffused among a small cohort of pioneers, despite no transnational coordination strategy or master plan. Capelli and Ubertazzi borrowed from their German counterparts and from Stendardi's example in *Costa*; Meier borrowed from Wendt and his example in *Lütticke*; Funck-Brentano borrowed from Modest and colleagues, and so forth. As first-generation Euro-lawyers crossed paths with colleagues in court, associational meetings, restaurants, and European institutions, this modular template could be gradually picked up by younger practitioners. In Italy, we saw how this inter-generational transmission is personified by Wilma Viscardini's son, and in Chapter 7 we will unpack another exemplary case. One final example among many from Germany places this process in sharp relief.

Wienand Meilicke became interested in European law after obtaining law degrees in three countries and briefly working at a law firm in the United States.[163] Like most second-generation (and all first-

---

[158] Alter, "Jurist Advocacy Movements," at 15–16.
[159] Interview with Peter-Christian Müller-Graff, November 28, 2017.
[160] Alter interview with Meier, November 8, 1993.
[161] Ibid.; The magazines were *Der Betrieb* and *Außenwirtschaftsdienst des Betriebs-Beraters*.
[162] Capelli, *Scritti di Diritto Comunitario Vol. II*, at 444.
[163] Meilicke received his *licence en droit français*, his doctorate from the University of Bonn, and his LLM in from NYU. In New York, he practiced at Shearman & Sterling from 1973 to 1975.

generation) Euro-lawyers, he never studied EU law. Rather, he trained himself as a practitioner in Bonn. Meilicke shared a clear participatory drive with his predecessors: "Judges at the European Court of Justice ... set up the infrastructure, but it's my generation which implemented it."[164] And like Wendt before him, in the 1980s Meilicke began publishing articles identifying national laws violating EU law. His first referral to the ECJ was constructed precisely to put these affirmations into practice.

The matter is rather technical: under German law, noncash contributions to a public limited company are subject to stricter publication and verification requirements than cash contributions.[165] But in a 1990 case litigated by Meilicke, the Federal Court of Justice held that some cash contributions were "disguised contributions in kind," if made before or after the company made a transaction to a subscriber discharging debts it owed. In such instances, companies not complying with the stricter requirements would be unable to discharge their debt.[166] As a result of the decision, Meilicke's client was unable to discharge some five million Deutsche Marks. Meilicke vehemently disagreed, publishing a book lambasting the Federal Court.[167] But after discovering that the case law arguably violated a 1976 European directive,[168] he took matters into his own hands. He identified a company – ADV/ORGA – that had discharged its debt exactly like his previous client. Intent on inviting the ECJ to overrule the Federal Court, Meilicke not only sued the company for the very behavior that he believed was legitimated by EU law; he also found an ingenious way to bring the case himself:

> [Reading] newspaper articles ... in 1990 I discovered that Commerzbank had signed a capital increase by waiving [ADV/ORGA]'s debt by exactly the same method. So what I did is I purchased some shares of that company ... I went to the next shareholders' meeting and asked for information [about] how they had exactly paid up the debt and repaid the Commerzbank loan. And then they didn't want to give that

[164] Interview with Wienand Meilicke, Meilicke Hoffman & Partner in Bonn, January 17, 2018 (via Skype).
[165] Case C-83/91, *Meilicke v. ADV-ORGA* [1992], ECR I-4871, at I-4921, paras. 3–5.
[166] Judgment of the Bundesgerichtshof of January 15, 1990, II ZR 164/88, DB 1990 at 311.
[167] Meilicke, Wienand. 1989. *Die "verschleierte" Sacheinlage*. Stuttgart: Schärfer Verlag.
[168] Council Directive 77/91/EEC of December 13, 1976 (*Official Journal* 1977 L 26, at 1).

information, [because in Germany] it was a "disguised contribution." And then I went to a court [the Hannover regional court] and sued for the information, and told them: "Look, here's this decision from the German Bundesgerichtshof, the German Supreme Court, but there are so many articles saying it's wrong. Please submit [to the ECJ]." Then I got together with a lawyer ... from Commerzbank ... [who] said wonderful, we will both argue that this should get to European Court ... I was quite optimistic that I would win.

The ECJ, however, thought that Meilicke had been too clever for his own good: "The Court wouldn't take the case because it said it was hypothetical, it was constructed."[169] Indeed, ECJ Advocate General Giuseppe Tesauro noted his discomfort that "the main action seemed to have been mounted by Mr. Meilicke purely in order to secure a ruling from the Court on the views put forward in his writings" and to overturn "the judgement of the *Bundesgerichtshof*."[170] Meilicke was disappointed but undeterred. He continued to solicit (and, as we will see, to ghostwrite) preliminary references from German lower courts in subsequent years. The most renown were the 2007 and 2011 *Meilicke* cases, which he again lodged himself to successfully challenge the denial of tax credits to shareholders of dividend-paying companies established in other member states, producing up to €10 billion in tax losses for the German state.[171] But this analysis also demonstrates that if Euro-lawyers are too brazen in constructing test cases – if the "hidden

---

[169] Interview with Wienand Meilicke, January 17, 2018; Case C-83/91, *Meilicke*, at I-4934.

[170] Arnull, Anthony. 1993. "Case C-83/91, *Wienand Meilicke v. ADV/ORGA FA Meyer AG*, Judgment of 16 July 1992." *Common Market Law Review* 30(3): 613–622, at 616–617.

[171] See: Case C-292/04, *Meilicke and Others* [2007], ECR I-1835; Case C-262/09, *Meilicke and Others* [2011], ECR I-5669. For a political analysis of these cases, see: Schmidt, Susanne K. 2018. *The European Court of Justice and the Policy Process: The Shadow of Case Law*. New York, NY: Oxford University Press, at 175–180. That Euro-lawyers sometimes take on the role of litigant is clear. For instance, a second-generation Euro-lawyer in France recounts the origins of a taxation-related reference he participated in constructing: "I had a dispute with the Social Security [administration] concerning some fairly special French taxes on general social contributions ... Some colleagues in other law firms had consulted with me ... It was serial litigation, and I had prepared the pleadings for the whole series for my colleagues, and when it was clear we had to go to the ECJ, my colleagues asked me to be the party to the suit. So we hired other lawyers to help us, and we went to the ECJ." See: Case C-103/06, *Derouin* [2008], ECR I-1853; Interview with Philippe Derouin, September 12, 2017.

transcript" is made public – their efforts risk backfiring. A case study of the canonical constructed EU lawsuit brings this message home.

### 5.4.2 The Perils of Taking Lawsuit Construction Too Far

Usually analyzed doctrinally,[172] what is truly notable in the famous *Foglia* v. *Novello* cases (1979 and 1980) is that they were pioneered by two first-generation Euro-lawyers we have already encountered, who got a bit carried away.

Emilio Cappelli and Paolo De Caterini first met in the mid-1960s in a pizzeria in Brussels while working at the European Commission. They had since become members of the Italian FIDE branch and opened a partnership in Rome. Their precise intent was to construct test cases to "dismantl[e] laws before the ECJ ... We had crazy fun, crazy fun!" Like other Euro-lawyers, their strategy in their combined twenty-five preliminary reference cases was to forge relationships with national agricultural associations – particularly Coldiretti and Confiagricoltura – and provincial agricultural cooperatives. They would "book a hotel room," travel to small agricultural villages, "schmooze ... visit with farmers," and scout the local *pretori* (small claims judges). In their division of labor, Cappelli would nurture relationships with the associations, and De Caterini would seek out clients: "I scouted all of Umbria to find someone willing to bring suit on tobacco matters," he recalls; "On grain matters, I scouted all of Puglia!" Their targeting of the humblest of lower courts was equally intentional. "All agricultural entrepreneurs feared the length of proceedings," so it was easier to convince them to play along at first instance (where proceedings would only last a few months). Further, many *pretori* were also practicing lawyers or members of the agricultural cooperatives, so they were more approachable. "We'd go to the honorary *pretori*, who knew people at the Confiagricoltura, or who perhaps held property of their own, and we'd explain things really well! ... the local *pretore* ... has the durum wheat growing outside his door! He gets it."[173]

All of this worked splendidly, producing seven (sometimes pathbreaking) references to the European Court from local *pretori* through 1978 that left legal scholars stupefied at how the "initiative of vigilant individuals" was empowering the ECJ to "contro[l] the powers of

---

[172] See, for instance: Bebr, Gerhard. 1982. "The Possible Implications of *Foglia* v. *Novello II*." *Common Market Law Review* 19(3): 421–441.

[173] Interview with Paolo De Caterini, December 27, 2017.

Member States [and] make further rules on community matters."[174] Then Cappelli and De Caterini pushed their "trickery" too far in *Foglia* – "the maximum fantasy that we were able to put into practice." They committed the diplomatic *faux pas* of targeting the laws of a foreign state.

The mischief begins as it so often does in Europe: with wine. Under French law, domestic fortified wines like Vermouth were classified as "natural sweet wines" subject to a lower consumption tax, while equivalent wines from other states were classified as "liquor wines" subject to an import tax.[175] Cappelli and De Caterini believed that this constituted a discriminatory tax violating Article 95 of the Treaty of Rome. But when they approached French judges to see if they were willing to punt a case to Luxembourg, they got a cold reception: "We were cruder, we were foreigners, after all . . . so we said, 'Now we'll stick it to them!'"

They turned to a fellow lawyer in Rome whose secretary, Mariella Novello, had an aunt living in Menton, a small town on the French riviera just past the Italian border. "'Let's just ship over a case [of wine]. Who'll do it?' 'What about the secretary of so and so, could she? The one [working for] the counterparty's lawyer? Can he ship it?' 'Ah, yes, to Menton! Come on, come on! We'll make it!'"[176] Mrs. Novello struck up a contract with a wine trader based in Piedmont – Pasquale Foglia – to ship Vermouth to her aunt. Crucially, the contract contained a clause that Mrs. Novello would "not be liable for any duties which were claimed by the Italian or French authorities contrary to the [Community] provisions on the free movement of goods."[177] In turn, Mr. Foglia struck up his own contract with an international shipping company – Danzas SpA – containing the exact same clause. When the cases of Vermouth reached the French border, Danzas was charged an import tax, which Mr. Foglia then asked Mrs. Novello to pay. When

---

[174] Schermers, "Law as It Stands against Treaty Violations by States," at 133. Schermers here references the *Leonesio* case, which in truth was constructed by Cappelli and De Caterini who, as we will see, also ghostwrote the local *pretore's* referral to the ECJ (see Figure 5.12). See: Case 93/71, *Leonesio* v. *Ministero dell'Agricoltura e Foreste* [1972], ECR 287.

[175] Case 104/79, *Foglia* v. *Novello I* [1980], ECR 746, at 749–750. The applicable French legislation originated from 1898, and had been last amended by Article 24 of the Finance Law No. 78–1239 approved on December 29, 1978 (*Journal Officiel de la République Française* No. 304 of December 30, 1978).

[176] Interview with Paolo De Caterini, December 27, 2017.

[177] 104/79, *Foglia* v. *Novello I*, at 758, para. 3.

she refused, Mr. Foglia sued before the local *pretore*, employing Cappelli and De Caterini to represent him, while Mrs. Novello turned to her own boss. The Euro-lawyers drafted a preliminary reference, and the judge used it to punt the case to Luxembourg.

The ECJ wanted nothing to do with this hot potato of a case. So they found a procedural means to dismiss it: given that "two private individuals who are in agreement ... inserted a clause in their contract in order to induce the Italian court to give a ruling," the dispute was of "an artificial nature" and the ECJ lacked jurisdiction to resolve it.[178] But Cappelli and De Caterini were stubborn. They drafted a second reference for the *pretore* to submit to the ECJ, arguing that it was the exclusive competence of national courts to adjudicate questions of fact. De Caterini recalls what happened next:

> We constructed lawsuit number two, pissing everyone off! We were mean! Saying that in Italy there are no fake lawsuits, that a lawsuit is a lawsuit, etc. please respond! The French state summoned the son of [famed Italian lawyer] Carnelutti to defend it in Italian, it was really tense. There was a whole public in attendance, and when we entered we were greeted with applause! These were students.[179]

The ECJ judges were livid. They held that "the circumstance referred to by the Pretore, Bra, in his second order for reference does not appear to constitute a new fact which would justify the Court of Justice in making a fresh appraisal of its jurisdiction."[180] In response, the Euro-lawyers planned to punt the case to the supreme civil court[181] – the Court of Cassation – and have *it* submit a third reference that the ECJ could not refuse: "Now we'll send a heck of a reference to those assholes!" In the meantime, however, France abrogated its import tax, and Italy's national Vermouth producer – Martini & Rossi – contacted De Caterini and Cappelli urging them to drop their combative campaign. In subsequent conferences, the duo's most prestigious friend at the European Court – Pierre Pescatore – refused to greet them. In retrospect, De Caterini acknowledges that they had taken their agency too far: "The offense was the following: We attacked France ... These rapports also mattered. We had offended the ECJ."[182]

[178] Ibid., at 759–760, paras. 10–12.
[179] Interview with Paolo De Caterini, December 27, 2017.
[180] Case 244/80, *Foglia v. Novello II* [1981], ECR 3047, at 3068, operative para. 4.
[181] Via a special procedure under Italian law known as the *ricorso per saltum*.
[182] Interview with Paolo De Caterini, December 27, 2017.

### 5.4.3 Step 2: Judicial Ghostwriting

Constructing test cases was only half the battle. Once in court, the first Euro-lawyers confronted judges who were often overworked, who ubiquitously lacked training in European law, and who disfavored what they took as quixotic solicitations of a faraway court "tucked away in the fairyland Duchy of Luxembourg."[183]

In Chapter 3, we unpacked how judges remain institutionally constrained and ill-equipped to enforce EU law. These barriers were exponentially more pronounced in 1960s and 1970s. The European Community was in its infancy, and even judges in big cities needed to be lobbied to participate in its construction. In Paris, Robert Saint-Esteben recalls why "the role of lawyers was determinative":

> I knew the era, the beginning. Which now appears far away, but you must understand that these were years following the birth of European law ... I remember an anecdote from the time which [Pierre-Henri Teitgen] told me, which was very true, from the courts of Paris ... One of the first times that a lawyer raised ... a question under the Treaty of Rome in his pleading, the [commercial court] President interrupted him and said: "What treaty are you talking about?" "Well the Treaty of Rome that was signed in 1957 in Rome founding ... " So we really had to fight! You see, us lawyers.[184]

In Milan, a cofounder of one of the first Italian firms to specialize in European law in the 1970s notes that "in the past it was virtually impossible" for national judges to invoke European law on their own; "it didn't happen because judges didn't study this topic, they didn't know it, they looked at you funny as you talked!"[185] In Munich, well into the 1980s some judges had "apparently never been confronted with European law" and had "no idea" how to apply it.[186] And in Hamburg, the first lower court judge to repeatedly dialogue with the ECJ in the 1970s lamented his colleagues' "ignorance" of EU law and deemed crucial lawyers' efforts to familiarize them with the preliminary reference procedure.[187]

---

[183] Stein, Eric. 1981. "Lawyers, Judges, and the Making of a Transnational Constitution." *American Journal of International Law* 75(1): 1–27, at 1.

[184] Interview with Robert Saint-Esteben, November 13, 2017.

[185] Interview with Roberto Jacchia, De Berti Jacchia Franchini Forlani Studio Legale in Milan, November 17, 2016 (in person).

[186] Interview with Peter Behrens and Thomas Bruha, January 25, 2018.

[187] Voss, Reimer. 1993. "The National Perception of the Court of First Instance and the European Court of Justice." *Common Market Law Review* 6: 1119–1134, at

The burden of embedding national judges within a fledgling transnational network of European courts thus rested upon the shoulders of practicing lawyers. "But of course," confides a former ECJ member, "judges weren't great specialists of European law, so they had lots of work and also a certain humility vis-à-vis EU law, inclining them to adopt the lawyer's reference. This is the reality."[188]

Yet simply "inclining" judges to solicit the ECJ once again understates matters. The first Euro-lawyers supplied more than mere "nudges"[189] or whisper passing suggestions in the ears of eager judges. Rather, they acted like shadow judicial clerks. By this, I mean that since the 1960s Euro-lawyers *consistently motivate and draft ready-made texts of preliminary references to the ECJ that are copied – sometimes verbatim – by national judges in their judicial orders.* In its increasingly rare form, lawyers may even dictate or type up the entire judicial order for the judge, whose only contribution is to sign it. Combined with constructing the "perfect" test case, the logic of ghostwriting is to cajole judges into deeming it necessary to solicit the ECJ, and to make this habit-disrupting act as easy and least labor-intensive as possible. Figure 5.8 places this form of agency on a conceptual continuum, highlighting the practices that substitute the lawyer for the judge as the bottom-up motor of the judicial construction of Europe.

I first became aware that only inexperienced lawyers trust judges to enforce European law and solicit the ECJ on their own accord in my conversations with veteran Italian practitioners. Wilma Viscardini recalls that "in my very first lawsuits, when I invoked a European law in court and asked for a preliminary reference, I had to provide a sort of crash course in European law ... it's certainly important to this day to suggest to the judge the interpretive questions to submit to the Court ... and sometimes to even draft the order of reference."[190] When I relayed these insights to Alberto Dal Ferro – a second-generation

1124; Voss, Reimer. 1986. "Erfahrungen und Probleme bei der Andwendung des Vorabentscheidungsverfahrens nacht Art. 177 EWGV." *Europarecht* 1: 95–111, at 97–98.

[188] Interview with Roger Grass, September 29, 2017.

[189] A nudge is "any aspect of the choice architecture that alters people's behavior in a predictable way without forbidding any options ... the intervention must be easy and cheap to avoid." See: Thaler, Richard, and Cass Sunstein. 2009. *Nudge: Improving Decisions about Health, Wealth, and Outcomes.* New York, NY: Penguin Books, at 6.

[190] Interview with Wilma Viscardini, September 29, 2017.

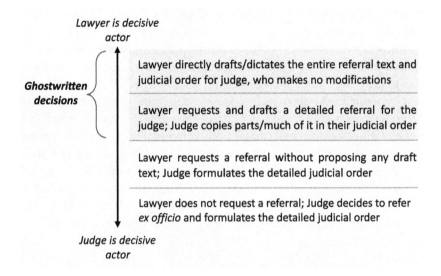

Figure 5.8 Conceptualizing lawyers' role in judicial decision-making

Euro-lawyer who brokered the pathbreaking 1991 *Francovich* case[191] by soliciting a referral from a local judge who did not even know where the ECJ was located – he was emphatic: "When I say: 'You must explain', it's absolutely necessary. It's an essential element. You must explain why EU law must prevail over national law, that the judge must disapply the latter ... you must thus interpose a proposal for a preliminary reference: A, B, C, D, E, F, if necessary ... in my experience it's essential."[192] Dal Ferro should know: he has since argued over 100 cases in Luxembourg.

Paolo De Caterini's experience is no different: "I remember our first lawsuit before the Tribunal of Brescia [in 1971]. The [judge] shot up! 'A Treaty? Sorry, but you should know that we don't apply Treaties! Why do you keep insisting on this Treaty?' And he was a notable jurist! From then on, every single memo we wrote would be preceded by two pages, where: 'In 1957, six states decided blah, blah, blah!'"[193] Although the judge did not solicit the ECJ in this instance, Cappelli and De Caterini's crash course cajoled one of the first rulings by an Italian

[191] In *Francovich*, the ECJ first held that EU member states could be held liable for damages to individuals suffered when the state fails to transpose EU law into national law. See: Joined cases C-6/90 and C-9/90, *Francovich*.

[192] Interview with Alberto Dal Ferro, March 6, 2017.

[193] Interview with Paolo De Caterini, December 27, 2017.

court recognizing the supremacy and direct effect of European law, "based ... entirely on the case law of the Court of Justice." In response, an enthusiastic member of the Commission Legal Service mused that Italian judges seemed to be "recognizing the specific characteristics of Community law" after "hesitat[ing] for a long time."[194]

This conclusion proved hopelessly premature. In interview after interview, even contemporary practitioners are adamant that without judicial ghostwriting, most national courts remain unlikely to invoke EU law and exceptionally unlikely to solicit the ECJ. And when they do, they are liable to make mistakes. While sometimes bordering on hubris, this view is usually ground in a pragmatic realism bordering on empathy. The best Euro-lawyers intuit the limited training and bureaucratic constraints afflicting their judicial interlocutors, particularly in lower courts. They know they must "present something that's pre-packaged ... [to] reduce the risk of an erroneous formulation and stimulate the judge to make [the reference] because the workload is reduced."[195] They must "do the homework"[196] and "spoon-feed" courts.[197] Judges often do not know "where the [ECJ] is located,"[198] they do not "exactly understand what to ask,"[199] and they "fear ... making a bad impression" by having their referrals declared inadmissible.[200] Since judges "almost never turn to the EU judge,"[201] ghostwriting referrals ready for copy and paste – "open parentheses, closed parentheses"[202] – remains a necessary staple of Euro-lawyering.

While the rule is that "you write [the judge] a draft" and "hope that he would copy yours,"[203] this outcome requires interpersonal finesse.

---

[194] Maestripieri, Cesare. 1972. "The Application of Community Law in Italy in 1972." *Common Market Law Review* 10: 340–351, at 340. The case concerned the direct applicability of Council Regulation 1975/69 and Commission Regulation 2195/69.

[195] Interview with Patrick Ferrari, Fieldfisher in Milan, December 13, 2016.

[196] Interview with Riccardo Sciaudone, Grimaldi Studio Legale in Rome, September 19, 2016 (in-person).

[197] Interview with Fabio Ferraro, law professor at the University of Naples and lawyer at De Berti Jacchia Franchini e Forlani in Naples, February 6, 2017 (in-person).

[198] Interview with Vincenzo Cannizzaro, law professor at La Sapienza University of Roma and lawyer, Cannizzaro & Partners in Rome, June 17, 2015 (in-person).

[199] Interview with Riccardo Sciaudone, September 19, 2016.

[200] Interview with Fabio Ferraro, February 6, 2017.

[201] Interview with Aristide Police, law professor at the University of Rome-Tor Vergata and lawyer at Clifford Chance in Rome, October 4, 2016 (in-person).

[202] Interview with Cristoforo Osti, Chiomenti Studio Legale in Rome, September 29, 2016 (in-person).

[203] Interview with Giuseppe Giacomini, October 24, 2016.

Particularly in years past, Euro-lawyers were liable to be perceived as snake oil salesmen. Hence in their interactions with judges, the goal of attacking the state's policies was best advanced via a strategically softer and collaborative predisposition. Viscardini recalls that some judges could be blindsighted by ready-made referrals, "risking to strike their susceptibility."[204] Capelli and Ubertazzi diffused these tensions by stressing how European law "was a novelty, and after all it was about going to the ECJ, it's not like we were convicting someone."[205] "Part of the game was explaining to the judge that this was serious stuff," echoes a Genoese pioneer, "but also really elegant and innovative."[206] Forging trust with more approachable first-instance judges was also key.[207] Viscardini wrote the entire reference in the 1976 *Donà* v. *Mantero* case because she knew the *pretore* and he "placed maximum trust" in her.[208] Bruno Nascimbene ghostwrote his first order of referral in the 1975 *Watson and Belmann* case[209] because the first-instance judges in Milan "were approximately my age, and we knew each other."[210]

Preparing the groundwork for ghostwriting was especially key when the first Euro-lawyers confronted semiprofessional judges in small, rural communities. The story of one preliminary reference is telling in this regard. In 1975, the small claims court of Bovino – a tiny village perched atop the sun-drenched hills of Puglia – audaciously referred a case to the ECJ challenging the Italian government's macroeconomic policy. As part of its anti-inflationary agenda, the Christian Democratic government had frozen the price of durum wheat, a key ingredient in dried pasta. Despite a "very significant increase" in world market prices for wheat, farmers were obliged to sell it "below the purchase price."[211] One of these – Mr. Russo – deemed this contrary to European law[212] and sued. Agreeably, the Justice referred the case to the ECJ, which declared the policy "incompatible with the common organization of

---

[204] Interview with Wilma Viscardini, September 29, 2017.
[205] Interview with Fausto Capelli, November 23, 2016.
[206] Interview with Giuseppe Giacomini, October 24, 2016.
[207] On the undertheorized role of trust in the judicial construction of Europe, see: Mayoral, Juan. 2017. "In the CJEU Judges Trust: A New Approach in the Judicial Construction of Europe." *Journal of Common Market Studies* 55(3): 551–568.
[208] Interview with Wilma Viscardini, September 29, 2017.
[209] Case 118/75, *Watson and Belmann* [1976], ECR 1185.
[210] Interview with Bruno Nascimbene, November 22, 2016.
[211] Case 60/75, *Russo* v. *AIMA* [1976], ECR 46, at paras. 2–3.
[212] Regulation No. 120/67 of the Council of June 13, 1967 on the common organization of the market in cereals (*Official Journal*, Special Edition 1967, at 33).

the markets" and directed the state to bear "the consequences" if "an individual producer has suffered damage."[213]

In truth, Mr. Russo was a member of an agricultural association (Confiagricoltura) with close ties to two Euro-lawyers we have already met: De Caterini and Cappelli. The duo had devised a strategy to challenge the government's anti-inflationary policy, and Mr. Russo agreed to serve as protagonist. But how to get a local part-time judge to refer the case to the ECJ? In a raspy voice punctuated by hearty chuckles, De Caterini recounts it all as if reading a playscript:

> It's a village atop of this [hill]. I travelled all night crossing train tracks to get there, where people were still in their bathing suits! There, there was a lawyer and *pretore* ... who was a friend of Confiagricoltura! We were interested in one thing: speed. For if this guy ... set[s] the hearing date correctly, the *avvocatura dello stato* [state legal service] won't be able to show up in time! They will raise so many objections that we'll be here all year!
>
> So we said: "Get ready, I'm on my way up!"
>
> The [judge] was up to speed on everything. I gave him the materials. "Yes, I'm fine with it." The preliminary reference, too! I mean, I was the one who wrote the preliminary references! It's obvious! I do it to this day. Trust them? No, no. I wrote the references myself! ... After that, a huge problem arose! I said: "Look, we must mail this to the ECJ."
>
> "Mail this to the ECJ?!" So he called the chancellery.
>
> They replied: "No, we've never done this! We have to send this through the international affairs department of the Ministry of Foreign Affairs."
>
> And I said, "No, no, no! For goodness sake, not the Ministry of Foreign Affairs! Let's not be silly!"
>
> "So wait, how do we do it?"
>
> "Well, you take an envelope and a postage stamp!"
>
> "An envelope and a postage stamp? How – are you sure? You're not going to get me thrown in jail for this?" In the end he convinced himself, because this was the way, after all!
>
> ... And after all of this: "Phew! We did it!"[214]

Suggestive of the affair's hurriedness to prevent the state legal service from opposing a referral to the ECJ is the fact that the judicial order was hastily handwritten[215] "as we dictated it," De Caterini confides.[216]

---

[213] 60/75, *Russo v. AIMA*, at operative parts (a) and (c).

[214] Interview with Paolo De Caterini, December 27, 2017.

[215] I confirmed this by obtaining the original file: CJUE-1715, *dossier de procedure originale, affaire* 60/75, Carmine Russo contro AIMA. HAEU, at 5–8.

[216] Interview with Paolo De Caterini, December 27, 2017.

De Caterini and Cappelli did not act as judicial ghostwriters once or twice. They did so systematically. For instance, in the landmark 1978 *Simmenthal* case,[217] the duo pounced upon a "fundamental error" of their opponents in the state legal service. Wanting to transplant the dispute from the small-town *pretore* of Susa to a more favorable forum, the state lawyer requested that the case be referred to the Italian Constitutional Court. After all, before 1984[218] the Constitutional Court clearly instructed judges to refer to it all matters concerning the validity Italian law under Community law such that it – and not the ECJ – could adjudicate the validity of national legislation. That is when the Euro-lawyers coyly approached the judge to cajole trouble: "'No, look. There's this problem, and it's intolerable, [the position] of the Constitutional Court.' So I wrote the preliminary reference for him … knowing full well that I was setting a bomb and even lighting the match!" In the key passage of De Caterini's ghostwritten reference, he asked the ECJ if Community law requires that "national measures which conflict with [European] provisions must be forthwith disregarded without waiting until those measures have been eliminated by … other constitutional authorities." The ECJ agreed, affirming that lower courts could submit references and disapply national legislation without awaiting directions from constitutional courts or parliaments.[219] In a conference in Luxembourg shortly after *Simmenthal*, the ECJ's Pierre Pescatore descended from the dais to appreciatively shake De Caterini's hand. "Everyone was looking at me like 'Who the heck is this guy!' … [Pescatore] really loved me, he'd tell me, because we all knew each other, the conferences were few, it was always the same people."[220]

The ghostwriting that produced the ECJ's pathbreaking *Simmenthal* ruling illustrates how judge-centric narratives can lead us astray. For instance, Alec Stone Sweet uses the case to highlight how "some Italian judges, apparently hoping to gain a measure of autonomy from the ICC [Italian Constitutional Court], worked to undermine [its] jurisprudence" by "request[ing] the ECJ to declare the ICC's … jurisprudence incompatible with the supremacy doctrine!"[221] Yet the

---

[217] 106/77, *Simmenthal*, ECR 629.

[218] See: Italian Constitutional Court, judgment No. 170 of June 8, 1984, *SpA Granital v. Amministrazione delle Finanze dello Stato.*

[219] 106/77, *Simmenthal*, at 632, 645–646.

[220] Interview with Paolo De Caterini, December 27, 2017.

[221] Stone, "Constitutional Dialogues in the European Community," at 10.

choreographers of this pugnacious campaign were not innately defiant judges, but mischievous lawyers who dexterously cajoled courts into playing their game.

### 5.4.4 "The Way to the Sentence Leads through the Pre-sentence"

Was judicial ghostwriting unique to Italy? In truth, the evidence suggests that French and German Euro-lawyers made use of the same repertoire for court-driven change for the same reasons, producing "pre-sentences," as one lawyer put it.[222]

In Paris, long-standing judges are the first to set the scene: "Before the 1980s," Guy Canivet recalls, "when European law was not well known, a certain number of law firms made it their trademark ... Ryziger's law firm, Funck-Brentano's firm ... and it's true that for judges like myself, who encountered these cases, they functioned as a motor."[223] Indeed, the first time the French Court of Cassation considered soliciting the ECJ in light of state noncompliance was in the 1966 *Promatex* case. Novel archival evidence reveals that the entrepreneurship of Paul-François Ryziger was key. Intent on having the ECJ strike down certain French custom barriers, the pioneering Euro-lawyer asked to "stay the proceedings until the ECJ pronounced itself on the affair. Ryziger went so far as to draft the preliminary questions such that the European judges could not avoid sanctioning the government law."[224] Writing in the 1980s, a colleague of Ryziger who solicited some of the first references from Paris' lower courts confided that because his interlocutors found it "difficult to perceive" EU law in cases "where all the parties are French," "the French judge will rarely apply Community law on his own initiative. He will also rarely draft a question himself *ex nihilo*. The role of the parties and of their counsel is therefore essential," particularly "if counsel drafts preliminary questions himself."[225]

Outside the halls of Paris' supreme courts, the absence of judicial training rendered first-instance judges even more dependent upon

[222] Interview with Rolf Gutmann, Guttmann, Pitterle, Zeller & Behl in Stuttgart, December 6, 2017 (via phone).
[223] Interview with Guy Canivet, October 2, 2017.
[224] Bernier, "France et le Droit Communautaire," at 129–130.
[225] Desmazières de Séchelles, Alain. 1987. "Experiences and Problems in Applying the Preliminary Proceedings of Article 177 of the Treaty of Rome, as Seen by a French Advocate." In *Article 177 EEC: Experiences and Problems*, Henry Schermers, Christiaan Timmermans, Alfred Kellermann, and J. Stewart Watson, eds. New York, NY: Elsevier, at 155–157.

lawyers' political entrepreneurship. In Lille, for instance, the first instance court president turned to Marcel Veroone – the region's first Euro-lawyer – to train judges on how to draft "preliminary references and to indicate how they should proceed when lawyers formulated these requests." That in the 1970s Veroone was the only lawyer in Lille to repeatedly request referrals from local courts meant that this training was as beneficial to him as for his judicial interlocutors. Even so, ghostwriting remained necessary. In an interview with me two years before his death, Veroone illustrated this by recalling a typically exasperated small-town judge, who pleaded that he ghostwrite the entire order of referral to the ECJ.[226]

Jean-Pierre Spitzer recounts first noticing French lawyers ghostwriting references while he clerked at the ECJ in the 1970s. "There was a case that's really important for specialists" he recalls, "[a] case where the lawyer was just fabulous. Fabulous! Because for the first time in the [European] Court's history, [a] judge who hadn't even gotten to the decision phase … decided to pose a ton [of] questions to the ECJ. And the lawyer who played this role! … I was blown away!"[227] When I interviewed the Euro-lawyer in question, they proudly showed me their faded personal copy of the original dossier, recounting how they "convinced the judge … that we needed to pose the question to the ECJ. Now, I'm not sure if I can tell you this because I don't know if the judge is still alive, but I'll tell you off the record." I followed the gesture to turn off the beeping device and switched to handwritten transcription: "The judge replied: 'You've convinced me, but I don't know how to do this. Write it for me.'"[228]

Having witnessed how the pioneers ghostwrote referrals, Spitzer put this repertoire to use upon returning to France to practice law. He is particularly proud of a 1985 tariff dispute,[229] where he cajoled the first instance judge in the tiny town of Béthune to solicit the ECJ for the first time:

> The whole Béthune bar was there at the end of my pleading. Everyone saying, "What is this, an extraterrestrial? I don't really understand what he's talking about, it's something bizarre." And the judge said, "counsel, you've convinced me, but I cannot answer your question." … I said,

[226] Interview with Marcel Veroone, ex-lawyer in Lille, September 4, 2018 (via phone).
[227] Interview with Jean-Pierre Spitzer, September 20, 2017.
[228] Interview with French lawyer, 2017 (in-person; date and name redacted).
[229] Case 385/85, S.R. Industries v. Administration des douanes [1986], ECR 2929.

"in my view, national law is contrary to European law. You should therefore first solicit the ECJ ... here is the question that you will pose." I had drafted it, because you had to do the work! I even drafted the motivations for him. I submitted a file, and said: "Here's the motivation, I don't request that you copy it, of course it's your discretion" – but he didn't change a thing. Because you had honest judges who said, "I don't know this at all, [and] this guy was a clerk [at the ECJ]" ... The French authorities got worried that a judge from Béthune could refer to the ECJ! In a centralized state this is impossible![230]

Spitzer's experience is not unique. Other French second-generation Euro-lawyers affirm ghostwriting detailed orders of referral to the ECJ.[231] After all, judges "have a restrained sensibility vis-à-vis EU law" and "lack the habit, so they will be happy to have a ready-made thing."[232]

In Germany, oral histories point in the same direction. Consider the last person you would expect to credit the entrepreneurship of lawyers over judicial activism: Reimer Voss, a pugnacious judge at Hamburg's fiscal court. Voss repeatedly figures in Karen Alter's narrative of judicial empowerment,[233] and for good reason: he was the ECJ's most prolific lower court interlocutor in the 1970s. Yet in a 1987 article, Voss cautioned that:

[L]arge areas of Community law either do not receive any attention at all from German judges ... it is obvious that a preliminary ruling to the Court of Justice is frequently not sought. The conditions necessary for a reference to the Court of Justice may not be known ... I would like to draw your attention to a particular phenomenon that seems to operate in other countries, too. What is so striking is that the same persons or companies frequently participate as plaintiffs in reference proceedings. In my experience one of the reasons for this is that the plaintiffs are advised by lawyers who are well-experienced in Community law and who suggest that the court make a reference to the Court of Justice.[234]

---

[230] Interview with Jean-Pierre Spitzer, Cabinet Saint Yves Avocats, September 20, 2017 (in-person).

[231] Interview with Philippe Derouin, September 12, 2017; Interview with Frédéric Manin, Altana Avocats in Paris, September 22, 2017 (in-person); Interview with Philippe Guibert, September 21, 2017.

[232] Interview with Eric Morgan de Rivery, September 12, 2017.

[233] Alter, "European Court's Political Power," at 464; Alter, *Establishing the Supremacy of European Law*, at 102.

[234] Voss, Reimer. 1987. "Experiences and Problems in Applying Article 177 of the EEC Treaty – From the Point of View of a German Judge." In *Article 177*

Even though no judge in Germany in the 1960s and 1970s was as eager to serve as motor of European integration, and even though he was less burdened by an onerous workload than other lower court judges, Voss confessed that "formulating the question for reference demands an especially high level of intellectual effort," hence it was crucial that "a small group of barristers familiar with European law" would "frequently urge us to make a reference."[235] It was undoubtedly Fritz Modest and the protagonists of this chapter that Voss had in mind.

To be sure, conversations with Euro-lawyers do suggest that particularly lower fiscal courts in Germany have occasionally been more open to efforts to Europeanize national law than their Italian and French counterparts, consistent with Chapter 4. Yet in line with Voss' experience, ghostwriting often remained necessary. As late as the 1980s, a first-generation Euro-lawyer in Cologne lamented how "the capacity of most national judges (courts) is limited and concentrated on their day-to-day work … [for] the number of judges (courts) sufficiently familiar with EEC law is rather small."[236] To this day, interviewees confirm that German judges care "to avoid the exposure if they ask the wrong questions," so they "normally try to get around" referring to Luxembourg.[237] Off-the-record, a first-generation Euro-lawyer relayed having to draft the entirety of one of their first orders of referral for a big city tax court whose judges did not know what European law was in the first place.[238] Recounting his participation in eighty-eight preliminary references since 1965, Dietrich Ehle shares that "still today I formulate the questions that should be referred … courts were not by themselves inclined the refer cases … I [can] convince the courts in 30–40 percent of all cases to refer."[239] At Fritz Modest's firm and its successor, lawyers "want to make it easier for the judge to make referrals … so what we normally do in our writs is to draft the questions … saying 'you could

_EEC: Experiences and Problems_, Henry Schermers, Christiaan Timmermans, Alfred Kellermann, and J. Stewart Watson, eds. New York, NY: Elsevier, at 57–58.

[235] Ibid., at 66–67; Voss, "Erfahrungen und Probleme," at 97–98.

[236] Deringer, Arved. 1987. "Some Comments by a German Advocate on Problems Concerning the Application of Article 177 EEC." In _Article 177 EEC: Experiences and Problems_, Henry Schermers, Christiaan Timmermans, Alfred Kellermann, and J. Stewart Watson, eds. New York, NY: Elsevier, at 210.

[237] Interview with Manja Epping, Christian Frank, and Thomas Raab, Taylor Wessing in Munich, December 12, 2017 (in-person).

[238] Interview with one of the first Euro-lawyers in Germany, name and date redacted (in-person).

[239] Interview with Dietrich Ehle, December 13, 2017.

ask this, or that, or almost the last one' ... in 50% [of cases] you would see big similarities between the proposals and the decision."[240]

An evocative aphorism capturing this practice of judicial ghost-writing is shared by Rolf Gutmann, a labor lawyer in Stuttgart who brokered over a dozen preliminary references since the early 1980s: "The way to the sentence leads through the pre-sentence."[241] Indeed, a local judge from whom Gutmann solicited the first-ever reference to the ECJ from the Stuttgart Administrative Court credits his discovery of European law to that 1981 encounter: "I was very happy that he did this work [drafting a preliminary reference] for us, because I didn't know anything about it, so I had to learn a lot."[242] Driven by his newfound European legal consciousness, the judge in question – Michael Funke-Kaiser – became the most prolific interlocutor of the ECJ that I met in my year and a half of fieldwork.[243]

Conversations with second-generation Euro-lawyers underscore how a "draft of the right questions is best practice" and can "actually [be] expected by the judges."[244] "You cannot trust the local judges [to] see the real problems, that they phrase it correctly, that they send it to the ECJ, you have to help them in that still today, especially in rural areas ... you really have to encourage them." Hence the dictum: "Formulate the questions and the matters that should be referred as precisely as possible."[245] A practitioner in Berlin who has argued over three dozen cases before the ECJ agrees that since "it's not part of the daily diet" of most judges to collaborate with the ECJ, one must pique their interest – "to contribute to the development of EU law" – and lessen their workload: "if the parties already presented on this topic, you can actually copy, or use [it so] it's not really much work."[246] For example, in the 1990 *Meilicke* case described previously, the Euro-lawyer not only constructed the case; Meilicke also "had a very nice,

---

[240] Interview with Klaus Landry and Lothar Harings [quoted], Graf von Westphalen, January 9, 2018 (in-person).

[241] Interview with Rolf Gutmann, December 6, 2017.

[242] See: Case 65/81, *Reina* [1982], ECR 34.

[243] Funke-Kaiser estimates referring ten cases to the ECJ since his interactions with Gutmann: Interview with Michael Funke-Kaiser, November 30, 2017.

[244] Interview with Rene Grafunder and Jorg Karenfort, Denton's in Berlin, November 7, 2017; See also: Interview with Manja Epping, Christian Frank, and Thomas Raab, December 12, 2017.

[245] Interview with Jürgen Lüdicke and Bjorn Bodenwaldt, PwC in Hamburg, January 8, 2018 (in-person).

[246] Interview with Thomas Luebbig, November 1, 2017.

wonderful session where the [Hannover regional] court copied all my questions, submitted all my questions to the Court of Justice." Like his French and Italian counterparts, Meilicke acknowledges that his ghostwriting serves a political strategy. Pushing "lower court judges to present a case directly to the European Court of Justice, bypassing their national court of last resort ... [creates] an incentive for national judges of last resort to present a case to the European Court of Justice themselves; for they do not like be shamed by a lower court judge."[247]

What are we to make of this oral history consensus? On the one hand, lawyers have reason to *underreport* their ghostwriting, as belied by those who only confided these actions off-the-record. In civil law countries wary of the lawyer-driven adversarial legalism of common law countries,[248] "the drafting of preliminary questions is considered to be essentially, if not exclusively, a judicial task,"[249] making ghostwriting "impossible to imagine."[250] Even some ECJ judges and Commission lawyers embraced this view. In a 1985 conference, ECJ judge Thijmen Koopmans cautioned that "the judge can not rely on the imaginative powers of the parties and their counsel. The question must find its place in the intellectual process the judge intends to use."[251] A representative of the Commission added that "it is for the national court to select and draft the questions," for lawyers would "draft them from a standpoint of partiality."[252]

On the other hand, some lawyers may be biased by the problem of "exaggerated roles ... [since] all of us like to think that what we do has an impact."[253] This is particularly plausible in purposive interviews with key informants, since the first Euro-lawyers derived pleasure from

---

[247] Interview with Wienand Meilicke, January 17, 2018; January 31, 2018 (via e-mail).

[248] Kagan, "Should Europe Worry about Adversarial Legalism?"

[249] Schermers, "Introduction." In *Article 177 EEC: Experiences and Problems*. Henry Schermers, Christiaan Timmermans, Alfred Kellermann, and J. Stewart Watson, eds. New York, NY: Elsevier, at 12.

[250] Interview with Christian Roth, September 25, 2017.

[251] Koopmans, "Technique of the Preliminary Question," at 328.

[252] Bebr, Gerhard. 1987. "The Preliminary Proceedings of Article 177 EEC: Problems and Suggestions for Improvement." In *Article 177 EEC: Experiences and Problems*. Henry Schermers, Christiaan Timmermans, Alfred Kellermann, and J. Stewart Watson, eds. New York, NY: Elsevier, at 346.

[253] Berry, "Validity and Reliability Issues in Elite Interviewing," at 680–681; Tansey, "Process Tracing and Elite Interviewing," at 769.

exercising their agency. In such instances, the best way to corroborate lawyers' insights is to be "relentless in gathering diverse and relevant evidence" by triangulating oral histories.[254] Judges testifying to lawyers' influence, as we have seen, enables one form of triangulation. The 2015 opening of the ECJ's historical archives permits another.

## 5.5 ARCHIVAL ANATOMIES

From 2016 to 2018 I obtained access to the original dossiers for 108 of the preliminary references to the ECJ between 1964 and 1979 (24 percent of the 447 referrals over the period). Since all access requests were vetted by the European Court's staff (to decide whether to redact any pages), I had to be selective about which files I sought: I focused disproportionately on referrals by lower courts located in (or near) the field sites I visited wherein one of the first Euro-lawyers represented a party to the suit. Almost all of these documents were "opened" for the first time by my requests, and I obtained permission to reproduce excerpts. The *dossiers* are only as complete as the materials supplied by national courts, and most only supplied their final signed reference. As a result, most of these archival documents reproduce the "public transcript" and make it impossible to compare judicial decisions to lawyers' pleadings – this was the unfortunate case for all of the German dossiers. But in several instances the materials from French and Italian courts are more complete, allowing us to peek behind the curtain.

Let us begin with the 1971 *SAIL* case: the first referral to the ECJ by a southern Italian court, and a veritable masterclass in judicial ghostwriting. The reference spurred the ECJ to strike down two 1929 and 1938 national regulations[255] establishing state "milk centers." These held a monopoly on local milk production and distribution: milk could only be imported from elsewhere when local demand exceeded supply, and state officials (prefects) could determine the boundaries of the centers' market control. So when a farmer from a hillside town imported some cases of milk "within the boundary of the 'prohibited' urban area of Bari," he was reported by two city officials and criminal proceedings were lodged. The first instance judge (*pretore* of Bari)

---

[254] Bennett, Andrew, and Jeffrey Checkel. 2015. *Process Tracing: From Metaphor to Analytic Tool.* New York, NY: Cambridge University Press, at 21.

[255] Royal Decree No. 994 of May 9, 1929; Law No. 851 of June 16, 1938.

doubted that national law complied with Article 37 of the Rome Treaty. So he punted the case to the ECJ.[256]

This rendition parallels the ECJ's official record of an audacious judge coming to rescue of a vigilant farmer. But by now we should be able to smell the makings of a constructed case: an individual's defiant boundary crossing, a surprisingly knowledgeable local judge. Indeed, the case's ghostwriter is none other than Italy's first Euro-lawyer: Nicola Catalano. How did Catalano persuade the judge to take the unprecedented step of inviting the European Court to strike down Italian law? The original dossier demonstrates that he did it (at least in part) via a twenty-eight-page memo providing an introduction to European law, appealing to the judge's legal imperatives, and subsidizing almost all of his work.

Step 1: a crash course in European law and its bearing on the dispute. Notice (i) how Catalano uses cogent language, underlining, and adjectives like "certain," "definitive," and "total" to quell doubts and make his memo easy to skim, and (ii) renders these claims credible by subtly invoking his insider expertise as ex-ECJ judge and member of the Italian delegation in negotiations over the Rome Treaty:

> We could ask the Illustrious Pretore to refer to the Constitutional Court ... but we prefer to base our defense upon the much more certain grounds of the monopoly's incompatibility ... with the Treaty of Rome ...
>
> The European Economic Community, is first of all based upon a customs union implying the definitive and total suppression – within a transition period happily expired on 31.12.1969 – of customs duties and quantitative restrictions ... and all "measures having equivalent effect" to a quantitative restriction.
>
> In this vein art. 37 of the treaty "progressively adjusts any State monopolies of a commercial character in such a manner as will ensure the exclusion, at the date of the expiry of the transitional period, of all discrimination between the nationals of Members States in regard to conditions of supply or marketing of goods."
>
> The rationale of the foregoing provision is evident. The authors of the Treaty realized that the abolition of quantitative restrictions would be insufficient to eliminate discriminations brought by state monopolies of a commercial character ... Any monopoly, especially a local one, is certainly incompatible if its sole objective and effect is to prevent market exchange ... "

[256] Case 82/71, SAIL, ECR 120, at 120–121.

Step 2: appealing to (i) the judge's sense of justice by casting national law in the poorest possible light and (ii) invoking the force of his obligations under European law. Catalano begins by admonishing the monopoly, variously characterizing it as outdated, a fascist legacy, a corrupt political machine, and a suicidal policy:

> ... this anachronistic monopoly of the milk centers ... this absurd monopoly ... the corporative origins of this system during the full-fledged fascist regime ... represent local centers of power with notable bearing for politics- or, more precisely, for local sub-politics ... Despite perky financing ... there is a very great gap between production costs (90 lire) and consumption price (150 lire) that is certainly unjustified...
>
> The vigorous opposition to the milk centers' monopoly by <u>all</u> agricultural associations proves that these arguments are no personal understanding ... applying criminal sanctions to protect these very monopolies is in truth a <u>suicidal violation</u>, in that it conflicts with the agricultural, economic, and even public health interests of this Country.

Catalano then outlines the judge's obligation – his "imperative" and "binding" "requirement" – to recognize the primacy of European law over national law:

> We must now demonstrate the reach and imperative of Art. 37 EEC, even within the national legal order and particularly before national courts.
>
> It must first be recalled that, unlike traditional international law, the EEC Treaty not only contains obligations binding upon member states and laws that are directly applicable and operable without implementing legislation, but it forbids (art. 5, section 2) member states from adopting any laws which compromise the realization of the Treaty's objectives ...
>
> This structure – which is a federal-type structure – is indeed characterized by the transfer of sovereignty and new powers to the Community ... the Court of Justice ... affirmed that contraventions of the foregoing provisions constitute violations of the rights of citizens, rights which national courts are required to protect ... the national judge is required to disapply national law if it contrasts with the Community rule that must prevail.

Finally, step 3: cajoling the judge into soliciting the ECJ by agreeably laboring to ghostwrite the reference. To strengthen his proposal, Catalano highlights the novelty of the issues raised by the dispute, the risks and imprudence of deciding them directly, and the pragmatic reasons to ask the ECJ to pronounce itself:

The authors of the Treaty recognized the difficulties of interpretation by national courts and the dangers of conflicting interpretations. In its wise arrangement, art. 177 attributed the competence of preliminary interpretation of Community law to the European Court of Justice ...

The Pretore charged [with the dispute] would certainly have the discretion to decide the question. However, in good conscience and while being fully convinced of his abilities – we believe that due to the delicate nature and the novelty of this very question, a judgment that eschews the light of the only specialized court in this domain could be deemed unwise ... Reasons of opportunity, prudence, and procedural economy advise soliciting the Court of Justice right now ...

Given the novelty of the matter we believe it is opportune to clarify the competences of the Court of Justice and the national courts.

The first reserves the competence to interpret Community law. But ... it is up to the national court to resolve the dispute, on the basis of the Court of Justice's interpretation, which is binding ... This logic must be applied in the current case ...

With this premise ... we will permit ourselves to suggest the questions of interpretation to submit to the Court of Justice ...

We need not reproduce the full text of Catalano's queries for the ECJ (see Figure 5.9 for excerpts). Suffice it to say that the local judge's version would fail any plagiarism test, and that Catalano achieved the desired outcome in Luxembourg. In many ways, Catalano was literally teaching the bench how to think and write like a European judge: the Euro-lawyer acknowledged as much in an article he penned in Italy's leading law review, *Il Foro Italiano*, wherein he called on national courts to mimic the reasoning and "style" of ECJ judgments.[257]

The most eye-popping archival evidence of ghostwriting consists of a Euro-lawyer's memo literally serving as the judicial order of referral itself. In 1975 Bruno Nascimbene had yet to become one of the most respected professors of EU law in Italy. An active member of the European Federalist Movement, at the time he was a twenty-seven year-old lawyer fresh out of law school, having written his thesis on the treaty-making power of the European Community. Then one day the husband of a university classmate – Alessandro Belmann – got hit with criminal charges. He had hosted a seventeen-year-old British woman – Lynn Watson – as a babysitter in his home without officially reporting her presence within the three-day period mandated by a 1931

---

[257] Catalano, Nicola. 1965. "Lo stile delle sentenze della Corte di giustizia delle Comunità europee." *Il Foro Italiano* 92(10): 141–148.

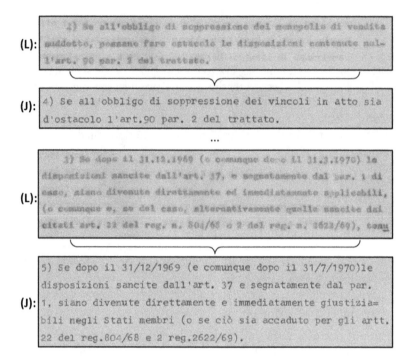

Figure 5.9 Excerpts of a ghostwritten reference: the Euro-lawyer's proposed draft **(L)** and judge's nearly identical official text **(J)** in the 1971 *SAIL* case
*Source:* HAEU CJUE-1277, affaire 82/71, Società Agricola Industria Latte SAIL, at 12, 44.

criminal law.[258] Ms. Watson faced up to three months of detention and the prospect of deportation, regardless of conviction.[259] Nascimbene was intent on transforming the dispute into a vehicle to push the ECJ to sanction the criminal law and affirm that protections for the free movement of workers in articles 48–66 of the Rome Treaty were directly applicable by national courts.

"I had to convince the judge," Nascimbene tells me. "I practiced frequently before the *Pretura*, and I don't hide the fact that its judges were approximately my age, and we knew each other … they trusted me … their sensibility for European law, I transmitted it to them, if I may say so. Not to brag, but I've realized this in frequenting them."

[258] Royal Decree No. 773 of June 18, 1931 ("Testo Unico Legge di Pubblica Sicurezza").
[259] Case C-188/75, *Watson and Belmann* [1976], ECR 1186, at 1188.

*Watson and Belmann* is a case in point: Nascimbene crafted a motivated memo capable of standing alone as an order of reference to the ECJ:

> We question that these laws' obligations are compatible with the foregoing rules of Community law ... we deem it opportune – or, rather, necessary – that the illustrious Pretore, in light of Article 177 of the EEC Treaty endowing the Court of Justice with the competence to decide <u>via a preliminary ruling</u> ... make use of this procedure, staying the proceeding underway until the Court has pronounced itself ... The questions that the illustrious Mr. Pretore can submit to the Court could be indicated as follows: ...

The judge was so convinced, the archives reveal (see Figure 5.10), that instead of writing a judicial order, he forwarded Nascimbene's memo and its five questions to the court chancellery, which referred *it* to Luxembourg! A few months later, the ECJ affirmed that, in response to Nascimbene's questions "which the *pretore* made his own" (how is that for a euphemism?), the Treaty's free movement protections were directly effective and restrictions could only be compatible if reasonable, proportionate, and forbearing from deportation.[260]

The original dossiers also contain direct evidence that other first-generation Euro-lawyers – including the Funck-Brentanos in France, and Capelli, Ubertazzi, Cappelli, and De Caterini in Italy – drafted preliminary references that were copied verbatim by local judges. Capelli and Ubertazzi even did so across borders – before Italian and French judges – confirming the modularity of this strategic repertoire. Such ghostwriting was often premised on walking judges through the As, Bs, and Cs of European law. In the 1978 *Union Latière Normande* case,[261] Lise and Roland Funck-Brentano did not merely motivate their proposed order of referral and draft the questions to be submitted to the ECJ. After all, they were before judges at the Commercial Court of Paris, infamous amongst Euro-lawyers for once querying what the Treaty of Rome was. To ensure that their interlocutors understood what they were talking about, the Funck-Brentanos held the judges by the hand. They provided annotated excerpts of the relevant provisions of the Rome Treaty, including Article 177 describing what the preliminary reference procedure is, and how it works (Figure 5.11). It worked in turn: the judges copied all five proposed questions and punted their first case to the ECJ.

---

[260] C-188/75, *Watson and Belmann*, ECR 1185, at 1187, 1199.
[261] Case 244/78, *Union laitière normande v. French Dairy Farmers* [1979], ECR 307.

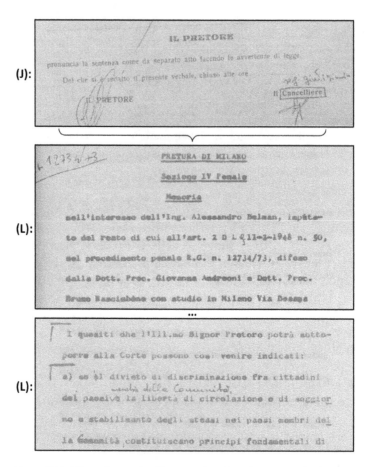

Figure 5.10 The judge's order (**J**) notes that the ruling is attached separately; The attachment (**L**) is the lawyer's memo in the "Watson and Belmann" case *Source:* HAEU CJUE-1780, affaire 118/75, Lynne Watson et Alessandro Belmann, at 7–8, 26.

Parallel occurrences are documented in the dossiers for over a dozen referrals by national courts. Excerpts of the ghostwritten judicial orders from six French and Italian courts are provided in Figure 5.12. One of these is the 1971 *Eunomia di Porro* case,[262] whose construction by Capelli and Uberazzi was described in the previous section. Knowing that the judges at the Tribunal of Turin had never referred a case to the ECJ, the Euro-lawyers typed up a comprehensive and motivated memo ready for cut and paste. Putting pen to paper, the judge scribbled

---

[262] 18/71, *Eunomia di Porro*, ECR 811.

Attendu subsidiairement qu'il y aurait lieu de surseoir à statuer sur la demande principale et saisir la Cour de Justice des Communautés Européennes, siégeant à Luxembourg, des questions relatives à l'interprétation du Traité et de la réglementation dérivée, et ce en vertu de l'article 177 du Traité qui prévoit :

*" La Cour de Justice est compétente pour statuer*
*" à titre préjudiciel*
*" a) sur l'interprétation du présent Traité*
*" b) sur la validité et l'interprétation des*
*" actes pris par les institutions de la*
*" Communauté..."*

*" Lorsqu'une telle question est soulevée devant une*
*" juridiction d'un des Etats membres, cette juridic-*
*" tion peut, si elle estime qu'une décision sur ce*
*" point est nécessaire pour rendre son jugement,*
*" demander à la Cour de Justice de statuer sur cette*
*" question."*

Figure 5.11 Baby steps: Euro-lawyers providing the national judge with annotated excerpts of the Treaty of Rome in the "Union Latière Normande" case
*Source:* HAEU CJUE-2324, affaire 244/78, Union Latière Normande, at 27.

Ubertazzi and Capelli's questions verbatim in a one-page order, stapled it to the lawyers' memo, and asked the chancellery to mail the file to Luxembourg. Formalities aside, the reference was authored by the lawyers themselves.

Behind the scenes, the ECJ's own members recognized and largely celebrated the first Euro-lawyers' efforts – as we previously saw in the personal praise they garnered from Judge Pescatore (when they did not get too carried away). Indeed, one of the Court's first clerks recalls how "in various preliminary references submitted to the Court in the 1960s–1980s, [Capelli and Ubertazzi] played an important role not only in their juridical treatment before the Court, but even before in convincing the Italian judge to refer the questions; Many of which led to Court judgments that, by basically obligating the national judge to disapply domestic law, pushed the Italian state to modify or remove statutes."[263] And on April 22, 1981, Capelli received a thankful letter that he has cherished and kept in his safe ever since. It was authored

263 Interview with Paolo Gori, April 6, 2017.

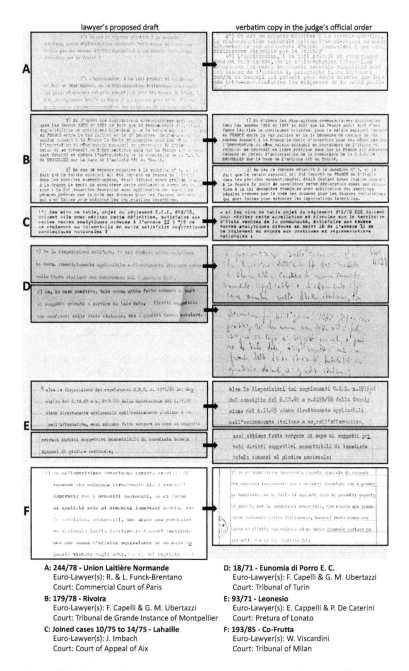

Figure 5.12  Copy and paste: excerpts of six ghostwritten referrals to the ECJ
*Sources:* From HAEU: CJUE-2324, affaire 244/78, at 7, 29; CJUE-2270, affaire 179/78, at 10–11; CJUE-1663-1664, affaires 10-14/75, at 62, 65; CJUE-1233, affaire 18/71, at 8–11; CJUE-1286, affaire 93/71, at 9–12; From the archives of Wilma Viscardini: Case 193/85.

by one of the recently retired leaders of the European Court's federalist faction, Alberto Trabucchi: "Dearest Capelli, you are one of the few persons in Italy who understands the significance of Community law" and can testify to the "events that witnessed the "invention" of this legal order."[264]

The ECJ imposes a forty-year gag rule on its records, so the trail of original dossiers ends in 1980. Yet the ghostwriting proceeds. Wilma Viscardini provides a closing example via her personal records of the 1985 Co-Frutta case. The case concerned the validity of a national consumption tax on bananas, which in practice was only applicable to imports given that Italian banana production is, shall we say, negligible.[265] Viscardini recounts how she leveraged the ghostwriter's repertoire to construct the case and draft the Tribunal of Milan's preliminary reference to the ECJ:

> Another important "test" case was the one that allowed us to dismantle the consumption tax on bananas ... Here too I had the opportunity to speak with an entrepreneur who lamented the tax's existence. I proposed that we ask for a refund on the tax payment after importing bananas that were freely circulating in other Member States ... The client gave me a blank slate, so we lodged a proceeding that sparked a preliminary reference and a judgement by the [European] Court in case 193/85, which fully embraced my position ... as you'll see, the questions referred by the Tribunal are exactly the same as those I had proposed in my closing pleading [see Figure 5.12].[266]

## 5.6 THE RADIATING EFFECT OF LAWYERS AND ITS LIMITS

Couched behind clients and judges that had yet to develop a European legal consciousness, the first Euro-lawyers invented a repertoire of lawsuit construction and judicial ghostwriting. They put this repertoire to use to mobilize civil society and national courts into punting noncompliance cases to the ECJ and expand the horizons of judicial review. Far from "not [being] politically motivated in bringing their

[264] Alberto Trabucchi to Fausto Capelli, April 22, 1981. Shared by Mr. Capelli from his archives.
[265] Case 193/85, Co-Frutta v. Amministrazione delle finanze dello Stato [1987], ECR 2085, at 2107.
[266] Interview with Wilma Viscardini, September 29, 2017.

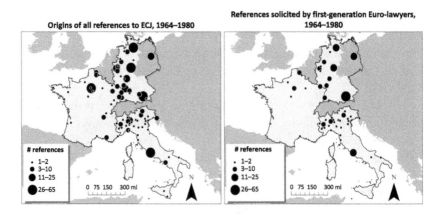

Figure 5.13 Referrals to the ECJ and the subset in cases solicited by the first Euro-lawyers, 1964–1980

actions," proceeding "willy-nilly,"[267] and riding a wave of surprisingly "vigilant" litigants,[268] Euro-lawyers played a decisive, labor-intensive, and very much intentional role in jump-starting the judicial construction of Europe.

Yet the same indicators that attest to the radiating effect of the first Euro-lawyers are also harbingers of the limits upon their repertoire of institutional change. Consider Figure 5.13, which maps the distribution of national court referrals to the ECJ during the 1960s and 1970s, visualizing these data as graduated point symbols. The figure compares the emergent geographies when the universe of all referrals ($n = 497$) is mapped versus the subset of references solicited by the first-generation Euro-lawyers ($n = 206$) listed in Figure 5.3. Two inferences readily stand out. First, geospatial data corroborate oral histories: the 1960s and 1970s truly were the age of the pioneers. The first Euro-lawyers not only participated in at least 41.5 percent of all preliminary references through 1980, but they influenced the emergent geography of national court referrals to the ECJ. Second, these maps highlight that French Euro-lawyers were less dominant (soliciting 19 of 98 referrals (19 percent)) than their colleagues in Germany (122 of 293 referrals (42 percent)) and Italy (65 of 106 referrals (61 percent)). Why?

---

[267] As Joseph Weiler presumes of lawyers and litigants' behavior: Weiler, "Transformation of Europe," at 2421.

[268] Schermers, "Law as It Stands against Treaty Violations by States," at 133.

There is little doubt that cross-national variation in the first Euro-lawyers' impact is of a piece with France's more restrictive political and legal opportunity structures. In Chapter 4, we traced how the French judiciary – particularly the administrative courts – institutionalizes comparatively mightier forms of bureaucratic domination that have long dissuaded judges from soliciting the ECJ and Europeanizing domestic policy. Through the 1970s, these hierarchical judicial relations were exploited by successive Gaullist governments to protect national sovereignty and block French judges from serving as motors of European integration. Charles de Gaulle set a particularly infamous set of precedents in the 1960s by threatening to disband the Council of State if it ruled against favored government policies, lowering the judicial retirement age to force out dissident judges, and packing both the Council of State and the Constitutional Council with loyalists.[269] The Gaullists even subsequently introduced an amendment in the National Assembly that would have made judges' enforcement of European law supremacy illegal.[270] Only with the 1981 election of socialist François Mitterand to the presidency did the government cease supporting legal and judicial obstructions to European integration. But by that time, the age of the pioneers was coming to a close.

Yet there is one additional factor that has continued to limit the impact of French Euro-lawyers, and it lies in the more restrictive and hierarchical organization of the French bar. Not only has France had only half to a third as many lawyers per capita as Germany and Italy, respectively;[271] it is also unique in that a tiny number of practitioners (the cassation bar) have historically monopolized legal representation before the state's supreme courts.[272] To this day, unless a Euro-lawyer can persuade a member of this group of 100 or so elites to play ball, they cannot represent their client before either the Court of Cassation or the Council of State. And because cassation lawyers regularly practice before both jurisdictions, they tend to be generalists rather than EU

---

[269] Moeschel, Mathias. 2019. "How 'Liberal' Democracies Attack(ed) Judicial Independence." In *Judicial Power in a Globalized World*. Paulo Pinto de Albuquerque and Krzysztof Wojtyczek, eds. Cham: Springer. at 138; Stone, Alec. 1992. *The Birth of Judicial Politics in France: The Constitutional Council in Comparative Perspective*. New York, NY: Oxford University Press, at 51.

[270] Bernier, "France et le Droit Communautaire," at 145; 244.

[271] Kelemen, "Suing for Europe," at 113.

[272] Karpik, Lucien. 1999. *French Lawyers: A Study in Collective Action, 1274–1994*. New York, NY: Oxford University Press, at 26–35.

specialists, whose interest lies in cultivating a favorable rapport with supreme court judges by not rocking the boat and limiting requests to solicit the ECJ.[273]

Consider the revealing experience of three of this chapter's protagonists. Given lower courts' reticence to enforce European law and solicit the ECJ, Lise and Roland Funck-Brentano struck up a collaboration with Paul-François Ryziger, the only Europeanist lawyer on the cassation bar. As a mentee of the Funck-Brentanos recalls, "Ryziger brought cases before the Court of Cassation that we fed him, such that he would then force the Court of Cassation to submit preliminary references."[274] While Ryziger relied on the fact that supreme courts are obligated to solicit the ECJ when doubting the compatibility of national and EU law,[275] his stubborn efforts did wear on supreme court judges. In the words of former Court of Cassation President Guy Canivet:

> The Funck-Brentanos and Ryziger, who as cassation lawyer collected the demands of all the [ordinary] lawyers who wanted to seize [the ECJ] ... after having played the role of pioneers, they became enclosed in a practice – well, especially Ryziger – that was a bit sterile, always the same thing. Plus, by front-loading his activism in European matters, he provoked some skeptical reactions by judges.[276]

Yet the geographies captured in Figure 5.13 point to a deeper story still. For they also highlight stark *subnational* variation *within* Italy, France, and Germany. Such localized spatiotemporal patterns cannot be explained by legal opportunity structures varying at the national level. Unearthing how Euro-lawyering (and the judicial enforcement of EU law) evolves, and why it becomes rooted in some communities and not others, is the focus of Chapter 6.

---

[273] Interview with Hélène Farge, September 21, 2017; Interview with Louis Boré, lawyer in the Ordre des Avocats au Conseil d'État et à la Cour de Cassation, September 15, 2017 (in-person).

[274] Interview with Christian Roth, September 25, 2017.

[275] Bernier, "France et le Droit Communautaire," at 129.

[276] Interview with Guy Canivet, October 2, 2017.

## CHAPTER SIX

# HOT SPOTS AND COLD SPOTS

## Euro-Lawyering's Uneven Corporatization

> *We should distinguish between international law firms . . . and those smaller, traditional firms where knowledge of EU law is much more limited . . . the second distinction is geographic . . . in smaller hubs, knowledge of this field is significantly reduced. And if you sum both dimensions – smaller law firms plus localization in provincial space – the result for EU law is that you plunge into an extraordinary black hole.*
> —Patrick Ferrari, lawyer at Fieldfisher's Milan office[1]

## 6.1 GROUND TRUTH

The protagonists of Chapter 5 exemplify how lawyers can forge their own opportunities to advance institutional change. Theirs was a master class on how to corner local judges into collaborating with a supranational court to Europeanize domestic public policies and bulldoze obstructions to regional integration. Yet new institutions and practices seldom survive on the backs of a few entrepreneurs. So as we move from the 1980s toward the present day, a key question arises: how does the practice of Euro-lawyering evolve, and under what conditions does it come to have a sustained impact on judicial policymaking?

This puzzle invites us to investigate a classic "big, slow-moving, and . . . invisible" social process.[2] At the macro-historical level, this can prove an arduous inferential task. Yet a "close-to-the-ground account"[3] helps us get a better grip of why the distribution of Euro-lawyers has become as uneven as the reach of the European Union's (EU's) judicial authority. A parable from Sicily provides a glimpse of this "ground truth."[4]

---

[1] Interview conducted on December 13, 2016 (in-person).

[2] Pierson, "Big, Slow-Moving, and . . . Invisible."

[3] For a similar approach in a dissimilar context, see: Stern, *Environmental Litigation in China*, at 1.

[4] By "ground truth," I borrow an expression from meteorologists describing on-the-ground verifications of forecasts and model predictions, supplied by individuals in the

"I don't fear the recorder," relays Giuseppe Di Rosa, an ambitious young lawyer in Palermo. Having gotten to know one another, I am now sitting in Di Rosa's office to document the *fil rouge* of our conversations. After receiving his law degree in Palermo, in the mid-2000s he enrolled in the European College of Parma.[5] He found himself immersed for the first time in an environment where "everything was interpreted from the perspective of European law ... I became convinced of this message." In the subsequent years Di Rosa completed a doctorate and interned at the European Commission. Yet "from a sociological point of view, what's really interesting" is what happened when he then returned home:

> When you came back here, you felt strangely alone. It's an incredible sensation, right? ... You realized that here, as you spoke to friends and lawyers, you were a sort of extraterrestrial ... When I joined [the Palermo] bar, my sister gifted me some business cards that read: "Lawyer specializing in European law." If I handed out those business cards, I would have never been able to work in Palermo again. I'm not joking! ... Today, nothing has changed. If you go out there and introduce yourself as an EU law specialist, it's anything but a comparative advantage! It's an *ad excludendum* activity! ... People say: "All right, he does international law, what the heck is he doing here?"[6]

Di Rosa's account begs for an explanation. After all, functionalist theories of judicialization in Europe posit that as national courts began dialoguing with the European Court of Justice (ECJ) in the 1960s, 1970s, and 1980s, they set off a growing flood of opportunities for litigation that could be mobilized to feed further judicial policymaking.[7] Some even claim that such a feedback loop proved to be unstoppably "self-reinforcing,"[8] a sentiment echoed by a prominent British jurist who famously cast EU law as an incoming tide: "It flows into the estuaries and up the rivers. It cannot be held back."[9] But where is

field. See: Fine, Gary Alan. 2009. *Authors of the Storm: Meteorologists and the Culture of Prediction*. Chicago, IL: University of Chicago Press, at 173–208.
[5] The College was founded by one of the first Euro-lawyers animating Chapter 5: Fausto Capelli.
[6] Interview with Giuseppe Di Rosa, April 18, 2017.
[7] Stone Sweet and Brunell, "European Court and National Courts"; Fligstein and Stone Sweet, "Constructing Polities and Markets"; Stone Sweet, *Judicial Construction of Europe*; Cichowski, *European Court and Civil Society*.
[8] Kelemen and Stone Sweet, "Assessing the Transformation of Europe," at 204.
[9] Lord Denning, quoted in: Kelemen and Pavone, "Political Geography of Legal Integration," at 362–363.

this tide in Palermo? If the first Euro-lawyers had set the fuse, why do practitioners like Di Rosa still struggle to light the match?

The puzzle deepens. For if functionalist theories of judicial policy-making are hard-pressed for an answer, Di Rosa's ground truth also cannot be easily reconciled with sociological accounts of professionalization. For instance, Andrew Abbott influentially argues that a new profession or specialization emerges when an emergent social need creates a vacuum that fails to be filled by a calcified hierarchy of practitioners. Invaders then rush in and successfully compete to assert their monopoly over a new form of professional labor.[10] In this view, turf wars among professional groups should drive the diffusion of Euro-lawyering. The gap between the expansion of EU rules and local practice should have induced a young class of EU law specialists to invade the bars of cities like Palermo.

Complementarily, theories drawing on Pierre Bourdieu's sociology[11] trace the evolution of EU law specialists to the production of symbolic capital and competitions for legitimacy. Intent on developing a "virtuous" skill set valued by wealthy international clients, lawyers in national markets of declining prestige should turn to EU law to capitalize on their expertise and position as brokers.[12] As bar associations in cities like Palermo evolve from elite clubs to bloated registries, lawyers have an incentive to embed themselves in an increasingly autonomous European legal field where "the continual circulation between the different poles of the European polity [becomes] an essential mechanism" in the production of a symbolic capital with substantial cash value.[13]

What these accounts miss is the spatial and material factors that can keep lawyers anchored to particular places and ways of doing. For even if the profusion of ECJ rulings, professional competition, and desire for symbol capital incentivize Euro-lawyering, most practitioners will only act upon this stimulus where local clients value and subsidize the costs of specialization. This intuition builds upon structuralist

---

[10] Abbott, *System of Professions*, at 248–254; Liu, "Legal Profession as a Social Process," at 672.

[11] Bourdieu, Pierre. 1986. "The Force of Law." *Hastings Law Journal* 38: 805–853.

[12] Dezelay and Garth, *Dealing in Virtue*, at 8; Dezelay and Madsen, "Force of Law and Lawyers"; Vauchez, *Brokering Europe*, at 72–115.

[13] Vauchez, *Brokering Europe*, at 110–111. See also: Dezelay, Yves, and Bryant Garth. 2011. "Introduction: Lawyers, Law, and Society." In *Lawyers and the Rule of Law in an Era of Globalization*, Dezelay and Garth, eds. New York, NY: Routledge, at 2–4; Dezelay and Garth, *Dealing in Virtue*.

sociologies of the legal profession and resource mobilization theory. The first studies posit that the legal profession's form mirrors the local client market. Practitioners are thus stratified into "hemispheres" of corporate lawyers and generalists.[14] In Lucien Karpik's pithy phrase, "[t]ell me what kind(s) of law you practise and I will tell you what kind(s) of clients you have."[15] The second studies claim that organized legal mobilization hinges on lawyers tapping into resource-rich business or civic networks.[16] As Charles Epp puts it, these arguments emphasize "the difficulty with which those resources are developed, and [the] key role of those resources in providing the sources and conditions for sustained rights-advocacy litigation."[17]

This chapter advances these theories by tracing in textured detail how spatial and economic inequities condition the evolution of Euro-lawyering and judicial policymaking by "situating legal conscious-ness."[18] I unpack how Euro-lawyers who began practicing since the late 1980s differ from the pioneers past, why they clustered in particular sites, and how they develop place-based identities shaping if and how they (and their judicial interlocutors) mobilize European law.

To wit, in rural regions or cities like Palermo – client markets at the peripheries of globalization balkanized into individuals and small businesses – Euro-lawyering has proven stillborn. In order to make a living and tend to a wide spectrum of mundane, localized disputes, lawyers embrace what I call a *logic of partition* from specialized fields like EU law: a type of place attachment[19] wherein European law is

---

[14] See: Heinz, John, and Edward Laumann. 1982. *Chicago Lawyers: The Social Structure of the Bar*. New York, NY: Russell Sage; Heinz, John, Edward Laumann, Robert Nelson, and Ethan Michelson. 1998. "The Changing Character of Lawyers' Work." *Law & Society Review* 32(4): 751–776.

[15] Karpik, *French Lawyers*, at 216; See also: Hoevenaars, Jos. 2018. *A People's Court? A Bottom-Up Approach to Litigation before the European Court of Justice*. The Hague: Eleven International.

[16] Galanter, "Why the 'Haves' Come out Ahead"; Conant, *Justice Contained*; Börzel, "Participation through Law Enforcement."

[17] Epp, *Rights Revolution*, at 3.

[18] Nielsen, "Situating Legal Consciousness."

[19] The concept of place attachment refers to people's rootedness "to space that has been given meaning through personal, group, or cultural processes." See: Altman and Low, *Place Attachment*, at 5; Relph, Edward. 1985. "Geographical Experiences and Being-in-the-World." In *Dwelling, Place, and Environment*, David Seamon and Robert Mugerauer, eds. Dordrecht: Nijhoff; Butz, David, and John Eyles. 1997. "Reconceptualizing Senses of Place: Social Relations, Ideology and Ecology." *Geografiska Annaler: Series B, Human Geography* 79(1): 1–25.

deemed neglectful of and irrelevant for local practice. By functioning as a mirror to the entrenched practices and habits among national judges traced in Chapter 3, this logic of partition favors the emergence of cold spots or "brown areas"[20] in the EU's judicial authority: places where lawyers seldom push courts to enforce EU law and solicit the ECJ.

Conversely, in "global cities" like Paris[21] where transnational businesses increasingly cluster, Euro-lawyering has evolved and become entrenched.[22] Since EU legal expertise enables lawyers to charge hefty legal fees and tend to the specialized needs of a resourceful clientele, an elite subset of practitioners has emerged and embraced a *logic of integration* with EU law: a place-based identity treating local practice, national law, and European law as one inseparable and professionally advantageous ecology. By agglomerating into larger "Euro-firms" infrastructurally suited to navigate this ecology, lawyers can regularly push specialized chambers of local courts to apply EU law and solicit the ECJ if necessary, fomenting hot spots of EU judicial enforcement. The picture that emerges is one of uneven corporatization that engenders an increasingly "variable geometry"[23] of access to the EU's judicial system and "contains"[24] the tide of Europeanization.

The rest of this chapter is organized as follows. In Section 6.2, I use geographic information systems (GIS) to map the corporatization of Euro-lawyering. A number of subnational hot spots of EU law litigation are revealed, whose distribution is increasingly congruent with where Euro-firms have agglomerated over time. Next, I unpack the mechanisms driving where Euro-lawyering and the judicial enforcement of EU law becomes entrenched through a comparative case study of four cold spots – Palermo, Naples, Bari, and Marseille (Section 6.3) – and five hot spots – Rome, Hamburg, Paris, Munich, and Milan (Section 6.4). I conclude in Section 6.5 by arguing that the resulting evidence points to a disconcerting trend: the growing confluence of

---

[20] O'Donnell refers to brown areas as gaps where a state legal system fails to penetrate: O'Donnell, Guillermo. 2004. "Why the Rule of Law Matters." *Journal of Democracy* 15(4): 32–46.

[21] Sassen, "Global City."

[22] Other studies also trace these gradual shifts to the late 1980s/early 1990s: Kelemen, *Eurolegalism*, at 143–194; Vauchez and France, *Neoliberal Republic*, at 22–25.

[23] Weiler, Joseph H. H. 1987. "The European Court, National Courts and References for Preliminary Rulings – The Paradox of Success." In *Article 177 EEC*, Henry Schermers, Christiaan Timmermans, Alfred Kellermann, and J. Stewart Watson, eds. New York, NY: Elsevier, at 371.

[24] Conant, *Justice Contained.*

Euro-lawyering and corporate interests which, by displacing the first Euro-lawyers, has tended to relegate their idealism to the ash heap of history.

## 6.2 THE RISE OF THE EURO-FIRM

Through the early 1980s, Euro-lawyers were few and scarcely stratified from the rest of the bar in perceptible ways. Almost all of the previous chapter's protagonists worked as solo-practitioners or in small boutiques throughout their careers. What distinguished them was scarcely visible – their ideational commitment to European integration, their frequent trips to Luxembourg, and their pleasure in exercising their agency to Europeanize national policies. Yet if today we parachuted into a French, Italian, and German city in search of a Euro-lawyer, all we would have to do is to visit the opulent offices of Cleary Gottlieb, Graf von Westphalen, BonelliErede, or Gide Loyrette Nouel. As we will see, the evolution of Euro-lawyering is of a piece with the rise of these corporate "Euro-firms."

Within the walls of Euro-firms (see Figure 6.1), we find an elite network of practitioners vastly different from the rest of the bar. Their education is likely to include not just a degree from a local law school, but also a masters or doctorate from prestigious institutions such as Harvard or the College of Europe in Bruges. When they represent clients, they speak not with the clients themselves, but with corporate in-house counsel. Instead of working from their homes, they occupy refurbished aristocratic villas or prime office space in the ritziest parts

Figure 6.1 The opulent Euro-Firm: the Munich office of Gleiss Lutz spans four floors (a); Cleary Gottlieb's Rome office occupies prime real estate in Piazza Di Spagna (b); Jones Day's Paris office overlooks Place de la Concorde (c)

of town. And when they solicit advice from their colleagues, they are as likely to launch a video conference with a foreign branch as they are to turn to the partner working next to them. Just as some have detailed the stratification of the American, French, and Chinese bars,[25] the Euro-firm lawyer and the generalist practitioner occupy different hemispheres of professional work.

Euro-firms proliferated particularly since the late 1980s, as a series of national regulatory reforms allowed lawyers to merge and agglomerate, and as the arrival of British and American big law in some European cities diffused new "logics of profitability and business development."[26] We will unpack this process in more detail shortly, but is there any evidence that the rise of the Euro-firms has impacted the dialogue between national courts and the ECJ to enforce and develop European law? Spatial statistics do point to a growing congruence between where Euro-firms open their offices and the propensity of local judges to solicit the European Court. Figure 6.2 displays decade-by-decade heat maps of referrals from non-supreme courts across Italy, France, and Germany from 1964 to 2013, where the darker grey shading denotes more preliminary references from courts in those locations.[27] Superimposed upon the heat maps is the distribution of corporate law firms specializing in EU law. These Euro-firms comprise those ranked by two influential surveys – the *Legal 500* or *Chambers Europe*[28] – for their expertise in European and competition law, and they are geocoded according to when and where they opened a branch office. These data are then aggregated as graduated point symbols, where larger circles denote more branch offices.

Figure 6.2 suggests a clear story. The judicialized enforcement of EU law has evolved as a patch-worked tapestry with evident signs of local spatial autocorrelation. A few locations have come to boast high densities of referrals to the ECJ: North Rhine-Westphalia and

---

[25] See: Heinz and Laumann, *Chicago Lawyers*; Karpik, *French Lawyers*; Liu and Halliday, *Criminal Defense in China*.

[26] Vauchez and France, *Neoliberal Republic*, at 23.

[27] These maps are created using kernel densities, which calculate the density of geocoded point features (preliminary references) within a search radius, fitting a curved surface over each point. For comparability, the shading scale is pinned as the highest point value across maps.

[28] The *Legal 500* and *Chambers Europe* use client surveys, interviews, and firm submissions to produce rankings by specialization and jurisdiction that firms frequently advertise: Vauchez and France, *Neoliberal Republic*, at 36; Avril, "Costume Sous la Robe", at 286.

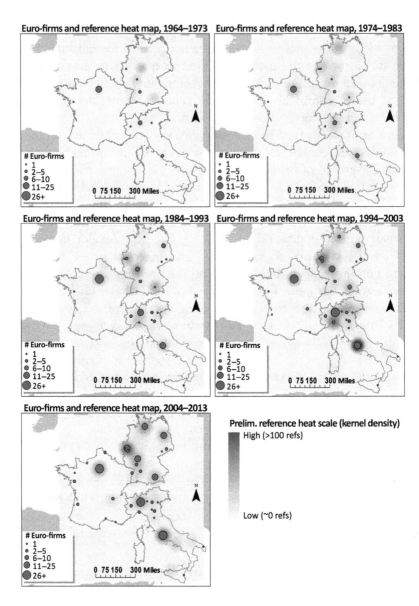

Figure 6.2 Heat maps of preliminary references to the ECJ and Euro-firm locations, 1964–2013

Hessen in Germany, Liguria and Lombardy in Italy, and cities such as Rome and Paris. Courts rarely dialogue with the ECJ elsewhere. Second, the distribution of Euro-firms increasingly aligns with these referral patterns. While in the 1960s and 1970s the entrepreneurship of the first Euro-lawyers fostered clusters of referrals in places without any Euro-firms (such as Hamburg), by the 1990s and 2000s all heat map areas of darker shading were also home to six or more corporate firms specializing in EU law.

To more precisely measure the growing congruence between Euro-firms and national courts' dialogue with the ECJ, Figure 6.3 aggregates national court referrals into a grid of polygons, each approximately 50 square kilometers in size. This allows us to then compute statistically significant clusters of preliminary references. In particular, by computing a commonly-used measure of spatial autocorrelation – the Getis-Ord $G_i^*$ statistic[29] – we can reveal where significantly higher numbers of preliminary references[30] occur compared to the global average. These areas are then classified as "hot spots," denoted by gradated grey shadings. To visualize the overlap between these hot spots and Euro-firm offices, Figure 6.3 overlays circular buffers of locations within commuting distance (a 50 km radius) of firms ranked by the *Legal 500* or *Chambers Europe*.

The resulting maps corroborate the story in Figure 6.2. First, about a dozen statistically significant hot spots of national court referrals to the ECJ emerge across each decade. Their distribution shifts somewhat over time as the baseline mean and polygon reference levels rise and evolve. Second, the territorial coverage of Euro-firms increasingly overlaps with the statistically significant hot spots. More precisely, Figure 6.4 traces the growing territorial congruence between preliminary reference hot spots and locations within 50 km of a Euro-firm from 1964 to 2013. While in the 1960s the percentage of hot spot territory lying within commuting distance of a Euro-firm was 41.2 percent, the overlap grows rapidly to 81.9 percent for the 2004–2013 period. Today, law firms ranked by the *Legal 500* or *Chambers Europe* lie within a

---

[29] See: Getis, Arthur, and J. K. Ord. 1992. "The Analysis of Spatial Association by Use of Distance Statistics." *Geographical Analysis* 24(3): 189–206. The Getis-Ord $G_i^*$ statistic is computed as: $G_i^* = \dfrac{\sum_{j=1}^{n} w_{i,j}x_j - \bar{X}\sum_{j=1}^{n} w_{i,j}}{S\sqrt{\dfrac{\left[n\sum_{j=1}^{n} w_{i,j}^2 - \left(\sum_{j=1}^{n} w_{i,j}\right)^2\right]}{n-1}}}$, where $x_j$ = the attribute value (number of referrals) for polygon $j$, $w_{i,j}$ = the spatial weight between polygons $i$ and $j$, and $n$ = the total number of polygons. Here, $\bar{X} = \dfrac{\sum_{j=1}^{n} x_j}{n}$ (mean referrals per polygon), and $S = \sqrt{\dfrac{\sum_{j=1}^{n} x_j^2}{n} - (\bar{X})^2}$ (standard deviation).

[30] Within a fixed distance band set to 15 km using incremental spatial autocorrelation analysis.

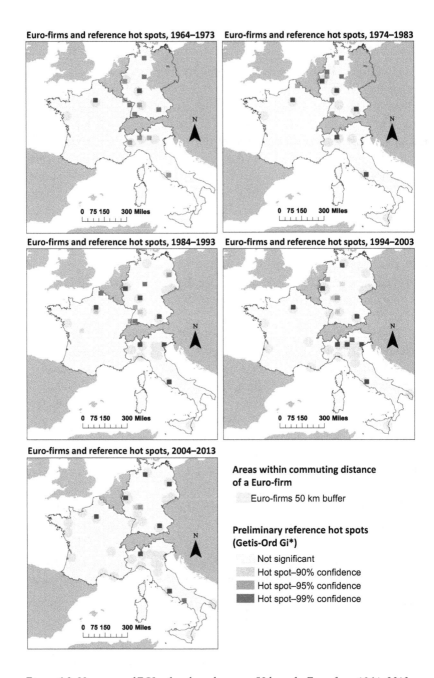

Figure 6.3  Hot spots of ECJ referrals and areas <50 km of a Euro-firm, 1964–2013

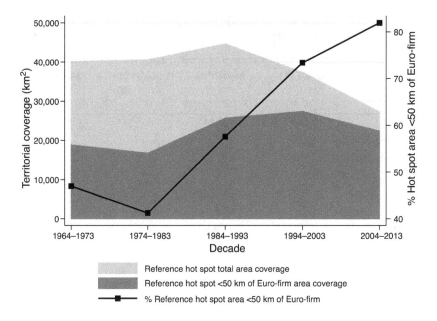

Figure 6.4 Congruence of reference hot spots and Euro-firm buffers, 1964–2013

half an hour drive of almost all locations where national courts are significantly more inclined to solicit the ECJ.

To be sure, these maps surface patterns and correlations rather that demonstrating causal relationships. Yet controlling for factors that may also impact litigation and judicial behavior does not eliminate the positive association between Euro-firms and referral activity. Table 6.1 displays the results of four regressions of the number of Euro-firms in a given locality at the lowest administrative unit (the Italian province, French department, and German district) on the number of yearly referrals to the ECJ by judges in the same locality. The data comprise over 16,000 region-year observations from 1980 to 2013. Models 1 and 2 are a standard panel regression, whereas Models 3 and 4 account for the overdispersion in national court referrals[31] via a zero-inflated negative binomial regression.[32] The number of Euro-firm offices is

---

[31] Across all region-year observations, 93 percent had zero preliminary reference counts.

[32] On using overdispersed count models to analyze referrals to the ECJ, see: Kelemen and Pavone, "Political Geography of Legal Integration"; Dyevre, Arthur, and Nicolas Lampach. 2018. "The Origins of Regional Integration: Untangling the

TABLE 6.1. Regression of number of Euro-firms on number of yearly referrals to ECJ, 1980–2013

| | Model (1) Panel reg. DV: Prelim. refs | Model (2) Panel reg. DV: Prelim. refs | Model (3) ZINB reg. DV: Prelim. refs | Model (4) ZINB reg. DV: Prelim. refs |
|---|---|---|---|---|
| # Euro-firms (t − 1) | 0.174** (25.04) | 0.173** (3.70) | 0.0224* (2.25) | 0.0313** (3.12) |
| ln(Population) | 0.0304 (0.64) | −0.0698 (−1.32) | −0.922** (−7.40) | −0.377 (−0.68) |
| # Patent apps. | −0.000218 (−1.10) | −0.0000189 (−0.02) | −0.000407 (−1.32) | −0.0000256 (−0.03) |
| Financial empl. | 0.00875** (13.85) | 0.00852** (3.10) | 0.00224* (2.12) | 0.00286 (1.57) |
| ln(GDP) | −0.00283 (−0.07) | 0.126 (1.95) | 1.393** (8.63) | 1.125* (2.01) |
| Country FEs? | – | Y | – | Y |
| Year FEs? | – | Y | – | Y |
| Cluster-robust SEs? | – | Y | – | Y |
| Constant | −0.373 (−0.69) | 0.560 (0.88) | 7.933** (6.13) | −0.428 (−0.07) |
| N | 16,060 | 16,060 | 16,060 | 16,060 |

$t$ statistics in parentheses for Models 1 and 2; $z$ statistics in parentheses for Models 3 and 4.
$*p < 0.05$, $**p < 0.01$

lagged by a year to account for the time it takes to set up a firm and begin to lodge court cases that can produce referrals to the ECJ.

Controlling for population, economic innovativeness,[33] levels of employment in financial services, and gross domestic product (GDP),[34] Table 6.1 reveals a positive correlation between Euro-firms and local

Effect of Trade on Judicial Cooperation." *International Review of Law and Economics* 56: 122–133.

[33] Proxied as the number of patent applications submitted to the European Patent Office (EPO).

[34] Control variables are from the EU Commission's Statistical Service (Eurostat). Additional prospective covariates that are not disaggregated at the lowest administrative unit (NUTS3 level) or that do not extend to the 1980s were excluded from the analysis.

court referrals to the ECJ that is statistically significant across all models.[35] These results are unchanged when year and country fixed effects (FEs) are included in the analysis,[36] and when standard errors are clustered by administrative units.[37] In the fully specified model – Model 4 – the number of Euro-firms is the most significant predictor of judges' propensity to solicit the European Court: that is, five additional Euro-firm branch offices increase the expected number of local court referrals to the ECJ in the subsequent year by 15 percent.[38]

This analysis is not meant to suggest that Euro-firms exert independent and monocausal influence on national judges' propensity to solicit the ECJ and apply EU law. As we will see, the corporatization of Euro-lawyering is deeply ensconced within particular socioeconomic ecologies.[39] But these findings do invite us to probe more deeply: to unpack how and why Euro-firms have become important bottom-up motors conditioning the judicial construction of Europe. To this end, I conduct a comparative case study of five hot spots and four cold spots of EU legal practice. The hot spots comprise the Italian, French, and German cities from which lower courts submitted the greatest number of preliminary references to the ECJ over the past six decades: Rome ($n = 246$), Hamburg ($n = 178$), Paris ($n = 129$), Munich ($n = 127$), and Milan ($n = 102$). Correlatively, the cold spots comprise the cities I visited with the fewest number of referrals: Marseille ($n = 4$), Bari ($n = 12$), Naples ($n = 15$), and Palermo ($n = 19$).

It is not only the vastly divergent propensity of local judges to solicit the ECJ that distinguishes these cities: they are also separated by an economic ocean (see Figure 6.5). While the four cold spots have relatively comparable levels of population to the five hot spots, measures of economic vitality and wealth reveal a deep chasm. Hot

---

[35] Namely, significant at the 95% ($p < 0.05$) or 99% ($p < 0.01$) confidence levels.

[36] Year fixed effects are included to account for time-variant shocks across jurisdictions, such as the ratification of an EU Treaty; country fixed effects are included to account for unobserved country-level characteristics, such as constitutional tradition.

[37] This approach accounts for potential within-locality correlations over time.

[38] Put differently, opening an additional Euro-firm office increases referrals by local courts in the subsequent year by a factor of $exp(\beta_{Eurofirms}) = exp(0.0313) = 1.03$, or by 3%.

[39] Heinz and Laumann reach a similar conclusion: "The legal profession, in our view, is what quantitatively oriented sociologists call an 'overdetermined' social system." See: Heinz and Laumann, *Chicago Lawyers*, at 69.

| Site type | Cases | # Prelim. refs (1964–2013) | | Avg. population (1975–2013) | | Avg. GDP in €2005bn (1980–2013) | | Avg. yearly EPO applications (1977–2012) | | Avg. # employed in finance (1980–2013) | | Avg. # ranked Euro-firms (1975–2013) | |
|---|---|---|---|---|---|---|---|---|---|---|---|---|---|
| | | NUTS3 | Avg. | NUTS3 | Avg. | NUTS3 | Avg. | NUTS3 | Avg. | NUTS3 | Avg. | NUTS3 | Avg. |
| Hot spots | Rome | 246 | | 3,764,169 | | 117 | | 128 | | 289,144 | | 16 | |
| | Hamburg | 178 | 156 | 1,689,230 | 2,532,235 | 77 | | 233 | | 218,886 | | 3 | |
| | Paris | 129 | | 2,180,848 | | 155 | 106 | 629 | 392 | 500,824 | 312,089 | 32 | 15 |
| | Munich | 127 | | 1,271,890 | | 71 | | 590 | | 254,683 | | 5 | |
| | Milan | 102 | | 3,755,039 | | 111 | | 383 | | 296,909 | | 17 | |
| Cold spots | Palermo | 19 | | 1,230,454 | | 18 | | 5 | | 32,671 | | 0 | |
| | Naples | 15 | 13 | 3,037,257 | | 48 | | 24 | | 94,626 | | 0 | |
| | Bari | 12 | | 1,554,971 | 1,908,406 | 22 | 33 | 15 | 42 | 45,793 | 70,526 | 0 | 0 |
| | Marseille | 4 | | 1,810,941 | | 45 | | 123 | | 109,013 | | 0 | |

Figure 6.5 Litigation and economic indicators across hot spot and cold spot fieldsites
*Note*: City-level statistics are gathered at the lowest administrative unit used by Eurostat – the NUTS3 level (comprising cities and small regions).

spots boast GDPs and financial employment levels that are an average of three and four times greater than cold spots, respectively. The average yearly number of applications submitted to the European Patent Office (EPO) is almost ten times higher in hot spot locations than in the cold spots. And most importantly, these divergences go hand in hand with variegated hemispheres of legal service provision. Whereas the hot spots hold an average of 15 Euro-firms each, none of the cold spots are home to a firm ranked by the *Legal 500* or *Chambers Europe* for specializing in EU law.

How do these divergent socioeconomic contexts condition where practitioners embrace Euro-lawyering and agglomerate into Euro-firms? Over the course of 15 months of field research, I conducted 235 interviews with practitioners across these 9 fieldsites to answer this question. Specifically, I conducted 144 interviews in hot spots (75 with practicing lawyers) and 91 across cold spots (43 with practicing lawyers). The breakdown of interviewees is provided in Figure 6.6. Following the method of purposive interview sampling described in Chapter 2, in each site I disproportionately sought to speak with lawyers with some knowledge of EU law and how cases might be referred to the ECJ. While I managed to speak to two dozen practitioners within corporate Euro-firms in the hot spot sites, I could not locate a single lawyer embedded in a similar structure across the cold spot sites. More than anything else, it is the impossibility of breaking into the world of Euro-firms that situates a very different legal consciousness among practitioners in the cold spots than in the hot spots, with profound consequences for judicial policymaking and the mobilization of European law.

## 6.3 COLD SPOTS AND THE LOGIC OF PARTITION

Across Marseille, Naples, Bari, and Palermo, legal practitioners articulate four interrelated themes across interviews. These themes delineate a roughly sequential *logic of partition* that functions as a mirror bolstering the institutional consciousness resisting Europeanization among judges elucidated in Chapter 3. First, lawyers convey a sense of resource deprivation and of being embedded within poor client markets. Second, the fragmentation and material scarcities of these markets are described as barriers to specialization and agglomeration. Third, these constraints foment a perception of EU law as an inapplicable luxury and the EU legal order as distant, even neglectful, of lived experience. Finally, this sense of partition is expressed in terms of a place-based

| Site type | Cases | # Interviewees (lawyers, judges, professors) | # Lawyers interviewed | | | |
|---|---|---|---|---|---|---|
| | | | Small firm ($n \leq 10$) | Mid firm ($n = 11$–$99$) | Large firm ($n \geq 100$) | Other |
| Hot Spots | Rome | 42 | 11 | 1 | 6 | 6 |
| | Hamburg | 18 | 3 | 1 | 5 | 3 |
| | Paris | 33 | 8 | 2 | 6 | 0 |
| | Munich | 15 | 1 | 0 | 5 | 0 |
| | Milan | 36 | 9 | 5 | 3 | 0 |
| Cold Spots | Palermo | 26 | 10 | 2 | 0 | 0 |
| | Naples | 20 | 8 | 2 | 0 | 4 |
| | Bari | 29 | 14 | 0 | 0 | 0 |
| | Marseille | 16 | 3 | 0 | 0 | 0 |

Figure 6.6  Interview sample across hot spot and cold spot fieldsites
Notes: The "other" category comprises government lawyers or retired practitioners.

identity situated in binary opposition to hot spots such as Rome, Milan, and Paris.

### 6.3.1 Resourceless Client Markets and the Travails of Specialization

The first two elements of a logic of partition illuminate what appears paradoxical at first glance: given a local context swarmed with thousands of competitors, why do not some practitioners master the Euro-lawyer's repertoire to gain a competitive advantage?

The answer is that professional competition and the percolation of EU law within member states are insufficient incentives for specialization. Resource mobilization and regular engagement with a niche of deep-pocketed clients is also necessary. Yet the client markets in cold spots of EU judicial enforcement are fragmented into countless "one-shotters": private persons and small businesses who engage with the EU's regulatory framework with little awareness or regularity. As Marc Galanter has argued, lawyers serving one-shotters "tend to be drawn from lower socio-economic origins, to have attended local, proprietary or part-time schools, to practice alone rather than in large firms ... to have problems of mobilizing a clientele ... [and] to elicit a stereotyped and uncreative brand of legal services."[40] Often disparaged as ambulance chasers in local dialects,[41] it is primarily their

[40] Galanter, "Why the 'Haves' Come Out Ahead," at 116–117.
[41] Including *azzeccagarbugli* ("knot-seekers"), *cavalocchio* ("eye-removers"), *mozzorecchi* ("earless scoundrels"), and *paglietta* ("straw hats") in Italy alone. See: Tacchi,

drive for professional survival – not a lacking moral ethic[42] – that incentivizes clinging to whatever mundane dispute happens upon their doorstep.

Lawyers across Marseille, Naples, Bari, and Palermo are determined to convey this distressing lived reality. Rostane Mehdi, an EU law professor who directs Sciences-Po Aix, shares that during his legal training initiatives in Marseille, even lawyers with degrees in EU law complain that "there is little litigation of EU law. There are no disputes, there are insufficient disputes, to imagine the full activities of a law firm."[43] "In Marseille the market is really weak," confirms one of these lawyers who would want to make use of his PhD in EU law. "It's difficult. My own firm is a generalist firm. I do a little European law when the occasion presents itself but ... there is no market."[44] And in a city where many law firms are "in a state of bankruptcy" and 49 percent of lawyers are solo-practitioners,[45] "when we ask how a lawyer in a port city ends up being less specialized, we can reply, 'why not'? Because he seeks at all costs to enlarge the spectrum of his activities to have enough income, but that will also diminish his competences."[46]

In Naples, where lawyers earn an average yearly income that is three times lower than their Milanese counterparts,[47] some interviewees speak of "sacrifice" and "survival." Many represent destitute clients under the state's restrictive legal aid regime:[48] "Our economy is still focused on small-time business, which is itself disappearing ... [so]

Francesca. 2002. *Gli Avvocati Italiani dall'Unità alla Repubblica*. Bologna, IT: Il Mulino, at 86.

[42] In other words, these findings suggest that lawyers do not reject EU law because of cultural or moral "backwardness," as may be deduced from narratives like: Banfield, Edward. 1958. *The Moral Basis of a Backward Society*. New York, NY: Free Press.

[43] Interview with Rostane Mehdi, Director of Sciences-Po Aix, Jean Monnet Professor, Centre d'études et de recherches internationales et communautaires (CERIC), Aix-Marseille University, October 11, 2017 (in-person).

[44] Interview with Pierre-Olivier Koubi-Flotte, Koubi-Flotte Avocats in Marseille, October 9, 2017 (in-person).

[45] Moreau, Caroline. 2012. "Statistique Sur La Profession D'Avocat." Paris, FR: Ministère de la Justice, at 26.

[46] Interview with Christian Rousse, Rousse & Associés in Marseille, October 17, 2017 (in-person).

[47] Statistics are from the 2018 annual review of the body running Italian lawyers' social security scheme: CENSIS. 2018. *Percorsi e scenari dell'Avvocatura Italiana*. Rome, IT: CENSIS, at 18.

[48] Known as *gratuito patrocinio* and established under law of December 30, 1933, n. 3282, this regime is very restrictive and limited to supporting litigation by the indigent. See: Olgiati and Pocar, "Italian Legal Profession," at 352; Canestrini,

many colleagues, due to the economic conditions, are taking on state legal aid cases, so we can compensate for our sacrifices with the income the state procures us for representing poorer clients."[49] A fellow practitioner who was able to absorb the costs of representing his clients before the ECJ underscores that this would be impossible for most of his colleagues:

> My clients were workers who had faced bankruptcy and were on unemployment insurance, so they definitely didn't have the means to be able to pay up-front ... the majority of Neapolitan lawyers would have been unable to proceed similarly ... they cannot deal with it. If a traffic accident arises, or a divorce, they'll have to take it to try to survive.[50]

This logic of professional survival inhibits collaboration and foments what some describe as a sort of clinginess: "In this difficult context ... usually the lawyer tries to deal with it on his own, even if they lack the competence, without turning to specialists."[51] Consider the experience of Roberto Mastroianni, a professor of EU law who spoke to me before being nominated judge at the General Court of the EU: while occasionally consulted by his colleagues, Mastroianni emphasized that "for the practice I can still undertake ... I work for non-Neapolitan businesses ... it's difficult to work in such an overcrowded context. Those dealing with a dispute do their best to cling to it, without collaborating."[52]

In Bari, where in 2016 lawyers earned a mean annual income of just € 25,000,[53] practitioners perceive a market that "has no points of entry for this field" of EU law.[54] For instance, the bar's efforts to create a committee on international affairs to sponsor EU legal training quickly unbuckled due to resource scarcities. "The Council of the Bar redirected the funds," relays a former committee member; "It's like organizing [events on EU law] is something of a luxury ...

Nicola. 2017. "Legal Aid in Italy." Available at: https://canestrinilex.com/en/readings/legal-aid-in-italy/.

[49] Interview with Ferdinando Del Mondo, lawyer in Naples, February 23, 2017 (in-person).

[50] Interview with Giovanni Nucifero, Studio Legale Nucifero in Naples, February 23, 2017 (in-person).

[51] Interview with Fabio Ferraro, February 6, 2017.

[52] Interview with Roberto Mastroianni, lawyer and law professor at the University of Naples (now judge at the General Court of the EU), February 13, 2017 (in-person).

[53] Piccolo, Francesco. 2017. "Quanti sono gli avvocati in Italia? E quanto guadagnano?" L'Occhio di Salerno, February 28.

[54] Interview with Giuseppe, lawyer in Bari, March 6, 2017 (in-person; name redacted).

The Tribunal of Bari ... is faced with disputes that aren't rich, I'm not sure how else to put it."[55] And when bar-sponsored initiatives collapse, practitioners are seldom able to pick up the pieces. In the words of a group of administrative lawyers, "to see the supranational dimension of lawsuits ... you not only need to be sensitive, but also dexterous in finding the resources to make it possible. Because the internet doesn't solve everything. You need databases, law reviews, and to participate in coursework and conferences."[56] Even when lawyers locate clients well-placed to invoke EU rules relevant to more depressed economies – such fundamental rights or employment and consumer protections – these parties "must raise the economic funds to sustain litigation. So it rarely happens."[57] In this context, lawyers who "lack work" may hedge their bets by soliciting many small-claims suits without deepening the legal issues of any particular one.[58]

In Palermo, where lawyers' income plummeted by 35 percent during the 2010–2014 economic crisis,[59] interviewees repeatedly tie "a depressed economy"[60] to lawyers' inability to specialize in EU law. Maria Bruccoleri, who heads the Sicilian chapter of the European Lawyer's Union (UAE), described Palermo's client market as "asphyxiated," such that lawyers still "interpret our profession in the old ways."[61] Similarly, one pair of corporate lawyers explain that "for there to be this demand [for EU law], you need there to be a substratum of corporations. Palermo does not offer a sufficient entrepreneurial fabric to enable you to gain this sort of competence," for "we're still stuck in the days of when people used to be small town lawyers, like 30 years ago. They used to practice criminal law, civil law, a bit of everything ...

---

[55] Interview with Angela Romito, professor of EU Competition Law at the Università di Bari, March 6, 2017 (in-person).

[56] Interview with Fabrizio Lofoco, Claudia Pironti, and Rosaria Russo, lawyers at Studio Legale Lofoco in Bari, March, 2017 (in-person).

[57] Interview with Ernesto Capobianco, lawyer at Studio Legale Associato Capobianco, Nocera e Romito, and professor of civil law at the Università del Salento, March 20, 2017 (in-person).

[58] Interview with Fabrizio Lofoco, Claudia Pironti, and Rosaria Russo, March, 2017.

[59] Specifically, from € 38,258 in 2010 to € 24,726 in 2014. See: Piccolo, "Quanti sono gli avvocati in Italia?"

[60] Interview with Giuseppe Verde, law professor at the Università di Palermo and judge at the Consiglio della Giustizia Amministrativa Per la Regione Siciliana, April 19, 2017 (in-person).

[61] Interview with Maria Bruccoleri, lawyer and president, Delegazione Sicilia dell'Unione Degli Avvocati Europei, April 4, 2017 (in-person).

because that's the market."[62] A professor at the University of Palermo who practices law confirms this logic of "putting pasta in the pot":

> The economic and social fabric shapes what is useful to me in my work ... I must keep training myself in fields that are useful to keep putting the pasta in the pot, right? Thus specialization, in the absence of socioeconomic dynamism and in the presence of enormous competition, focuses on things of extremely immediate relevance ... It's not clear that behind the preliminary reference procedure there can be a concrete return for your pockets ... [it's] perceived as luxury knowledge, responsive to luxury disputes.[63]

The absence of specialized lawyers is confirmed by local judges, who admit that their own reluctance to apply EU law and solicit the ECJ is exacerbated when lawyers never push them to do so. In Chapter 3, we saw how judges in Marseille perceive their city as having "an extremely difficult economic life ... so, there are certainly business lawyers in Marseille but we don't see them in court," and those who remain "never raise" points of EU law.[64] At the nearby Court of Appeal of Aix, the situation is similar: if "the lawyers are very good," explains a judge in the commercial chamber,

> they enormously aid the judge in their work, that's certain. But here in Provence this is very rarely the case, except in highly specific disputes where Parisian lawyers in very meticulous law firms come down ... we have some [lawyers] who are more dominant, but they're still generalists ... [so] the dimension of EU law is really not present in the lawyers' case files.[65]

This experience is shared by colleagues in Marseille's administrative court: "We are only seized of the issues invoked by the parties' briefs," notes an administrative judge, "so if there is no invocation of EU law, we won't go looking for it ... I can only recall one file where EU law was invoked by the lawyer. It's rare, yeah."[66]

[62] Interview with Valentina Giarrusso and Pietro Alosi, Kenton & Miles Legal in Palermo, April 4, 2017 (in-person).
[63] Interview with Alessandra Pera, lawyer and professor of EU and Comparative Law, Università degli studi di Palermo, April 5, 2017 (in-person).
[64] Interview with six judges, Tribunal de Grande Instance de Marseille, October 25, 2017 (in-person, names redacted).
[65] Interview with Lise Leroy-Gissinger, October 24, 2017.
[66] Interview with Hélène Rouland-Boyer, October 23, 2017. Colleagues echoed the sentiment, for instance: "No, no, almost never [are we solicited to apply EU law

The experience of judges in Marseille is shared by lower court colleagues in Naples, Bari, and Palermo. The absence of Euro-lawyers is frequently cited, lamented, and perceived as an obstacle to enforcing EU law and mobilizing the ECJ. At the Tribunal of Palermo, two judges elucidate that "if we had lawyers who said 'look at this, look at that', as we said about lawyers who propose how to articulate a preliminary reference, it would already lead us. But a reciprocal stimulation is missing ... those who do this, unfortunately, don't come from our territory."[67] "If the parties don't request [preliminary references] in a way that sufficiently clear, you don't understand," adds an appellate colleague, and "in the end you exclude the possibility to refer ... speaking for myself, lawyers have never solicited it."[68] In Bari, civil judges describe how "the bar that matters [for EU law litigation] isn't ours, but maybe that of Milan,"[69] for local lawyers' briefs "lack any hook to EU law ... I've not witnessed any lawyers articulate this."[70] A first instance colleague confirms that there are "really very few" solicitations to apply EU law, and this is problematic, since "our ability to invoke it depends upon how the lawyers frame the lawsuit ... jurisprudence isn't made by judges, it's made by lawyers!"[71] In Naples, a Euro-enthusiastic judge concludes that "preliminary references from Naples were and remain few. This is explained first of all ... by the nature of Neapolitan litigation ... our Tribunal deals with an extremely limited number of business disputes, whereas it deals with tons of bankruptcy suits" featuring generalist practitioners.[72] Indeed, the only Neapolitan judge to regularly refer cases to the ECJ – Paolo Coppola – emphasizes that without lawyers mobilizing EU law, it becomes extremely difficult for judges to find "vehicles" for breaking entrenched habits and soliciting the European Court.[73]

---

by lawyers]. There was only a single case recently..."; Interview with Christophe Cirefice, October 19, 2017.

[67] Interview with Giuseppe de Gregorio and Michele Ruvolo, Tribunal of Palermo, April 3, 2017 (in-person).

[68] Interview with Tania Hmeljak, April 21, 2017.

[69] Interview with two judges, Court of Appeal of Bari, March 7, 2017 (in-person; names redacted).

[70] Interview with Teresa Liuni, Court of Appeal of Bari, March 13, 2017 (in-person).

[71] Interview with Ernesta Tarantino, March 20, 2017.

[72] Interview with Raffaele Sabato, ex-judge at the Tribunal of Naples, Court of Cassation & Tax Commission of Campania, and since 2019 judge at the European Court of Human Rights, February 17, 2017 (in-person).

[73] Interview with Paolo Coppola, February 13, 2017.

### 6.3.2 The Logic of Partition

Depressed client markets and the disincentives to specialize foment a sense of distance to the project of European integration. EU law becomes perceived as a playground for the rich limited to those hot spots where corporate Euro-firms agglomerate. In turn, this situated legal consciousness leads practitioners to disavow the boundary-blurring role that is so central to Euro-lawyering.

One telling indicator of the perceived separation between EU law and lived experience is the common view that EU legal training is a waste of time. In Marseille, an established corporate lawyer mocks his younger colleagues who pursue LLMs or PhDs in EU law: "These masters provide them with expertise in areas where they'll never find a client! ... What are those people doing here? ... They should head to Paris."[74] Unsurprisingly, that is exactly the reflex of those law graduates who write their theses on EU law. According to a law professor at Aix-Marseille University, "the majority of our students, those I know, have left. They got their masters in international and European law, and they left for Brussels, the international organizations ... and this prevents us from forging links with local practitioners."[75] This dynamic is brought to life by an exchange between three lawyers in Bari. When Rosanna, a member of the UAE, makes the case for specialization, her younger counterparts jump in to supply a hefty dose of skeptical resignation, claiming that their EU legal training proved worthless:

**Pietro**: "When I decided [to study EU law in law school], I was the only one, and people made fun of me! They would tell me: 'It'll be worthless'! And they were right. It's a fact! ... When I tell people that I wrote my thesis on EU law, who cares? In Italy, in southern Italy, and in Bari, given what we do? It's true that that those who deepen this, who complete their doctorates, have the ambition to jump away from Italy. But to learn these fields here is very rare, because those who do find themselves having undertaken worthless work... "
**Rosanna**: "This is Pietro's point of view. What do you all think?"
**Giuseppe**: "Yes. Certainly those who want to deepen their knowledge of these fields leave for a different bar. That is, I don't know. Certainly the labor market for lawyers in Bari has no points of entry for this field..."
**Rosanna**: "Ok, I believe in specializing while keeping your feet on the ground, while participating in lawyers' associations ... forging networks

---

[74] Interview with Christian Rousse, October 17, 2017.
[75] Interview with Estelle Brosset, professor at Aix-Marseille University, October 19, 2017 (in-person).

with foreign colleagues brings you to deal with cases or consultations or work that are not just from Bari ... you become a lawyer specialized in EU law who works throughout Italy!..."

**Pietro:** "In our reality of the south, it is perceived as something distant that is not professionally useful. I hate to say it, but it's true. Any interest in it, which my colleague locates within lawyers' associations, does exist, yes, but it remains purely academic. A curiosity, right? Pure curiosity. Since it's of little practical use ... In other bars and other contexts it's different."[76]

Pietro and Giuseppe's sentiments are broadly shared, to the chagrin of Euro-enthusiastic law professors like Ennio Triggiani, the longtime chair of EU law at the University of Bari: "There remains a broad deficit of knowledge on behalf of lawyers. This can be an issue, because if you don't know the field, then oftentimes judges won't realize it ... [So] over the past 10 years I've edited a quarterly journal on EU law. And we thought, we hoped, that many more lawyers would subscribe, but this didn't happen!"[77] In Palermo, when Giuseppe Di Rosa – the aspiring Euro-lawyer opening this chapter – invited an ex-ECJ judge to deliver a lecture, he "had to fill up the hall personally, by calling individual lawyers one by one" to avoid the embarrassment of an empty room.[78] In this context, those few lawyers who do stubbornly invoke EU law can be left feeling like theirs is more of a personal passion than a useful tool: "You live it as something like a passion, something extraneous. So you see the pathology that you develop? You live it as if you're passionate about EU law, not as if you're a well-rounded jurist!"[79]

In these conversations, lawyers often transpose a sense of vertical distance to the EU legal order into a horizontal opposition of "our reality" to that of cities where wealthy interests and Euro-firms agglomerate. Euro-lawyering is thus thickened in the form of a place – a very *different* place. Here, place attachment has a negative resonance,[80] as when two administrative judges in Palermo excuse local lawyers' ignorance of European law by arguing that "it also depends upon the differences between us and Milan. If you just look at the average worth of disputes,

---

[76] Interview with four lawyers in Bari, March 6, 2017 (in-person, names redacted).

[77] Interview with Ennio Triggiani, professor of EU law at the Università degli studi di Bari, March 20, 2017 (in-person).

[78] Interview with Giuseppe Di Rosa, April 18, 2017.

[79] Ibid.

[80] As human geographers have long argued, "senses of place could be negative or positive." See: Butz and Eyles, "Reconceptualizing senses of place," at 14.

the type of litigation ... Eh! They're well-equipped there."[81] Nestled within these statements is often a sense of distributive injustice, as when one consumer protection lawyer conveys that "the Tribunal of Milan is usually seized with important disputes, economically and thus also juridically, and is always getting published in law reviews. Here in poorer Palermo, the court and the lawyers suffer a bit."[82] This sentiment is sometimes described as a personal and spatial "gap." "If I were a Milanese lawyer I'd certainly be even better," claims a Neapolitan practitioner, for "the ability to specialize is always tied to the economic context. So we live the Italian south's gap not just from an economic point of view, but also from a legal one!"[83]

By far the most common characterization, however, is that the opposition of cold spot to hot spot is not static. Just as sociologists have noted that "hub cities" are rife with business-as-war rhetoric "striving for total market conquest,"[84] so too do interviewees characterize hot spots as magnets sucking up resources and knowledge from their own communities.[85] Christian Rousse, a lawyer in Marseille, eloquently puts it this way: "Internationalization – or Europeanization when it's governed by EU legislation – displaces: the more you extend the field of law, the more that field will retreat to the primary authorities."[86] For instance, in places such as Marseille free movement disputes and maritime transport litigation have shifted elsewhere. According to the director of the legal service of the Port of Marseille, "the end of maritime law firms in Marseille is linked to the evolution of the insurance market, since insurance is very cartelized and everything was transferred to London and Paris."[87] In conversations with Italian practitioners, the gravitational pull of "London and Paris" is replaced by the draw of "Milan and Rome." Cristoforo Osti, a lawyer at

[81] Interview with Federica Cabrini and Giuseppe La Greca, Regional Administrative Court in Palermo, Tuesday, April 4, 2017 (in-person).
[82] Interview with Alessandro Palmigiano, Studio Legale Palmigiano in Palermo and lawyer for ADICONSUM, April 12, 2017 (in-person).
[83] Interview with Giovanni Nucifero, February 23, 2017.
[84] Aran, Núria Arbonés. 2016. "Hub Cities 2.0 for the 21st Century." In *Urban Europe*, Virginie Mamadouh and Anne van Wageningen, eds. Amsterdam: Amsterdam University Press, at 106–107.
[85] Sometimes this perception borders on a resentment toward global cities, echoing the findings in: Cramer-Walsh, "Putting Inequality in Its Place"; Cramer, *Politics of Resentment*, at 77.
[86] Interview with Christian Rousse, October 17.
[87] Interview with Claire Merlin, director of the Port of Marseille Legal Service, October 20, 2017 (in-person).

Chiomenti (one of Rome's leading Euro-firm offices), embodies this "pull" when teaching law students in southern Italy:

> There are niches of people constantly involved in [EU law] issues ... primarily in Milan and also a bit in Rome. Beyond that, I teach at the University of Lecce ... when the students I mentor – who might be really good – ask me to supervise their theses ... I tell them: "Keep in mind that if you want to specialize in this field, as soon as you graduate you must pick up, leave, and go elsewhere." And usually their reply is, "I know."[88]

Interviewees usually attribute the "brain drain" dynamic described by Osti to the financial and recruitment power of Euro-firms. "In France," professor Rostane Mehdi explains, "the firms who practice EU law are the big international firms, which have a sufficient infrastructure ... Jeantet, Gide, the big American firms, obviously, and these firms are scarcely present in Marseille."[89] In Palermo, two of the few lawyers practicing in a transnational firm explain that "Milan and Rome boast a density of international law firms that is not just superior – they're almost all exclusively focalized there ... the [traditional law firm] has a harder time recruiting lawyers who were specialized abroad. Because the specialized lawyer trained abroad knows that he can go work at Chiomenti or Cleary Gottlieb and immediately earn a vast monthly income."[90] In Naples, Amedeo Arena – an EU law professor and lawyer – explains that without his university activities, as an attorney he would have "a really hard time. The alternative is to join a big law firm, but those are in Rome and Milan."[91] Picking up and leaving are usually a one-way street. In the words of a colleague at the University of Naples, "those who begin working in Brussels – where you especially practice EU law – or in Milan or Rome, once they've moved elsewhere they'll hardly return to Naples, where disputes are more traditional."[92]

It is hard to ignore how a logic of partition among lawyers in these cities echoes the oral histories of the first Euro-lawyers recounting the ubiquitous obstacles to Europeanizing change they faced in decades past. Fieldwork in these cold spots serves as something of a time

---

[88] Interview with Cristoforo Osti, September 29, 2016.
[89] Interview with Rostane Mehdi, October 11, 2017.
[90] Interview with Valentina Giarrusso and Pietro Alosi, April 4, 2017.
[91] Interview with Amedeo Arena, lawyer and EU law professor at the Università di Napoli Federico II, January 9, 2017 (in-person).
[92] Interview with Fabio Ferraro, February 6, 2017.

machine, reminding us that in many places the barriers to the judicial construction of Europe remain steep indeed.

## 6.4 HOT SPOTS AND THE LOGIC OF INTEGRATION

In cities like Milan, Paris, and Hamburg, interviewees speak not of stasis, but of transformation. In these hot spots, the transition from the "age of the pioneers"[93] to the age of the Euro-firms is deeply felt. Consider the top-down view of Guy Canivet from the Paris judiciary: whereas into the early 1980s, it was individual Euro-lawyers like Funck-Brentano, Ryziger, and Collin who ran the show,

> They've been displaced over time by a new generation ... [today] it's all about the diffusion of knowledge between these big law firms and the courts ... these big firms that are capable of launching investigations, producing pleadings based on EU law that are much more sophisticated than what judges can do.[94]

This mirrors the bottom-up view of Christian Roth, an established Euro-lawyer:

> In [the 1970s], we had judges at the ECJ and lawyers who were persuaded that through preliminary references we could advance the law via the *grands arrêts*, because in those years we didn't have the degree of Europeanization we have today ... Afterwards, we clearly perceived that beginning around 1990 to 1995 there was a transformation in the practice of EU law, where EU law began to turn much more on the practice of competition law. And competition law became the prerogative of specialized English law firms, who mostly saw a business opportunity in taking charge of EU law, as a tool for professional work.[95]

This gradual shift – which the *New York Times* described as "a quiet revolution among European law firms"[96] – is hardly unique to Paris. Across western Europe, the number of lawyers and branch offices of US law firms rose from 394 and 43 in 1985 to 2,236 and 99 by 1999, respectively.[97] In turn, "European [law] firms have adopted

---

[93] Interview with Charles-Henri Leger, September 12, 2017.

[94] Interview with Guy Canivet, October 2, 2017.

[95] Interview with Christian Roth, September 25, 2017.

[96] Tagliabue, John. 2007. "Law Firms from U.S. Invade Paris." *The New York Times*, July 25, Sec. C, Col. 0, at 1.

[97] See: Kelemen, R. Daniel, and Eric Sibbitt. 2004. "The Globalization of American Law." *International Organization* 58(1): 103–136, at 114. See also: Aronson, Bruce. 2007. "Elite Law Firm Mergers and Reputational Competition: Is Bigger Really

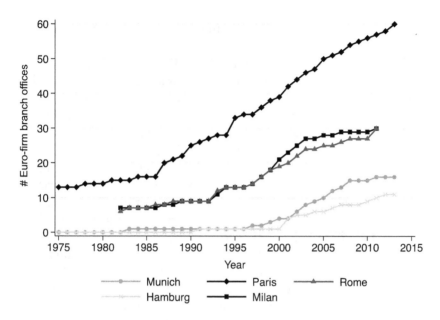

Figure 6.7 Euro-firm branch offices in hot spot fieldsites, 1975–2013

many of their [Anglo-American competitors'] legal techniques and
have increased their size significantly," with the goal of tending to
"corporate clients in the increasingly liberalized market."[98] Figure 6.7
depicts the rising number of branch offices of Euro-firms ranked for
their EU legal expertise in the *Legal 500* or *Chambers Europe* across the
five hot spot fieldsites. As all remaining national regulatory barriers
to partnerships, interfirm mergers, and Anglo-American big law were
lifted, an agglomeration process began in earnest in Paris at the dawn
of the 1990s, replicating itself in Milan and Rome by the late 1990s
and in Hamburg and Munich by the early 2000s.[99] Whereas none of
the four cold spot fieldsites are home to a single ranked Euro-firm to

---

Better – An International Comparison." *Vanderbilt Journal of Transnational Law* 40:
763–831; Dezelay, Yves, and Bryant Garth. 2012. "Corporate Law Firms, NGOs,
and Issues of Legitimacy for a Global Legal Order." *Fordham Law Review* 80(6):
2309–2345.

[98] Kelemen, "Suing for Europe," at 112.

[99] The slower entry of large firms in Germany is due to delayed regulatory reform:
"Until 1989, regulations limited partnerships and thus law firms to a particular
Lander ... In 1989 this restriction was lifted ... [because] in order to compete
in corporate and international markets, German law firms were already openly
breaking existing regulations." See: Faulconbridge, James, and Daniel Muzio. 2015.

this day, their numbers now range from 11 in Hamburg to as many as 60 in Paris.

There is no doubt that client markets in these hot spots are resource-rich, enabling Euro-firms to charge remarkable fees. In Italy, the Milan metropolitan area accounts for almost a fifth of the country's GDP.[100] Corporate lawyers thus almost exclusively agglomerate within larger Milanese firms or their affiliated offices in Rome. Among these, the leading thirty practitioners – the "magnificent 30," as GQ Magazine once called them – charged a combined €1.6 billion in fees in 2014.[101] Their junior partners are not doing too badly either: starting salaries in Milanese and Roman Euro-Firms skyrocketed to $160,000 by 2015.[102] That is over six times greater than the average practitioner stands to earn in a southern Italian city such as Bari.

In France, all of the country's businesses with over 1,500 employees have offices in Paris, which accounts for 31 percent of national GDP.[103] Little wonder that recent studies[104] confirm a stratification between an elite of practitioners in big Parisian firms – le barreau d'affaires – and the more generalist mass dispersed elsewhere – le barreau classique. While French law firms with over 100 practitioners make up less than 1 percent of the market, these are almost exclusively located in Paris. There, the average lawyer charges over €258,000 in annual fees,[105] and those at the top of their game at Linklaters, Cleary Gottlieb, or Freshfields may charge €700 an hour and earn €200,000 per month.[106] That is, they may earn more in four weeks than their non-Parisian counterparts make over five years.[107]

"Transnational Corporations Shaping Institutional Change." Journal of Economic Geography 15(6): 1195–1226, at 1203, 1213.

[100] Roberts, Hannah. 2016. "Milan, Italy's Most Business-Focused City, Looks to Rival London." Financial Times, November 11.

[101] Iacobini, Gianpaolo. 2014. "I 30 Avvocati Più Potenti." Il Giornale, November 8.

[102] Li Vigni, Ilaria. 2015. Avvocate Negli Studi Associati e Giuriste D'Impresa. Milan, IT: Franco Angeli, at 26.

[103] "Dynamics of the Paris Region Economy." IAU Île-de-France, September 2016, p. 7. Available at: www.iau-idf.fr/fileadmin/NewEtudes/site_anglais/KnowHow/Studies/Study_1303/Trajectoires_ANGLAIS_12octobre_intranet.eps.

[104] Karpik, French Lawyers, at 216; Vauchez and France, Neoliberal Republic.

[105] Bessy, Christian. 2016. "Organisation des cabinets d'avocats et marchés des services juridiques." Revue d'économie industrielle 155(3): 41–69, at 54, 61–62.

[106] Décugis, Jean-Michel, and Mélanie Delattre. 2012. "L'Argent des Maîtres." Le Point, February 9.

[107] Assuming an annual income of approximately €34,900, as reported in: Bessy, "Organisation des cabinets d'avocats," at 62.

In Germany, too, the rise of the Euro-firms has been concentrated in trade-intensive cities such as Hamburg – whose port consistently ranks among Europe's top three for container traffic[108] – or in dynamic financial centers like Munich, which accounts for 10–15 percent of all German patents.[109] The "sight of the Americans coming" for these markets in the 1980s and 1990s galvanized German firms to emulate the Anglo-Saxon model by tying themselves to corporations, growing in size, raising salaries, and bolstering their "proximity to, and understanding of, European law."[110] Today, lawyers within these Euro-firms can expect their starting salaries of €125,000 to surpass €500,000 once they make partner.[111]

### 6.4.1 Resourceful Client Markets and Specialized Agglomeration

While the foregoing bars are no more competitive than in cold spot locations, their density of deep-pocketed clients transforms the outcome of professional competition. The conversations I had across the five hot spots reveal how lawyers feel pressure to tend to their clientele via an arms race to (1) specialize in EU economic law and (2) agglomerate into corporate Euro-firms.

While the outcome of this process – the diffusion of Euro-lawyering – is the reverse of that in the cold spots, the underlying logic remains the same: "When it comes to preliminary references or relations with EU institutions ... specialists can exist in any town where there is a client market."[112] As one lawyer and law professor in Rome explains, his colleagues' push to master EU law and solicit its application "depends on the types of clients you have. If you think that clients are interested in this field, you'll invest your time."[113] As in the cold spots, lawyers describe these markets in spatial and materials terms. "Why did I live my life in Paris?" queries Robert Saint-Esteben, one of France's long-standing Euro-lawyers; "I would have much rather lived in Biarritz,

---

[108] "Top 50 World Container Ports." *World Shipping Council.* March 19, 2019. Available at: www.worldshipping.org/about-the-industry/global-trade/top-50-world-container-ports.

[109] Clark, Greg, and Tim Moonen. 2014. "Munich: A Globally Fluent Metropolitan Economy." *Global Cities Initiative*, Brookings Institution and JPMorgan Chase, p. 5.

[110] Morgan, Glenn, and Sigrid Quack. 2005. "Institutional Legacies and Firm Dynamics." *Organizational Studies* 26(12): 1765–1785, at 1771–1772; Faulconbridge and Muzio, "Transnational Corporations Shaping Institutional Change," at 1209.

[111] "Salary Survey 2019 – Europe." Robert Walters Global Salary Survey 2019, p. 92.

[112] Interview with Charles-Henri Leger, September 12, 2017.

[113] Interview with Luigi Daniele, September 27, 2016.

my home on the Atlantic ... but to practice EU law and competition law, I was obligated to come to Paris," where "economic activity, steel trade, transport routes, politics" agglomerate in a "mirror image of the political-economic structure of the country."[114]

In Italy and Germany, too, the tale is much the same. At Chiomenti in Milan, a Euro-lawyer recalls his own migration north from Palermo:

> A great part of the practical application of EU law – what lawyers do – is ... practiced in essentially two cities [Milan and Rome]. So any attempts to return to Naples or Palermo to practice competition law would be deleterious ... the clients for law firms like this one are here, and it's they who require technical, cutting-edge legal services.[115]

At the nearby offices of Fieldfisher, two colleagues explain that EU law "is hard enough to practice in Milan and Rome; in Naples you can't practice it ... [for these] issues are usually managed from a multinational firm's central headquarters."[116] Euro-firm lawyers in German cities such as Munich and Hamburg tell a similar story. In Munich, we find many "huge German corporations [and] multinationals" due to the presence of the Federal Patent Court and the EPO, and "the facts they present us don't allow us to say, 'well it's only German law'."[117] In Hamburg "there are many lawyers specializing in European-influenced law ... [for] Hamburg is a trade city. And so transportation, shipping, trade" disputes agglomerate,[118] in contrast to rural regions where businesses "are rather small and medium-sized. And there you just don't have these international cases."[119] Two professors at Hamburg's Europa-Kolleg similarly posit that you could never find a leading EU jurist "in, say, [places] like Passau or Marburg! ... [conversely] Hamburg is a big commercial place with many many international contacts on a commercial basis."[120]

[114] Interview with Robert Saint-Esteben, November 13, 2017.
[115] Interview with Emilio Cucchiara, Chiomenti Studio Legale in Milan, November 28, 2016 (in-person).
[116] Interview with Patrizia Gozzoli and Patrick Ferrari [quoted], Fieldfisher in Milan, December 13, 2016 (in-person).
[117] Interview with Daniel Petzold, Gleiss Lutz in Munich, December 1, 2017 (in-person).
[118] Interview with Klaus von Gierke, January 5, 2018.
[119] Interview with Jürgen Lüdicke and Bjorn Bodewaldt, lawyers at PwC in Hamburg, January 8, 2018 (in-person).
[120] Interview with Peter Behrens [quoted] and Thomas Bruha, January 25, 2018.

But why precisely does it matter that clients be resource rich? First, Euro-firm lawyers frequently trace their incentive and capacity to master EU rules to their interactions with clients' in-house legal departments.[121] In-house counsel may foment a business' European legal consciousness, and even if they perceive preliminary references to the ECJ "narrowly as a strategic tool amongst many others,"[122] they will expect the lawyers they hire to be ready to weaponize it. In Paris, one long-standing Euro-lawyer puts it this way:

> If the client is big and rich or if they're poor and single, they don't solicit you in the same way ... I handled cases for big French businesses, and I dealt with in-house counsel where within them there was a specialist in EU law that knew as much as I. So for these clients, they come to you saying: "Evidently there's an aspect of EU law, that's why we come to you, dear lawyer, you who was a clerk [at the ECJ]."[123]

Clearly when interviewees speak of clients that are big and rich, they mean *really* big and *really* rich. Even "a corporation that has €200 or €250 million of revenue will rarely have this in-house competence," a practitioner in a Milanese Euro-firm confides; but "if you have a client who is important and has a structured in-house legal service, then things are good, we can understand each other."[124] Conversations with Euro-firm lawyers are riddled with tales of epic battles between the likes of Alitalia,[125] Uber,[126] Eurobet,[127] Daimler,[128] and

---

[121] For instance: Interview with Fabio Cintioli, lawyer at Cintioli and Associati in Rome and ex-judge at the Consiglio di Stato, September 30, 2016 (in-person); Interview with Luigi Daniele, September 27, 2016; Interview with Claire Lavin and Eric Morgan de Rivery, Jones Day in Paris, September 13, 2017; Interview with Philippe Guibert, September 21, 2017; Interview with Frédéric Manin, September 22, 2017; Interview with Jan Tolkmitt, January 25, 2018.

[122] Interview with Roberto Jacchia, November 17, 2016.

[123] Interview with Jean-Pierre Spitzer, September 20, 2017.

[124] Interview with Roberto Jacchia, November 17, 2016.

[125] Interview with Philippe Derouin, lawyer at SCP Derouin in Paris, September 12, 2017 (in-person), concerning the case: Conseil d'Etat, Assemblée, du 3 février 1989, 74052, recueil Lebon.

[126] Interview with Robert Saint-Esteben and Hughes Calvet, Bredin Prat in Paris, November 13, 2017 (in-person), and interview with Philippe Guibert, September 21, 2017 (in-person), concerning Case C-320/16, *Uber SAS France* [2018], ECLI:EU:C:2018:221.

[127] Interview with Enrico Raffaelli, Rucellai & Raffaelli Studio Legale in Milan, December 14, 2016 (in-person).

[128] Interview with Daniel Petzold, December 1, 2017.

Maersk.[129] One judge at the Regional Court of Hamburg who is frequently seized of these disputes memorably describes them as "one [party] owns one half of the world, and the other owns the other half of the world! ... so of course they have lawyers who are competent in European law ... and they come with five lawyers in the hearings."[130]

Not only can big businesses afford in-house counsel capable of setting the stage for an EU lawsuit, they can also pay for the extra research and time costs necessary for lawyers to labor to convince national courts to solicit the ECJ. "There needs to be an economic interest behind it," affirm three Euro-firm lawyers in Munich; "If there is no economic interest, your personal legal ambition will not carry you to the ECJ."[131] At the Hamburg Fiscal Court, a judge and ex-Graf von Westphalen lawyer emphasizes the necessity of resource mobilization: "You have cases involving a lot of money. That is another fact that I wanted to mention, and that contributes to this court bringing cases to the ECJ ... you had large international companies ... they all had an interest in that multi-billion euro business, and they were looking for lawyers who could help them."[132] A colleague at the regional court confirms that local lawyers are "highly competent" in EU law because their clients "are able to pay their high fees!"[133] And when I spoke to two lawyers at Jones Day's Paris office about the disillusioned Euro-lawyer in Palermo of this chapter's opening, they confirmed his inferences:

> EU litigation is lengthy and costly! It takes years, and it's very expensive! ... So who can pay for this? It's the big businesses. This matters too! When you look at the conjunction of those lawyers who interest themselves in EU law – like your friend in Palermo, which is a really beautiful city – most will say: "I'm going to go to a law firm that will value my experience and my training, so I'm going to Paris, or London, or Brussels, or Frankfurt!"[134]

---

[129] Interview with Stephanie Zöllner, judge at the Landgericht Hamburg and ex-practicing lawyer, January 10, 2018 (in-person), in discussing a case seizing her chamber at the time involving EU law.

[130] Ibid.

[131] Interview with Manja Epping, Christian Frank [quoted], and Thomas Raab, December 12, 2017.

[132] Interview with Tobias Bender [quoted] and Corina Kögel, January 17, 2018.

[133] Interview with Stephanie Zöllner, January 10, 2018.

[134] Interview with Claire Lavin and Eric Morgan de Rivery [quoted], September 13, 2017.

Practitioners within Euro-firms thus share with their more generalist colleagues a perception that EU law is a luxury economic service for the rich. "Its margins [of profitability] are elevated," a corporate lawyer in Milan relates matter-of-factly; "because it's substantively a legal luxury ... it's a body of law that, since it requires knowledge, study, research, and facilities, generates a service fee that normally only undertakings of a certain size could afford."[135]

When large clients comprise the main repeat players in a field of law, lawyers face their own "isomorphic" pressure[136] to capture the returns to size. The drive to agglomerate was a near-universal leitmotif across conversations. One Roman Euro-lawyer recalls that "I would have never chosen to enter a bigger firm," but "today, let's say that the logic of the legal services market almost requires it."[137] A colleague in Paris echoes how "especially from the 1950s to the 2000s, you couldn't practice international law, it was impossible to work across countries, without working in a transnational firm."[138] And in Munich a Euro-firm lawyer claims that "without [EU law], we wouldn't be as big as we are."[139] But why? Vincenzo Cannizzaro – a renown EU law professor in Rome – answers by contrasting the limits of his boutique firm with the capacities of Euro-firms:

> The differences are abyssal ... [Think of] due diligence, mergers and acquisitions: I can't do it, I don't have the resources. You need authorizations, and a developed organization of the firm. And also vis-à-vis EU law, complex issues require a certain infrastructure ... The big firms have more interactions between departments. So a client in one department with a problem relevant to another department can circulate between departments. For me, clients only come when they have a particular issue, I can never satisfy the entire spectrum of client exigencies ... the big firm often strikes contracts with multinationals at an international and European level, and I would never be able to do this! Right? ... I can't make big investments. This is obvious.[140]

Cannizzaro's list of benefits to agglomerating into Euro-firms is hardly exhaustive. Larger firms are hoarders of reputation and prestige, not

[135] Interview with Roberto Jacchia, November 17, 2016.
[136] See: DiMaggio and Powell, "Iron Cage Revisited," at 149–150.
[137] Interview with Francesco Samperi, LS Lejus Sinacta in Rome and ex-President of the European Lawyer's Union (UAE), October 11, 2016 (in-person).
[138] Interview with Olivier Freget, Freget-Tasso de Panafieu Avocats in Paris, September 15, 2017 (in-person).
[139] Interview with Daniel Petzold, December 1, 2017.
[140] Interview with Vincenzo Cannizzaro, October 4, 2016.

least by capitalizing on the name brand of their founders and getting themselves ranked in the *Legal 500* and *Chambers Europe*.[141] Hence "big clients turn to big law firms ... [because it] enables the directors of these corporations to say tell their clients, 'look, don't worry, we chose the top [law firm] in the market'."[142] At Gleiss Lutz' Munich office, a lawyer explains how the firm built upon the reputation of Alfred Gleiss[143] to stake its claim over EU competition law, thus attracting "very good cases ... involv[ing] really huge corporations, and they're not looking for a single person sitting somewhere in Munich."[144] At Cleary Gottlieb – often considered the "first Euro-law firm"[145] due to founding partner George Ball's friendship to Jean Monnet – lawyers in its Rome office share how "a firm of this size, on a global scale, expands the pool of clients, which as you've noted are in great part corporations ... this creates a virtuous cycle: you're more exposed, so you deal with these issues more often, you deepen the issues, you gain expertise, and this in turn attracts more interesting disputes your way."[146]

In addition, Euro-firms are structured as transnational networks with a hub in Brussels and spokes radiating outward to foreign offices and state antitrust authorities, "promoting cross-fertilization and exchange of expertise in EU law."[147] Thus lawyers at Chiomenti in Milan routinely "organize practice-focused meetings" with Euro-lawyers in "other excellent and big firms in other countries ... [such as] Gide in France, Gleiss Lutz in Germany."[148] Finally, Euro-firms can mobilize vast resources to produce niche knowledge for internal safekeeping. Size permits a division of labor, and "these firms are organized into departments, those on corporate law, on finance, on regulation, banking, intellectual property," with practitioners holding cross-cutting EU

---

[141] Interview with Philippe Guibert, September 21, 2017.

[142] Interview with Luigi Daniele, September 27, 2016.

[143] Alfred Gleiss was arguably Germany's first lawyer to specialize principally in European competition law, publishing commentaries on the matter by the early 1960s. For instance, see: Oberdorfer, Conrad, and Alfred Gleiss. 1963. *Common Market Cartel Law*. New York, NY: Commerce Clearing House.

[144] Interview with Daniel Petzold, December 1, 2017.

[145] Vauchez, *Brokering Europe*, at 64–65.

[146] Interview with Pietro Merlino and Mario Siragusa, Cleary Gottlieb in Rome, September 26, 2016 (in-person).

[147] Interview with Patrick Ferrari, December 13, 2016; Interview with Francesco Rossi Dal Pozzo, Studio Legale Associato Levi-Dal Pozzo and ex-Euro-firm lawyer in London, November 22, 2016 (in-person).

[148] Interview with Emilio Cucchiara, November 28, 2016.

expertise consulting across departments.[149] Young lawyers and interns may be treated to their own summer school featuring the latest developments in EU economic law, as in the Munich office of Milbank.[150] When he left his boutique firm and joined DS Avocats in Paris, Jean-Paul Montenot recalls being stunned by "the law reviews arriving fresh off the press at least once a day. So nothing escapes me."[151]

Central among the niches of knowledge guarded within Euro-firms is the ghostwriter's repertoire detailed in Chapter 5. Although these firms can also devote substantial resources to lobbying and non-litigation activities, All Euro-firm lawyers interviewed across the five hot spots have either "systematically draft[ed] the preliminary reference questions in their entirety"[152] or witnessed colleagues doing so for local judges. They are adamant that "this is a practice that is now broadly entrenched" and taken for granted.[153] Yet the most reliable confirmation comes from the judges themselves, who highlight lawyers' driving role in pushing them to solicit the ECJ.

Consider qualitative evidence from the EU law hot spot *par excellence*: Paris. There, three judges at the Court of Appeal confide that "it's certain that it's [lawyers] that craft the pleadings, and so effectively it's them that cite the case law, and when there's a preliminary reference it's because it was raised by the parties."[154] At the court of first instance, judges confirm that "it's the lawyers that are going to be the motor, because they're extremely specialized. In fact, they're oftentimes more specialized – though I shouldn't probably tell you this – than the judges!"[155] This striking deference is even discernible at the Court of Cassation and Council of State. One Cassation judge explains that "if they come before us with a full draft of a preliminary reference ... Frankly, you'd have to have really strong convictions to think you'd be able to do better!"[156] And recall how ex-Cassation President

---

[149] Ibid.

[150] Interview with Alexander Rinne, Milbank, Tweed, Hadley & McCloy LLP in Munich, December 1, 2017 (in-person).

[151] Interview with Jean-Paul Montenot, September 13, 2017.

[152] Interview with Francois Molinié, SCP Piwnica-Molinié Avocats & Associés in Paris, September 27, 2017 (in-person).

[153] Interview with Aristide Police, October 4, 2016.

[154] Interview with Chantal Arens, Marie-Caroline Celeyron-Bouillot, and N. Boureois De-Ryck, October 4, 2017.

[155] Interview with judge at the French Court of Cassation and ex-judge of first instance, September 2017 (in-person; name/date redacted).

[156] Interview with Thierry Fossier, October 3, 2017.

Canivet stresses that "big firms are capable of launching investigations, producing pleadings based on EU law that are much more sophisticated than what judges can do."[157] In the words of Council of State judge Patrick Frydman:

> We have a bar that is more competent ... there are lots of specialized law firms, lots of Anglo-Saxon firms ... which can bring forth much more pointed questions than the average lawyer ... This plays a big role, and it explains the numeric concentration of preliminary reference questions from the Paris region. Because effectively it's very much the lawyers who identify the problem. After all, we pronounce ourselves on the basis of their requests. We won't deem something incompatible with EU law of our own motion ... so if the lawyers don't think about raising these questions, then we won't respond to them and there won't be a preliminary reference to the ECJ.[158]

What holds for Paris holds for other hot spots as well. At the Regional Administrative Court in Rome – which refers more cases to the ECJ than any other Italian, French, or German lower administrative court – a judge explains that "these [law] firms follow all the issues that arise and are constantly keeping themselves up to date ... it's not that [some] judges are better prepared, it depends upon the lawsuits brought before them! It's the lawsuit that brings the judge to study, not the studying that attracts the lawsuit!"[159] In Milan, judges at the Tribunal's corporate law chamber also convey that "the push to interest oneself more in this unification with EU law ... came from the lawyers,"[160] such that "those [cases] we referred [to the ECJ] were all requested by the parties ... they were well formulated."[161] And in Hamburg, the construction of test cases and the proposal of detailed preliminary references is confirmed by judges at the Fiscal Court[162] and at the

[157] Interview with Guy Canivet, October 2, 2017.
[158] Interview with Patrick Frydman, September 25, 2017.
[159] Interview with Rosa Perna, Regional Administrative Tribunal for Lazio, October 10, 2016 (in-person). A colleague at the Council of State agrees that "lawyers certainly helped overcome judges' inexperience in submitting preliminary references." See: Interview with Roberto Chieppa, Secretary General of the Italian Antitrust Authority (AGCM) and judge at the Consiglio di Stato, October 12, 2016 (in-person).
[160] Interview with Francesca Fiecconi, December 2, 2016 (Fiecconi served on the Tribunal's corporate law chamber).
[161] Interview with Claudio Marangoni, Tribunal of Milan (specialized corporate chamber), December 12, 2016.
[162] Interview with Tobias Bender and Corina Kögel, January 17, 2018.

Regional Court, who admit that "it's very helpful if you have well prepared files, well prepared from the lawyers," since "often the lawyers propose a preliminary request" and "write something, and we ask them: 'If you have questions we should ask the European Court of Justice, write them down'."[163]

### 6.4.2 The Logic of Integration

The entrenchment of Euro-lawyering in cities such as Paris, Milan, and Hamburg not only transforms legal practice: it reworks and situates legal consciousness too. In opposition to the logic of partition rooted in cities where EU legal practice is negligible, lawyers practicing where Euro-firms agglomerate tend to embrace a two-part *logic of integration*: (1) a mindset fusing two domains of knowledge – EU law and national law – by treating them as inseparable; and (2) a sense of incestuous attraction between the worlds of big business, big law, and specialized court chambers that foments a corporate ecology favorable for Euro-lawyering.

First, rather than interpreting knowledge of EU law as superfluous, a waste of time, or distant from lived reality, interviewees within Euro-firms perceive it as impossible to divorce themselves from EU law and the ECJ's jurisprudence. Exemplary is the following reaction of an EU law specialist in Hamburg. When I convey that some practitioners elsewhere deem it impractical to specialize in EU law, he quickly rebuts:

> If a colleague in a bar were to tell me, "I don't care about European law, or it's just sort of a little bit of luxury knowledge," I would say, "this is not appropriate"... If you go to Palermo or Marseille, or I don't know where, and the lawyers say "we can't specialize as much in European law," I want to re-emphasize, that statement in my mind is questionable ... the question is whether you specialize in French or Italian law, and European law is part of French and Italian law.[164]

This logic conveys a place attachment where what is taken for granted *here* is opposed to what is absent in practitioners *there*. And it is a broadly shared perspective. Compare the parallel views of Euro-firm lawyers in Munich, – "I'd challenge the proposition [of a distinction between EU and national law] ... you can't practice competition

---

[163] Interview with Stephanie Zöllner, January 10, 2018.

[164] Interview with Klaus von Gierke, Norton Rose Fulbright in Hamburg, January 5, 2018 (in-person).

law without being involved in European competition law"[165] – in Paris, – "if you practice competition law, you're necessarily practicing EU law … the two are so closely juxtaposed and proximate"[166] – in Milan, – "you avail yourself of Italian law in exactly the same way as you avail yourself of EU law … I treat them as one"[167] – and in Rome: "A traditional lawyer … says 'everything I need is in the statute.' By contrast … I would consult it and then look at the [EU] directive, they're on the same plane."[168] What is distanced as extraneous in the cold spots is integrated as professionally useful knowledge in the hot spots.

Crucially, a legal consciousness that collapses the partition between national and European law is rarely undergirded by idealism. A more prevalent theme across conversations with Euro-firm lawyers is a sense of professional self-interest: the same utilitarian logic that drives lawyers in more depressed client markets *away* from Europe. Telling, in this regard, is the fact that when interviewees discuss the gravitation pull of EU law, they almost always mean those economic rules of interest to the "haves" (those governing competition, taxation, and intellectual property) rather than those that advance the public interest and the standing of the "have nots" (rules governing the environment, consumer protection, employment, and fundamental rights).[169] Competition is "the field where you practice EU law the most," one Parisian Euro-lawyer explains, hence "it's not a question of idealism, [that is] something you'll find with the professors."[170] Two colleagues add that "you can't be a good competition lawyer in the Paris Bar if you haven't perfectly master EU law," for "the clients who come to us expect that we know EU law, should it be useful."[171] In Rome, lawyers handling commercial or corporate disputes echo how "it's become fundamental to confront yourself with European law,"[172] for "you can't

---

[165] Interview with Alexander Rinne, December 1, 2017.
[166] Interview with Frédéric Manin, September 22, 2017.
[167] Interview with Patrick Ferrari, December 13, 2016.
[168] Interview with Riccardo Sciaudone, September 19, 2016.
[169] On the growing hegemony of competition lawyers, see: Avril, "Costume Sous la Robe".
[170] Interview with Frédéric Manin, September 22, 2017.
[171] Interview with Francois Molinié, September 27, 2017; Interview with Philippe Guibert, September 21, 2017.
[172] Interview with Fabio Cintioli, September 30, 2016.

assist clients ably if you don't know how much that supranational law influences the daily life of businesses."[173]

It would therefore be misleading to infer that Euro-lawyering becomes entrenched where local lawyers and judges are more ideationally committed to European integration. Even a jurist like Bruno Nascimbene – a first-generation Euro-lawyer who sponsors training in the Milan bar – is under no illusion of the motives driving enrollment: while "in the past … it was more about idealism," today for lawyers "the ends are utilitarian," even if "they might not or would not ever admit to it."[174] A Parisian judge similarly observes how EU law disputes attract "big law firms highly structured to make a lot of money. That's their prerogative, to each his own!"[175] One law professor and practicing lawyer confirms that economic interest undergirds large Euro-firms "to the nth degree, to the point that profitability sometimes trumps quality."[176] More idealist law school graduates in these hot spots may thus struggle to accept the instrumentalization of EU law within firms that will "do anything for money."[177] I even met a couple of judges in Hamburg who renounced €400 in hourly fees within big law firms because they felt that they were compromising on their principles. Colleagues "were more career oriented," one of these jurists explains, so "I knew I had to advise clients … I didn't like, or [whose] trade they were in I would find repulsive."[178] "You feel a bit uncomfortable to look at your [work]," another ex-Euro-firm lawyer recalls; "You feel like you betray your own knowledge and your own principles!"[179]

As Euro-lawyers are interwoven in an agglomeration economy of corporate in-house counsel, specialized court chambers, and big law firms' transnational networks, a logic of integration tends to assume the form of a spatial ecology. One judge at the Council of State in Rome describes this as a "necessary attraction" in places where wealthy disputes tend to arise: "The lawyer almost always includes a motivation

[173] Interview with Francesco Samperi, October 11, 2016.
[174] Interview with Bruno Nascimbene, November 22, 2016.
[175] Interview with Thierry Fossier, October 3, 2017.
[176] Interview with Aristide Police, October 4, 2016.
[177] Tommaso Valletti, former chief competition economist at the European Commission, quoted in: "The European System of Monopoly." *The Counterbalance*, April 20, 2021. Available at: https://thecounterbalance.substack.com/p/the-european-system-of-monopoly.
[178] Interview with judge at a German lower court and ex-lawyer (in-person; date/-name redacted).
[179] Interview with Jan Tolkmitt, January 25, 2018.

related to EU law," the judge explains, for "those that are qualified are put to work on questions of greater economic relevance ... so there's a necessary attraction between these two worlds."[180] In the corporate law chamber of the Tribunal of Milan – which handles most of Italy's copyright and competition disputes – judges similarly stress their repeated interactions with corporate Euro-lawyers: "After a year or two, you get to know them quite well. And their specialization helps our own; they are detailed, specific, they push the court."[181] In Paris, a leading Euro-lawyer at a global law firm was intent on conveying the "incestuous ... micro-world" in which he became embedded:

> In Paris, there's a part of the bar – about 200 lawyers, I'd say – who are really knowledgeable of EU law ... it's a social group. As a sociologist, it must be really interesting, because I haven't seen this so much elsewhere, this incestuous aspect. Because in truth, the judges, the lawyers, and those who are judged – that is, the in-house counsel of the big businesses – they frequently meet up with each other ... after [the hearings] they go to dinner together ... everyone knows each other, sociologically it's a micro-world.[182]

Hamburg exemplifies this transition where past Euro-lawyers' ideational ties to local judges (between Fritz Modest's firm and judges like Reimer Voss), have been displaced by interactions between Euro-firms and specialized court chambers. Institutional isomorphism is bolstered by a career pipeline linking specialists from these firms into the city's judiciary.[183] Consider how a lawyer who became judge at the Hamburg Fiscal Court stresses his interactions with former colleagues in discussing his referrals to the ECJ:

> We talked about constructing cases, and specialized lawyers and special-ized courts ... we meet at conferences, and they talk about like parallel

---

[180] Interview with Claudio Contessa, judge at the Council of State in Rome, October 6, 2019 (in-person).

[181] Interview with Alima Zana, Tribunal of Milan (specialized corporate chamber), November 28, 2016 (in-person, rough written transcript); This view was corrobo-rated by: Interview with Claudio Marangoni, December 12, 2016; Interview with Francesca Fiecconi, December 2, 2016.

[182] Interview with Eric Morgan de Rivery, September 12, 2017.

[183] See, for instance: Interview with Stefanie Kohls, judge at the Landgericht Hamburg (ex-lawyer at Heuking, Kühn, Lüer, Wojtek), January 25, 2018 (in-person); Interview with Jan Tolkmitt, January 25, 2018 (ex-lawyer at Allen & Overy). An early case is that of Jürgen Gündisch, who left Graf von Westphalen to serve as judge at the Hamburg Constitutional Court for twenty-five years.

cases they bring in different fiscal courts. And then they select or decide: "Where should we bring a leading case?" And they say, for instance, [about a court] ... "Well, you can forget about it! They don't understand, they have no expertise in customs law, and they would never refer a case to the ECJ".... So at a conference where we met, I said, "well, why don't you bring the case to us?"[184]

These interminglings with Euro-firms are perceived by judges as crucial for keeping up with the rules of the game. As a patent judge in Munich confides, EU law disputes have become "so complicated, and there's so much money involved" that what appears as a "national case" is usually "much bigger at the international level. And you don't understand this if you don't have contact [with] the parties and the attorneys" who "come to my court every time ... this is essential for me to understand how the game is played ... you have to hear it again and again."[185]

## 6.5 FROM CORPORATIZATION TO POLITICIZATION

The passing of the pioneers of Euro-lawyering, the rise of the Euro-firms, and the way this process situates legal consciousness mark a profound evolution of legal mobilization and judicial policymaking in Europe.[186] By routinizing liaisons between businesses, national courts, and the ECJ, Euro-firm lawyers have at once become architects of the EU's capacity to govern through law and stratifiers of access to transnational justice.

The passage from the idealism of a few entrepreneurs pre-1980s to the interests of a corporate elite post-1980s may to some extent be an inevitable progression, but it also invites critical reflection. For this passage contributes to the perception that European integration primarily benefits resourceful interests agglomerating in some communities while neglecting the rights of others. That EU laws on paper also undeniably seek to advance the public interest – fundamental rights, environmental protections, and consumer benefits[187] – scarcely matters in practice if the political economy of legal mobilization treks

---

[184] Interview with Tobias Bender [quoted] and Corina Kögel, January 17, 2018.
[185] Interview with Matthias Zigann, December 19, 2017.
[186] On how these findings are part of a broader trend, see: Liu, Sida. 2008. "Globalization as Boundary-Blurring: International and Local Law Firms in China's Corporate Law Market." *Law & Society Review* 42(4): 771–804.
[187] Pavone, Tommaso. 2016. "Democracy by Lawsuit: Or, Can Litigation Alleviate the EU's 'Democratic Deficit?'" *Constitutional Studies* 2: 59–80.

along a counter-current: if lawyers and judges on the ground treat access to European justice as a luxury service for the privileged few. One might even feel some nostalgia for a bygone era when even an unpaid $3 electricity bill sufficed to inspire the fight for a transnational rule of law.[188]

It is in this light that the corporatization of Euro-lawyering and the big, slow-moving, and "quiet revolution among European law firms"[189] risks "containing justice"[190] and the mobilization of European laws that could advance broader public interests. However, none of this is set in stone. Beginning in the 1990s, a less incremental and more disruptive political shift has also been reshaping the judicial construction of Europe: the politicization of European integration and the rise of contentious politics. As we will see in Chapters 7 and 8, this eventful shift generates its own challenges for Euro-lawyering and judicial policymaking. Yet it also opens novel opportunities for a less elite-centric and more public-facing mode of legal advocacy.

[188] See: 6/64, *Costa* v. *ENEL*, ECR 587; Arena, "From an Unpaid Electricity Bill."
[189] Tagliabue, "Law Firms from U.S. Invade Paris."
[190] Conant, *Justice Contained.*

# PART FOUR

# LAWYERS AND THE RISE OF CONTENTIOUS POLITICS

## CHAPTER SEVEN

# EURO-LAWYERING GOES PUBLIC
## Interpretive Mediation and the Politics of Compliance

*The ruling handed down yesterday by the European Court of Justice in Luxembourg . . . [is] even more disruptive than expected, to the point of sweeping away all of the anachronistic organization of labor on Italian ports . . . [and] fully endorsing the position advocated by the Genoese law firm of Giacomini and Conte.*
—*Il Sole-24 Ore*, December 11, 1991[1]

*Do they really think they'll be able to dismantle our union on the basis of a ruling from Luxembourg? After all, it would be quite the problem, a huge socio-political clash. Do they want to get into it?*
—Dockworkers on the Port of Genoa, December 11, 1991[2]

## 7.1 WHEN WAR IS WAGED ON EUROPEAN LAW

In normal times, Paride Batini did not like talking to journalists. But 1992 was not a normal year for the port city of Genoa, so the charismatic leader of the city's dockworkers' union took to the press to issue a threat: "The port appears headed towards an ever-more inevitable clash whose seriousness is without precedent ... if forced, we will defend ourselves, in concrete form."[3] Batini's pugnaciousness betrayed newfound vulnerability: a few months earlier, national law protecting his union's control over port labor was rebuffed by a faraway European Court. Newspapers soon predicted a "war" that would "bring Genoa to its knees."[4]

---

[1] Dardani, Bruno. 1991. "La Corte di Lussemburgo Spazza il Monopolio del Lavoro Nei Porti." *Il Sole-24 Ore*, December 11, p. 11.
[2] Rizzi, Massimo. 1991. "CULMV: 'Lavoro, Non Sentenze'." *Il Lavoro*, December 11.
[3] Valentino, Piero. 1992. "Genova, Da La Spezia Un Attacco Ai Camalli." *La Repubblica*, June 14.
[4] Minella, Massimo. 1992. "Genova in Ginocchio, Camalli e Camionisti Assediano La Città." *La Repubblica*, October 15.

Two decades later and 500 km to the south, a language of contention[5] surfaced anew. "This is a declaration of war!" shouted one hundred farmers before the city hall in Bari, "and we're ready to fight." In the rural hinterlands, protesters blocked highway traffic and triggered a police roundup.[6] Their anger targeted a decree implementing a European decision mandating the eradication of olive trees suspected of being infected by a deadly pathogen. Conspiracy was in the air, and tips began flooding local police that the researchers who diagnosed the disease had deliberately infected the plants. Warrants were drawn up, the scientists were called in for questioning, and their computers were confiscated.[7]

As we will see, these contentious events produced remarkably divergent legacies of compliance and court-driven change. Yet both were triggered by similarly disruptive efforts to reform local practices by mobilizing European law. As judicial policymaking and international law have expanded since the 1990s, these types of controversies have become more frequent, fueling backlash to polities like the European Union (EU) and courts like the European Court of Justice (ECJ). Some observers even posit the dawn of a populist era threatening to unravel the judicialization of politics. In this chapter and in Chapter 8, I problematize this view and evaluate the capacity of lawyers to serve as brokers of compliance when controversy erupts. By tracing how Euro-lawyering can adapt to moments of heightened contestation of judicial policymaking, I illuminate how legal entrepreneurs can exploit controversy and social mobilization to steer it toward compliance or toward defiance.

To do so, these pages abandon the domain of everyday judging, concealed litigation, and big, slow-moving evolutions for what William Sewell calls *eventful temporalities*: a "relatively rare subclass of happenings that significantly transform [social] structures."[8] We are now in the rapidly shifting world of breaking news, protest and counterprotest, and the public rush to "make sense of the ruckus."[9] Lawyers intent

---

[5] Tarrow, Sidney. 2013. *The Language of Contention: Revolutions in Words, 1688–2012.* New York, NY: Cambridge University Press.

[6] "Il Tar del Lazio blocca le ruspe, ma la rabbia dei contadini non si placa." *LecceNews24.it*, October 13, 2015.

[7] Abbott, Alison. 2015. "Italian Scientists Vilified in Wake of Olive-Tree Deaths." *Nature*, June 1, 2015.

[8] Sewell, William. 2005. *Logics of History: Social Theory and Social Transformation.* Chicago, IL: University of Chicago Press, at 100.

[9] Cramer, *Politics of Resentment*, at 35, 168–169.

on sustaining judicial policymaking and Europeanization in these conditions cannot fall back solely on behind-the-scenes ghostwriting. Rather, they must go public and assume an additional political role: that of *interpretive mediators* in the public sphere.

To set the analytic stage for for this chapter and Chapter 8, Section 7.2 theorizes how moments of contentious politics can forge collective identities premised on obedience or disobedience of the law. It then outlines a comparative sequential approach to trace how the politics of lawyers can tip the scales toward one outcome over the other. In so doing, I challenge the assumption that "revolts" and "backlashes"[10] targeting international laws and courts are inherently regressive and destined to exacerbate noncompliance. For contentious politics are mutable, and under certain conditions backlash can counterintuitively expand opportunities for legal mobilization and judicial policymaking that is more socially embedded, publicly engaged, and ultimately "real"[11] to communities of stakeholders.

## 7.2 LEGAL MOBILIZATION AND CONTENTIOUS COMPARISONS

Through the 1990s, the conventional wisdom about the judicial construction of Europe was that it proceeded apace because it was sheltered by the "mask and shield" of the law.[12] Judicial policymaking transformed Europe because it unfolded as a "quiet revolution" and a "less visible constitutional mutation."[13] The gradualism of judicial decisions clothed in technocratic garb rendered them difficult to detect and to politically contest. The ECJ's transformative judgments were handed down in yawn-inducing cases on the regulation of cheeses and the shape of wine bottles.[14] In short, Europe's political development through law hinged on lawyers and judges banishing their agency from public scrutiny.[15]

---

[10] Rasmussen, "Present and Future European Judicial Problems"; Voeten, "Populism and Backlashes against International Courts"; Turnbull-Dugarte and Devine, "Can EU Judicial Intervention Increase Polity Scepticism?"

[11] Vanhala, *Making Rights a Reality?*

[12] Burley and Mattli, "Europe before the Court," at 72–73.

[13] Weiler, "Transformation of Europe," at 2453; Weiler, "Quiet Revolution."

[14] Maduro, Miguel Poiares. 1998. *We the Court: The European Court of Justice and the European Economic Constitution*. New York, NY: Hart.

[15] Vauchez, "Force of a Weak Field," at 130.

These efforts were bound to provoke controversy sooner or later. Indeed, in the past two decades scholars have made a 180-degree turn. Instead of probing how judicial policymaking hides from politics, they have pivoted to how politics unmasks and increasingly protests judicialization.[16] First, as national courts, the ECJ, and the EU accrue authority and engage in expansive policymaking, politicization has followed suit, including "the growing salience of European governance ... polarisation of opinion, and ... expansion of actors and audiences engaged in monitoring EU affairs."[17] Second, as "political awareness of the outcomes of integration through law has grown significantly," recalcitrant policymakers and interest groups "have become more skillful in penetrating the shield of law."[18] A "permissive consensus" supportive of integration has given way to the "constraining dissensus" of populist politics.[19] In particular, the judicial construction of Europe "reinforce[s] local populist mobilization narratives"[20] because it can be cast as an "external interference" protecting elite interests and as "zero-sum," in that it "increase[s] awareness and understanding among citizens regarding the sovereignty-diluting effects of EU integration."[21] Finally, these narratives render citizens prone to protest, emboldening governments and supreme courts to revolt against the ECJ,[22] provoke a "judicial retreat,"[23] and erode the EU's capacity to govern through

[16] Zürn, "Opening up Europe," at 164; Blauberger and Martinsen, "Court of Justice in Times of Politicisation."

[17] Zürn, "Opening up Europe," at 166; Schmitter, Philippe. 2009. "On the Way to a Post-functionalist Theory of European Integration." *British Journal of Political Science* 39(1): 211–215, at 211–212.

[18] Blauberger and Martinsen, "Court of Justice in Times of Politicisation," at 395.

[19] Hooghe and Marks, "Postfunctionalist Theory of European Integration."

[20] Voeten, "Populism and Backlashes against International Courts," at 407.

[21] Turnbull-Dugarte and Devine, "Can EU Judicial Intervention Increase Polity Scepticism?" at 7. See also: Blauberger, Michael, and Susanne Schmidt. 2017. "Free Movement, the Welfare State, and the European Union's Over-Constitutionalization." *Public Administration* 95: 437–449.

[22] Imig, Doug, and Sidney Tarrow. 2000. "Political Contention in a Europeanising Polity." *West European Politics* 23(4): 73–93; Rasmussen, "Present and Future European Judicial Problems"; Madsen, Mikael Rask, Henrik Palmer Olsen, and Urška Šadl. 2017. "Competing Supremacies and Clashing Institutional Rationalities: The Danish Supreme Court's Decision in the *Ajos* Case and the National Limits of Judicial Cooperation." *European Law Journal* 23: 140–150; Madsen et al., "Backlash against International Courts"; Hofmann, Andreas. 2018. "Resistance against the Court of Justice of the European Union." *International Journal of Law in Context* 14: 258–274.

[23] Conant, "Failing Backward?"

law. In this view, the EU typifies a broader wave of backlashes foreshadowing a "dejudicialization of international politics."[24]

This emergent consensus perceptively highlights that "judicialization should not be considered a teleological process."[25] Ironically, it also risks trading one teleology for another. Treating politicization, protest, and backlash as "regressive contentious politics" – and asking how much targeted institutions are constrained or corroded – ignores how contentious events open multiple opportunities for agency and change.[26] After all, elite-driven or concealed processes of judicial policymaking are no panacea – they have serious limits of their own. The previous chapters revealed that as a "quiet revolution,"[27] the judicial construction of Europe arguably proved *too* quiet, leaving EU law opaque to citizens, civic associations, and even judges who could otherwise mobilize it. From this street-level viewpoint, public controversies not only provide kindling for backlash; they also open opportunities to "vernacularize"[28] EU law and make it tangible to a broader array of prospective "compliance constituencies."[29] Indeed, those who have dedicated their lives to studying cycles of contentious mobilization emphasize that their outcomes are more contingent than predetermined,[30] as people are forced to negotiate "which ideas are considered 'sensible,' which constructions of reality are seen as 'realistic,' and which claims are held as 'legitimate.'"[31]

From this alternative perspective, when recalcitrant actors organize contentious backlash to laws or judicial decisions, they constitute critical junctures where "structural ... influences on political action are significantly relaxed for a relatively short period."[32] As mobilization

---

[24] Abebe, Daniel, and Tom Ginsburg. 2019. "The Dejudicialization of International Politics?" *International Studies Quarterly* 63(3): 521–530.

[25] Ibid.

[26] Alter and Zürn, "Theorising Backlash Politics," at 740.

[27] Weiler, "Quiet Revolution."

[28] On this process of translation and vernacularization more broadly, see: Merry, *Human Rights and Gender Violence*, at 193–194; Simion, Kristina. 2021. *Rule of Law Intermediaries: Brokering Influence in Myanmar*. New York, NY: Cambridge University Press.

[29] Alter, *New Terrain of International Law*, at 19.

[30] For instance, see: Tarrow, Sidney. 1989. *Democracy and Disorder: Protest and Politics in Italy, 1965–1975*. New York, NY: Oxford University Press; McAdam et al. 2001. *Dynamics of Contention*. New York, NY: Cambridge University Press.

[31] De Wilde, Pieter, and Michael Zürn. 2012. "Can the Politicization of European Integration Be Reversed?" *Journal of Common Market Studies* 50: 127–153, at 143.

[32] Capoccia and Kelemen, "Study of Critical Junctures," at 343.

spills over from the courtroom to the public sphere, protest and public controversy broadens participation from a small network of institutional insiders to an expansive web of citizens, journalists, civic associations, and politicians. As people begin questioning the local practices that they previously took for granted, they can reshape their orientations to public institutions and the law.[33] Legal rules are discovered and their political salience deepens during moments of contentious politics,[34] and consequently so does public demand for ways to frame the prospect of socio-legal change.[35] This opens an opportunity to wage what Frank Fisher calls a "politics of local knowledge":[36] public advocacy aimed at reconciling people's quotidian objectives, expectations, and loyalties with disruptive laws and court decisions.

Enclosed within courthouses and banned from launching media-savvy public relations campaigns, judges are ill-suited to this task. But as mediatory actors, Euro-lawyers are uniquely positioned to wage a politics of local knowledge. Provided that they supplement strategic litigation with public advocacy, lawyers gain a political opportunity to mobilize as "interpretive mediators."[37] They can reconcile local narratives with newfound knowledge of European laws to promote

[33] Brubacker, Rogers. 1994. "Rethinking Nationhood." *Contention* 4: 3–14; Sewell, William. 1996. "Historical Events as Transformations of Structures: Inventing Revolution at the Bastille." *Theory and Society* 25(6): 841–881; Beissinger, Mark. 2002. *Nationalist Mobilization and the Collapse of the Soviet State.* New York, NY: Cambridge University Press, at 147–199.

[34] See: Zürn, Michael. 2014. "The Politicization of World Politics and Its Effects." *European Political Science Review* 6: 47–71, at 48–50; Hooghe, Liesbet, and Gary Marks. 2013. "Politicization." In *The Oxford Handbook of the European Union*, Erik Jones, Anand Menon, and Stephen Weatherill, eds. New York, NY: Oxford University Press.

[35] Frames constitute "schemata for interpretation," and framing processes are often essential for social mobilization: Snow, David, and Robert Benford. 1988. "Ideology, Frame Resonance, and Participant Mobilization." *International Social Movement Research* 1: 197–217.

[36] Fisher, *Citizens, Experts, and the Environment.*

[37] In Fisher's conception, "the postpositivist expert must function as an interpretive mediator operating between the available analytical frameworks of social science and competing local perspectives ... Given the reduced distance between the experts and the citizens, the role of both can be redefined. In effect, whereas the citizen becomes the 'popular scientist,' the analyst takes on the role of a 'specialized citizen.'" See: Ibid., at 80.

compliance and cultivate a legal consciousness that blurs the boundaries pitting lived experience against transnational legality.[38]

The impact of this strategy, however, is contingent upon lawyers "play[ing] a role in creating their own legal opportunities"[39] in a well-timed sequence. First, by mobilizing clients and ghostwriting a national court's referral to the ECJ, lawyers can convert a salient but intractable local controversy into a judicially resolvable dispute at the European level. As first movers, Euro-lawyers can control the timing of legal mobilization to blindsight potentially recalcitrant actors and take advantage of favorable shifts in the political climate. By then working their social embeddedness to relocalize a judicial ruling and mobilize the local press, lawyers can anticipate, promote, and "amplify the impact of judicial decisions"[40] to preempt backlash. Conditional upon mobilizing quickly in a context with some diffuse support for a supranational intervention, contentious politics amplify lawyers' capacity to rally local stakeholders into compliance constituencies. A politics of backlash might then backfire, broadening "the radiating effects of courts"[41] by spurring citizens and interest groups to claim European laws and rights they previously ignored.

I empirically illustrate this argument by comparing the two explosive controversies opening this chapter, which sparked litigation before the ECJ and contentious backlash: the 1991/1992 *Port of Genoa* case (in this chapter), which quashed the monopoly rights over port labor of a centenarian union of dockworkers, and the 2015/2016 *Xylella* case (in Chapter 8), which mandated the eradication of thousands of centenarian olive trees across Puglia. While equally contentious, *Port of Genoa* produced a legacy of Europeanization and compliance whereas *Xylella* undermined the EU's legal authority and entrenched noncompliance. In the language of Chapter 6, *Port of Genoa* created a "hot spot" of European legal mobilization and judicial policymaking, whereas *Xylella* deepened a "cold spot" instead. How can we assess if lawyers lent a hand in tipping the scales?

To answer, I combine comparison, process tracing, and the triangulation of evidence. First, I draw upon the case selection logic known

---

[38] Liu, "Globalization as Boundary-Blurring."
[39] Vanhala, "Legal Opportunity Structures," 525.
[40] Hamlin, Rebecca. 2016. "'Foreign Criminals,' the Human Rights Act, and the New Constitutional Politics of the United Kingdom." *Journal of Law & Courts* 4: 437–461, at 458.
[41] Galanter, "Radiating Effects of Courts."

as the "methods of agreement and difference."[42] I compare *Port of Genoa* and *Xylella* because these otherwise similar cases witnessed divergent legacies of compliance and Europeanization that covary with whether Euro-lawyers mobilized public support via interpretive mediation. I then buttress this comparison by tracing the sequence of events and "entities engaging in activities" in each case that exacerbated backlash or steered contention toward compliance.[43] "By fusing these two elements, [this] comparative sequential method"[44] facilitates linking Euro-lawyering to variation in the outcome of backlash politics. Finally, to reconstruct the rapidly unfolding events animating contention in each case, I account for the "potential bias of evidentiary sources" by "gathering diverse and relevant evidence."[45] In particular, I triangulate between dozens of on-site interviews, court records, public opinion data, and historical newspaper coverage spanning across the ideological spectrum.[46]

The resulting case comparison is summarized in Figure 7.1. Both the *Port of Genoa* and *Xylella* cases emerged as social controversy and political gridlock triggered attempts to mobilize EU law and judicial review by the ECJ. In both cases, the result was the application of EU laws already in the books: these cases hardly constitute "turning points in the development of the law."[47] Yet complying with these rules meant massive disruption to deeply-rooted local practices, so unsurprisingly, in both instances recalcitrant interest groups mobilized contentious backlash to thwart compliance. What made the difference is that whereas in *Port of Genoa* Euro-lawyers preempted backlash via

[42] Pavone, "Selecting Cases for Comparative Sequential Analysis."

[43] Beach, Derek, and Rasmus Pedersen. 2019. *Process-Tracing Methods*. Ann Arbor, MI: University of Michigan Press, at 99–101.

[44] Falleti, Tulia, and James Mahoney. 2015. "The Comparative Sequential Method." In *Advances in Comparative-Historical Analysis*, James Mahoney and Kathleen Thelen, eds. New York, NY: Cambridge University Press, at 225–226; 236.

[45] Lustick, Ian. 1996. "History, Historiography, and Political Science: Multiple Historical Records and the Problem of Selection Bias." *American Political Science Review* 90: 605–618, at 616; Bennett, Andrew, and Jeffrey Checkel (eds.). 2015. *Process Tracing: From Metaphor to Analytic Tool*. New York, NY: Cambridge University Press, at 21.

[46] From left-wing outlets like *Il Lavoro* and *La Repubblica* to the more conservative *Il Sole-24 Ore* and *Il Giornale*, to those with local knowledge, like Genoa's *Il Secolo XIX* and Bari's *La Gazzetta del Mezzogiorno*.

[47] Vauchez, Antoine. 2017. "EU Law Classics in the Making." In *EU Law Stories: Contextual and Critical Histories of European Jurisprudence*, Fernanda Nicola and Bill Davies, eds. New York, NY: Cambridge University Press, at 26–29.

| Cases and outcomes ↓ | Possible explanatory variables → | | | | | |
|---|---|---|---|---|---|---|
| | **A:** ECJ solicited to resolve a local controversy? | **B:** ECJ decision disrupts existing EU law? | **C:** ECJ decision disrupts salient local practices? | **D:** ECJ decision sparks contentious backlash? | **E:** Euro-lawyers wage proactive litigation? | **F:** Euro-lawyers mobilize as interpretive mediators? |
| **Case 1–*Port of Genoa*:** Europeanization and compliance | Yes | *No* | Yes | Yes | *Yes* | *Yes* |
| **Case 2–*Xylella*:** Euroskepticism and noncompliance | Yes | *No* | Yes | Yes | *No* | *No* |

Figure 7.1 Comparative case study design for the analysis of the *Port of Genoa* (Chapter 7) and *Xylella* (Chapter 8) cases

proactive litigation and media-savvy public advocacy, *Xylella* involved a reactive group of nationally-oriented lawyers whose litigation efforts emboldened civil disobedience.

## 7.3 THE PORT OF GENOA CASE

The year 1992 was always supposed to be a moment of rebirth for Genoa. But it was not supposed to happen contentiously via European law; it was supposed to happen festively via Christopher Columbus.

The timing could have hardly been better: the year coincided with Columbus' 500th anniversary, and the city was hosting the World Expo. For the occasion, a massive urban renewal project was commissioned. Renzo Piano – the city's most famous architect – was tasked with rebuilding the abandoned warehouses on the old port's docks and constructing Europe's largest aquarium. As William Weaver chronicled in *The New York Times*, "it is not just another world's fair. . . . The old focus of the city would be restored; Genoa's heart would beat again."[48]

Yet for over a century, what propelled Genoa into rivalry with Marseille and Barcelona over control of Mediterranean trade was not the old port, but the industrial port just to its west: some 25 kilometers' worth of cranes, containers, heaps of coal and steel, gigantic ships, and internal highways and railways spanning from the city's medieval lighthouse, the *Lanterna*, westward to the town of Voltri. And it was in this setting that, while Expo festivities unfolded on the old port, a clash between the liberalizing thrust of European law and the protectionist practices of local labor activists ensued.

### 7.3.1 A Crisis Engulfs a "Utopia That Would Make Marx Proud"

The "critical antecedents"[49] of the *Port of Genoa* case can be traced to the economic decline of Italy's largest industrial port and the political gridlock that frustrated reform efforts.

---

[48] Weaver, William. 1992. "Genoa Holds an Expo, Too." *The New York Times*, June 7, 1992, p. 8.

[49] By "critical antecedents," I mean background conditions that combine with people exercising their agency in subsequent events to produce divergent legacies of social change. See: Slater, Dan, and Erica Simmons. 2009. "Informative Regress: Critical Antecedents in Comparative Politics." *Comparative Political Studies* 43(7): 886–917, at 889.

Life had not always been difficult on Genoa's docks. From the 1950s through the early 1970s, the port witnessed remarkable expansion and became a motor of Italy's postwar "economic miracle."[50] With its geographically favored location at the southern tip of the "industrial triangle" comprising Turin and Milan, demand for imports from these industrial hinterlands fueled the port's economic boom. From 1950 through 1973, total loaded and unloaded goods increased by 669 percent (from 8.3 to 61.5 million tons).[51] Growth was driven primarily by imports of coal and oil alongside steel destined for Lombardy's steelworks industry (see Figure 7.2).[52] The boom in traded goods went hand-in-hand with important innovations. Genoa was the first Mediterranean port to invest in the infrastructure for the shipping and handling of containers, and in 1971 only Rotterdam surpassed Genoa in common market container traffic.[53] Burgeoning employment was another spillover effect: from 1950 to 1964, the number of dockworkers grew from 3,000 to 8,059.[54]

Yet the global recession and stagflation of the 1970s began to turn the economic tide against Genoa. From 1973 through 1990, loaded and unloaded goods dropped by 29.6 percent (from 61.5 to 43.6 million tons; see Figure 7.3).[55] As the center-left newspaper *La Repubblica* lamented, "to write about the woes of Genoa has almost become a literary genre."[56] Even more worrying was the gridlock frustrating a political response. At the Consorzio Autonomo del Porto (CAP) – the state authority responsible for the port's management since 1903[57] – the crisis became such a "hot potato" that when its longtime president's mandate concluded in 1981, nobody wanted to serve as his replacement, forcing him to reluctantly serve another term.[58] In Parliament, the mantra of "port reform" proved a nonstarter: ten different drafts of port reform legislation were drawn up from the

---

[50] Ginsborg, Paul. 2003. *A History of Contemporary Italy*. New York, NY: Palgrave Macmillan, at 210–253.
[51] Comune di Genova. 2003. *I Numeri e La Storia del Porto di Genova*. Genoa: Sistema Statistico Nazionale, at 145.
[52] Ibid., at 12; 22.
[53] Ibid., at 13.
[54] Musso, Bruno. 2008. *Il Porto di Genova*. Turin: Celid, at 21.
[55] Comune di Genova, *Numeri e La Storia del Porto di Genova*, at 145.
[56] Bozzo, Gianni Baget. 1991. "Il Primato di Genova." *La Repubblica*, May 24.
[57] Musso, *Porto di Genova*, at 18.
[58] Ibid., at 45.

Figure 7.2 The port in its prime: (a) the "Ponte Libia" container terminal – the first in the Mediterranean, 1969; (b) Genoese dockworkers, 1960s
*Source:* Comune di Genova (2003: 20; 315).

1970s through 1991, but none got past the drawing board.[59] "Years of statements and debates over port reform," port operators decried, "were sterile from the start."[60]

What were the sources of economic decline in Genoa, and why was a policy response so politically intractable? There is little doubt that external macroeconomic forces played a large role. As Saskia Sassen has written, the shift to services and finance underlying postwar globalization created new "geographies of centrality" and "hierarchies

---

[59] Dardani, Bruno. 1991. "Alla Camera la legge antimonopoli." *Il Sole-24 ore*, July 25, p. 10.
[60] Dardani, Bruno. 1991. "Gli Utenti all'attacco." *Il Sole-24 ore*, July 25, p. 10.

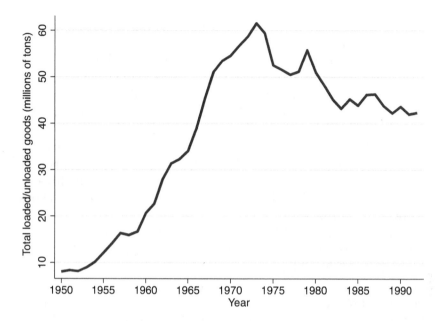

Figure 7.3 Total loaded and unloaded goods in the Port of Genoa, 1950–1992
*Source:* Comune di Genova (2003: 144).

of cities," wherein "a multiplicity of formerly important manufacturing centers and port cities have lost functions and are in decline."[61] This analysis was frequently invoked by the local press, which described Genoa as "a city that has departed the industrial age without entering the postindustrial age."[62] Yet there is also one critical cause of the decline of Genoa's competitiveness that is innate to local labor politics and that explains why reform efforts proved intractable: the monopolistic organization of dockwork by the state-sanctioned labor union, the *Compagnia Unica Lavoratori Merci Varie* (CULMV, or "exclusive labor union for various goods").

The CULMV's roots run deep through Genoa's history. The statute founding its progenitor dates back nearly seven centuries to 1340.[63] Known in Genoese dialect as *camalli*, dockworkers became the objects of folklore and served as the oft-romanticized embodiments of the city's history. Residents were well aware of how "the port and the entire

---

[61] Sassen, Saskia. 1994. *Cities in a World Economy.* Thousand Oaks, CA: Pine Forge Press, at 4–5.

[62] Bozzo, "Primato di Genova."

[63] Costamagia, Giorgio. 1965. *Gli Statuti della Compagnia dei Caravana del Porto di Genova, 1340–1600.* Turin: Accademia della Scienza.

253

city depended upon the *camalli* ... sooner or later, all needed to settle their debts with them: the Republic of Genoa, the French, the Savoy, the Kingdom of Italy, the fascist regime, the second and the third Republic."[64] "For seven hundred years" – one journalist concludes – only the *camalli* and a few privileged others could "live the perfume and mystery of the sea."[65] The CULMV's leaders (or *console*) were similarly hailed as protagonists in Genoese historiography, imbuing their labor union with a classic "charismatic authority."[66] In particular, the *console* from 1984 through 2009, Paride Batini, became a "romantic symbol,"[67] a larger-than-life figure "legendary for his intransigence and for his epic look: Jeans, dark turtleneck, Eskimo-style coat, a slender build, and the air of an American actor."[68]

With time, the CULMV's social control of port labor was codified into law by Article 110 of the 1942 Italian Navigation Code.[69] This outcome – and the CULMV's political power – stemmed from a history of working class contention. With their meeting hall adorned with portraits of Marx, Lenin, and Guido Rossa, the labor union's members had organized one of Italy's first major labor strikes in 1900.[70] Batini had been dubbed "the last communist" by prominent politicians and as "Genoa's Mao Tse Tung" by the local press.[71] It thus did not take long for the *camalli* and "their striped shirts ... [to become] a symbol, a postcard of 'Red' Genoa": a fraternal order whose *lingua franca* remains a thick Genoese dialect[72] and whose collective pride lies in having "played a decisive role in the history of [Italy]." As one of their retired old guard explained, "it's true, here we are all communists. We know how to give life a sense of purpose."[73]

---

[64] Musso, Bruno. 2017. *Il Cuore in Porto*. Milan: Mursia Editore, at 20, 23.

[65] Cevasco, Francesco. 2009. "Tra i finti docks dove i camalli sono quasi spariti." *Corriere della Sera*, November 8, p. 35.

[66] Weber, *Economy and Society*, vol. II, at 1111–1123.

[67] Marchesiello, Michele. 2010. *La Città Portuale*. Rome: Aracane Editrice, at 153.

[68] Imarisio, Marco. 2009. "Morto Batini, il 'camallo' che sfidava la storia." *Corriere della Sera*, April 24, p. 21.

[69] Under Article 110 of the Navigation code, the loading, unloading, shipment, storage, and movement of materials goods within the port were reserved to dockwork companies whose members had (under Articles 152 and 156 of the Regulation on Maritime Navigation) to also be of Italian nationality. See: Regio Decreto 30 marzo 1942, no. 327.

[70] Musso, *Porto di Genova*, at 18.

[71] Imarisio, "Morto Batini."

[72] Musso, *Porto di Genova*, at 17.

[73] Cevasco, "Tra i finti docks."

Sense of purpose, indeed! For at its apex, the CULMV could exercise decisive influence over national politics. Consider the so-called events of Genoa of 1960. Giuseppe Giacomini – a Genoese lawyer whom we will return to shortly – was twelve years old when in 1960 the *camalli* took to the streets to oppose Prime Minister Tambroni's decision to allow the neofascist Movimento Sociale Italiano (MSI) party to hold its annual congress in Genoa.[74] The protests culminated in a "revolutionary moment" that brought down Tambroni's parliamentary coalition.[75] Giacomini recalls: "Some people died. The dockworkers were very driven. They waited for the police cars.... The police jeeps would drive up at high speed, the *camalli* would wait for them, with metal hooks, they hooked them from below as they sped by, and they overturned them! ... they were difficult people to control."[76]

The CULMV leveraged its monopoly rights and pugnacious reputation to its bargaining advantage. Special cranes had to be developed with seating for two workers instead of one, because the CULMV "imposed the presence of a number of laborers [for a given task] that was double that of other ports."[77] Shipments of liquid, which are less labor intensive to handle than dry goods, were charged as if they were dried goods. When it would rain, "all work would be halted, in the Port of Genoa. And [the *camalli*] were paid all the same."[78] CULMV dockworkers were allegedly paid 172 percent more per shift than the average worker at other Italian ports, with their shift capped at six hours instead of eight.[79] And most fatefully of all, union membership was strictly limited to Italian citizens.[80]

While for some the CULMV represented a sort of "utopia that would make Marx proud,"[81] its bargaining victories exacerbated Genoa's competitive disadvantage in the European common market. Even left-wing newspapers lamented how the "monopoly of dockwork at above-

---

[74] Benna, Alessandro, and Lucia Compagnino. 2005. *30 Giugno 1960*. Genoa: Frilli.
[75] Musso, *Porto di Genova*, at 17.
[76] Interview with Giuseppe Giacomini, November 2, 2016.
[77] Interview with Alessandro Vaccaro, president of the Genoa Bar Association, November 2, 2016 (in-person).
[78] Interview with Giuseppe Giacomini, November 2, 2016.
[79] Conte, Giuseppe, and Giacomini, Giuseppe. 1990. "Memoria ai sensi dell'art. 20 del protocollo sullo statuto della Corte di Giustizia C.E.E." September 20, Genoa, IT, p. 4. Shared from Giuseppe Giacomini's personal archives.
[80] See: Case C-179/90, *Merci Convenzionali Porto di Genova v. Siderurgica Gabrielli* (*"Port of Genoa"*) [1991], ECR I-5889, at 5925.
[81] Interview with Giuseppe Giacomini, November 2, 2016.

market rates" had "caused the Port to miss out on the transport of containers."[82] As Alessandro Vaccaro – the president of Genoa's bar association – recalls, "there were shippers … who preferred to dock in Rotterdam and then proceed [south] by land rather than to come to Genova, which was more expensive."[83] Local journalists claimed that efforts to honor shippers' request to open dockwork to outside competition[84] might allow the "Port of Genoa to really breathe in the air of renewal and rebirth."[85] The socialist president of the port authority (CAP) – Rinaldo Magnani – similarly stressed that "Genoa has thus remained the only port where, due to a total opposition by the CULMV, any experiment [for reform] has drowned before even being attempted."[86] Having repeatedly demonstrated their capacity to project their pugnacious political influence well beyond the city limits, "nothing and no one [was] able to break their monopoly."[87]

By the early 1990s, the Port's economic situation had become unsustainable. In 1991, it lost millions of dollars in revenue due to a decline of 200,000 tons of transported goods. In spite of multiyear state subsidies of over $800.5 million, the Port was on the brink of bankruptcy.[88] In just a couple of decades, the Port of Genoa had degenerated from motor of the postwar economic miracle into "the voice of the national debt."[89]

### 7.3.2 Mobilizing the Ghostwriter's Repertoire

It was in this historical moment that two second-generation Euro-lawyers decided to turn to Europe. The late Giuseppe Conte[90] was an established Genoese civil lawyer with iconoclastic inclinations. He believed that when innovative policy solutions to disputes or controversies were foreclosed by national law, they could be opened via

---

82 Bozzo, "Primato di Genova."
83 Interview with Alessandro Vaccaro, November 2, 2016.
84 Valentino, Piero. 1991. "Gli Industriali Alla Riconquista del Porto di Genova." *La Repubblica*, May 25.
85 Valentino, Piero. 1991. "Pace d'Agosto a Genova tra Porto e Camalli." *La Repubblica*, August 25.
86 Dardani, Bruno. 1991. "'I camalli sono un caso nazionale'." *Il Sole-24 ore*, June 13, p. 10.
87 Bozzo, "Primato di Genova."
88 Valentino, "Gli Industriali Alla Riconquista"; Valentino, "Pace d'Agosto."
89 Bozzo, "Primato di Genova."
90 The lawyer discussed here should not be confused with a fellow lawyer by the same name who would become Prime Minister of Italy in 2018.

European law. A fluent French and Spanish speaker, he held personal connections to Brussels and was a close friend with Enrico Traversa, then a young lawyer at the European Commission who would climb the ranks of its Legal Service. Giuseppe Giacomini was a younger criminal lawyer, who "in one of those contingencies of life" began collaborating with Conte on cases that intersected between their areas of practice. Giacomini was captivated by how his senior colleague "had a way of confronting juridical issues that was completely different from mine and that of all the lawyers that I knew," and he became convinced that mastering European law could represent a "Copernican revolution" for his professional identity and advocacy.[91]

Like the first Euro-lawyers in Chapter 5, Conte and Giacomini were ideationally committed to European integration, drawing inspiration from famous pro-European declarations like the 1941 Ventotene Manifesto. Yet like later generations of Euro-firm lawyers in Chapter 6, Giacomini sought to complement Conte's "cultural passion" for EU law with a more pragmatic "business sense": the conviction that expertise in EU law could provide a competitive advantage in a legal services market saturated with nationally-oriented practitioners.[92]

By 1990 the duo had already pioneered multiple referrals to the ECJ from Genoese courts – the first being the 1982 *Luisi and Carbone* case[93] aimed at liberalizing capital flows in Europe. Like other Euro-lawyers they derived pleasure from exercising their agency: their goal, Giacomini recalls, was "to collaborate in the creation of this new [European legal] system via national jurisdictions … and through that genius institution, that truly supreme chapel of quality that the ECJ has always been." A "provincial approach" to the resolution of social problems, Conte and Giacomini believed, often led to political paralysis and stagnation, leaving EU law as "the only path forward" to promote change.[94] In other words, Conte and Giacomini knew that European judges might well "act when elected officials won't."[95]

In response to the port's economic crisis, the duo thus began to read up on the ECJ's case law concerning public monopolies,

---

[91] Interview with Giuseppe Giacomini, October 24 and 26, 2017.
[92] Ibid.
[93] Case 286/82, *Luisi and Carbone* v. *Ministero del Tesoro* [1984], ECR 377.
[94] Interview with Giuseppe Giacomini, October 24 and 26, 2017 (via phone).
[95] Frymer, Paul. 2003. "Acting When Elected Officials Won't: Federal Courts and Civil Rights Enforcement in U.S. Labor Unions, 1935–85." *American Political Science Review* 97(3): 483–499.

abuse of dominant market position, and freedom of establishment. These antitrust laws were altogether novel domestically: until October 1990,[96] competition rules were absent from Italian law. Yet thanks to their previous lawyering experience before the ECJ, Conte and Giacomini knew that antitrust rules were an established cornerstone of European law. For instance, under Article 86 of the Treaty of Rome, "any abuse by one or more undertakings of a dominant position within the common market ... shall be prohibited." And under Article 90, "Member States shall neither enact nor maintain in force any measure contrary to the rules" of Article 86, even "in the case of public undertakings and undertakings to which Member States grant special or exclusive rights."

"In these conditions," Giacomini recalls, "my partner and I ... asked ourselves ... if, given a ship ... adorned with cranes that could load and unload shipments, it could possibly still be legitimate to mandate the services of the CULMV." Thus the idea of constructing a test case to be referred to the ECJ was born. Yet two difficulties remained. First, Conte and Giacomini had to identify a dispute vividly illuminating the conflicts between EU competition law and local labor practices. Second, they had to find a client willing to take on the city's most powerful labor union. And "in a very politically tense situation, we couldn't find a client willing to raise this issue. They were all scared to raise this issue!"[97] So Conte and Giacomini took the matter into their own hands, proactively pushing the ghostwriter's repertoire to its limits.

A serendipitous opportunity for the Euro-lawyers to exercise their agency emerged in 1988 with a ship named *Wallaroo*. The vessel was carrying a consignment of 5.5 tons of steel worth 6 billion lire ($4.6 million) from Hamburg destined to an Paduan steelworks company: Siderurgica Gabrielli SpA. *Wallaroo* docked in the Port of Genoa on December 22, 1988, and although it was adorned with four cranes and its own crew, it was prevented by Merci Convenzionali SpA (one of the public companies comprising the port authority) from unloading the steel on its own. The *coup de grâce* arrived in early 1989, when the CULMV engaged in a series of strike actions. For three months, the shipment of steel lay frozen on Genoa's docks. And Siderurgica Gabrielli, to whom the steel was due, sued.[98]

---

[96] See: Legge No. 287 del 10 Ottobre 1990, "Norme per la tutela della concorrenza e del mercato."

[97] Interview with Giuseppe Giacomini, November 2, 2016.

[98] For documentation of these facts, see: Tribunale di Genova, Ordinanza nella causa civile, Merci Convenzionali Porto di Genova SpA contro Siderurgica Gabrielli SpA

This public transcript suggests a rather organic origin of a legal dispute. But the reality is that the suit had been meticulously choreographed by Conte and Giacomini. Given widespread reticence to take on the CULMV, the Euro-lawyers (i) lodged the suit at their own risk, and (ii) devised an ingenious way "sue" the *camalli* without actually suing them. As Giacomini confides in an interview,

> we found a legal case that has a characteristic that has never been written about, but it's really important ... we couldn't find a client willing to raise this issue ... so we invented the case ... we asked Siderurgica Gabrielli to authorize us to raise the legal case at our own risk, as lawyers. That is, not only did we lack a client paying us, but we bore the risk!
>
> We constructed it in the following way. The ship, *Wallaroo*, arrives ... we asked Merci Convenzionali, one of the constitutive public companies in the [Port Authority], to unload the ship ... to realize this, it was obliged to turn to the CULMV. But the CULMV was on strike! So Merci Convenzionali told us: "No, you have to wait because the ship can't be unloaded, because only the *camalli* can do so, and they're on strike." We replied, "no problem! We can unload on our own, because we are adorned with our own cranes." "You can't do that," they retorted. And so a lawsuit before the Tribunal of Genoa was born.[99]

The Euro-lawyers' timing was also intentional, coinciding with a favorable moment of political reckoning: even as the Port was on the brink of bankruptcy, the *camalli* were engaging in another series of disruptive strikes. But Conte and Giacomini made another key strategic move: they sued Merci Convenzionali – the state-run port authority – rather than the dockworkers. Why?

First, the Euro-lawyers knew that Merci would be more supportive of efforts to solicit the ECJ. Just a couple of years prior in a dispute between Merci and the dockworkers concerning a series of unpaid bills, Merci had suggested that national law protecting the *camalli*'s monopoly rights over port labor contrasted with the Treaty of Rome.[100] Indeed, once the dispute was lodged before the Civil Court in Genoa, Merci's unenthusiastic defense was that its hands were tied by Article 110 of the Navigation Code.[101] Its lawyers ultimately endorsed Conte

(Dimundo, relatore), May 28, 1990, pp. 1–3. Shared from Giuseppe Giacomini's personal archives.

[99] Interview with Giuseppe Giacomini, November 2, 2016.

[100] "CULMV 'torna' a Settembre." *Corriere Mercantile*, July 10, 1991.

[101] Filippo Schiaffini, the director of Merci, stated in September 1991 that "the breaking of the monopoly of port dockworkers unions is an enormous advantage

and Giacomini's argument that a referral to the ECJ would be desirable, and even the *avvocatura dello stato* (state legal service) declined to defend a law that, after all, had been subjected to countless reform efforts in Parliament.[102]

Second, Conte and Giacomini mobilized their expertise to exploit a more favorable legal opportunity structure at the supranational level. They knew that if the *camalli* could be excluded as a party to the domestic dispute, the ECJ's rules of procedure would preclude them from defending themselves in Luxembourg. "This was our own ingenious invention, it must be said," Giacomini recalls with a grin; for when the CULMV "became aware that there had been a preliminary reference to the ECJ that concerned it … it couldn't intervene before the European judges!"[103] By suing the port authority, Conte and Giacomini blindsighted the dockworkers and ensured that all the parties to the suit would support a European intervention before the ECJ and, later, before the local press.

The final obstacle to mobilizing the European Court was the President of the Tribunal of Genoa: Antonino Dimundo. A short man with a "vivacious" character, Dimundo was visibly torn. Tickled by the idea of challenging the CULMV, he was also wary of the political consequences and the impact that might befall his professional reputation. So when Conte and Giacomini ghostwrote a proposed reference to the ECJ, Dimundo cautioned: "I don't know this area of law. I understand what you are asking of me. Make no mistake, counsel, don't make me make a bad impression!" The Euro-lawyers' response sought to assuage these reticences by stressing their linked fate: "Mr. President," Giacomini replied, "I have no incentive to have you make a bad impression because I, too, am building my future in this way."[104]

### 7.3.3 From Ghostwriting to Public Advocacy

In the end, Dimundo collaborated, referring the case to the ECJ on May 28, 1990. At this point, Conte and Giacomini moved beyond their behind-the-scenes role as ghostwriters and became interpretive mediators in the public sphere. In-between their trips to Luxembourg to argue the case, they preemptively engaged the local press in a "very

for port companies like ours." See: Minella, Massimo. 1991. "Porto aperto ai non-cittadini." *Il Lavoro*, September 20, at 10.

[102] "Monopolio in banchina, ultimo atto." *Il Secolo XIX*, July 10, 1991.

[103] Interview with Giuseppe Giacomini, November 2, 2016.

[104] Interview with Giuseppe Giacomini, October 24 and 26, 2017.

deliberate media strategy" to lay the groundwork for compliance with ECJ's decision. As Giacomini explains:

> Our strategy was legally well-founded, but it was so new that it wouldn't have been understood at first glance ... [so through] multiple interviews with Genoese journalists, I tried to explain in simple, clear, and correct terms what the goal of our actions were ... [given] the impact this lawsuit would have on public opinion ... it was indispensable to work to prepare things ahead of time, and to accompany them after this legal action, which was ... charged with cultural, sociological, and political meaning.[105]

While Genoa was a context with diffuse public support for European integration, as we will see, Conte and Giacomini realized it was hardly a foregone conclusion that a court decision disrupting long-standing labor relations would be welcomed. By getting ahead of the forthcoming blitzkrieg of news through a media-savvy framing campaign, the Euro-lawyers decreased the probability that the backlash to come would prompt confusion and rally the public to resist compliance.

This was no straightforward task. Even seasoned journalists had a difficult time understanding the procedures and logics of European law. As the lawsuit was punted to Luxembourg, some journalists incorrectly described the ECJ's Advocate General – a fellow judge who offers a preliminary opinion on how the case might be decided – as a member of the European Community's "public ministry," thereby conjuring up images of an intrusive bureaucracy.[106] Others erroneously claimed that the Advocate General's opinion was "binding" rather than advisory.[107] And even local interest groups, like the CEOs of shipping companies, confessed their lack of knowledge of core EU legal principles like direct effect and supremacy, prompting confusion about whether the ECJ's ruling "would be binding in Italy."[108]

In a context where most local stakeholders lacked a European legal consciousness, the seeds a Euroskeptic revolt were germinating. "In Italy and in Genoa in particular," journalists warned, "these mechanisms of the EEC still strike us as mysterious. And they are

---

[105] Ibid.
[106] See: "Il pubblico ministero Cee." *Il Giornale*, September 20, 1991; "CULMV alla sbarra." *Corriere Mercantile*, September 19, 1991; Carozzi, Giorgio. 1991. "Eurosberla per Batini e l'organizzazione portuale." *Il Secolo XIX*, September 20, 1991, p. 11.
[107] Minella, "Porto aperto ai non-cittadini"; Carozzi, "Eurosberla per Batini."
[108] Musso, *Porto di Genova*, at 60.

perceived with suspicion."[109] Ominous portrayals of European power politics – "What is circling around the EEC Court? What interests and forces are at play? And to what ends?"[110] – and of an asymmetric war pitting Europe against the dockworkers – "European cannonballs against the CULMV" read one headline[111] – were beginning to emerge in newspapers.

So Conte and Giacomini quickly mobilized the local press to promote clarity, diffuse their view that European law was the only way to overcome bottlenecks to reform, and cast the predicted ECJ judgment as an opportunity for the city's rebirth. In their rhetoric, they tapped preexisting efforts by local newspapers and the national shippers' association to "sensitize public opinion" and "confront the real problems" of the port by "liberating [it] from ideological clashes."[112] The Euro-lawyers plainly described their strategy and goals. Their objective had always been "to raise an international lawsuit [and] force the Genoese judiciary to pronounce itself," namely by convincing the city tribunal "to delegate the judgment to the Court of Luxembourg."[113] In speeches before local civil associations they emphasized that "what the national legislator has been incapable of doing will be done by the European Court," for once "the ruling is read out it will enter into force, and it will be immediately binding ... rendering inapplicable any law that contrasts with it."[114] Confident of their mastery of EU law by publicizing that they had never lost a case before the ECJ, they presciently predicted the result: "Article 110 on the port reserves will no longer exist," and the dockworkers and port authority will be forced into negotiations to comply with the European Court's ruling.[115]

Giacomini even preemptively rebutted the inevitable protests of the dockworkers. While the CULMV was unlikely to be persuaded via rhetoric alone, his logic was that "if you expect bad news with substantial advance notice, you can begin to prepare yourself ... and when it arrives you're probably better able to deal with it."[116] To soften

[109] Malatto, Costantino. 1991. "Cannonate Europee contro la CULMV." *Il Lavoro*, July 31.
[110] *Il Secolo XIX*, "Monopolio in banchina."
[111] Malatto, "Cannonate Europee."
[112] Musso, *Cuore in Porto*, at 159.
[113] *Il Secolo XIX*, "Monopolio in banchina."
[114] "Porto, imminente la decisione CEE." *Il Giornale*, October 4, 1991, p. 22.
[115] Ibid.
[116] Interview with Giuseppe Giacomini, October 24 and 26, 2017.

the forthcoming blow, he underscored to labor-friendly newspapers that they were attacking national law and not the dockworkers, who had merely made the most of the domestic legal regime.[117] And he emphasized that "the dockworkers have nothing to fear, and they know it. They're undoubtedly capable as professionals, so in the free market they surely won't have any problems."[118] The result of this public advocacy was that Giacomini was often the only party to the suit quoted in newspaper coverage. So when the ECJ delivered its judgment on December 10, 1991, most local observers had seen it coming, and newspapers were able to make sense of it.

The European Court's decision crystallized the argument proposed by Conte and Giacomini and broadly endorsed by Merci Convenzionali, the ECJ's Advocate General, and their friend Enrico Traversa, who acted on behalf of the Commission's Legal Service in the dispute. The ECJ held that Article 90 of the Treaty of Rome "precludes rules of a Member State which confer on an undertaking established in that State the exclusive right to organize dockwork and require it for that purpose to have recourse to a dock work company formed exclusively of national workers."[119] In so doing, the Court underscored Europe's interest in the dispute given that the Port of Genoa "constitut[es] a substantial part of the common market," adding that a state-sanctioned dockworkers union was not part of those "services of general economic interest" allowed some leeway from the strict application of EU competition rules.[120]

From the standpoint of black letter law, the decision was an important albeit linear application of the existing case law of the ECJ. This was precisely why Conte and Giacomini had been confidently predicting the outcome in the press. But the domestic policy consequences are hard to overstate: "In one instant," Giacomini recalls, "Article 110 became illegitimate."[121]

The consensus in the local and national press was that the ruling was at once pathbreaking and thoroughly expected. Genoa's leading newspaper, *Il Secolo XIX*, described it as a "Euro-revolution" that was as

---

[117] Minella, Massimo. 1991. "Imputata la legge, non Batini." *Il Lavoro*, December 11.
[118] Minella, Massimo. 1991. "Una rivoluzione targata Cee." *Il Lavoro*, September 21, p. 8.
[119] See: C-179/90, *Siderurgica Gabrielli* ("Port of Genoa") at operative part, para. 1.
[120] Ibid., at para. 15; operative part, para. 3.
[121] Interview with Giuseppe Giacomini, November 2, 2016.

"predictable" as it was "certainly resounding."[122] "A 'historic' ruling," noted journalists at the left-wing *Il Lavoro*, "but also a ruling we largely anticipated."[123] Leading Euro-lawyers throughout Italy – like Fausto Capelli in Milan – rushed to the press to publish their own elucidations and push for compliance,[124] a strategy soon mimicked by representatives of the European Commission.[125] Should anyone have any remaining questions, Conte and Giacomini wrote their own plain language explanation of the ruling[126] and once again made themselves available for countless interviews. "Why is this judgment so important?" – Giacomini rhetorically inquired as he spoke to the press the day after the ECJ's decision – "Because I've not yet had a minute to stop talking to journalists."[127]

The success of these framing efforts did not hinge solely on promoting knowledge of European law. A key "permissive condition"[128] for the success of Conte and Giacomini's public advocacy was the fact that they were able to mobilize diffuse public support for a European intervention. While admittedly latent and amorphous, tapping into this reservoir of support bolstered the likelihood that the ECJ's intervention would be well received by local stakeholders.

Three complementary forms of evidence point to the mobilization of public support for court-driven reforms. At the narrowest level, the parties to the suit publicly welcomed the intervention with varying degrees of enthusiasm. They argued that the ECJ had bolstered legal certainty and provided a blueprint for reform. The vice president of the national employers' association (Confindustria) underscored that the ECJ ruling "has the virtue of pushing away all the uncertainties

---

[122] Carozzi, Giorgio. 1991. "In porto finisce il monopolio." *Il Secolo XIX*, December 11; Carozzi, Giorgio. 1991. "Alla Cee picconate al buio." *Il Secolo XIX*, December 11, p. 11.

[123] Minella, Massimo. 1991. "Ecco le picconate della Cee." *Il Lavoro*, December 11.

[124] Capelli, Fausto. 1991. "Porti, alt Cee al monopolio dei camalli." *Il Giornale*, December 11.

[125] Dardani, Bruno. 1991. "Bangemann 'presenta' a Genova il piano Cee per la politica del mare." *Il Sole-24 ore*. December 14, p. 10.

[126] Conte, Giuseppe, and Giuseppe Giacomini. 1991. "Stop Europeo al monopolio nei porti." *Italia Oggi*, December 11, p. 12.

[127] Minella, "Imputata la legge."

[128] According to Soifer, "permissive conditions can be defined as those factors or conditions that change the underlying context to increase the causal power of agency or contingency and thus the prospects for divergence." See: Soifer, Hillel. 2012. "The Causal Logic of Critical Junctures." *Comparative Political Studies* 45(12): 1572–1597, at 1574.

and perplexities ... that conditioned political behavior working to reform the Italian port sector."[129] Leading shippers hailed the ruling as "clarifying the rules of the game, which had been costly and confused."[130] The president of the port authority told the press that "Genoa now has a unique opportunity to return to being an essential tool ... at the service of the economy of the EEC."[131] Even the leader of the *camalli* – Paride Batini – refrained from directly attacking the ECJ's judgment: "It's about time!" he declared a day after scrambling to make sense of the decision; the "game will now be played in the open."[132] That a diverse set of interested parties interpreted the ECJ's ruling as clarifying the rules of the game points to how pro-European framings were beginning to pierce through the opacity of EU law.

Second, newspapers across the ideological spectrum cast the ECJ's ruling in a broadly positive light. From the left, *La Repubblica* argued that "the preliminary ruling is essential" for "the most ancient heart of Genoese production [to] return to being the biggest industry of the city."[133] From the right, *Il Sole-24 ore* hailed the ruling as "ten extremely cogent and clear pages that reply to all the questions that for years have hung over the inefficiency of Italian ports."[134] And Genoa's *Il Secolo XIX* described general sentiment as hopeful that the "EEC judgment might translate itself into a clarifying driving force," since "the monopoly was misused. Today, it sounds like old language devoid of content, a social and economic anachronism."[135] Notice how these frames channeled Conte and Giacomini's advocacy by inverting the status quo: what was cast as "devoid of content" was no longer EU law, but local labor politics that had run their course.

Finally, diffuse support extended to the broader public as well. Conte and Giacomini underscored the "great interest" and "broad breath that [the ECJ ruling] has found in the people," hoping that it would "help them know our work" and convince them to support reform.[136] Even though this support was superficial, public opinion and street-level

---

[129] Dardani, Bruno. 1991. "Linea dura degli utenti portuali." *Il Sole-24 ore*, December 18, p. 10.

[130] Razzi, Massimo. 1991. "Il buio oltre la banchina." *Il Lavoro*, December 12.

[131] Dardani, "Bangemann 'presenta' a Genova."

[132] Carozzi, Giorgio. 1991. "Batini: Era ora!" *Il Secolo XIX*, December 13.

[133] Valentino, Piero. 1992. "Alt alla Concorrenza nel Porto di Genova." *La Repubblica*, April 19.

[134] Dardani, "Corte di Lussemburgo spazza il monopolio."

[135] Carozzi, "Era ora!"

[136] Minella, "Imputata la legge."

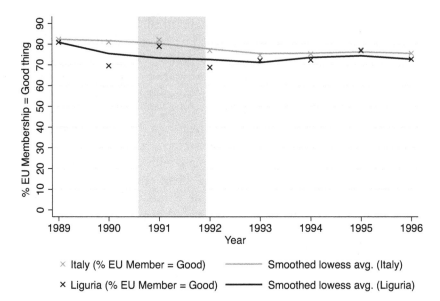

Figure 7.4 Percentage of Italians and Ligurians believing that EEC membership is a "good thing," 1989–1996
Notes: The gray shading denotes the dates from lodging of ECJ proceedings to judgment.
Source: Eurobarometer (1989–1996).

surveys confirmed that residents of Genoa were broadly supportive of European integration. First, *Eurobarometer* surveys taken as the Port of Genoa case unfolded suggest that approximately seven out of ten residents in the Liguria region deemed EEC membership to be "a good thing" (see Figure 7.4).

Second, everyday citizens interviewed by journalists in the streets of Genoa displayed remarkable awareness of the lawsuit and welcomed the ECJ's ruling. "We asked dozens of people … about their opinion of the judgment of the European Court of Justice," *Il Secolo XIX* reported the day after the decision was released; "Almost all those asked agreed to reply, and they often did so with an awareness of the lawsuit … on the merits, the general opinion is that this revolution can be a singular opportunity for rebirth, for the economy of the port, and thus for the entire city." Interview excerpts suggest as much: "It's a marvelous thing," declared the director of a public medical clinic; "I'm very favorable about the EEC ruling," a high school teacher responded; "I agree with the EEC judgment. The politics of the monopoly are unjust," noted the commander of the city firefighters; "We don't look too good, us Genoese, when it's the EEC that has to tidy things up for us," added the president of a retirement home; "In any case, this news has given me new faith in the future of our port."[137]

As *Il Secolo XIX* explained, Genoese residents were not only positively "judging the [ECJ's] judgment," but simultaneously "rediscovering traditions" of port-driven trade and labor politics. In so doing, they weaved the decontextualized language of the ECJ's judgment – which referred to the CULMV as if it were any other labor union and Genoa's port as if were any other important trade hub – within the fabric of local knowledge. This integration rendered the European Court's ruling intelligible and meaningful, cultivating a newfound awareness for transnational law and embedding it in the long shadow of local practice.[138] Even as the distant nature of EU law was perceived as the key to the speedy technocratic resolution of a local political quagmire, its "relocalization"[139] converted it back into meaningful knowledge to daily life.

Diffuse support for compliance bore the feedback effect of strengthening the ambitions of the resourceful interest groups that had been lobbying for port reform for years. The president of Genoa's port authority audaciously called on the Italian Parliament to enact an "urgent government law" to generalize the ECJ's ruling, transforming all public dockworkers' unions into "companies operating in a regime of free competition."[140] The leader of local shippers, Ugo Serra, claimed a mandate in the broadest possible terms: "The winner isn't us, but rather the law and the principles of the free market."[141] Indeed, some thirty shipping and transport associations would likely have foregone launching a political campaign titled "Genoa: Europe's Port" if they doubted that the public would be receptive.[142] And Genoa's social democratic mayor, Romano Merlo, would not have forcefully declared that "the judgment of Luxembourg should auspiciously bring newfound

---

[137] Carozzi, Giorgio.1991. "Caro, vecchio porto." *Il Secolo XIX*, December 12.
[138] On conceptualizing how new identities and practices are integrated within past cultural repertoires, see: Sewell, "Historical Events as Transformations of Structures."
[139] Miller, Clark. 2004. "Resisting Empire: Globalism, Relocalization, and the Politics of Knowledge." In *Earthly Politics*, Sheila Jasanoff and Marybeth Martello, eds. Cambridge, MA: MIT Press, at 83.
[140] Conte and Giacomini, "Stop Europeo."
[141] Ibid.
[142] Valentino, Piero. 1992. "La Guerra del Porto Deve Finire." *La Repubblica*, July 5.

serenity and new opportunities" if center-left voters did not generally side with the European Court.[143]

Local public support was thus bolstered by policymakers and interest groups rallying into compliance constituencies. In turn, this shifting political context marginalized dockworkers' delayed grumblings. After two days of vigorous internal debate over how to respond to the ruling, the CULMV was reduced to trying to turn the ECJ's decision against shippers by defining them as the "true" monopolists.[144] But when such delayed counter-framings gained little traction, the *camalli* resorted to their repertoire of contentious resistance, with stark unintended consequences.[145]

### 7.3.4 Europe's "Prima Donna": From Contention to Compliance

Having lost control of the way the ECJ decision was being framed in the public sphere, dockworkers decided to flex their muscles and make their displeasure clear. In March 1992, they sent a shot over the bow by organizing a brief strike that shut down all trade on the industrial port. Yet even as dockworkers grew intransigent, import–export and shipping companies began to the test the post-*Port of Genoa* waters.[146]

First, in April an association of shippers cited the "many damages that they incur from the *ancien regime*'s monopoly" by lodging a complaint with the European Commission requesting that it open an infringement proceeding against the Italian state.[147] Second, some shipping operators sought revenge for past defeats. None was more audacious than Bruno Musso, the CEO of Tarros. In 1970, Musso had attempted to dock one of his ships with his own crew, but "the CULMV threateningly surrounded him and his attempt failed." Musso had since transferred his activities to the nearby Port of La Spezia, and the ECJ's ruling was an irresistible opportunity "to return for a do-over."[148] So in June, he dispatched his fleet of ships for Genoa. This provoked "episodes of intimidation and violence"[149] – including a dockworker's

[143] Mattei, Elio. 1991. "Genova, regole di mercato anche per i 'camalli'." *Avanti!*, December 14, p. 22.
[144] Carozzi, "Era ora!"
[145] Mattei, "Regole di mercato."
[146] "Genova, l'Europa non va a Camallo." *La Repubblica*, March 6, 1992.
[147] Valentino, "Alt alla Concorrenza."
[148] Valentino, "da La Spezia un attacco ai camalli."
[149] Arcuri, Camillo. 1992. "Il fronte del porto in azione, nave bloccata." *Corriere della Sera*, June 18, p. 16.

attempt to hit Musso over the head with a large log.[150] The *camalli* forged human shields and disrupted the ships' entry (see Figure 7.5), forcing three of Musso's vessels to turn around within the span of a week.[151]

Despite such initial victories, the judicial winds were not in the dockworkers' favor. With national politics disrupted by the *Mani Pulite* (Clean Hands) anti-corruption investigations in Milan and Parliament characteristically slow to debate reforms of the Italian navigation code, a "government of judges" emerged to enforce the new legal regime.[152] So when dockworkers sued Musso before a local small claims judge – as Musso had strategically anticipated[153] – their plan backfired. Not only did Musso summon Conte and Giacomini to argue his case,[154] but the duo proved victorious once again as the judge, Alvaro Vigotti, "recognized Musso's right to [employ his own dockworkers] ... [because] the ruling of the ECJ in Luxembourg against port monopolies is valid, even in the absence of national antitrust legislation."[155] The fact that local public opinion was broadly supportive of compliance gave judges cover to apply EU law even if they were sympathetic to the dockworkers' cause. "That was truly a cultural moment, a cultural turn," Giacomini recalls, "because even judges who leaned left politically ... applied [EU] law! Even if they didn't like it very much."[156]

Having lost in courts of public opinion and courts of law, dockworkers resorted to an extreme, last-ditch act of contentious disobedience. For eighty grueling days from late August into early November of 1992, the CULMV orchestrated an unprecedented strike that shut down the nation's largest port.[157] The strike may have been cathartic for dockworkers, but with time it backfired spectacularly. After all, they might have still hoped for solidarity from other port employees and working class laborers. But by freezing dockwork for months, the

[150] Musso, *Cuore in Porto*, at 187.
[151] Valentino, Piero. 1992. "Porto di Genova, Tregua Tra Camalli e Armatori." *La Repubblica*, July 1.
[152] Valentino, "La Guerra del Porto."
[153] Arcuri, "fronte del porto in azione."
[154] Musso also retroactively paid the expenses the Euro-lawyers' incurred in the *Port of Genoa* case with support of the national shippers' association. See: Musso, *Porto di Genova*, at 58.
[155] "Il Pretore da Ragione a Musso." *La Repubblica*, July 21, 1992.
[156] Interview with Giuseppe Giacomini, November 2, 2016.
[157] Minella, Massimo. 1992. "La Pace è Arrivata in Porto, I Camalli Tornano al Lavoro." *La Repubblica*, November 7.

Top: Dockworkers blocking the arrival of one of Bruno Musso's ships, June 26, 1992;
Middle: CULMV leader Paride Batini addresses members, October 16, 1992;
Bottom right: Truckers protesting the CULMV's strike in Genoa, October 12, 1992

Figure 7.5 The CULMV's strike makes headlines in the *Corriere Della Sera*
*Sources:* Historical Archive of Fondazione Corriere Della Sera: Arcuri, Camillo. 1992.
"I camalli scaricati dalla storia." *Corriere Della Sera*, June 26, 1992, p. 16; Grondona,
Daniela. 1992. "A Genova cade il muro dei camalli." *Corriere Della Sera*, October 16,
1992, p. 24; Grondona, Daniela. 1992. "Genova invasa da autotreni per la protesta
anticamalli." *Corriere della Sera*, October 14, 1992, p. 14.

*camalli* threatened the jobs of all workers dependent on the port's supply chain. Thus in October truck drivers decrying how the CULMV's "arrogance" was placing their own livelihoods in jeopardy[158] protested in the streets for three days, blocking city traffic and calling for abolishing the dockworkers' monopoly rights. Other port laborers followed suit, threatening to indefinitely suspend their services lest the CULMV continue its strike. The police were dispatched to "avoid a confrontation," for "*camalli* and truckers clashed with their fists. Insults, shoving ... a few days later tensions escalated" anew.[159]

Rather than rallying the working class, the *camalli*'s reactive backlash campaign splintered it instead. Public calls to end the "war" on Genoa's docks grew as protest diffused to the city streets and impacted the lives of citizens with no direct ties to the port.[160] One interviewee recalls dumpsters being set on fire throughout the city.[161] Residents no longer perceived this as clash between righteous laborers and elite interests, which was a battle that the *camalli* had repeatedly won in the past. The dominant narrative had shifted: an entire city rallying around European law and against the perceived arrogance of a monopolistic enterprise endangering the public interest.

Eventually, Batini and the CULMV acquiesced, ending the strike and joining the bargaining table on November 7, 1992. Perhaps the tipping point proved to be the promise of a $7.5 million payment from Port Authority President Magnani.[162] Perhaps it was the threat of shippers abandoning Genoa altogether, taking 60,000 containers' worth of annual traffic with them.[163] Regardless, what is clear is that the CULMV had sustained nearly a year's worth of bad press, alienated public opinion, and turned natural working class allies against it. In just over a year, the CULMV's status as custodian of local history had been disenchanted.

November 1992 thus marked the transition from contestation to compliance, culminating in the 1994 reform of the Italian Navigation

[158] Grondona, Daniela. 1992. "Genova invasa da autotreni per la protesta antica-malli." *Corriere della Sera*, October 14, p. 14.
[159] Minella, "Genova in Ginocchio"; Razzi, Massimo. 1992. "I Camalli in Mare Aperto." *La Repubblica*, November 29.
[160] Valentino, "La Guerra del Porto."
[161] Interview with Gerolamo Taccogna, lawyer and law professor at the University of Genoa, October 28, 2016 (in-person).
[162] Minella, "Pace è Arrivata in Porto."
[163] Minella, "Genova in Ginocchio."

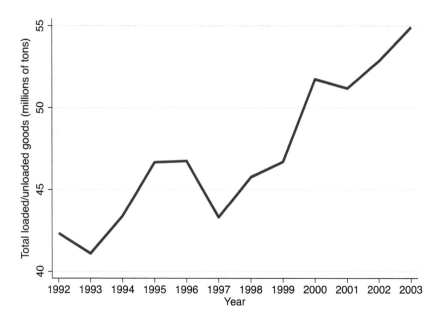

Figure 7.6 Total loaded and unloaded goods in the Port of Genoa, 1992–2003
*Source:* Comune di Genova (2003: 145).

Code[164] after "two nightmare years ... [when] every two months ...
the text would change."[165] The reform finalized the liberalization of
the Port of Genoa along the model of an Anglo-Saxon port authority.[166] Like other north European ports, private shipping operators were
allowed to compete for control of specialized sections of the Port.[167]
And dockworkers from across Europe were allowed to organize into
their own unions and compete with the CULMV over the provision of
labor.

Yet policy change was just the tip of the iceberg, for *Port of Genoa*
became a catalyst for economic reform and legal mobilization. In the
decade following the ECJ's ruling, the port experienced an increase
in traffic of 30 percent (from 42.3 million to 54.9 million tons of
goods; see Figure 7.6). A city council report argued that the port

---

[164] See: Legge 28 gennaio 1994, no. 84, "Riordino della legislazione in materia
portuale."

[165] Musso, *Cuore in Porto,* at 187.

[166] Carbone, Sergio, and Francesco Munari. 1994. "La legge italiana di riforma dei
porti ed il diritto comunitario." *Il Foro Italiano* 114(4): 367–392.

[167] Musso, *Cuore in Porto,* at 147.

had "exited from the long and dark tunnel of the recession and its 'numbers' had returned to being those of a great European port."[168] In 1994, Genoa surpassed Marseille in container traffic and beat all Mediterranean competitors in passenger traffic.[169] By 1997, even left-wing newspapers were lauding the "brilliant results" of liberalization.[170] By 2001 the port had grown to directly or indirectly employ 35 percent of the city's working population and to comprise 11 percent of its GDP.[171] And with revenues on the increase, the late 1990s witnessed the "transformation and technological updating of the port infrastructure."[172]

Unfortunately the tide did not raise all boats: dockworkers bore the brunt of the distributional consequences of socio-legal change. With their monopoly rights gone, rising competition from foreign laborers, and the port authority investing in new technologies that replaced manpower with machine power, membership suffered. From 1991 to 1995, the CULMV's numbers plummeted from 1,497 to 689.[173] And when their legendary *console* – Paride Batini – passed away in 2009, journalists realized that, in fact, "the *camalli* have nearly disappeared."[174]

If the port's modest economic recovery proved a gradual transformation, *Port of Genoa*'s crash course in European law immediately diffused a transnational legal consciousness among local practitioners. Giacomini is unsurprisingly adamant that EU law only became "real" in Genoa after the lawsuit: "*Port of Genoa* is so well-known that it certainly drew the attention even of those lawyers who didn't even know that EU law existed.... If we hadn't existed, Conte and Giacomini, EU law would have arrived here with at least a decade of delay."[175] But we need not take Giacomini's word for it. In interviews with a diverse array of practitioners – including a maritime lawyer, competition lawyer, family lawyer, administrative lawyer, and

---

[168] Comune di Genova, *Numeri e La Storia del Porto di Genova*, at 145.
[169] Minella, Massimo. 1994. "Il Porto di Genova Risorge, Traffici Record Nel 1994." *La Repubblica*, December 14.
[170] Minella, Massimo. 1997. "Genova, Prima nel Mediterraneo." *La Repubblica*, April 1.
[171] Lampani, Aldo. 2001. "Un Genovese su Tre Lavora sui Moli." *La Repubblica*, February 3.
[172] Comune di Genova, *Numeri e La Storia del Porto di Genova*, at 14.
[173] Musso, *Porto di Genova*, at 46.
[174] Cevasco, "Tra i finti docks."
[175] Interview with Giuseppe Giacomini, October 24 and 26, 2017.

labor judge[176] – all stressed that the lawsuit "transformed a city" and persuaded them to take EU law seriously.[177] The president of Genoa's bar association recalls how he and his colleagues recognized the lawsuit's importance: "Its importance was immediately understood because ... the port is the heart of the city ... Newspapers debated it, because there were historical precedents everyone knew about ... and [the *camalli*'s practices] were known to everyone. They held the port back."[178]

Across conversations with Genoese jurists, *Port of Genoa* was repeatedly referenced as a blueprint for legal mobilization. Consider the representative views of two lawyers – Gerolamo Taccogna, who teaches and practices administrative law, and Andrea La Mattina, who teaches and practices competition law:

> The ruling of the Court of Justice transformed a city ... then there were preliminary references in the wake of that judgment.... The problematics of the port first and most completely taught the judges of the Tribunal of Genoa how to do these things. And once you know how, you also have more occasions to do so.[179]

> When talking about preliminary references [to the ECJ], undoubtedly the so-called *Port of Genoa* ruling played an important and driving role.... It transformed the Italian approach to port law. Other important preliminary references always dealt with the same sector ... that is, a whole series of further precisions that were fundamental and all originated from Genoa.[180]

Some lawyers went so far as to sketch the contours of a hybrid field of law rooted in the city in the post-*Port of Genoa* era: "Genoese EU competition law."[181] That some would recognize this as a coherent

---

[176] Interview with Pierangelo Celle, Studio Legale Turci and law professor at the University of Genoa, October 19, 2016 (in-person); Interview with Francesco Munari, Munari Giudici Maniglio Panfili Associati and law professor at the University of Genoa, October 24, 2016 (in-person); Interview with Alberto Figone, Studio Figone, October 27, 2016, (in-person); Interview with Roberto Damonte, Studio Legale Damonte, October 28, 2016 (in-person); Interview with Marcello Basilico, judge at the Tribunal of Genoa, October 18, 2016 (in-person).

[177] Interview with Gerolamo Taccogna, October 28, 2016.

[178] Interview with Alessandro Vaccaro, November 2, 2016.

[179] Interview with Gerolamo Taccogna, October 28, 2016.

[180] Interview with Andrea La Mattina, BonelliErede and law professor at the University of Genoa, November 14, 2016 (in-person).

[181] Interview with Enrico Vergani, Studio Legale Garbarino Vergani and law professor at the University of Genoa, October 27, 2016 (in-person).

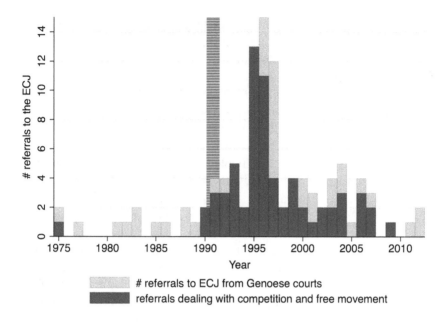

Figure 7.7  Referrals to the ECJ from Genoese courts, 1975–2013
*Notes:* The gray dashed shading denotes the dates spanning ECJ proceedings.

legal field is a testament to the ways that Euro-lawyers had incorporated EU law and the ECJ's ruling within the "social ordering that is indigenous" to Genoa.[182]

Litigation statistics corroborate lawyers' perceptions that the *Port of Genoa* case proved a catalyst of a "feedback loop" of litigation and judicial policymaking.[183] In the decade following the case (1992–2002), Genoese courts referred sixty-four preliminary references to the ECJ, or five times the number ($n = 12$) that they had submitted over the prior three decades (see Figure 7.7). Furthermore, 78 percent ($n = 50$) of these references dealt with those EU competition and free movement rules at the heart of *Port of Genoa*. Some of the most important cases in this period witnessed the return of this chapter's protagonists. For example, Conte and Giacomini were once again on the attack in the 1993/1994 *Corsica Ferries* case[184] expanding the freedom to provide maritime transport services, and Alvaro Vigotti –

---

[182] Galanter, "Radiating Effects of Courts," at 129.
[183] Stone Sweet and Brunell, "European Court and National Courts," at 16–22.
[184] Case C-18/93, *Corsica Ferries Italia Srl v. Corpo dei Piloti del Porto di Genova* [1994], ECR I-1812.

the labor judge who first enforced the ECJ's ruling against the *camalli* – was the referring judge in the pathbreaking 2003/2006 *Traghetti del Mediterraneo* case[185] that broadened the state's liability for breaches of EU law. Importantly, however, legal mobilization expanded, as 77 percent of local court referrals to the ECJ in the decade following *Port of Genoa* were solicited by lawyers other than Conte and Giacomini. As one Genoese lawyer puts it, EU law became "a lived reality, and not just an exam one took at the university."[186]

Unsurprisingly, the most reliable allies were those judges at the Tribunal of Genoa who had witnessed their president collaborate with Conte and Giacomini in the *Port of Genoa* case. One judge in particular – Michele Marchesiello – became a reliable entrepreneur:[187] to "measure oneself" with the ECJ was "prestigious," "pique[d] his curiosity, and also energize[d] him," he recalls.[188] Crediting Euro-lawyers like Conte and Giacomini for "opening the prospective" of soliciting the ECJ, Marchesiello even wrote a book about globalization arguing that "the European Court of Justice had to intervene to awaken Italian ports – Genoa's first and foremost – from their sleep," thereby promoting a "dramatically inevitable transformation."[189] And before retiring, Marchesiello played an important role in "transmitting" his passion for EU law to his colleagues.[190] In the two decades following *Port of Genoa*, the Tribunal referred sixty cases to the ECJ. To put this in perspective, that is more than twice the number issued by any other Italian civil court of first instance during the entire sixty-year span of the Treaty of Rome.[191]

And so it was that Genoa was transformed into a laboratory for Europeanization and judicial policymaking. After *Port of Genoa*, local law firms became "trendy" when they "surface[d] EU law-related questions," and lower court judges referred cases to the ECJ "with great

---

[185] Case C-173/03, *Traghetti del Mediterraneo SpA v. Repubblica Italiana* [2006], ECR I-5177.

[186] Interview with Pierangelo Celle, October 19, 2016.

[187] Interview with Paolo Canepa, Studio Legale Roppo Canepa, November 3, 2017 (in-person).

[188] Interview with Michele Marchesiello, November 10, 2016.

[189] Marchesiello, *La Città Portuale*, at 165–166.

[190] Interview with Lorenza Calcagno, Tribunal of Genoa, November 8, 2016 (in-person).

[191] The second-most referring lower court is the Tribunal of Milan, with twenty-nine references.

frequency ... [for] the judges were happy, as it were, to serve as the ECJ's *prima donna.*"[192]

## 7.4 THE COMPLICATED LEGACIES OF COMPLIANCE

I want to close this chapter by acknowledging the complicated legacy of compliance and Europeanization that *Port of Genoa* left behind, a legacy that is hardly unique. Even when court-driven change triumphs over a politics of backlash, unintended consequences may only surface with the passing of time.

For instance, in the United States during the 1960s and 1970s, civil rights lawyers called for the enforcement of the 1964 Civil Rights Act to desegregate labor unions. Elected officials stonewalled and resisted these demands, so lawyers turned to the courts.[193] Judges proved more receptive to lawyers' calls for change, yet they did not fully appreciate how "even the most discriminatory of unions, if reformed, could serve to benefit civil rights causes down the road."[194] As unions' court losses and financial penalties piled up, the unintended consequence proved to be the "weakening of the chief opposition to free market capitalism."[195]

A strikingly similar leitmotif suffuses the *Port of Genoa* case. To be sure, the city's modest economic recovery and the ability of foreign laborers to work in Italy's largest port were profound achievements. Yet it did not turn out to be true that Genoa's centenarian union of dockworkers would survive liberalization unscathed, and that the tide of court-driven change would lift all boats.

In January 2018, I was invited to discuss an early draft of this chapter at Genoa's city hall, where dockworkers and truckers had clashed nearly three decades prior. The *Port of Genoa* case clearly continues to conjure up powerful memories. Midway through the conference, the longtime journalist for *Il Secolo XIX*, Giorgio Carozzi, delivered his prepared remarks. Carozzi lamented how the more pragmatic touch of political negotiation had been unable to resolve the port's crisis, such that the only way out was to turn to the adversarial rigidity of European

---

[192] Interview with Francesco Munari, October 24, 2016.

[193] Frymer, "Acting When Elected Officials Won't."

[194] See: Frymer, Paul. 2008. *Black and Blue: African Americans, the Labor Movement, and the Decline of the Democratic Party.* Princeton, NJ: Princeton University Press, at 41, 15.

[195] Ibid., at 25.

law.[196] Twenty years ago, Carozzi's lament would have seemed out of place. Today, it strikes a more perceptive note: as the winners and losers of the judicial construction of Europe crystallize over time, the legacies of court-driven change can instead become cloudier, as law's triumphs are complicated and reinterpreted by "the light of new history making."[197]

---

[196] For local coverage of the event, see: Scorza, Angelo. 2018. "Occhi americani puntati sul porto di Genova." *Ship2Shore*, January 19.

[197] Castells, Manuel. 1997. "An Introduction to the Information Age." *City* 6: 2–16, at 16.

CHAPTER EIGHT

# EURO-LAWYERING GOES SILENT
## Resistance, Conspiracy, and the Politics of Backlash

> *Not that I hadn't understood that my brother was refusing to come down*
> *for now, but I pretended not to understand in order to force him to*
> *declare himself, to say, "Yes, I wish to remain in the trees until teatime,*
> *or until sunset, or until dinnertime, or until it's dark" – something that,*
> *in other words, would mark a limit, a proportion to his act of protest.*
> *But he said nothing of the sort, and I felt a little afraid.*
> —Italo Calvino, *The Baron in the Trees*[1]

## 8.1 THE DEATH OF A GIANT

In an olive grove near Alliste – a tiny sun-drenched town nestled within the heel of Italy's boot – Enzo Manni, the director of an olive oil cooperative, leads a group of Americans toward a baobab-like tree whose trunk's circumference spans 25 feet. It is the "Giant of Alliste," a living monument thought to be 1,500 years old that attracts a small yearly following of tourists and olive oil aficionados.[2] But these Americans are neither: they are journalists covering an emergent crisis.

"There are many ... here, here," remarks Manni, pointing down to tiny drops of spit on the grass. Within the globs lie nascent spittlebugs, the vectors of a deadly pathogen that, until two years prior in 2013, had never been detected in Europe: *Xylella fastidiosa*. Just like coronaviruses "kee[p] oxygen from reaching our vital organs," this bacterium restricts water flow in the plant it infects, turning its leaves brown as it slowly dries to death.[3] Manni gestures back up at the giant: glorious and healthy at first glance, one branch's curled-up leaves foreshadow its fate. It is as if the tree were "having a slow stroke" notes Ettore, a local

---

[1] Calvino, Italo. 2017. *The Baron in the Trees*. New York, NY: Houghton Mifflin Harcourt, at 31.
[2] Yardley, Jim. 2015. "Fear of Ruin as Disease Takes Hold of Italy's Olive Trees." *The New York Times*, May 11; Serravezza, Flavia. 2016. "*Xylella*, il 'gigante' di Alliste in agonia." *La Gazzetta del Mezzogiorno*, August 18.
[3] Kakissis, Joanna. 2020. "Southern Europe Could Lose $22 Billion Fighting Deadly Olive Tree Disease." *NPR*, May 3.

279

Figure 8.1 Olive groves in Puglia in 2016 (a) and 2019 (b) after dying of *Xylella*
*Sources:* "File:Ostuni olive grove SS379-3339.jpg" by Isiwal; "File:Olivenhain mit
Xylella fastidiosa bei Surano LE 190710.jpg" by Sjor. Both photos licensed with
CC BY-SA 4.0.

olive oil producer; "It is devastating ... apocalyptic," Manni adds.[4]
A year later, the Giant of Alliste had shriveled to death.[5]

The giant was hardly alone. It lay at the epicenter of an epidemic
afflicting the Salento region of Puglia that would kill 10 million olive
trees, cost 100,000 jobs, produce 1.2 billion euros in damages, and surge
world olive oil prices by 20 percent.[6] As vast expanses of formerly lush
groves desiccated into sickly cemeteries (see Figure 8.1), apocalyptic
analogies proliferated. "The drama of *Xylella fastidiosa,*" a local judge
told me, "is lived by farmers ... as a sort of biblical plague."[7]

Yet biblical comparisons were not the only narratives that diffused
to make sense of crisis. A "language of contention"[8] soon directed its
ire at the European Union (EU) and the European Court. But why?
The answer reveals the bottom-up politics via which EU law is cast as
a threat to daily life, provoking rebellions in public squares and local
courthouses. Compared to the *Port of Genoa* case in Chapter 7, the
*Xylella* case illuminates how failures to reconcile disruptive laws with

---

[4] Yardley, "Fear of Ruin."
[5] Serravezza, "il 'gigante' di Alliste in agonia."
[6] Borunda, Alejandra. 2018. "Italy's Olive Trees Are Dying." *National Geographic,*
August 10; Vasilopoulos, Costas. 2019. "Thousands of Jobs Lost in Italian Olive Oil
Sector, Farmers Group Warns." *Olive Oil Times,* May 6; "Xylella, già 1,2 mld di danni,
tempi certi per il decreto." Coldiretti, January 8, 2019. Available at: www.coldiretti.it/
economia/xylella-gia-12-mld-danni-temp-certi-decreto; Kinver, Mark. 2016. "Olive
Disease Arrives on Mallorca." *BBC News,* November 21.
[7] Interview with Teresa Liuni, May 18, 2017.
[8] Tarrow, *Language of Contention.*

local knowledge can foment conspiracy, foster backlash, and frustrate compliance with seemingly well-entrenched legal orders.

The outbreak of *Xylella* amid Puglia's olive groves sparked controversy and local political gridlock. At the supranational level, the European Commission and the European Court of Justice (ECJ) soon stepped in to forestall the pathogen's march to other member states by mandating the eradication of thousands of olive trees. Yet given their limited outreach to local stakeholders and lackluster appreciation of olive trees' cultural significance, the EU's containment efforts backfired, sparking a farmers' revolt that reframed an epidemic as a massacre and called for deliberate acts of resistance. At first glance, this sequence of events mirrors the *Port of Genoa* case. Just as Genoa's centenarian union of dockworkers was ready to fight to defend its place in local history, centenarian olive trees in Puglia have long served as symbolic embodiments of local culture and agricultural life. It is hardly surprising that farmers would reflexively rally to protect their groves from legal decisions "descend[ing] on the everyday as an all-powerful outsider."[9]

Yet as the *Port of Genoa* case illustrates, noncompliance in the wake of backlash is hardly an inevitable legacy. Contentious resistance became entrenched in Puglia because nobody sought to negotiate the controversy through interpretive mediation until it was too late. After all, the *Xylella* case germinated in a "cold spot" of European legal mobilization (see Chapter 6) where local lawyers seldom invoke EU law and judges habitually ignore the authority of the ECJ. This time there were no Euro-lawyers to proactively solicit a European intervention, to vernacularize EU law in the press in a way that resonated with local stakeholders, and to rally judges and the public toward compliance by framing it as an opportunity for rebirth. In fact, some local lawyers and judges even joined resistance efforts and began to traffic in conspiracy. By the time the devastating consequences of inaction became clear, a legal consciousness forged upon everyday acts "against the law"[10] was as commonplace in court as in the streets.

In short, it was not just sickly olive trees that desiccated across southern Italy. The *Xylella* case places in sharp relief how the top-down

---

[9] Sarat and Kearns, *Law in Everyday Life*, at 5.
[10] Ewick, Patricia, and Susan Silbey. 1998. *The Common Place of Law: Stories from Everyday Life*. Chicago, IL: University of Chicago Press, at 28.

application of disruptive European rules can trigger a "politics of resentment"[11] corroding the EU's capacity to govern through law and courts.

## 8.2 THE *XYLELLA* CASE

### 8.2.1 Crisis, Gridlock, and "the Coronavirus of Olive Trees"

What plant virologists describe as "the coronavirus of olive trees"[12] arrived in Europe through the import of infected plants from Costa Rica into Italy.[13] In other words, just as the global shift to services and finance deepened an economic crisis underlying the *Port of Genoa* case, so did the globalization of trade in plants underlie the phytosanitary crisis in the *Xylella* case. Yet in both cases, the critical antecedents of a politics of backlash were predominantly local. In Genoa, it was the conflict between the protectionist practices of a local labor union and the liberalizing thrust of EU law. In Puglia, it was the chasm between the speedy yet dispassionate management of the *Xylella* crisis at the European level and the political gridlock and communal trauma festering at the local level.

Well before the *Xylella* outbreak had claimed the Giant of Alliste, the pathogen had raised serious alarm among plant virologists at the University of Bari. The researchers had first detected its presence near Gallipoli in September 2013 using a battery of tests.[14] "We were hoping it was a laboratory artifact,"[15] one of these scientists recalls, yet "unfortunately they found it," another adds somberly.[16]

The scientists' sense of alarm was warranted. In the Americas where *Xylella* originated,[17] it diffused so rapidly that eradication became impossible. In Brazil, annual crop losses amount to a staggering 36

---

[11] Cramer, *Politics of Resentment.*

[12] Kakissis, "Southern Europe Could Lose $22 Billion."

[13] Colella, Christian, Roberto Carradore, and Andrea Cerroni, 2019. "Problem Setting and Problem Solving in the Case of Olive Quick Decline Syndrome in Apulia, Italy." *Phytopathology Review* 109(2): 187–199, at 191.

[14] See: Saponari, Maria, Donato Boscia, Franco Nigro, and Giovanni Martelli, 2013. "Identification of DNA Sequences Related to *Xylella fastidiosa* in Oleander, Almond and Olive Trees Exhibiting Leaf Scorch Symptoms in Apulia (Southern Italy)." *Journal of Plant Pathology* 95: 668.

[15] Colella et al., "Problem Setting and Problem Solving," at 191.

[16] The scientist quoted here is Giovanni Martelli of the University of Bari. See: *Terra!* "A Macchia d'Olio," directed by Claudio Branchino. Mediaset [Rete 4], November 6, 2017.

[17] See: Wells, John, Bligala Raju, Hsueh-Yun Hung, William Weisburg, Linda Mandelco-Paul, and Don Brenner, 1987. "*Xylella fastidiosa* gen. nov., sp. nov.: Gram-

percent and cause $100 million in annual damages to its citrus industry alone.[18] In California the price tag for crop losses to its vineyards is $104 million.[19] The pathogen's transatlantic crossing to a EU whose *raison d'être* lay in dismantling barriers to trade and free movement was akin to lighting a match in a barn full of kindling.

This threat was hardly lost on EU officials. The European Commission describes *Xylella* as "one of the most dangerous plant bacteria worldwide."[20] Alarmed by the devastation it wrought upon the Americas, in 2000 the Council of the EU classified the pathogen as a prohibited "organis[m] harmful to plants or plant products" in Annex I of Council Directive 2000/29/EC. The directive requires member states to inform the Commission should *Xylella* be detected in their territory (Article 16.1), empowering the latter to decide which measures should be taken to contain or eradicate the pathogen (Articles 16–19).[21] Hence once the Commission was alerted of *Xylella's* presence in Puglia on October 21, 2013, it quickly mobilized its repertoire for technocratic management of the EU's single market.[22]

The Commission's first response was to solicit an urgent scientific opinion from the European Food Safety Authority (EFSA) following the procedure laid down in Regulation 178/2002.[23] It asked EFSA to identify the list of potential host plants, the vectors of diffusion, and proposed countermeasures. EFSA responded a few weeks later, concluding that "there is an urgent need to put in place measures to prevent the spread of this harmful organism into other parts of the Union." It identified hundreds of plant species as potential hosts, spittlebugs with a flight range of 100 meters as the natural vector of diffusion, and it sought additional time to recommend countermea-

Negative, Xylem-Limited, Fastidious Plant Bacteria Related to *Xanthomonas* spp." *International Journal of Systematic and Evolutionary Microbiology* 37(2): 136–143.

[18] Luivisi, Andrea, Francesca Nicolì, and Luigi de Belli, 2017. "Sustainable Management of Plant Quarantine Pests: The Case of Olive Quick Decline Syndrome." *Sustainability* 9: 659–678, at 666.

[19] Yardley, "Fear of Ruin."

[20] Borunda, "Italy's Olive Trees Are Dying."

[21] Council Directive 2000/29/EC of 8 May 2000. *Official Journal of the European Communities*, L169/1.

[22] EFSA. 2013. "Statement of EFSA on Host Plants, Entry and Spread Pathways and Risk Reduction Options for *Xylella fastidiosa* Wells et al." *EFSA Journal* 11(11): 3468, at 4.

[23] Regulation 178/2002 of the European Parliament and the Council of 28 January 2002. *Official Journal of the European Communities*, L31/1.

sures.[24] In the meantime, in February 2014 the Commission issued a provisional decision prohibiting the "movement, out of the province of Lecce, region of Apulia, Italy, of plants" to other areas of the common market, since the pathogen was "likely to spread rapidly and widely."[25] Following scientific reports confirming the spread of Xylella,[26] in July the Commission established a buffer zone around the outbreak epicenter where phytosanitary testing had to immediately take place.[27]

By January 2015, EFSA had solicited dozens of scientists to update the Commission. Confirming that the Italian Xylella strain was a variant of a preexisting American subspecies,[28] it explained that since "the literature yielded no indication that eradication is a successful option once the disease is established," the Commission should refocus its efforts on preventing diffusion.[29] In particular, eradication of "asymptomatic plants found infected based on sensitive laboratory tests and [of] neighbouring plants" would have a "high" degree of effectiveness if implemented quickly.[30] The result was another – and ultimately the most fateful – Commission decision in May 2015. While all hope of eradication was lost in the outbreak epicenter, the Commission directed Italian authorities within the surrounding buffer zone to "immediately remove" all plants "within a radius of 100 meters around the plants which have been tested and found to be infected."[31]

The Commission's decision to prioritize consultations with EFSA scientists made sense from a legal and technocratic point of view. Yet its negligible outreach of local stakeholders blinded it to the social trauma that widespread tree eradication would unleash. First, the on-the-ground optics of removal measures were far from favorable: they would predominantly target healthy-looking plants in the buffer zone rather

[24] EFSA, "Statement of EFSA on Host Plants," at 3; 8; 26.
[25] Commission Implementing Decision of 13 February 2014. *Official Journal of the European Union*, L45/29.
[26] Cariddi, Corrado, et al. 2014. "Isolation of a Xylella fastidiosa Strain Infecting Olive and Oleander in Apulia, Italy." *Journal of Plant Pathology* 96: 425–429.
[27] Commission Implementing Decision of 23 July 2014. *Official Journal of the European Union*, L219/56.
[28] EFSA. 2015. "Scientific Opinion on the Risk to Plant Health Posed by Xylella fastidiosa in the EU Territory, with the Identification and Evaluation of Risk Reduction Options." *EFSA Journal* 13(1): 3989, at 39.
[29] Ibid., at 117–118.
[30] Ibid., at 96–97; 102.
[31] Commission Implementing Decision (EU) 2015/789 of 18 May 2015. *Official Journal of the European Communities* L125, at Article 6.

than sickly trees in the outbreak epicenter, since newly afflicted trees often do not show visible symptoms of *Xylella* during their incubation period.[32] And a 100 meter radius not only encompassed spittlebugs' flight distance; it also cut across many family-owned groves.

But most importantly, treating olive trees exclusively as an object of phytosanitary regulation ignored their symbolic resonance in Italian society. When the country's party system collapsed in the early 1990s, the center-left's political leader, Romano Prodi, famously invoked the olive tree's image of resilience in the face of crisis: the olive "is the outcome of hundreds of years of human labor, [and] is contorted because it has the strength to resist even the most severe weather."[33] Such sentiments are especially deeply rooted in the southern region of Puglia, where 60 million olive trees outnumber people by 15 to 1.[34] Not only do these trees generate 40 percent of Italy's olive oil,[35] but they lie at the heart of communal identity and agricultural life. Puglia's regional flag features a single olive tree, "representing not only one of the most precious resources of Puglia's agriculture, but also a constant element of the landscape that becomes a symbol of unity of the entire region, from north to south."[36] This official status is reinforced by the many daily rituals revolving around olive trees. "These olive trees have sustained and enriched us for centuries," explains Corrado, a farmer in the town of Ostuni in a 2017 interview; "They're the ones that constituted me, my parents, my grandparents. All of us have lived thanks to these trees."[37] Many southern Italian farmers plant an olive tree to mark the birth of a child, converting their groves into living embodiments of their own families.[38]

Local policymakers thus found themselves caught in a bind to which the Commission remained blissfully unaware. To be sure, Puglia's elected officials initially hoped that a European intervention could "justify measures that would have [otherwise] been politically

[32] Colella et al., "Problem Setting and Problem Solving," at 192.
[33] Gilbert, Mark. 1996. "The Oak Tree and the Olive Tree." *Italian Politics* 111: 101–117, at 103.
[34] Donati, Silvia. 2016. "On the 'Olive Oil Road' in Puglia." *Italy magazine*, July 14.
[35] Pergament, Danielle. 2015. "Italy's Treasured Olive Oil, at the Source." *The New York Times*, May 22.
[36] "Stemma Della Puglia." Regione Puglia, December 1, 2012. Available at: www.regionepuglia.org/stemma/.
[37] Quoted in: *Terra!* "A Macchia d'Olio," November 6, 2017.
[38] Martin, Glen. 2016. "What's Killing the Great Olive Groves of Apulia?" *California Magazine*, August 15.

incomprehensible and certainly lacking in public consensus."[39] Videoconferences between regional and Commission officials were described as an "SOS to Europe."[40] Two members of the European Parliament from Puglia wrote a letter to the Commission "to ask Europe for an immediate intervention,"[41] while another local politician traveled to Brussels to lobby for "the EU's contribution, in terms of scientific and economic support."[42]

Yet this political behavior was less indicative of diffuse public support for the EU than a smoke screen from the gridlock that was frustrating local efforts to respond to crisis. The platform of the ruling center-left Democratic Party (PD) seemed premised on doing nothing in the absence of "scientific certainty."[43] The center-right Forza Italia (FI) party deplored the "interminable empty roundabouts" that had precluded "a single euro [from being] sent to farmers."[44] Yet amid growing "disorder and tumult" in the regional parliament, legislation to raise funds to assuage farmers' damages was repeatedly defeated.[45]

As Puglia's parliament devolved into a circular firing squad, concerned farmers criticized Italian officials "for reacting too slowly"[46] and only offering up "words and superficiality."[47] Yet at the same time they were equally suspicious of a transnational intervention coordinated from Brussels, particularly in the aftermath of the sovereign debt crisis and the painful EU-backed austerity measures that followed.[48] In contrast to *Port of Genoa* where political gridlock unfolded as 70–80 percent of the local population supported EU membership, as the *Xylella* outbreak began less than 40 percent of local respondents viewed the EU in a positive light (see Figure 8.2). Thus it did not

[39] Interview with Giovanni Pesce, Studio Legale BDL in Rome, August 18, 2017 (via Skype).
[40] "Peste degli ulivi in videoconferenza l'Sos all'Europa." *La Repubblica*, November 19, 2013.
[41] "Dal Governo 5mln per l'emergenza degli ulivi salentini." *Gazzetta del Mezzogiorno*, December 1, 2013.
[42] "Stefano (Sel): dossier a Bruxelles." *Gazzetta del Mezzogiorno*, November 14, 2013.
[43] "Non toccate gli ulivi, e no a bombardamento con farmaci e pesticidi." *Gazzetta del Mezzogiorno*, August 23, 2014.
[44] "Mozione di sfiducia di Fi." *Gazzetta del Mezzogiorno*, October 22, 2014.
[45] "Contro la moria degli ulivi." *Gazzetta del Mezzogiorno*, 31 July, 2014.
[46] Yardley, "Fear of Ruin."
[47] "Troppi ritardi per fronteggiare la 'Xylella fastidiosa'." *Villaggio Globale*, August 12, 2014.
[48] Bull, Martin. 2018. "In the Eye of the Storm." *South European Society and Politics* 23(1): 13–28.

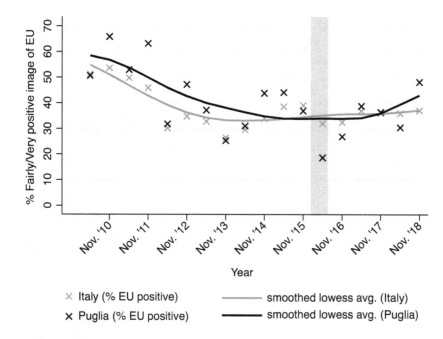

Figure 8.2 Percentage of Italians and Apulians with a positive image of the EU, 2010–2018
*Notes*: The gray shading denotes the dates spanning ECJ proceedings in the *Xylella* case.
*Source*: Eurobarometer (2010–2018).

take long for local grievance to refocus on Europe as soon as the Commission began ordering tree eradications in 2015.

### 8.2.2 Mobilizing Resistance and Reframing Epidemic as Massacre

As residents in rural communities harbor a growing sense of distributive injustice and of not being heard, they constitute a fertile terroir for populist indignation channeling what Katherine Cramer calls "politics of resentment."[49] It is precisely such a contentious politics that was triggered by efforts to enforce European law in the *Xylella* crisis.

Storm clouds began to gather over compliance efforts when a local environmental NGO released a highly publicized report to the EU health commissioner refuting EFSA's findings and accusing the

---

[49] Cramer, *Politics of Resentment*; Call, Samantha, and Seth Jolly. 2020. "Euroscepticism in the Populism Era." *The Journal of Politics* 82(1): e7–e12.

Commission of "condemning to death the whole Apulia eco-system."[50] The NGO supported its claims with undated YouTube videos claiming to demonstrate that better soil treatment and tree pruning would suffice to nurse sick trees back to the health.[51] The report prompted EFSA to reiterate that "an excessive pruning might enhance the contamination … since [it] can infect the plant through wounds if the wounds are unprotected."[52] Yet these top-down rebuttals belied a bottom-up trend: the profusion of local framings contesting claims to expertise and attributing blame to European institutions.

Even more alarming were anonymous allegations that *Xylella* had been deliberately unleashed by local and EFSA-affiliated scientists that began flooding Bari's police headquarters by summer 2014.[53] While national scientific associations[54] defended their colleagues, these conspiracies were reported by local newspapers and crystallized popular distrust of scientific claims to authority.

These narratives began reframing *Xylella* from an epidemic into a transnational massacre aided and abetted by the EU. As these frames diffused, local judges and politicians faced increasing pressure from "all sides" to call EU legal obligations into question.[55] For instance, when farmers confronted the president of the Puglia region – the center left's Michele Emiliano – in front of reporters, Emiliano flipped from declaring "no alternative"[56] to compliance to promising to "go to Brussels himself to defend Salento's olive trees."[57] Politicians affiliated with the anti-establishment Five Star Movement organized a march through olive groves to mobilize opposition to tree removal.[58] And a few mayors joined the ruckus by calling on local prosecutors to inves-

---

[50] Armellini, Alvise. 2015. "EU Divided over Italy's Olive Tree Disease." *EU Observer*, March 2015.

[51] EFSA. 2015. "Response to Scientific and Technical Information Provided by an NGO on *Xylella fastidiosa*." *EFSA Journal* 13(4): 4082, at 4.

[52] Ibid., at 9.

[53] Abbott, "Italian Scientists Vilified."

[54] Ibid.; "La xylella dagli insetti, i laboratori non c'entrano." *La Repubblica*, June 14, 2016.

[55] Drogo, Giovanni. 2019. "Xylella, la Procura di Lecce smentisce se stessa e l'inchiesta viene archiviata." *Next Quotidiano*, May 7.

[56] Chiumarulo, Vincenzo. 2015. "Xylella, il Tar blocca anche il Piano Silletti bis." October 13.

[57] Spagnolo, Chiara. 2016. "Xylella, la Ue mette di nuovo sotto accusa l'Italia." *La Repubblica*, July 22.

[58] Chiumarulo, "il Tar blocca anche il Piano Silletti bis."

tigate allegations that some entities "meant to permit the diffusion of the epidemic."[59]

Judges succumbed to these calls to action when Lecce's public prosecutor (a judicial office in the Italian legal system) opened a criminal investigation against scientists at the University of Bari and Giuseppe Silletti, the special commissioner appointed in February 2015[60] to manage the epidemic. In a fiery press conference, prosecutors charged that "there is no causal nexus between the drying [of olive trees] and infection by *Xylella fastidiosa*," adding that collusion with powerful multinationals was plausible.[61] While the investigation would ultimately "refute itself" and exonerate all accused, for four years it undermined the scientific consensus upon which EU intervention rested.[62] And by promptly sequestering all infected trees scheduled for removal as evidence in the criminal probe, prosecutors effectively forbade compliance with the Commission's decisions.[63] Prominent politicians like Michele Emiliano celebrated the move as a "liberation ... casting total doubt" on "the EU's strategy."[64]

Farmers capitalized on these developments by waging a campaign to humanize olive trees and equate their eradication with murder. A confrontation with municipal authorities in the town of Oria in April 2015 highlights their increasing reliance on contentious action and frames. Seventy farmers and environmental activists set up tents, forged human shields, and climbed atop trees marked for eradication, shouting: "Assassins, those olive trees have more history than us all!"[65] The owner of the trees in question, a lawyer named Giovanni Pesce to whom we will return shortly, wrote a letter published by Puglia's leading newspaper, *La Gazzetta Del Mezzogiorno*, which dramatized it as "call for help" against "savage" EU measures.[66] Carnival festivities

---

[59] Castellaneta, Bepi, and Francesca Mandese. 2015. "Xylella, Siletta gela I sindaci, 'Il piano tagli non si tocca'." *Corriere del Mezzogiorno*, October 13.

[60] Following a declaration of a state of emergency by Prime Minister Matteo Renzi on February 10, 2015. See: Opinion of Advocate General Bot in joined cases C-78/16 and C-79/16, *Pesce and Others v. Presidenza del Consiglio dei Ministri ("Xylella")*, ECLI:EU:C:2016:340, at paras. 15–16.

[61] "Xylella, 10 indagati." *Corriere della Sera*, December 19, 2015, at p. 23.

[62] Drogo, "la Procura di Lecce smentisce se stessa."

[63] Spagnolo, Chiara. 2016. "Xylella, la Corte UE dà il via libera all'abbattimento ulivi nel Salento." *La Repubblica*, June 9.

[64] "Silletti indagato e ulivi sequestrati." *Corriere della Sera*, December 18, 2015.

[65] "Xylella, ulivi secolar abbattuti a Oria." *Famiglia Cristiana*, April 13, 2015.

[66] "Lettera ad Emiliano: Aiuto contro le eradicazioni selvagge per la Xylella." *La Gazzetta del Mezzogiorno*, June 6, 2015.

Figure 8.3 (a) Funeral march for olive trees in Copertino, February 2016; (b) an activist attempting to obstruct the removal of olive trees in Oria, April 2015
*Source: La Repubblica* and ©Federica Masella for (a); *Fame di Sud* and ©Valerio Saracino for (b). Photos reproduced with permission.

in city squares were soon replaced with funeral marches as families of farmers dressed up as olive trees and held up signs reading: "I'm healthy … xylella is in your head" (see Figure 8.3).[67] A nationally televised special on the *Xylella* crisis featured a desperate farmer affirming, "I'd rather die myself, instead of a tree … they don't have the courage to tell us to kill ourselves on our own."[68] And local papers were flooded by indignant letters, one of which suggested that Puglia's olive trees would surely vote for Italy's exit from the EU.[69]

In turn, sympathetic journalists mimicked these narratives in their editorials. They embedded photos of trees with seemingly human features in their crisis news coverage.[70] They charged the EU's "diktats" with perpetrating a "massacre of olive trees"[71] that would "cancel a deep part of [the] local identity" of people who "cultivated, lived, and loved these plants like they were members of their family."[72] And a few

---

[67] "Xylella, il Carnevale salentino col funerale degli ulivi." *La Repubblica*, February 8, 2016.

[68] Quoted from: *Terra!* "A Macchia d'Olio," November 6, 2017.

[69] "Quando il Garda sembra l'autostrada." *La Repubblica*, July 5, 2016.

[70] "Puglia, lo spettacolo social dell'ulivo pensieroso." *La Repubblica*, March 9, 2016.

[71] Colluto, Tiziana. 2015. "Strage ulivi in Puglia, il diktat Ue." *Il Fatto Quotidiano*, March 17; Tondelli, Agnese. 2016. "Xylella: l'Ue impone la strage degli ulivi in Puglia." *Ambiente Bio*, June 20; "No al massacro degli ulivi in Puglia." *Il Cambiamento*, April 16, 2015.

[72] Gargiulo, Kasia Burney. 2015. "Caso Xylella: nel Salento scudi umani per difendere gli ulivi contro l'eradicazione." *Fame del Sud*, April 15.

even published conspiratorial websites and books purportedly exposing the EU's plan to "kill that forest ... [of] centennial olive trees."[73]

These popular narratives "highlighted the deep distrust lurking in" Puglia[74] alongside farmers' need to make sense of trauma, attribute blame, and privilege "experience-based-expertise" over the "imposition of mandatory policies."[75] Farmers sometimes interrupted news reportage to convey their need to make sense of crisis on their own terms: how could the EU claim that "the lands worked by [their] father[s] and grandfather[s] and the older generations could possibly be broken by a bacteria[?] No, somebody plotted to commit sacrilege."[76] Their sense that a massacre was underway lay in an embodied history where "every tree has a name here."[77] To threaten these anthropomorphic symbols was sure to trigger an emotional response, as highlighted by a farmer in Ostuni: "From a rational standpoint there's always something we can do. But it's from an emotional point of view that I don't know what will happen to me. Because one of my nightmares is that they'll come here with the bulldozers, right? It's truly unimaginable."[78]

For the first three years of the *Xylella* outbreak, these affective histories were only invoked by farmers and environmental activists, who recognized the importance of waging "a politics of local knowledge."[79] In the *Port of Genoa* case, the Euro-lawyers who orchestrated the EU's intervention similarly knew that "it was indispensable to work to prepare things ahead of time" via a "very deliberate media strategy."[80] Yet in Puglia, such public advocacy and interpretive mediation were conspicuously missing. By the time that EU institutions came to terms with these rapidly shifting on-the-ground politics, farmers had succeeded in supplanting passive submission to legal authority with a collective identity forged through contentious disobedience.

---

[73] As one of several examples see, the website – http://xylellareport.it/ – and self-published book authored by one of Bari's professional journalists: Mastrogiovanni, Marilù. 2015. *Xylella Report: Uccidete quella foresta. Attacco agli ulivi secolari del Salento*. Bari: Il Tacco d'Italia.

[74] Borunda, "Italy's Olive Trees Are Dying."

[75] Colella et al., "Problem Setting and Problem Solving," at 192.

[76] See: *Terra!* "A Macchia d'Olio," November 6, 2017.

[77] Interview with Leo Piccillo, president of *Coldiretti*'s Lecce chapter, quoted in ibid.

[78] Interview with Corrado Rodio, farmer in Ostuni, quoted in ibid.

[79] Fisher, *Citizens, Experts, and the Environment.*

[80] Interview with Giuseppe Giacomini, October 24 and 26, 2017.

### 8.2.3 Taking Resistance to the European Court

The stage was thus set for Act II of Italy's *Xylella* crisis, where lawyers mobilized national courts and the ECJ in ways that added fuel to the fire.

In late 2015 and 2016, some lawyers bolstered the farmers' revolt by waging a complementary and defiant litigation campaign. Unlike the Euro-lawyers in *Port of Genoa*, these practitioners were more nationally oriented, and they exercised their agency reactively rather than proactively. They turned to the courts after contentious backlash was well underway, and instead of appealing to judges and the public to comply with EU law, their goal was to stop it in its tracks.

The first lawsuit was lodged by Giovanni Pesce, a lawyer whose olive grove had served as the stage for the first clash between farmers and municipal authorities in April 2015. Pesce felt that he and his neighbors were victims of "a mass and indiscriminate eradication" of possibly nefarious origins, given the criminal inquiry launched by prosecutors in Lecce. The "forceful side" of "a fairly distant [European] law" was being weaponized "without sufficient explanation ... without considering the emotional and cultural aspect of the case. Only techno-cratic evaluations bore any weight."[81] The second lawsuit was lodged in October 2015 by three lawyers – Mariano Alterio, Mario Tagliaferro, and Nicola Grasso – on behalf of farmers from a town whose mayor had called for a criminal investigation into the management of the crisis.[82] They described their lawsuit as a "David vs. Goliath" battle pitting "18 farmers ... against the European Commission, Italy, Puglia, and Greece!"[83]

During a conversation with Alterio and Grasso, I was struck by how calls for resistance had diffused from the olive groves to the bar. Both lawyers rejected the boundary-blurring role central to Euro-lawyering in contentious times. Instead of trying to vernacularize EU law, they channeled farmers' grievances by reifying the conflict between "a thousand year-old cultural identity" and European diktats "arriv[ing] like a shot from above":

[81] Interview with Giovanni Pesce, August 18, 2017.

[82] Colluto, Tiziana. 2016. "Xylella, decide la Corte di Giustizia Ue." *Il Fatto Quotidiano*, January 22.

[83] Interview with Mariano Alterio, Studio Legale Alterio in Bari, and Nicola Grasso, law professor at the University of Salento, March 23, 2017 (in-person).

**Alterio:** "One perceives that the policies from Brussels exacerbate a very local situation ... they arrive like a shot from above against which you can't even confront yourself directly because their way of coming up with solutions is the same ... [this] is perceived as a decision of a technocratic authority..."

**Grasso:** "They couldn't care less. It's all the same. Am I clear? So this isn't right. It's a decision taken with an axe, period ... it's not like if you remove a 200 or 300 year old olive tree and you replace with a new plant that you have the same thing ... for the preservation of the landscape, of a thousand year-old cultural identity."

**Alterio:** "The Commission's intervention was very radical. That is, to give you an example, it's as if in a city like Bari – 330,000 plus people – there were a couple sick people from an unknown disease, and so it says: 'Perhaps it could diffuse very, very rapidly, so because the risk is that, in these months, you've all contracted the disease from these two people, we'll kill you all. We'll quarantine Bari.' This is what it is... "

**Grasso:** "And we must note that it's not yet been scientifically proven that these olive trees dry up due to *Xylella*[84] ... it's rather improbable that [it arrived] in 2011, with a little plant from Costa Rica ... it could be, but it's also possible that Santa brought it with his reindeer!"[85]

Alterio and Grasso thus tapped into a popular repertoire of "counter-knowledge."[86] By dexterously interweaving dramatization, indignation, and mockery, this repertoire legitimated resistance to an out-of-touch authority. To illustrate Europe's contemptuous neglect of local culture, during our conversation my interlocutors invoked long-standing rumors that the EU planned to ban wood-fire pizza ovens and the production of parmesan cheese.[87] In a context of aroused public passion where local stakeholders were desperate to navigate

[84] Grasso added that "the only scientific study ... of UC Berkeley ... affirms that olive trees are not a plant susceptible to *xylella*." Yet UC Berkeley researchers had defended this link. See: Almeida, Rodrigo. 2016. "Can Apulia's Olive Trees Be Saved?" *Science* 353(6297): 346–348.

[85] Interview with Mariano Alterio and Nicola Grasso, March 23, 2017.

[86] Colella et al., "Problem Setting and Problem Solving," at 190.

[87] The rumor of a ban on wood-fire pizza ovens originated with British tabloids and was reproduced by some Italian newspapers: Cianciullo, Antonio. 1999. "Forni a legna proibiti." *La Repubblica*, December 14; The EU health commissioner at the time underscored that such legislation had neither been proposed nor voted for: "Brussels to Ban Wood Fire Ovens." EU Commission's "Euromyths" Archive, December 16, 1999. Available at: http://blogs.ec.europa.eu/ECintheUK/brussels-to-ban-wood-burning-ovens/. The allegation that wooden containers or spoons were banned by Europe – for parmesan production or otherwise – is also characterized by the Commission as a "myth": "EU Bans Wooden Oars for Stirring the Christmas Pudding." EU Commission's "Euromyths" Archive,

uncertainty, rumor and conspiracy have a way of providing clarity, "hit[ting] the sweet spot where preexisting prejudices are confirmed."[88]

The three lawyers lodged separate lawsuits before the regional administrative court in Rome in October 2015, though they subsequently met to discuss their shared goals.[89] For litigation to succeed, they had to persuade their judicial interlocutors to take farmers' claims seriously. Alterio and Tagliaferro's memo alleged that "nobody really knows the content" of the "supposed 'investigations'" driving the Commission decisions, whose implementation would turn "the entire communal territory into a desert." And it added that tree eradication would be "futile, given the lack of scientific proof of the relationship between [tree] drying and the presence of *xylella*."[90] Citing similar concerns, Pesce's memo implored the judges to annul the national decree implementing the Commission decision and to refer the case to the ECJ, where they could challenge the validity of EU law outright.[91]

The lawsuits succeeded in persuading Italian judges: in January 2016 the Roman court suspended the regional implementation of the Commission decisions and solicited the ECJ, noting that it "shared the doubts brought forth by the plaintiffs" due to "an absence of scientific analysis."[92] The judges' five queries synthesized the lawyers' proposed arguments, asking whether tree removal around infected plants lacked motivation, was disproportionate, and violated the precautionary principle under EU environmental law.[93] For a second time, national judges intervened to block the implementation of European law.

Predictably, this defiant litigation campaign hit a wall as soon as the referral arrived in Luxembourg. During oral arguments, the

November 11, 1992. Available at: http://blogs.ec.europa.eu/ECintheUK/eu-bans-wooden-oars-for-stirring-the-christmas-pudding/; Regulation (EC) No. 1935/2004 of the European parliament and the Council of 27 October 2004. *Official Journal of the European Union* L338/4.

[88] I here borrow from Fintan O'Toole's brilliant analysis of UK Prime Minister Boris Johnson's tactics when he was a Brussels-based journalist, where he fabricated just these sort of Euroskeptic folktales that were then picked up by Italian tabloids: O'Toole, Fintan. 2019. "The Ham of Fate." *New York Review of Books* 66(13): 29.

[89] Interview with Giovanni Pesce, August 18, 2017.

[90] "Ricorso, Con Richiesta di Concessione di Misure Cautelari Monocratiche Provvisorie Ex. Art. 56 C.P.A." October 9, 2015 [TAR Lazio], at 14; 3; 29; 35; 7–8, shared from Mariano Alterio's personal archive.

[91] Interview with Giovanni Pesce, August 18, 2017.

[92] "Xylella, il Tar del Lazio invia gli atti alla Corte di Giustizia Ue." *Rai News*, January 22, 2016.

[93] Joined cases C-78/16 and C-79/16, "*Xylella*," at para. 21.

ECJ's Advocate General, the Commission, and the Italian and Greek governments defended the measures and stressed the need for speedy implementation. Yet instead of crystallizing a consensus in favor of compliance, these developments exacerbated a local optics of conspiracy. The hearing may have "betrayed the political interests of other member states," Pesce told me, since "for them it's a good thing, let's say, if measures lead to a mass and indiscriminate eradication" forcing Italian olive oil producers out of business.[94] In *Port of Genoa*, Euro-lawyers had acted deliberately to avoid this perception: they constructed their test case to the ECJ to exclude dockworkers from being a party to the case, so that it did not appear that they were being targeted. But the "David vs. Goliath" litigation campaign that lawyers waged in the *Xylella* case lent itself to a very different media portrayal. Journalists described the case as pitting "everyone against the farmers," with the Commission "breathing down the neck" of the ECJ to support a "cleaver-like" intervention.[95]

### 8.2.4 "Europe Feels Far Away": From Contention to Noncompliance

On June 9, 2016, the ECJ deferred to the Commission, exacerbating the chasm between how the *Xylella* crisis was being perceived locally and managed supranationally.

For the three lawyers representing indignant farmers, a "precautionary measure" intuitively meant that olive trees should not be removed unless their infection status was certain.[96] Conversely, the ECJ held that "where there is uncertainty as to the existence or extent of risks ... but the likelihood of real harm to public health persists should the risk materialise, the precautionary principle justifies the adoption of restrictive measures."[97] On the ground, farmers interpreted a "proportional" response as the use of "holistic" and "sustainable agronomic methods and traditional framing techniques aimed at reducing symptoms."[98] Conversely, for ECJ containing *Xylella* "requires that not only the infected plants but also nearby host plants be removed ... [and the

---

[94] Interview with Giovanni Pesce, August 18, 2017.

[95] "Xylella, contadini contro tutti." *Telerama News*, April 22, 2016; Colluto, Tiziana. 2016. "Xylella, Corte Giustizia Ue: 'Bruxelles puo chiedere all'Italia il taglio degli ulivi sani'." June 9.

[96] Interview with Mariano Alterio and Nicola Grasso, March 23, 2017; *La Gazzetta del Mezzogiorno*, "Lettera ad Emiliano."

[97] Joined cases C-78/16 and C-79/16, "*Xylella*," at para. 47.

[98] Colella et al., "Problem Setting and Problem Solving," at 194, 190.

Commission] is empowered to impose such a measure."[99] Elected officials in Puglia claimed that they did not compensate farmers because Brussels forbade it.[100] But the ECJ retorted that while the Commission did not provide "specifically for a compensation scheme," this could not "be interpreted as precluding such a right."[101] And whereas farmers argued that it was the olive groves of Puglia that required protection, the ECJ rebutted that these interests were counterbalanced by "the public interest in safeguarding effective protection of EU territory ... against the spread of the bacterium."[102]

In sharp contrast to the *Port of Genoa* decision, the ECJ's *Xylella* judgment "was certainly poorly received," not least "because it was never sufficiently explained" via "a dialogue with citizens."[103] Instead of welcoming the decision as opening an expected pathway forward, local journalists, politicians, and stakeholders were blindsighted and construed it as a shocking attack.

First, newspapers of all political stripes described the judgment in dramatic and unfavorable terms. The anti-establishment *Il Fatto Quotidiano* wrote that "in the blink of an eye, thousands of olive trees in Salento could be destroyed," because "now it's the EU Court of Justice" calling for "a mass eradication."[104] From the left *La Repubblica* wrote that the ECJ "extinguishe[d] the hopes of Puglia to find a way to save the trees."[105] Lecce's local paper described the judgment as an "axe" cascading "like lightning bolt from the blue sky" unloading a "frigid shower" upon the "people of the olive trees."[106] And in Bari *La Gazzetta del Mezzogiorno* published an evocative cartoon titled "the Scream," where an olive tree was made to resemble the angst-stricken figure in Edvard Munch's famous painting.[107]

Second, political backlash was equally swift and multi-partisan. Puglia's center-left President accused the ECJ of "confirming drastic measures that risk producing unimaginable consequences for our

---

[99] Joined cases C-78/16 and C-79/16, "*Xylella*," at para. 70.
[100] Interview with Giovanni Pesce, August 18, 2017.
[101] Joined cases C-78/16 and C-79/16, "*Xylella*," para. 86.
[102] Ibid., at para. 74.
[103] Interview with Giovanni Pesce, August 18, 2017.
[104] Colluto, "Bruxelles puo chiedere all'Italia il taglio degli ulivi sani."
[105] Spagnolo, "la Corte UE dà il via libera all'abbattimento."
[106] "Contro la scure della Corte di Giustizia Europea, il popolo degli ulivi scende in piazza." *Leccenews24.it*, June 11, 2016.
[107] Pillinini, Nico. 2016. "Il Nuovo Piano Anti-Xylella." *La Gazzetta del Mezzogiorno*, June 10.

Figure 8.4 A protest against the ECJ's decision in Lecce, June 11, 2016
*Source: Leccenews24.it.* Photo reproduced with permission.

landscape and economy." The center-right's FI party released an even more indignant statement: "We're truly at a loss of words: the decision of the European Court of Justice ... risks to irreversibly modify the landscape of Salento and Puglia of those elements most emblematic of our identity ... we're ready to block the demolition cranes and pit ourselves against the absurd and unthinkable decisions of EU judges." And the spokesman for the populist Five Star Movement charged that "Europe is first and foremost responsible for the *Xylella* disaster" and "the desertification of the territory."[108]

Finally, this political and media backlash emboldened the farmers' revolt. The local representative of a national farmers' association accused the ECJ of "acting like Pontius Pilate, washing its hands of responsibility for paying compensation to olive cultivators."[109] A day after the judgment farmers and environmental activists took to the streets in Lecce, holding up signs reading "Salento is once again under attack ... but we won't surrender" (see Figure 8.4).[110] And as their repertoire of contentious resistance comprising protests, tree "funerals,"[111] and the "most incredible conspiracy theories"

[108] "Xylella, la Corte UE: 'sì all'obbligo di eradicazione degli ulivi potenzialmente infetti." *Leccenews24.it*, June 9, 2016.
[109] Squires, Nick. 2016. "Europe orders Italians to cut down olive trees infected with bacteria." *The Telegraph*, June 9.
[110] *Leccenews24.it*, "Contro la scure della Corte di Giustizia Europea."
[111] Gioia, Sonia. 2016. "Xylella, abattuto l'albero infetto a Ostuni: 'Corsa contro il tempo per salvare gli ulivi millenari'." *La Repubblica*, October 26.

diffused,[112] popular support for the EU in Puglia plummeted to an abysmal 19 percent in May 2016 and 27 percent in November 2016 (see Figure 8.2).

Ultimately, the farmers' revolt achieved its obstructionist goals. The decisions of the European Commission and the ECJ's subsequent judgment have scarcely been complied with to this day. As a consequence, *Xylella* spread into a number of European states and deepened the reticence of local lawyers and judges to avail themselves of EU law and solicit the ECJ.

First, as the farmers' revolt was emboldened by criminal inquiries, injunctions, defiant litigation campaigns, and foot dragging by elected officials, EU law was never converted into local practice. While Lecce's prosecutors begrudgingly lifted their sequestration of thousands of trees two months after the ECJ's decision, in January 2018 prosecutors in Bari once again sequestered an olive grove by resurrecting conspiratorial charges.[113] It took three more years for judges in Lecce to lift criminal allegations hanging over the heads of the scientists they had accused of deliberately spreading the disease and diffusing misinformation.[114] And instead of the tens of thousands of trees identified for immediate removal through early 2015 alone, less than 2,000 were actually fallen by 2017.[115]

This inaction exacerbated the rift with the Commission, which sent repeated letters to the Italian government urging compliance to no avail. In 2018 Commissioners thus launched an infringement proceeding against Italy, threatening to withdraw crucial agricultural subsidies since "Italian authorities failed to fully comply with the EU rules."[116] In September 2019 the ECJ confirmed the Commission's

---

[112] Cassano, Antonello. 2016. "L'incubo xylella nell'eden degli ulivi." *La Repubblica*, October 21.

[113] Spagnolo, Chiara. 2016. "Xylella, la Procura dissequestra 2.223 ulivi infetti nelle campagne fra Brindisi e Lecce." *La Repubblica*, July 28; "Xylella, pm Bari dissequestra ulivo infetto ma non il terreno." *La Gazzetta del Mezzogiorno*, April 10, 2019.

[114] Drogo, "la Procura di Lecce smentisce se stessa."

[115] Borillo, Michelangelo. 2017. "Così si Batte la Xylella." *Corriere della Sera*, May 8, p. 26.

[116] European Commission. "Infringements: Commission Refers Italy to Court over Its Failure to Adequately Prevent Further Spread of the Quarantine Harmful Organism 'Xylella fastidiosa' in Apulia." May 17, 2018. Available at: http://europa.eu/rapid/press-release_IP-18-3805_en.htm.

charges, finding that Italy failed to remove infected plants and to sufficiently monitor the pathogen's advance.[117]

As *Xylella* spread uninhibited, it left a growing trail of devastation in its wake. By 2019 the estimated number of dead trees spun nearly 20 percent of Puglia's olive groves, with 10 million additional trees under imminent threat.[118] With nearly half a million acres of groves destroyed, Italian olive oil production plummeted by 50 percent (65 percent in Puglia) through 2019, contributing a loss of up to 100,000 jobs.[119] The *Xylella* crisis grew transnational in scale as the pathogen spread to France in 2015, Spain in 2017, and Portugal in 2019.[120] Scientists now believe that "southern Italy is becoming a reservoir" for *Xylella* in ways that will preclude the bacteria from ever being eradicated in Europe, producing up to $22 billion in economic losses over the next fifty years.[121]

Yet the failure to reconcile EU law with local knowledge also produced a more concealed effect. Instead of jump-starting a feedback loop of litigation and judicial policymaking like the *Port of Genoa* case, the interviews I conducted in Puglia shortly after the ECJ's *Xylella* ruling suggest a chilling effect. Several of the twenty-eight

---

[117] Case C-443/18, *Commission v. Italy* [2019], ECLI:EU:C:2019:676; Pagano, Mario. 2019. "Who Will Save the Olive Tree?" *European Journal of Risk Regulation* 10(4): 811–820.

[118] Borunda, "Italy's Olive Trees Are Dying."

[119] Dawson, Daniel. 2019. "UN Issues New Standards to Curb Spread of Xylella." *Olive Oil Times*, April 5; "Filiera olio da Di Maio, persi 100mila posti di lavoro." *Coldiretti*, April 1, 2019. Available at: www.coldiretti.it/lavoro/filiera-olio-maio-persi-100mila-posti-lavoro; Vasilopoulos, "Thousands of Jobs Lost in Italian Olive Oil Sector."

[120] Putinja, Isabel. 2016. "*Xylella fastidiosa* Continues to Spread in Corsica." *Olive Oil Times*, February 19; Atoui, Reda. 2016. "*Xylella fastidiosa* Bacterium Arrives in Spain." *Olive Oil Times*, November 27; "First Identification of *Xylella fastidiosa* in Portugal." *XF-ACTORS*, January 10, 2019. Available at: www.xfactorsproject.eu/press_review/first-identification-of-xylella-fastidiosa-in-portugal/.

[121] Strona, Giovanni, Carstens, Corrie Jacobien, and Pieter Beck. 2017. "Network Analysis Reveals Why *Xylella fastidiosa* Will Persist in Europe." *Scientific Reports* 7(71): 1–8, at 1; White, Steven, James Bullock, Danny Hooftman, and Daniel Chapman 2017. "Modelling the Spread and Control of *Xylella fastidiosa* in the Early Stages of Invasion in Apulia, Italy." *Biological Invasions* 19(6): 1825–1837, at 1830; Burdeau, Cain. 2018. "Can Xylella Be Stopped?" *Olive Oil Times*, May 4, 2018; Schneider, Kevin, Wopke van der Werf, Martina Candoya, Monique Mourits, Juan Navas-Cortés, Antonio Vincent, and Alfons Oude Lansink 2020. "Impact of *Xylella fastidiosa* Subspecies *Pauca* in European Olives." *PNAS* 117(17): 9250–9259.

jurists I spoke to confessed off-the-record that their sense of distance to European law deepened as the *Xylella* crisis unfolded. As Giovanni Pesce explains, backlash to the ECJ's decision was exacerbated by the fact that in southern Italy "the functioning of the European Court of Justice ... [is] deemed to be distant not just in a physical sense, but precisely because practically nobody is aware of basic notions of EU law."[122]

In this light, the conspiratorial crusades of local prosecutors were just the tip of the iceberg, betraying how farmers' defiant legal consciousness had silently taken root within local courts. Several judges I spoke to in Bari confided that they "don't have a propensity and a positive outlook" toward EU law and the ECJ, which they have come to perceive as disruptive and invasive forces.[123] Even those colleagues who supported the ECJ's *Xylella* decision confessed that most judges felt differently. Some expressed "fear that the perception ... won't be as benevolent ... [for] the Euroskeptic perspective is common to the local population and the judicial authorities."[124] Others added "that the ECJ decision could be instrumentalized as an 'interference' in administrative decisions and citizens' lives," predicting that it would be framed as "negatively impacting local interests."[125] Quantitative evidence (see Figure 8.5) supports the inference that the *Xylella* crisis damaged an already frail dialogue between local courts and the ECJ. In the four years following Commission Decision 2015/789 and the ECJ's 2016 judgment, judges in Bari and Lecce referred only a single case to the European Court, a sharp drop from the ten referrals made in the prior four years.

The *Xylella* case typifies the risks accompanying the politicization of European integration and judicial policymaking. Without interpretive mediation and public advocacy, the foundations of the judicial construction of Europe risk dessicating as fast as the olive trees of Italy. As ECJ decisions and European laws disrupt deeply rooted practices and provoke political controversy, negotiating compliance requires

---

[122] Interview with Giovanni Pesce, August 18, 2017.
[123] Interview with judge at the Tribunal of Bari, March 2017 (in-person, name/date redacted); Interview with two judges at the Court of Appeal of Bari, March 2017 (in-person, names/date redacted).
[124] Interview with Teresa Liuni, May 18, 2017.
[125] Interview with Giovanni Zaccaro, Tribunal of Bari, May 21, 2017 (via e-mail); Interview with Enrico Scoditti, ex-judge at the Tribunal of Bari, May 18, 2017 (via e-mail).

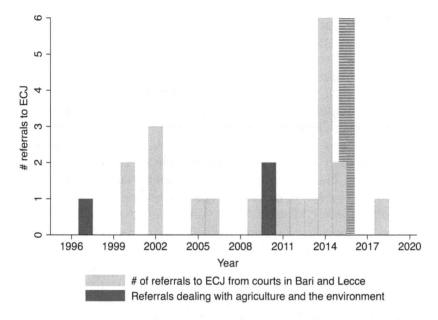

Figure 8.5 References to the ECJ from courts in Bari and Lecce, 1995–2020
*Notes:* The gray shading denotes the dates spanning Commission Implementing Decision (EU) 2015/789 and the ECJ's judgment in the *Xylella* case.

engaging local stakeholders on their own terms. In the poignant words of the former president of the Bari bar,

> in many parts of Italy [olive trees are] the "life" of the people, and they're thus highly protected ... We've been unable to explain, in clear terms, the current state of affairs. I'm not a conspiracy theorist and I don't like producing conspiracies. I look to the facts (and to the judges) and, in this instance, the facts leave me perplexed. This, too, makes Europe feel far away, far away from the people ... olive oil – as is known – floats on water.[126]

## 8.3 THE TRIUMPH OF BACKLASH AND ITS LIMITS

In Chapter 7, I noted that even the most triumphant cases of legal mobilization and judicial policymaking can yield unintended consequences surfacing with the passage of time. I want to conclude

---

[126] Interview with Emmanuele Virgintino, president (2008–2015) of the Bari bar association, May 26, 2017 (via e-mail).

this chapter with the reverse observation: even the most devastating politics of backlash can bear some silver linings.

As the dust settles in the wake of an initial bout of contentious mobilization, the material consequences of backlash can crystallize and cut through the fog of uncertainty and conspiracy. Indeed, the glaring devastation wrought by the *Xylella* crisis eventually forced self-reflection upon all parties concerned. On the EU's side, in late 2017 the Commission issued a new decision that walked back its top-down regulatory approach and extended a figurative olive branch to agricultural communities. The decision amended its tree removal requirements via a telling exception: "In order to respect the tradition and history of a particular location, Member States should have the option to decide that host plants officially designated as plants of historic value do not need to be removed if they are not infected."[127] This emphasis on "cultural and social value" was given a more permanent basis in a 2020 implementing regulation.[128] As EFSA-affiliated scientists conceded, "in retrospect, social turmoil should have been expected .... The [EU] aims to address the threats of *X. fastidiosa* as a plant pathogen ... but the reality to Apulians is different: cutting down their olive trees means destroying the physical embodiment of their families and history."[129]

To adjust to this lived reality, the Commission funded a new project, *XF-ACTORS*, aimed at containing *Xylella* by pairing a scientific advisory board with a "Stakeholder Board to ensure the consortium takes into account the interest of the stakeholders and end-users."[130] Since 2017, *XF-ACTORS* has sponsored regular joint seminars with farmers, environmentalists, and municipal authorities in Puglia: a belated recognition of the important role that public advocacy and interpretive mediation plays in a politics of compliance.

---

[127] Commission Implementing Decision (EU) 2017/2352 of 14 December 2017. *Official Journal of the European Union* L366, at 32.

[128] Article 13.2 of the Regulation notes: "[T]he Member State concerned may decide, for scientific purposes, not to remove plants which have been found to be infected by the specified pest in the sites of plants with particular cultural and social value." See: Commission Implementing Regulation (EU) 2020/1201 of 14 August 2020. *Official Journal of the European Union* L269, at 10.

[129] Almeida, "Can Apulia's Olive Trees Be Saved?"

[130] "A New EU Project Starts in November: XF-ACTORS." *XF-ACTORS*, December 2, 2016. The project comprises twenty-nine partners across fourteen countries, under coordination of the Institute for Sustainable Plant Projection of Bari. The project is funded by the Commission's Horizon 2020 program.

This policy shift helped foster a countermovement among the farmers themselves: the *gilet arancioni* ("orange vests"), inspired by the *gilets jaunes* ("yellow vests") protests that erupted in France in the fall of 2018. Three thousand of them rode tractors into Bari in January 2019, decrying obstructionist politics and the "immobilism" of Italy's then-populist government.[131] When in the same month a local judge once again issued an injunction to block tree removal, they organized another protest: "Enough is enough," they declared, "these sequestrations led the way to the pathogen's advance."[132] These counterprotests gained sufficient steam to prompt another about-face by Puglia's President, who now backed tree removals and characterized prosecutors' obstructionist criminal probes as "infelicitous."[133] A few months later thousands of *gilets* marched into Rome carrying olive branches and demanding compensation,[134] which was finally appropriated by the Italian Parliament in May 2019.[135]

None of these developments could turn back the clock on years of backlash and judicial noncompliance with European law. But they do suggest a lesson that might get lost amid the ruckus of contention: as interest groups and policymakers abandon legitimate grievance for illusion and conspiracy, sooner or later they too may be forced to reckon with the realities they unleash.

---

[131] Gabrieli, Giuseppe. 2019. "A Bari 3mila gilet arancioni, sfila la rabbia degli agricoltori contro il governo." *La Repubblica*, January 7.

[132] "Xilella, la rabbia di agricoltori e sindaci a Monopoli." *La Gazzetta del Mezzogiorno*, January 13, 2019.

[133] "Xylella, Emiliano: 'L'inchiesta della Procura di Lecce non è stata felice'." *Quotidiano di Puglia*, January 15, 2019.

[134] "Gilet arancioni invadono Roma." *La Gazzetta del Mezzogiorno*, February 14, 2019.

[135] Minerva, Maria Claudia. 2019. "Xylella, firmato il decreto emergenze." *Quotidiano di Puglia*, May 27.

# PART FIVE

# CONCLUSION

## CHAPTER NINE

# MAKING SENSE OF GHOSTWRITERS

> *Voluntaristic change will often take over after unintended change has done the spadework and created conditions in which the outline of previously hidden possibilities of change can begin to be perceived . . . Such, then, are some of the devices which the possibilist can use . . . to help defend the right to a nonprojected future as one of the truly inalienable rights of every person and nation; and to set the stage for conceptions of change to which the inventiveness of history and a "passion for the possible" are admitted as vital actors.*
>
> —Albert Hirschman, *A Bias for Hope*[1]

In politics and law as in literature and art, ghostwriters abound. For instance, lobbyists who favor particular legislation regularly propose draft bills for elected officials.[2] Street-level bureaucrats, too, can refract executive regulations and forge their own informal rules.[3] And behind every judicial decision lie the translators, registrars, and clerks vital to making law.[4]

---

[1] Hirschman, Albert. 1971. *A Bias for Hope*. New Haven, CT: Yale University Press, at 37.

[2] Hula, Kevin. 1999. *Lobbying Together: Interest Group Coalitions in Legislative Politics.* Washington, DC: Georgetown University Press, at 100; Earshaw, David, and David Judge. 2002. "No Simple Dichotomies: Lobbyists and the European Parliament." *Journal of Legislative Studies* 8(4): 61–79, at 62; 64; Chalmers, Adam. 2013. "Trading Information for Access: Lobbying Strategies and Interest Group Access to the European Union." *Journal of European Public Policy* 20(1): 39–58.

[3] Lipsky, *Street Level Bureaucracy*, at 13–23; Thierry, Jessica Sampson, and Dorte Martinsen. 2018. "Lost in Translation: How Street-Level Bureaucrats Condition Union Solidarity." *Journal of European Integration* 40(6): 819–834; Martinsen, Dorte Sindbjerg, Michael Blauberger, Anita Heindlmaier, and Jessica Sampson Thierry. 2019. "Implementing European Case Law at the Bureaucratic Frontline." *Public Administration* 97(4): 814–828.

[4] Latour, *Making of Law*; Rosenthal, Jeffrey, and Albert Yoon. 2010. "Judicial Ghostwriting: Authorship on the U.S. Supreme Court." *Cornell Law Review* 96(6): 1307–1344; Baetens, Freya. 2019. *Legitimacy of Unseen Actors in International Adjudication.* New York, NY: Cambridge University Press; Pauwelyn, Joost, and Krzysztof Pelc. 2019. "Who Writes the Rulings of the World Trade Organization?" SSRN working paper. Available at: https://papers.ssrn.com/sol3/papers.cfm?abstract_id=3458872.

These actors usually pass unnoticed until they face negative public-ity. As public scrutiny of policymaking grows and populist movements purport to unmask the powers behind the throne, ghostwriting takes on a "can't live with it, can't live without it" quality illuminating its Janus-faced implications for democracy and politics. Its air of unaccountable influence raises valid legitimacy concerns and renders it vulnerable to public criticism. Yet in a complex world beset by scarcities of time, expertise, participation, and leadership, ghostwriters can also function like trillions of gut bacteria "vital to keeping the body politic in good health."[5]

But not all ghostwriters are created equal as agents of institutional change. These last few pages take stock of this book's findings for the study of lawyers and political development, particularly in light of the mounting challenges plaguing the rule of law in Europe. I first suggest what is distinct about lawyers as agents of institutional change (Section 9.1) and how we might make normative sense of their repertoire of ghostwriting (Section 9.2). I then close in Section 9.3 by channeling political economist Albert Hirschman to sound a possibilist note in troubling times. As a wave of illiberalism and rule of law breakdowns sweeps across some European states, a growing number of lawyers have sought to reclaim the elusive promise of the judicial construction of Europe, to disavow the imperatives of the market, and to join a transnational struggle for political liberalism.

## 9.1 SOLVING "THE CASE OF THE MISSING AGENTS"

Many actors that we intuitively conceive as ghostwriters are prototyp-ical institutional insiders: judicial clerks, career bureaucrats, legislative aides, and the like. Partitioned from the outside world, these actors are well placed to bolster the autonomy of the institutions they inhabit.[6] They can serve as vital guardrails against political capture and custodians of institutional memory. At the same time, insiders

---

[5] I draw from Stokes' account of how democratic theorists grew to value political parties as mediatory actors between state and society: Stokes, Susan. 1999. "Political Parties and Democracy." *Annual Reviews of Political Science* 2: 243–267.

[6] For examples drawn from the American case, see: Cohen, Jonathan. 2002. *Inside Appellate Courts: The Impact of Court Organization on Judicial Decision Making in the United States Courts of Appeals*. Ann Arbor, MI: University of Michigan Press, at 85–125; Carpenter, Daniel. 2001. *The Forging of Bureaucratic Autonomy: Reputation, Networks, and Policy Innovation in Executive Agencies, 1862–1928*. Princeton, NJ: Princeton University Press, at 19–23; Romzek, Barbara, and Jennifer Utter. 1997.

may cultivate self-referential institutions that resist change and fail to respond to shifting political demands and social needs.

The lawyers animating this book embody a different type of ghost-writing. Instead of insiders acting as *boundary reifiers*, they are mediators who advance institutional change as *boundary blurrers*. Positioned at the junction of civil society, national judiciaries, and international institutions, their influence hinges on seizing opportunities for change that may be lost upon actors moored to only one of these spheres, while acquiring just enough situated knowledge in each to interlink them effectively.

In an increasingly interconnected world, judicial authority and political development stand on the shoulders of institutional boundary blurrers.[7] The construction of the world's sole supranational polity in Europe exemplifies this point. Lacking in coercive and administrative capacity, "the politics of everyday Europe"[8] could only be reshaped if private parties could be cajoled into acting as public enforcers, domestic courts as European courts, and national states as subnational units within a fledgling federated polity. These gradual and oftentimes tortuous transformations have at this point been meticulously documented,[9] and they may even be reproducing themselves within centralized states once thought to be impervious to boundary blurring.[10] Yet who is driving these institutional changes, and to what ends, often remains unclear. Some have even resigned themselves to "call off the search" for these "missing agents."[11]

In this book, I have tried to "solve" the case of the missing agents by illuminating how their "missingness" is partly a by-product of deliberate strategy. To the extent that national lawyers succeeded in advancing European integration, it was usually in their interest if it appeared that an amorphous complex of rights-conscious litigants, euro-enthusiastic judges, and supranational entrepreneurs was doing all the work. This approach cultivated the sense that European law

"Congressional Legislative Staff: Political Professionals or Clerks?" *American Journal of Political Science* 41(4): 1251–1279.

[7] Liu, "Globalization as Boundary-Blurring."

[8] McNamara, Kathleen. 2015. *The Politics of Everyday Europe: Constructing Authority in the European Union*. New York, NY: Oxford University Press.

[9] Kelemen, *Eurolegalism*.

[10] For instance, see: Vauchez and France, *Neoliberal Republic*; Pavone, "Lawyers, Judges, and the Obstinate State."

[11] Case, Rhonda Evans. 2011. "Eurolegalism and the Case of the Missing Agents: Should We Call Off the Search?" *Tulsa Law Review* 47(1): 195–204.

was something of a "messianic" force,[12] and it diverted attention from controversial practices like lawsuit construction and inconvenient problems like overworked judges lacking basic legal knowledge.

Understating the politics of lawyers did not just benefit attorneys. The European Court's own reputation as "the most effective supranational judicial body in the history of the world"[13] depends on the self-fulfilling prophecy of a rights-conscious civil society claiming European Union (EU) law before capacious national judiciaries eager to join forces with the European Court of Justice (ECJ). If the EU's compliance pull lies in rights revolutions blossoming organically, then critiques maligning Europe as a runaway "juristocracy" can be countered,[14] and the EU can more effectively serve as a model for transnational governance.[15]

While some scholars argue that just this sort of rights revolution has swept through Europe,[16] this narrative provoked a realist retort. In this less sanguine view, legal mobilization and judicial policymaking have been driven by the "haves" and neglected the interests of the "have nots."[17] Far from a broad-based rights revolution, the judicial construction of Europe is a process that the powerful can capture to contain justice. With time, these clashing perspectives have struck an ambivalent truce: "Until we understand more about how and why different parties mobilize law, it is difficult to respond to normative questions about whether European legal mobilization is a positive or negative development for democracy and rights."[18]

How does this book help us gain traction over this normative puzzle? What are we to make of parties and judges who mobilize the law not because of a burning rights-consciousness or activist ambition, but

---

[12] Weiler, "In the Face of Crisis."

[13] Stone Sweet, *Judicial Construction of Europe*, at 1.

[14] Hirschl, *Towards Juristocracy*, at 214–215.

[15] Alter, Karen, Laurence Helfer, and Osvaldo Saldias, 2012. "Transplanting the European Court of Justice: The Experience of the Andean Tribunal of Justice." *The American Journal of Comparative Law* 60(3): 629–664.

[16] See: Stone Sweet, Alec. 2000. *Governing with Judges*. New York, NY: Oxford University Press, at 37–38; Kelemen, "EU Rights Revolution"; Cichowski, Rachel. 2006. "Courts, Rights, and Democratic Participation." *Comparative Political Studies* 39(1): 50–75; Cichowski, *European Court and Civil Society*.

[17] Conant, *Justice Contained*; Börzel, "Participation through Law Enforcement"; Hoevenaars, *A People's Court?*

[18] Conant, Lisa, Andreas Hofmann, Dagmar Soennecken, and Lisa Vanhala, 2018. "Mobilizing European Law." *Journal of European Public Policy* 25(9): 1376–1389, at 1376.

because entrepreneurial lawyers stubbornly push them to do so? In my view, an ethical evaluation is only possible if we are clear-eyed about *what* lawyers do when they act as ghostwriters of institutional change, along with *when* and *why* they do it.

## 9.2 INSTITUTIONAL CHANGE AND THE ETHICS OF GHOSTWRITING

What do lawyers do when they ghostwrite the behavior of litigants and judges? Are they volunteering suggestions? Coercing action? Or something else?

There is little doubt that if "A has power over B to the extent that [they] can get B to do something that B would not otherwise do,"[19] then ghostwriting is an exercise of power. But this classic conception of power accommodates a wide range of actions, from "nudging" an actor toward a preferred choice while leaving alternatives open[20] to coercing compliance.[21] Along this spectrum, ghostwriting is surely closer to nudging than to coercion. Yet ghostwriting not only modifies people's choice architecture: it can more profoundly reshape their legal consciousness. In those communities where Euro-lawyering became entrenched, local courts and stakeholders were more likely to gradually view themselves as street-level compliance constituencies of a supranational legal order.

To be sure, lawyers often took matters into their own hands, making the most of their clients' blank checks and the occasional opportunity to draft a national court's referral to the ECJ. Yet ghostwriting was and remains a strategy of persuasion[22] whose effectiveness stems from the bricolage of local knowledge, legal expertise, and individual labor more than material incentives or force. I uncovered no evidence that Euro-lawyers coaxed clients and judges to perform involuntary actions harmful to their own interests. And even as some courts and

---

[19] Dahl, Robert. 1957. "The Concept of Power." *Behavioral Science* 2(3): 201–215, at 202–203.

[20] Thaler and Sunstein, *Nudge*, at 6.

[21] Baldwin, David. 2015. "Misinterpreting Dahl on Power." *Journal of Political Power* 8(2): 209–227; Lukes, Steven. 2015. "Robert Dahl on Power." *Journal of Political Power* 8(2): 261–271.

[22] In Robert Dahl's later work, he distinguished between power and coercion on the one hand, and influence and persuasion on the other. See: Stinebrickner, Bruce. 2015. "Robert A. Dahl and the Essentials of Modern Political Analysis: Politics, Influence, Power, and Polyarchy." *Journal of Political Power* 8(2): 189–207, at 196.

litigants began cooperating with Euro-lawyers, the contingent struggle to produce this outcome belies fears that it opens the door to runaway judicial activism.

The second factor impinging upon a normative evaluation of ghost-writing concerns *when* it occurs in a sequence of political development. When new rules and institutions are layered atop an existing tapestry – as when European laws percolate within national legal orders – most actors ensconced within preexisting relations of authority are likely to proceed with business as usual. A change in their behavior and legal consciousness is neither automatic, costless, nor self-reinforcing. New laws must be demystified, framed as directly applicable rights, and taken as authoritative even when they disrupt established practice. Institutional change would prove stillborn without entrepreneurs pushing the bounds of acceptable agency to question the status quo and illuminate previously hidden possibilities.

The first Euro-lawyers were defined by this challenge: to preclude ignorance and inertia from extinguishing what they saw as the imperative of forging a European community based on the rule of law. The ubiquity of on-the-ground indifference and passive resistance to this project of institutional change cannot be overstated during the founding decades of the European Community. The idea that from such a context a tide of rights-conscious litigants and national judges organically sprang forth is something of a founding myth, albeit one containing a grain of truth. And at the heart of that truth lie lawyers and their concealed struggles. For every success there were a dozen failures, but little by little the fruits of their labor began to bear fruit.

This brings us to the final relevant factor for an ethical evaluation of ghostwriting: the question of lawyers' shifting motives. The pioneers of Euro-lawyering may not have been the civil rights crusaders we usually think of as "cause lawyers," but the available evidence indicates that they still bore a deep ideational commitment to the cause of European integration and a vigorous participatory drive.[23] The repertoire of court-driven change that they invented, however, was both modular and content neutral: it could just as easily mobilize courts to tend to corporate interests as it could contribute to building a transnational

---

[23] On the differences between cause lawyers dedicated to specific rights causes and more institutionally-oriented political lawyers, see: Karpik, Lucien. 2007. "Political Lawyers." In *Fighting for Political Freedom: Comparative Studies of the Legal Complex and Political Liberalism*. Terence Halliday, Lucien Karpik, and Malcolm Feeley, eds. Portland, OR: Hart.

polity based on the rule of law. Over time, Euro-lawyering and judicial policymaking thus underwent a passage from idealism to interest. "At the time of the 60s," recounts a long-standing practitioner who joined one of France's first Euro-firms, it was "an admirable age of people who believed in Europe, who ... weren't there for careerist reasons, since [the European Community] was a new thing, so you had to want it, to believe in it ... this spirit evolved over time, it widened, it became advantageous for people with careerist motives."[24] As corporate Euro-firms increasingly took charge of Euro-lawyering and agglomerated in wealthier client markets, they spatially and economically stratified access to the EU's judicial system, perhaps signaling that European law is as vulnerable to cooptation as other legal fields.[25] Does this undermine Euro-lawyering's normative legitimacy?

On the one hand, the passage from idealism to interest is to some extent inevitable in any process of institutional change and political development. Change agents can seldom etch a legacy on the walls of political time if they place all their hopes in the idealism of others. Rather, a broader swath of more self-interested actors must come to find it advantageous to support change. On the other hand, this evolution speaks to whether the judicial construction of Europe rests on a broad-based rights revolution or represents another opportunity for "the 'haves' [to] come out ahead."[26] If we only look to the development of European law on paper, we would be heartened to see it eclipse the domain of trade to pay growing attention to social, environmental, and fundamental rights. But a close-to-the-ground perspective reveals that the political economy of litigation and judicial policymaking in Europe has simultaneously shifted along a countercurrent that threatens to exacerbate inequities in access to transnational justice.

## 9.3 POLITICAL LAWYERING AND DEMOCRATIC HISTORY MAKING

The recasting of legal mobilization and judicial policymaking in Europe by market inequalities has been patchworked, slow-moving, and invisible.[27] It has largely evaded public scrutiny even as the politicization

---

[24] Interview with Charles-Henri Leger, September 12, 2017.
[25] Dezelay and Garth, "Merchants of Law as Moral Entrepreneurs"; Dezelay and Garth, "Corporate Law Firms."
[26] Galanter, "Why the 'Haves' Come Out Ahead."
[27] Pierson, "Big, Slow-Moving, and ... Invisible."

of European integration has illuminated the expansive role that law and courts play in transnational governance.[28] Is market capture destined to narrow the promise and erode the legitimacy of the judicial construction of Europe?

This question has become more pressing in recent years as the world's sole supranational legal order is shaken by the most existential threat it has yet faced: a "rule of law crisis" prompted by the constitutional breakdown and the rise of authoritarianism in some European states like Hungary and Poland.[29] The EU's liberal promise of legality, mobility, and market-building was supposed to "end history," yet it unintentionally "open[ed] up a new realm of contradiction and conflict."[30] Today the judicial construction of Europe not only faces the festering risk of market capture from below; it also faces the imminent risk of authoritarian corrosion from within. With Europe on the front lines of a worldwide recession of democracy and the rule of law,[31] lawyers face a reckoning with history: a choice over whether to join a cross-national constellation of struggles for political liberalism to reclaim the normative ethos of European integration.

At this juncture, there are heartening developments that give us reason to be "biased for hope."[32] Yet before turning to these developments, I want to underscore an uncomfortable truth: lawyers are on both sides of Europe's rule of law crisis. Attorneys are not born liberal democrats, and the constitutional breakdowns of states like Hungary and Poland expose how lawyering can be weaponized to attack judicial independence and civil society while frustrating the capacity of international institutions to stand in the way.

Unlike mediatory Euro-lawyers who keep one foot within civil society, the attorneys at the forefront of a worldwide democratic recession have both feet planted in the executive apparatus of the

---

[28] Blauberger and Martinsen, "Court of Justice in Times of Politicisation."

[29] Kelemen, R. Daniel. 2019. "Is Differentiation Possible in Rule of Law?" *Comparative European Politics* 17(2): 246–260, at 247.

[30] See, respectively: Fukuyama, Francis. 2006. *The End of History and the Last Man*. New York, NY: Free Press, at 270–272; Castells, "Introduction to the Information Age," at 16.

[31] Diamond, Larry. 2021. "Democratic Regression in Comparative Perspective." *Democratization* 28(1): 22–42; Alizada, Nazifa, Rowan Cole, Lisa Gastaldi, Sandra Grahn, Sebastian Hellmeier, Palina Kolvani, and Jean Lachapelle, 2021. "Autocratization Turns Viral: Democracy Report 2021." University of Gothenburg, V-Dem Institute, at 10–19.

[32] Hirschman, *Bias for Hope*, at 37.

state. They are "lawyers-in-chief" like Hungarian Prime Minister Viktor Orbán, Polish Law and Justice (PiS) party leader Jarosław Kaczyński, and Russian President Vladimir Putin,[33] who cultivate an army of "autocratic legalists" within the bureaucracy.[34] While existing comparative studies acknowledge that lawyers are "limited liberals [who] too often have been impediments to liberalism,"[35] they have also resisted tying legalistic attacks on liberalism to the resurgence of autocracy.[36] Lawyers-in-chief have capitalized on this lapsus: they are not authoritarians but, in Orbán's words, "illiberal democrats" who, in Putin's words, recognize that "the liberal idea has become obsolete."[37]

The European experience shows us that illiberal democracy is a contradictory yet useful catchphrase for those seeking to partition a transnational rule *of* law into a series of states that rule *by* law.[38] For instance, upon winning elections in 2010 and 2015, Hungary's Fidesz party and Poland's PiS party claimed a democratic mandate to restructure the courts. They rammed legislation through Parliament that decapitated the judiciary's senior leadership by lowering their retirement age, packed constitutional courts and judicial governing councils with loyalists, ceased publishing disfavored court decisions, and created disciplinary bodies to punish disobedient judges and

---

[33] Scheppele, Kim Lane. 2019. "The Legal Complex and Lawyers-in-Chief." In *The Legal Process and the Promise of Justice: Studies Inspired by the Work of Malcolm Feeley*. Rosann Greenspan, Hadar Aviram, and Jonathan Simon, eds. New York, NY: Cambridge University Press, at 362.

[34] Corrales, Javier. 2015. "The Authoritarian Resurgence: Autocratic Legalism in Venezuela." *Journal of Democracy* 26(2): 37–51; Scheppele, Kim Lane. 2018. "Autocratic Legalism." *University of Chicago Law Review* 85: 545–584.

[35] Halliday, Terrence, and Sida Liu. 2007. "Birth of a Liberal Moment? Looking through a One-Way Mirror at Lawyers' Defence of Criminal Defendants in China." In *Fighting for Political Freedom*, Halliday, Karpik, and Feeley, eds. New York, NY: Cambridge University Press, at 66.

[36] For instance, see: Karpik, "Political Lawyers," at 469; Zakaria, Fareed. 1997. "The Rise of Illiberal Democracy." *Foreign Affairs* 76(6): 22–43.

[37] Buzogany, Aron. 2017. "Illiberal Democracy in Hungary." *Democratization* 24(7): 1307–1325; "Vladimir Putin says Liberalism Has Become Obsolete." *Financial Times*, June 28.

[38] Ginsburg, Tom, and Tamir Moustafa. 2008. *Rule by Law: The Politics of Courts in Authoritarian Regimes*. New York, NY: Cambridge University Press; Müller, Jan-Werner. 2016. "The Problem with Illiberal Democracy." *Project Syndicate*, January 21; Pech, Laurent, and Kim Lane Scheppele. 2017. "Illiberalism Within: Rule of Law Backsliding in the EU." *Cambridge Yearbook of European Legal Studies* 19: 3–47; Daly, Tom Gerald. 2019. "Democratic Decay: Conceptualising an Emerging Research Field." *Hague Journal on the Rule of Law* 11: 9–36, at 13–14.

prosecutors.[39] Classically authoritarian in intent, these reforms seek to forge a "dual state"[40] where politically sensitive cases are adjudicated by politically controlled courts and only the rest receive impartial judgment.[41]

These campaigns rely on transnationally savvy lawyers who know how to borrow Mohamed Morsi's template to forcibly retire senior judges in Egypt; transplant Recep Tayyip Erdogan's strategy to capture Turkey's Constitutional Court; and argue that blunting constitutional review is not so bad when democracies in good standing like Finland lack constitutional courts altogether.[42] They lean on jurists who know how to obstruct intergovernmental decision-making in Brussels and recast a supranational intervention as a breach of Europe's legal competences, despite the EU's Treaty-enshrined promise to safeguard "freedom, democracy, equality, [and] the rule of law."[43] These are Euro-lawyers' illiberal twins at work.

Is there hope that a vanguard of legal practitioners will launch a counteroffensive from within civil society? One promising starting point is to recognize the possibilist revisionism suffusing this book's take on the judicial construction of Europe. Europe's political development through law was neither decreed from above nor built overnight: it was a piecemeal ground-up trudge. It did not rely on the benevolence of states, a tide of heroic litigants, and an activist juristocracy: it stood on the shoulders of ordinary people and judges

---

[39] Scheppele, "Autocratic Legalism," at 549–556, 573; Sadurski, Wojciech. 2019. *Poland's Constitutional Breakdown*. New York, NY: Oxford University Press, at 96–126.

[40] The concept of a "dual state" was coined by Ernst Fraenkel in: Fraenkel, Ernst. 2017 [1941]. *The Dual State: A Contribution to the Theory of Dictatorship*. New York, NY: Oxford University Press.

[41] Stern, *Environmental Litigation in China*, at 97–122.

[42] Scheppele, "Autocratic Legalism," at 553–554; Scheppele, Kim Lane. 2019. "Autocracy under the Cover of the Transnational Legal Order." In *Constitution-Making and Transnational Legal Order*, Gregory Shaffer, Tom Ginsburg, and Terence Halliday, eds. New York, NY: Cambridge University Press, at 223–224; Emmons, Cassandra, and Tommaso Pavone. 2021. "The Rhetoric of Inaction: Failing to Fail Forward in the EU Rule of Law Crisis." *Journal of European Public Policy* 28 (10): 1611–1629.

[43] Under Article 2 of the Treaty on European Union. See: Scheppele, Kim, Dimitry Kochenov, and Barbara Grabowska-Moroz. 2021. "EU Values Are Law, After All: Enforcing EU Values through Systemic Infringement Actions by the European Commission and the Member States of the European Union." *Yearbook of European Law* 39: 3–121.

who could be persuaded to challenge their own governments. Nor has its subjection to heightened public scrutiny unequivocally provoked regressive backlash: it has also broadened citizens' awareness of their European legal rights. Denying this possibilist inheritance is critical to the success of those who seek to undermine the rule of law in Europe. They must hijack the state as the sole embodiment of "the people" and sever civil society from transnational policymakers.[44] They must foreclose European interventions from above and extinguish hope in social mobilization from below. They must co-opt or silence the legal professions through the Janus-faced deployment of the dual state.

These developments are undeniably troubling, yet the crises they unleash also have a way of bringing to light previously hidden possibilities for agency and institutional change.[45] It turns out that Euro-lawyers are neither destined to quiescent corporate servitude[46] nor to co-optation by the state. Faced with imminent threats to the rule of law, lawyers have gained a new *raison d'être*, an opportunity to be part of the vanguard of a transnational "resurrection of civil society."[47] From the democratization of Spain and Korea in the 1980s to political struggles for transitional justice in Latin America and the rule of law in Asia,[48] history is rife with examples of "lawyers, in particular, [who] stimulated the resurgence of civic groups" by connecting them with allies abroad and to international organizations.[49]

To start, attorneys can repurpose tried-and-true Euro-lawyering to enable the ECJ to expand the EU's rule of law enforcement toolkit. In the past few years alone, referrals from national courts have fueled a revolution in the European Court's case law. In the most pathbreaking series of rulings since proclaiming Europe a "community based on

---

[44] Müller, Jan-Werner. 2019. "Populism and the People." *London Review of Books* 41(10): 35–37.

[45] For an early iteration of this insight, see: Halliday, *Beyond Monopoly.*

[46] Multinational corporations have either been passive bystanders or even net benefactors as liberal democracy erodes across parts of Europe: Gray, Julia, R. Daniel Kelemen, and Terence Teo. 2019. "Pecunia Non Olet: The Political Economy of Financial Flows into Illiberal European Countries." Presented at the 11th Annual EU Workshop, Princeton University, April 29.

[47] O'Donnell, Guillermo, and Philippe Schmitter. 2013 [1986]. *Transitions from Authoritarian Rule*, Vol. 4. Baltimore, MD: Johns Hopkins University Press, at 55.

[48] See, for instance: González-Ocantos, *Shifting Legal Visions*; Tam, Waikeung. 2012. *Legal Mobilization under Authoritarianism: The Case of Post-Colonial Hong Kong.* New York, NY: Cambridge University Press.

[49] Halliday, Karpik, and Feeley, *Fighting for Political Freedom*, at 18.

the rule of law" in 1986,[50] the ECJ has held that all member states are required to maintain independent judiciaries,[51] that judges need not honor a European Arrest Warrant (EAW) if a lack of judicial independence would violate the defendant's right to a fair trial,[52] and that efforts to capture national court systems via government-controlled disciplinary chambers are illegal under EU law.[53] These rulings are a rallying cry for all national courts to act as guarantors of citizens' fundamental EU rights and resist illiberal reforms.[54] And Polish judges have heeded this call despite threats of repression, punting nearly two dozen cases to Luxembourg to challenge illiberal national laws.[55]

These expanding European legal opportunities are an invaluable resource for lawyers who seek to wrestle spokesmanship over civil society from the grips of an abusive state. As Kim Scheppele has argued, "a citizenry trained to resist the legalistic autocrats must be educated in the tools of law themselves."[56] In recent years, for instance, lawyers have exposed repression masked as law by representing dissident academics and publicizing the sham trials brought against them.[57] They have banded together into transnational associations to defend journalists and public watchdogs against legal harassment and intimidation.[58] They have worked with NGOs subject to state

[50] 294/83, *Les Verts*, at para. 23.
[51] Specifically under Article 19(1) of the Treaty on European Union. See: Case C-64/16, *Associação Sindical dos Juízes Portugueses* [2018], ECLI:EU:C:2018:117, at paras. 43–44.
[52] Case C-216/18 PPU, *Minister for Justice and Equality v. Celmer* [2018], ECLI:EU:C:2018:586.
[53] Joined cases C-585/18, C-624-18, and C-625/18, *A. K. and Others v Sąd Najwyższy* [2019], ECLI:EU:C:2019:982; see also case C-192/18, *Commission v. Poland* [2019], ECLI:EU:C:2019:924; case C-619/18, *Commission v. Poland* [2019], ECLI:EU:C:2019:531.
[54] Grabowska-Moroz, Barbara, and Jakub Jaraczewski. 2019. "High Expectations." *Verfassungsblog*, November 2019; Pech, Laurent, and Patryk Wachowiek. 2020. "1460 Days Later." *Verfassungsblog*, January 20.
[55] Jaremba, Urszula. 2020. "Defending the Rule of Law or Reality-Based Self-Defence?" *European papers* 5(2): 851–869.
[56] Scheppele, "Autocratic Legalism," at 582–583.
[57] For instance, see: Morijn, John, and Barbara Grabowska-Moroz. 2019. "Supporting Wojciech Sadurski in a Warsaw Courtroom." *Verfassungsblog*, November 28.
[58] One such organization is the "Coalition against SLAPPS (Strategic Lawsuits Against Public Participation) in Europe" (CASE). Founded in 2020, it works "on behalf of journalists, activists, whistle blowers, rights defenders and other watchdogs targeted by these tactics … to expose legal harassment and intimidation, protect the

repression to identify hooks to European law that can be publicized in the streets, invoked in the courts, and serve as counter-narratives to portrayals of the EU as a hostile foreign entity.[59] And they have complemented public advocacy with behind-the-scenes lobbying campaigns, supplying European institutions with rapid legal analyses and situation reports that cut through the fog of state disinformation.[60]

To be sure, none of these strategies are silver bullets, and their simultaneous deployment would certainly be unprecedented in EU history. But neither are they reinventions of the wheel. They represent extensions and reconfigurations of a politics of lawyers whose lineage has undergirded European integration since its inception. In its noblest moments, these politics have served less as a means for professional aggrandizement and more as a calling to empower a transnational community of citizens to become masters of their collective destiny.

I want to close this book with one of Albert Hirschman's most perceptive observations: "People enjoy and feel empowered by the confidence, however vague, that they 'have history on their side'."[61] I often think about this phrase as I write about those first Euro-lawyers who believed that uniting Europe through law was possible. Who labored to persuade citizens and judges to fight for this vision. I also think about it when those who foreshadow the collapse of a European community based on the rule of law claim history as their ally. For they are not the only actors who can assert themselves over an unprojected future. By stepping into the light of democratic history making, lawyers can still promote a future where freedom and legality continue to inspire the struggle for progress.

---

rights of those who speak out, and advocate for comprehensive protective measures and reform." See: www.the-case.eu/about.

[59] These efforts are hardly futile: In public opinion surveys in Poland and Hungary, citizens have consistently expressed higher support for the EU than their national governments. See: Scheppele, Kim, and Gabor Halmai. 2019. "The Tyranny of Values or the Tyranny of One-Party States?" *Verfassungsblog*, November 25.

[60] One example is the "Good Lobby Profs" initiative founded in 2021: a transnational group of lawyers and law professors who "act as a rapid response mechanism to uphold the rule of law across the [European] continent ... [by] provid[ing] pro bono expert analysis, support as well as engag[ing] in (good) lobbying activities." See: www.thegoodlobby.eu/thegoodlobbyprofs/.

[61] Hirschman, Albert. 1991. *The Rhetoric of Reaction*. Cambridge, MA: Harvard University Press, at 158.

# APPENDIX

LIST OF INTERVIEWEES

| Field site | Interviewee | Lawyer | Judge | Law Professor | Other | Interview date(s) | # Interviews |
|---|---|---|---|---|---|---|---|
| Rome | Roberto Reali | | 1 | | | 7/20/2015 | 1 |
| | Massimo Masella Ducci Teri | 1 | | | Public official | 6/25/2015 | 1 |
| | Giandonato Caggiano | | | 1 | | 6/23/2015 | 1 |
| | Luigi Moccia | | | 1 | | 6/16/2015 | 1 |
| | Luca Marini | | | 1 | | 6/17/2015 | 1 |
| | Luigi Daniele | 1 | | 1 | | 6/18/2015; 9/23/2016 | 2 |
| | Marta Cartabia | | 1 | 1 | | 6/24/2015; 10/5/2016 | 2 |
| | Gian Luigi Tosato | 1 | | 1 | | 6/25/2015; 10/5/2016 | 2 |
| | Cristoforo Osti | 1 | | 1 | | 6/22/2015; 9/29/2016 | 2 |
| | Sergio Fiorentino | 1 | | | | 6/25/2015; 9/28/2016 | 2 |
| | Gianni de Bellis | 1 | | | | 9/28/2016 | 1 |
| | Pietro Merlino | 1 | | | | 6/25/2015; 9/26/2016 | 2 |
| | Mario Siragusa | 1 | | | | 6/25/2015; 9/26/2016 | |
| | Riccardo Sciaudone | 1 | | | | 6/15/2015; 9/19/2016 | 2 |
| | Vincenzo Cannizzaro | 1 | | 1 | | 6/17/2015; 10/4/2016 | 2 |
| | Roberto Conti | | 1 | | | 8/4/2015; 10/12/2016 | 2 |
| | Amelia Torrice | | 1 | | | 8/3/2015; 9/19/2016 | 2 |
| | Antonino Galletti | 1 | | | | 9/26/2016 | 1 |
| | Gianpaolo Girardi | 1 | | | | 9/26/2016 | 1 |
| | Filippo Zinelli | 1 | | | | 9/26/2016 | |
| | Roberto Giovagnoli | 1 | 1 | | | 9/27/2016 | 1 |
| | Sergio Fidanzia | 1 | | | | 9/22/2016 | 1 |
| | Angelo Gigliola | 1 | | | | 9/22/2016 | |
| | Francesco Maria Samperi | 1 | | | | 10/11/2016 | 1 |
| | Silvana Sciarra | | 1 | 1 | | 10/13/2016 | 1 |

| Field site | Interviewee | Lawyer | Judge | Law Professor | Other | Interview date(s) | # Interviews |
|---|---|---|---|---|---|---|---|
| | Giuseppe Bronzini | | 1 | | | 10/3/2016 | 1 |
| | Antonella di Florio | | 1 | | | 10/7/2016 | 1 |
| | Margherita Leone | | 1 | | | 9/29/2016 | 1 |
| | Ernesto Lupo | | 1 | | Public official | 10/6/2016 | 1 |
| | Monica Velletti | | 1 | | | 10/7/2016 | 1 |
| | Fabio Cintioli | 1 | 1 | 1 | | 9/30/2016 | 1 |
| | Aristide Police | 1 | | 1 | | 10/4/2016 | 1 |
| | Eugenio Picozza | 1 | | 1 | | 10/4/2016 | 1 |
| | Claudio Contessa | | 1 | | | 10/3/2016 | 1 |
| | Daria de Pretis | | 1 | 1 | | 10/14/2016 | 1 |
| | Rosa Perna | | 1 | | | 10/10/2016 | 1 |
| | Roberto Chieppa | | 1 | | Public official | 10/12/2016 | 1 |
| | Lilia Papoff | | 1 | | | 10/13/2016 | 1 |
| | Paolo Cassinis | 1 | | | Public official | 10/7/2016 | 1 |
| | Serena la Pergola | 1 | | | Public official | 10/13/2016 | |
| | Amos Andreoni | 1 | | 1 | | 2/22/2017 | 1 |
| | Paolo de Caterini | 1 | | 1 | Member of EU Commission Legal Service | 12/27/2017 | 1 |
| Genoa | Marcello Basilico | | 1 | | | 10/18/2016 | 1 |
| | Marco Pelissero | | | 1 | | 11/14/2016 | 1 |
| | Alberto Figone | 1 | | | | 10/27/2016 | 1 |
| | Francesco Munari | 1 | | 1 | | 7/28/2015; 10/24/2016 | 2 |
| | Lara Trucco | | | 1 | | 10/20/2016 | 1 |
| | Paolo Canepa | 1 | | | | 11/3/2016 | |
| | Davide Ponte | | 1 | | | 10/20/2016 | 1 |
| | Daniele Granara | 1 | | 1 | | 11/12/2016 | 1 |
| | Gerolamo Taccogna | 1 | | 1 | | 10/28/2016 | 1 |
| | Sergio Maria Carbone | 1 | | 1 | | 10/21/2016 | 1 |
| | Giuseppe Giacomini | 1 | | | | 10/26/2017; 10/24/2016; 11/2/2016 | 3 |
| | Giorgia Scuras | 1 | | | | 10/24/2016 | |
| | Greta Demartini | 1 | | | | 11/8/2016 | 1 |
| | Pierangelo Celle | 1 | | 1 | | 10/19/2016 | |
| | Marco Turci | 1 | | | | 10/19/2016 | 1 |
| | Andrea La Mattina | 1 | | 1 | | 11/14/2016 | 1 |
| | Alessandro Vaccaro | 1 | | | | 10/2/2016 | 1 |
| | Lorenzo Schiano di Pepe | 1 | | 1 | | 10/25/2016 | 1 |
| | Stefano Savi | 1 | | | | 11/9/2016 | 1 |

| Field site | Interviewee | Lawyer | Judge | Law Professor | Other | Interview date(s) | # Interviews |
|---|---|---|---|---|---|---|---|
| | Lorenza Calcagno | | 1 | | | 11/8/2016 | 1 |
| | Maurizio Maresca | 1 | | 1 | | 11/2/2016 | 1 |
| | Roberto Braccialini | | 1 | | | 10/30/2016 | 1 |
| | Maria Teresa Bonavia | | 1 | | | 11/8/2016 | 1 |
| | Enrico Vergani | 1 | | 1 | | 10/27/2016 | 1 |
| | Roberto Damonte | 1 | | | | 10/28/2016 | |
| | Emanuela Boglione | 1 | | | | 10/28/2016 | 1 |
| | Federica Bianchi di Lavagna Passerini | 1 | | | | 10/28/2016 | |
| | Michele Marchesiello | | 1 | | | 11/10/2016 | 1 |
| | Carlotta Gualco | | | | Civic org. head | 11/14/2016 | 1 |
| Milan | Fabrizio Fracchia | | | 1 | | 10/12/2016 | 1 |
| | Cinzia Calabrese | 1 | | | | 11/28/2016 | 1 |
| | Bianca La Monica | | 1 | | | 12/7/2016 | 1 |
| | Giulia Turri | | 1 | | | 11/25/2016 | 1 |
| | Alima Zana | | 1 | | | 11/28/2016 | 1 |
| | Martina Flamini | | 1 | | | 11/24/2016 | 1 |
| | Federico Salmeri | | 1 | | | 12/13/2016 | 1 |
| | Ilaria Gentile | | 1 | | | 11/23/2016 | 1 |
| | Elena Quadri | | 1 | | | 12/13/2016 | 1 |
| | Antonio de Vita | | 1 | | | 11/21/2016 | 1 |
| | Angelo de Zotti | | 1 | | | 11/30/2016 | 1 |
| | Giuseppe Buffone | | 1 | | | 12/14/2016 | 1 |
| | Pierpaolo Gori | | 1 | | | 11/18/2016 | 1 |
| | Anna Gardini | 1 | | | | 12/2/2016 | 1 |
| | Dario Simeoli | | 1 | | | 12/12/2016 | 1 |
| | Alessandro Simeone | 1 | | | | 11/28/2016 | 1 |
| | Diana-Urania Galetta | | | 1 | | 11/17/2016 | 1 |
| | Antonio Papi Rossi | 1 | | | | 11/22/2016 | 1 |
| | Edoardo Gambaro | 1 | | | | 11/22/2016 | |
| | Francesco Rossi Dal Pozzo | 1 | | 1 | | 11/22/2016 | 1 |
| | Emilio Cucchiara | 1 | | | | 11/28/2016 | 1 |
| | Roberto Jacchia | 1 | | | | 11/17/2016 | 1 |
| | Enrico Raffaelli | 1 | | | | 12/14/2016 | 1 |
| | Laura Cossar | 1 | | | | 11/24/2016 | 1 |
| | Francesca Cunteri | 1 | | | | 12/1/2016 | 1 |
| | Giuseppe Franco Ferrari | 1 | | 1 | | 11/24/2016 | 1 |
| | Francesco Viganò | | | 1 | | 11/25/2016 | 1 |
| | Fausto Capelli | 1 | | 1 | | 11/23/2016 | 1 |
| | Francesco Mariuzzo | | 1 | | Public official | 12/6/2016 | 1 |

| Field site | Interviewee | Lawyer | Judge | Law Professor | Other | Interview date(s) | # Interviews |
|---|---|---|---|---|---|---|---|
| | Francesca Ruggieri | 1 | | 1 | | 12/2/2016 | 1 |
| | Patrick Ferrari | 1 | | | | 12/13/2016 | 1 |
| | Patrizia Guzzoli | 1 | | | | 12/13/2016 | |
| | Francesca Fiecconi | | 1 | | | 12/2/2016 | 1 |
| | Claudio Marangoni | | 1 | | | 12/12/2016 | 1 |
| | Stefano Cozzi | | 1 | | | 12/12/2016 | 1 |
| | Bruno Nascimbene | 1 | | 1 | | 7/8/2015; 11/22/2016 | 2 |
| Trento/ Bolzano | Barbara Marchetti | | | 1 | | 1/16/2017 | 1 |
| | Guglielmo Avolio | | 1 | | | 1/9/2017 | 1 |
| | Enrico Giammarco | 1 | | | | 1/18/2017 | 1 |
| | Gloria Servetti | | 1 | | | 1/24/2017 | 1 |
| | Roberta de Pretis | 1 | | | | 1/17/2017 | 1 |
| | Michele Maria Benini | | 1 | | | 1/23/2017 | 1 |
| | Roberto Beghini | | 1 | | | 1/25/2017 | 1 |
| | Giorgio Flaim | | 1 | | | 1/26/2017 | 1 |
| | Guido Denicolò | 1 | | | | 1/16/2017 | 1 |
| | Giandomenico Falcon | 1 | | 1 | | 1/20/2017 | 1 |
| | Giuseppe Nesi | | | 1 | | 1/12/2017 | 1 |
| | Federico Paciolla | | 1 | | | 1/13/2017 | 1 |
| | Andrea de Bertolini | 1 | | | | 1/18/2017 | 1 |
| | Armin Reinstadler | 1 | | | | 1/19/2017 | 1 |
| | Andreas Reinalter | 1 | | | | 1/19/2017 | |
| | Gian Antonio Benacchio | | | 1 | | 1/25/2017 | 1 |
| | Alma Chiettini | | 1 | | Public official | 1/18/2017 | 1 |
| | Roberta Sandri | 1 | | | | 1/23/2017 | 1 |
| | Massimo Zortea | 1 | | | | 1/23/2017 | |
| | Andrea Mantovani | 1 | | | | 1/16/2017 | 1 |
| | Monica Carlin | 1 | | | | 1/10/2017 | 1 |
| | Andrea Manca | 1 | | | | 1/4/2017 | 1 |
| | Michele Cozzio | 1 | | 1 | | 1/19/2017 | 1 |
| | Marco Dani | | | 1 | | 1/25/2017 | 1 |
| | Thomas Mathà | 1 | | | Public official | 1/28/2017 | 1 |
| | Antonino Ali' | 1 | | 1 | | 1/19/2017 | 1 |
| | Luisa Antoniolli | | | 1 | | 1/16/2017 | 1 |
| | Fulvio Cortese | | | 1 | | 1/9/2017 | 1 |
| | Luca Cestaro | | | 1 | | 2/7/2017 | 1 |
| | Ciro Faranga | 1 | | | Senator | 6/24/2015 | 1 |
| | Salvatore Veneziano | | 1 | | | 2/9/2017 | 1 |
| | Gianmaria Palliggiano | | 1 | | | 2/20/2017 | 1 |

| Field site | Interviewee | Lawyer | Judge | Law Professor | Other | Interview date(s) | # Interviews |
|---|---|---|---|---|---|---|---|
| Naples | Fabio Ferraro | 1 | | 1 | | 2/6/2017 | 1 |
| | Roberto Mastroianni | 1 | | 1 | | 7/21/2015; 2/13/2017 | 2 |
| | Umberto Aleotti | 1 | | 1 | | 7/29/2015; 2/17/2017 | 2 |
| | Mariangela Avolio | 1 | | | | 7/29/2015; 2/17/2017 | |
| | Maurizio Carrabba | 1 | | | | 7/29/2015; 2/17/2017 | |
| | Alessandro Senatore | 1 | | | | 7/29/2015 | |
| | Giuseppe Tesauro | 1 | 1 | 1 | ex-Advocate General at ECJ | 7/22/2015; 2/18/2017; 2/25/2017 | 5 |
| | Paolo Coppola | | 1 | | | 7/21/2015; 2/13/2017; 2/25/2017 | |
| | Massimo Fragola | | | 1 | | 7/30/2015; 2/14/2017 | 2 |
| | Raffaele Sabato | | 1 | | | 7/14/2015; 2/17/2017 | 2 |
| | Alberto Cinquegrana | 1 | | | | 2/7/2017 | 1 |
| | Giovanni Nucifero | 1 | | | | 2/23/2017 | 1 |
| | Ferdinando Del Mondo | 1 | | | | 2/23/2017 | |
| | Amedeo Arena | 1 | | 1 | | 2/9/2017 | 1 |
| | Raffaele Squeglia | 1 | | | | 2/24/2017 | 1 |
| | Marco Gagliotti | 1 | | | | 2/23/2017 | 1 |
| Bari | Fabrizio Lofoco | 1 | | | | 3/2/2017 | 1 |
| | Claudia Pironti | 1 | | | | 3/2/2017 | |
| | Rosaria Russo | 1 | | | | 3/2/2017 | |
| | Rosanna (anonymized) | 1 | | | | 3/6/2017 | 1 |
| | Giuseppe (anonymized) | 1 | | | | 3/6/2017 | |
| | Ilaria (anonymized) | 1 | | | | 3/6/2017 | |
| | Pietro (anonymized) | 1 | | | | 3/6/2017 | |
| | Angela Romito | | | 1 | | 3/6/2017 | 1 |
| | Alberto Capobianco | | | 1 | | 3/6/2017 | |
| | Luciano Garofalo | 1 | | 1 | | 3/7/2017 | 1 |
| | Paola (anonymized) | | 1 | | | 3/2017 | 1 |
| | Marta (anonymized) | | 1 | | | 3/2017 | |
| | Enrico Scoditti | | 1 | | | 3/8/2017 | 1 |
| | Vito Leccese | | | 1 | | 3/10/2017 | 1 |
| | Emmanuele Virgintino | 1 | | | | 3/13/2017 | 1 |

| Field site | Interviewee | Lawyer | Judge | Law Professor | Other | Interview date(s) | # Interviews |
|---|---|---|---|---|---|---|---|
| | Teresa Liuni | | 1 | | | 3/13/2017 | 1 |
| | Gennaro Notarnicola | 1 | | 1 | | 3/13/2017 | 1 |
| | Ennio Triggiani | | | 1 | | 3/20/2017 | 1 |
| | Angela Arbore | | 1 | | | 3/20/2017 | 1 |
| | Ernesta Tarantino | | 1 | | | 3/20/2017 | 1 |
| | Marcello Barbanente | | 1 | | | 3/20/2017 | 1 |
| | Ernesto Capobianco | 1 | | 1 | | 3/20/2017 | 1 |
| | Giacinta Serlenga | | 1 | | | 3/22/2017 | 1 |
| | Giovanni Zaccaro | | 1 | | | 3/22/2017 | 1 |
| | Francesco Tedeschi | 1 | | | | 3/23/2017 | 1 |
| | Nicola Grasso | | | 1 | | 3/23/2017 | 1 |
| | Mariano Alterio | 1 | | | | 3/23/2017 | |
| | Sebastiano Gentile | | 1 | | | 3/23/2017 | |
| | Giovanni Pesce | 1 | | | | 8/18/2017 | 1 |
| Florence | Filippo Donati | | | 1 | | 7/13/2015 | 1 |
| | Francesco Oliveri | 1 | | | Public official | 7/13/2015 | 1 |
| | Giovanna Ichino | | 1 | | | 7/14/2015 | 1 |
| | Adelina Adinolfi | | | 1 | | 7/14/2015 | 1 |
| | Bruno de Witte | | | 1 | | 7/14/2015 | 1 |
| | Valeria Piccone | | 1 | | | 7/16/2015 | 1 |
| | Niccolò Pecchioli | 1 | | | | 7/16/2015 | 1 |
| | Salvatore "Toto" Cordaro | 1 | | | Public official | 3/31/2017 | 1 |
| | Vito Patanella | 1 | | | | 3/31/2017 | |
| | Giuseppe Battaglia | | | | Public official | 3/31/2017 | 1 |
| | Michele Ruvolo | | 1 | | | 4/3/2017 | 1 |
| | Giuseppe de Gregorio | | 1 | | | 4/3/2017 | |
| | Luigi Raimondi | 1 | | 1 | | 4/3/2017 | 1 |
| | Antonello Tancredi | | | 1 | | 4/3/2017 | 1 |
| Palermo | Valentina Giarrusso | 1 | | | | 4/4/2017 | 1 |
| | Pietro Alosi | 1 | | | | 4/4/2017 | |
| | Maria Bruccoleri | 1 | | 1 | | 4/4/2017 | 1 |
| | Federica Cabrini | | 1 | | | 4/4/2017 | 1 |
| | Giuseppe La Greca | | 1 | | | 4/4/2017 | |
| | Giovanni Tulumello | | 1 | | | 4/5/2017 | 1 |
| | Alessandra Pera | | | 1 | | 4/5/2017 | 1 |
| | Rosanna de Nictolis | | 1 | | | 4/10/2017 | 1 |
| | Marco Mazzamuto | 1 | | 1 | | 4/11/2017 | 1 |
| | Daria Coppa | 1 | | 1 | | 4/11/2017 | 1 |
| | Claudio Zucchelli | | 1 | | | 4/12/2017 | 1 |

| Field site | Interviewee | Lawyer | Judge | Law Professor | Other | Interview date(s) | # Interviews |
|---|---|---|---|---|---|---|---|
| | Benedetto Romano | | | | civic org. head | 4/12/2017 | |
| | Alessandro Palmigiano | 1 | | | | 4/12/2017 | 1 |
| | Giuseppe di Rosa | 1 | | 1 | | 4/18/2017 | 1 |
| | Giuseppe Verde | | 1 | 1 | | 4/19/2017 | 1 |
| | Caterina Mirto | 1 | | | | 4/19/2017 | 1 |
| | Francesco Cancilla | | 1 | | | 4/21/2017 | 1 |
| | Chiara Gioè | 1 | | 1 | | 4/21/2017 | 1 |
| | Tania Hmeljak | | 1 | | | 4/21/2017 | 1 |
| Foggia | Vincenzo de Michele | | | 1 | | 3/25/2017 | 1 |
| Vicenza | Alberto Dal Ferro | 1 | | | | 3/6/2017 | 1 |
| Modena | Teresa Magno | | 1 | | | 7/25/2015 | 1 |
| Padova | Gabriele Donà | 1 | | | | 7/23/2015; 8/26/2017 | 2 |
| Brescia | Wilma Viscardini | 1 | | 1 | | 29/9/2017 | 1 |
| | Mara Bertagnolli | | 1 | | | 1/30/2017 | 1 |
| ECJ | Fabio Pappalardo | | | | Librarian | 2/10/2017 | 1 |
| | Fabrizio Barzanti | | | | Référendaire | 7/31/2015 | 1 |
| | Daniele Domenicucci | | | | Référendaire | 8/4/2015 | 1 |
| | Paolo Gori | | 1 | | Référendaire | 4/6/2017 | 1 |
| Paris | Philippe Derouin | 1 | | | | 9/12/2017 | 1 |
| | Charles-Henri Leger | 1 | | | | 9/12/2017 | 1 |
| | Eric Morgan de Rivery | 1 | | | | 9/12/2017 | |
| | Claire Lavin | 1 | | | | 9/12/2017 | 1 |
| | Hugues Calvet | 1 | | | | 9/13/2017 | 1 |
| | Robert Saint-Esteben | 1 | | | | 9/13/2017 | |
| | Christian Brugerolle | | | | Jurist | 9/15/2017 | 1 |
| | Olivier Freget | 1 | | | | 9/15/2017 | 1 |
| | Louis Boré | 1 | | | | 9/15/2017 | 1 |
| | Didier Theophile | 1 | | | | 9/19/2017 | 1 |
| | Jean-Pierre Spitzer | 1 | | | Référendaire | 9/20/2017 | 1 |
| | Bernard Stirn | | 1 | 1 | | 9/20/2017 | 1 |
| | Helene Farge | 1 | | | | 9/21/2017 | 1 |
| | Philippe Guibert | 1 | | | | 9/21/2017 | 1 |
| | Sophie Canas | | 1 | | | 9/22/2017 | 1 |
| | Frédéric Manin | 1 | | | | 9/22/2017 | 1 |
| | Christian Roth | 1 | | 1 | | 9/25/2017 | 1 |
| | Patrick Frydman | | 1 | | | 9/25/2017 | 1 |
| | Jean-Sébastien Pilczer | 1 | 1 | | | 9/25/2017 | 1 |
| | Julie Bailleux | | | 1 | | 9/27/2017 | 1 |
| | Laurent Truchot | | 1 | | Référendaire | 9/27/2017 | 1 |

| Field site | Interviewee | Lawyer | Judge | Law Professor | Other | Interview date(s) | # Interviews |
|---|---|---|---|---|---|---|---|
| | Francois Molinié | 1 | | | | 9/27/2017 | 1 |
| | Fabien Raynaud | | 1 | | Public official | 9/29/2017 | 1 |
| | Jacqueline Riffault-Silk | | 1 | | | 9/29/2017 | 1 |
| | Roger Grass | | 1 | | Référendaire, greffier | 9/29/2017 | 1 |
| | Guy Canivet | | 1 | | | 10/2/2017 | 1 |
| | Geraud Sajust de Bergues | | 1 | | Référendaire, public official | 10/2/2017 | 1 |
| | Alain Lacabarats | | 1 | | | 10/3/2017 | 1 |
| | Thierry Fossier | | 1 | | | 10/3/2017 | 1 |
| | Philippe Florès | | 1 | | | 10/4/2017 | 1 |
| | Chantal Arens | | 1 | | | 10/4/2017 | 1 |
| | Marie-Caroline Celeyron-Bouillot | | 1 | | | 10/4/2017 | |
| | Nathalie Bourgeois-de-Ryck | | 1 | | | 10/4/2017 | |
| | Mattias Guyomar | | 1 | | | 10/5/2017 | 1 |
| Marseille/ Aix | Pierre-Olivier Koubi-Flotte | 1 | | | | 10/9/2017 | 1 |
| | Rostane Mehdi | | | 1 | | 10/11/2017 | 1 |
| | Valérie Michel | | | 1 | | 10/16/2017 | 1 |
| | Christian Rousse | 1 | | | | 10/17/2017 | 1 |
| | Christophe Cirefice | | 1 | | Ex-civil sevant | 10/19/2017 | 1 |
| | Estelle Brosset | | | 1 | | 10/19/2017 | 1 |
| | Claire Merlin | 1 | | | Public official | 10/20/2017 | 1 |
| | Hélène Rouland-Boyer | | 1 | | Ex-civil sevant | 10/23/2017 | 1 |
| | Ghislaine Markarian | | 1 | | | 10/23/2017 | 1 |
| | Lise Leroy-Gissinger | | 1 | | | 10/24/2017 | 1 |
| | Ivonne (anonymized) | | 1 | | | 10/25/2017 | |
| | Felicia (anonymized) | | 1 | | | 10/25/2017 | |
| | Françoise (anonymized) | | 1 | | | 10/25/2017 | 1 |
| | Fabrice (anonymized) | | 1 | | | 10/25/2017 | |
| | Victor (anonymized) | | 1 | | | 10/25/2017 | |
| | Camille (anonymized) | | 1 | | | 10/25/2017 | |
| Lille | Marcel Veroone | 1 | | | | 8/20-8/22/2018 | 1 |
| | Thomas Luebbig | 1 | | | | 11/1/2017 | 1 |
| | Susanne Augenhofer | | | 1 | | 11/1/2017 | 1 |

327

| Field site | Interviewee | Lawyer | Judge | Law Professor | Other | Interview date(s) | # Interviews |
|---|---|---|---|---|---|---|---|
| Berlin | Heike Schweitzer | | | 1 | | 11/2/2017 | 1 |
| | Ingolf Pernice | | | 1 | | 11/3/2017 | 1 |
| | Rene Grafunder | 1 | | | | 11/7/2017 | 1 |
| | Jorg Karenfort | 1 | | 1 | | 11/7/2017 | 1 |
| | Helmut Aust | | | 1 | | 11/7/2017 | |
| | Christian Joerges | 1 | | 1 | | 11/8/2017 | 1 |
| | Georg Nolte | | | 1 | | 11/9/2017 | 1 |
| | Norbert Wimmer | 1 | | 1 | | 11/10/2017 | 1 |
| | Christoph Arhold | 1 | | | | 11/10/2017 | |
| | Stephan Gerstner | 1 | | | | 11/13/2017 | |
| | Matthias Kottmann | 1 | | | | 11/13/2017 | 1 |
| | Kathrin Dingermann | 1 | | | | 11/13/2017 | |
| | Christian Armbruester | | 1 | 1 | | 11/14/2017 | 1 |
| | Frederik Leenen | 1 | | | | 11/15/2017 | 1 |
| | Thomas Henze | 1 | | | Référendaire; Civil servant | 11/16/2017 | 1 |
| | Ralf Kanitz | 1 | | | Civil servant | 11/16/2017 | |
| | Dieter Grimm | | 1 | 1 | | 11/20/2017 | 1 |
| | Christoph Wagner | 1 | | 1 | | 11/21/2017 | 1 |
| | Andreas Gruenwald | 1 | | 1 | | 11/21/2017 | |
| | Carl-Wendelin Neubert | 1 | | | | 11/21/2017 | 1 |
| | Alexander Jannasch | | 1 | | | 11/22/2017; 11/30/2017 | 2 |
| | Monika Noehre | 1 | 1 | | | 1/22/2018 | 1 |
| Mannheim | Jan Bergmann | | 1 | 1 | | 11/28/2017 | 1 |
| | Michael Funke-Kaiser | | 1 | | | 11/30/2017 | 1 |
| Heidelberg | Peter-Christian Mueller-Graff | | 1 | 1 | | 11/28/2017 | 1 |
| Munich | Thomas Ackermann | | | 1 | | 11/29/2017 | 1 |
| | Alexander Rinne | 1 | | | | 12/1/2017 | 1 |
| | Rudolf Mellinghoff | | 1 | | | 12/11/2017 | 1 |
| | Manja Epping | 1 | | | | 12/12/2017 | 1 |
| | Christian Frank | 1 | | | | 12/12/2017 | |
| | Thomas Raab | 1 | | | | 12/12/2017 | |
| | Daniel Petzold | 1 | | | | 12/12/2017 | 1 |
| | Ansgar Ohly | | | 1 | | 12/14/2017 | 1 |
| | Marianne Grabrucker | | 1 | | | 12/15/2017 | 1 |
| | Wolfgang Schoen | | | 1 | | 12/18/2017 | 1 |
| | Erik Roeder | | | 1 | | 12/18/2017 | |
| | Markus Loeffelmann | | 1 | | | 12/19/2017 | 1 |

| Field site | Interviewee | Lawyer | Judge | Law Professor | Other | Interview date(s) | # Interviews |
|---|---|---|---|---|---|---|---|
| | Michael Schönauer | | 1 | | | 12/19/2017 | 1 |
| | Matthias Leistner | 1 | | 1 | | 12/19/2017 | 1 |
| | Matthias Zigann | | 1 | | | 12/19/2017 | 1 |
| Frankfurt | Frank Schreiber | | 1 | | | 12/4/2017 | 1 |
| Stuttgart | Rolf Gutmann | 1 | | | | 12/6/2017 | 1 |
| Cologne | Dietrich Ehle | 1 | | | | 12/13/2017 | 1 |
| City in | Christa | | 1 | | | 12/15/2017 | |
| populous | Hendrik | 1 | 1 | | | 12/15/2017 | 1 |
| Lander | Berta | | 1 | | | 12/15/2017 | |
| Bensheim | Carl Otto Lenz | 1 | 1 | | Ex-ECJ Advocate General; ex-MP (CDU) | 12/16/2017 | 1 |
| Muenster | Andreas Middeke | | 1 | 1 | | 12/19/2017 | 1 |
| | Svenja Kreft | | 1 | | | 12/19/2017 | |
| Duesseldorf | Ralf Neugebauer | | 1 | | | 1/8/2018 | 1 |
| Lueneburg | Joachim Tepperwien | | 1 | | | 1/19/2018 | 1 |
| | Sebastian Baer | | 1 | | | 1/19/2018 | |
| | Anna Miria Fuerst | | 1 | | | 1/19/2018 | |
| Leipzig | Ingo Kraft | | 1 | 1 | | 1/15/2018; 1/12/2018 | 2 |
| | Marion Eckertz-Hoefer | | 1 | | | 1/12/2018 | 1 |
| Hamburg | Klaus von Gierke | 1 | | | | 1/5/2018 | 1 |
| | Juergen Luedicke | 1 | | 1 | | 1/8/2018 | 1 |
| | Bjorn Bodewaldt | 1 | | | | 1/8/2018 | |
| | Klaus Landry | 1 | | | | 1/9/2018 | 1 |
| | Lothar Harings | 1 | | | | 1/9/2018 | |
| | Andreas Schulte | 1 | | | | 1/10/2018 | 1 |
| | Eva Liebich | 1 | | | | 1/10/2018 | |
| | Stephanie Zoellner | | 1 | | | 1/10/2018 | 1 |
| | Klaus Dienelt | | 1 | | | 1/11/2018 | 1 |
| | Tobias Bender | 1 | 1 | | | 1/17/2018 | 1 |
| | Corina Koegel | | 1 | | | 1/17/2018 | |
| | Weinand Meilicke | 1 | | | | 1/31/2018; 1/17/2018 | 2 |
| | Markus Kotzur | | | 1 | | 1/18/2018 | 1 |
| | Stefanie Kohls | 1 | 1 | | | 1/25/2018 | 1 |
| | Jan Tolkmitt | 1 | 1 | | | 1/25/2018 | 1 |
| | Peter Behrens | | | 1 | | 1/25/2018 | 1 |
| | Thomas Bruha | | | 1 | | 1/25/2018 | |
| | Ernst-Joachim Mestmaecker | 1 | | 1 | | 1/26/2018 | 1 |

## EUROPEAN COURT OF JUSTICE CASES CITED

| ECJ Case # | Case name | Year decided | Published in |
|---|---|---|---|
| 26/62 | Van Gend en Loos | 1963 | ECR 1 |
| 6/64 | Flaminio Costa v. ENEL | 1964 | ECR 587 |
| 44/65 | Hessische Knappschaft v. Singer and Fils | 1965 | ECR 965 |
| 56/65 | Société Technique Minière v. Maschinenbau Ulm | 1966 | ECR 235 |
| 57/65 | Lütticke v. Hauptollamt Sarrlouis | 1966 | ECR 205 |
| 1/67 | Ciechelsky v. Caisse régionale de sécurité sociale du Centre | 1967 | ECR 181 |
| 9/67 | Colditz v. Caisse d'assurance vieillesse des travailleurs salariés | 1967 | ECR 229 |
| 22/67 | Caisse régionale de sécurité sociale du Nord v. Goffart | 1967 | ECR 321 |
| 7/68 | Commission v. Italy | 1968 | ECR 424 |
| 11/70 | Internationale Handelsgesellschaft | 1970 | ECR 1126 |
| 34/70 | Syndicat national du commerce extérieur des céréales and Others v. O.N.I.C. | 1970 | ECR 1233 |
| 18/71 | Eunomia di Porro e. C. v. Ministry of Education of the Italian Republic | 1971 | ECR 811 |
| Joined Cases 51/71 to 54/71 | International Fruit Company | 1971 | ECR 1107 |
| 82/71 | SAIL | 1972 | ECR 120 |
| 93/71 | Orsolina Leonesio v. Ministero dell'Agricoltura e Foreste | 1972 | ECR 287 |
| 41/74 | Van Duyn v. Home Office | 1974 | ECR 1337 |
| Joined Cases 10/75 to 14/75 | Lahaille | 1975 | ECR 1053 |
| 36/75 | Roland Rutili v. Ministre de l'Intérieur | 1975 | ECR 1219 |
| 87/75 | Conceria Daniele Bresciani v. Amministrazione Italiana delle Finanze | 1976 | ECR 129 |
| 13/76 | Gaetano Donà and Mario Mantero | 1976 | ECR 1333 |
| 60/75 | Russo v. AIMA | 1976 | ECR 46 |
| 118/75 | Watson and Belmann | 1976 | ECR 1185 |
| 106/77 | Amministrazione delle Finanze dello Stato v. Simmenthal SpA | 1978 | ECR 629 |
| 120/78 | Rewe-Zentral AG v. Bundesmonopolverwaltung für Branntwein / "Cassis de Dijon" | 1979 | ECR 649 |
| 179/78 | Procureur de la République v. Michelangelo Rivoira and others | 1979 | ECR 1147 |
| 244/78 | Union laitière normande v. French Dairy Farmers | 1979 | ECR 307 |
| 104/79 | Foglia v. Novello I | 1980 | ECR 746 |
| 244/80 | Foglia v. Novello II | 1981 | ECR 3047 |
| 65/81 | Reina | 1982 | ECR 34 |
| 261/81 | Walter Rau Lebensmittelwerke v. De Smedt PVBA | 1982 | ECR 3961 |
| 283/81 | Srl CILFIT and Lanificio di Gavardo SpA v. Ministry of Health | 1982 | ECR 3417 |
| 286/82 | Luisi and Carbone v. Ministero del Tesoro | 1982 | ECR 377 |

| ECJ Case # | Case name | Year decided | Published in |
|---|---|---|---|
| 16/83 | Criminal proceedings against Karl Prantl | 1984 | ECR 1299 |
| 294/83 | Les Verts v. European Parliament | 1986 | ECR 1339 |
| 193/85 | Co-Frutta v. Amministrazione delle finanze dello Stato | 1987 | ECR 2085 |
| 385/85 | S.R. Industries v. Administration des douanes | 1986 | ECR 2929 |
| C-369/88 | Criminal proceedings against Jean-Marie Delattre | 1991 | ECR I-1487 |
| Joined Cases C-6/90 and C-9/90 | Andrea Francovich and others v. Italian Republic | 1991 | ECR I-5357 |
| C-179/90 | Merci Convenzionali Porto di Genova v. Siderurgica Gabrielli | 1991 | ECR I-5889 |
| C-83/91 | Meilicke v. ADV-ORGA | 1992 | ECR I-4871 |
| C-18/93 | Corsica Ferries Italia Srl v. Corpo dei Piloti del Porto di Genova | 1994 | ECR I-1812 |
| C-415/93 | Union Royale Belge des Sociétés de Football Association ASBL v. Jean-Marc Bosman | 1995 | ECLI:EU: C:1995:463 |
| Joined Cases C-240/98 to C-244/98 | Océano Grupo Editorial SA | 2000 | ECLI:EU: C:2000:346 |
| C-473/00 | Cofidis SA | 2002 | ECLI:EU: C:2002:705 |
| Joined Cases C-482/01 and C-493/01 | Georgios Orfanopoulos and Others and Raffaele Oliveri v. Land Baden-Württemberg | 2004 | ECR I-5257 |
| C-173/03 | Traghetti del Mediterraneo SpA v. Repubblica Italiana | 2006 | ECR I-5177 |
| C-292/04 | Meilicke and Others | 2007 | ECR I-1835 |
| C-429/05 | Rampion and Godard | 2007 | ECLI:EU: C:2007:575 |
| C-103/06 | Derouin | 2008 | ECR I-1853 |
| C-109/07 | Pilato v. Bourgault | 2008 | ECLI:EU: C:2008:274 |
| C-262/09 | Meilicke and Others | 2011 | ECR I-5669 |
| Joined Cases C-338/11 to C-347/11 | Santander Asset Management SGIIC | 2012 | ECLI:EU: C:2012:286 |
| C-22/13 | Raffaella Mascolo and Others v. Ministero dell'Istruzione, dell'Università e della Ricerca and Comune di Napoli | 2014 | ECLI:EU: :2014:2401 |
| C-319/15 | Overseas Financial and Oaktree Finance | 2016 | ECLI:EU: C:2016:268 |
| C-64/16 | Associação Sindical dos Juízes Portugueses | 2018 | ECLI:EU: C:2018:117 |
| Joined Cases C-78/16 and C-79/16 | Pesce and Others v. Presidenza del Consiglio dei Ministri | 2016 | ECLI:EU: C:2016:340 |
| Joined Cases C-124/16, C-188/16 and C-213/16 | Criminal proceedings against Ianos Tranca and Others | 2017 | ECLI:EU: C:2016:563 |

| ECJ Case # | Case name | Year decided | Published in |
|---|---|---|---|
| C-320/16 | *Uber SAS France* | 2018 | ECLI:EU: C:2018:221 |
| C-192/18 | *Commission v. Poland* | 2019 | ECLI:EU: C:2019:529 |
| C-216/18PPU | *Minister for Justice and Equality* | 2018 | ECLI:EU: C:2018:586 |
| C-443/18 | *Commission v. Italy* | 2019 | ECLI:EU: C:2019:676 |
| C-619/18 | *Commission v. Poland* | 2019 | ECLI:EU: C:2019:531 |
| Joined Cases C-585/18, C-624/18, and C-625/18 | *A. K. and Others v Sąd Najwyższy* | 2019 | ECLI:EU: C:2019:982 |

# BIBLIOGRAPHY

Abbott, Andrew. 1988. *The System of Professions: An Essay on the Division of Expert Labor*. Chicago, IL: University of Chicago Press.

2016. *Processual Sociology*. Chicago, IL: University of Chicago Press.

Abebe, Daniel, and Tom Ginsburg. 2019. "The Dejudicialization of International Politics?" *International Studies Quarterly*, 63(3): 521–530.

Abel, Richard. 1988. "Lawyers in the Civil Law World." In *Lawyers in Society, Volume II: The Civil Law World*. Richard Abel and Philip Lewis, eds., Berkeley and Los Angeles, CA: University of California Press.

Alizada, Nazifa, Rowan Cole, Lisa Gastaldi, Sandra Grahn, Sebastian Hellmeier, Palina Kolvani, and Jean Lachapelle. 2021. "Autocratization Turns Viral: Democracy Report 2021." Technical report, V-DEM Institute, Gothenburg.

Almeida, Rodrigo. 2016. "Can Apulia's Olive Trees Be Saved?" *Science*, 353(6297): 346–348.

Alter, Karen. 1996a. "The European Court's Political Power." *West European Politics*, 19(3): 458–487.

1996b. "The Making of a Rule of Law in Europe." PhD dissertation, MIT, Cambridge, MA.

1998. "Explaining National Court Acceptance of European Court Jurisprudence: A Critical Evaluation of Theories of Legal Integration." In *The European Court and National Courts: Doctrine and Jurisprudence*. Anne-Marie Slaughter, Alec Stone Sweet, and Joseph Weiler, eds., New York, NY: Hart.

2000. "The European Union's Legal System and Domestic Policy: Spillover or Backlash?" *International Organization*, 54(3): 489–518.

2001. *Establishing the Supremacy of European Law*. New York, NY: Oxford University Press.

2014. *The New Terrain of International Law: Courts, Politics, Rights*. New York, NY: Princeton University Press.

2016. "Jurist Advocacy Movements in Europe and the Andes." iCourts Working Paper Series, 65: 1–30.

Alter, Karen, and Laurence Helfer. 2017. *Transplanting International Courts*. New York, NY: Oxford University Press.

Alter, Karen, Laurence Helfer, and Osvaldo Saldias. 2012. "Transplanting the European Court of Justice: The Experience of the Andean Tribunal of Justice." *The American Journal of Comparative Law*, 60(3): 629–664.

Alter, Karen, and Sophie Muenier-Aitsahalia. 1994. "Judicial Politics in the European Community." *Comparative Political Studies*, 26(4): 535–561.

Alter, Karen, and Michael Zürn. 2020. "Theorising Backlash Politics." *British Journal of Politics and International Relations*, 22(4): 739–752.

Altman, Irwin, and Setha Low. 1992. *Place Attachment*. Boston, MA: Springer.

Aran, Núria Arbonés. 2016. "Hub Cities 2.0 for the 21st Century." In *Urban Europe: Fifty Tales of the City*. Virginie Mamadouh and Anne van Wageningen, eds., Amsterdam: Amsterdam University Press.

Arena, Amedeo. 2019. "From an Unpaid Electricity Bill to the Primacy of EU Law: Gian Galeazzo Stendardi and the Making of *Costa v. ENEL*." *European Journal of International Law*, 30(3): 1017–1037.

Arksey, Hilary, and Peter Knight. 1999. *Interviewing for Social Scientists*. Thousand Oaks, CA: SAGE.

Arnull, Anthony. 1993. "Case C-83/91, *Wienand Meilicke* v. *ADV/ORGA FA Meyer AG*, Judgment of 16 July 1992." *Common Market Law Review*, 30(3): 613–622.

Aronson, Bruce. 2007. "Elite Law Firm Mergers and Reputational Competition: Is Bigger Really Better – An International Comparison." *Vanderbilt Journal of Transnational Law*, 40(4): 763–831.

Arrington, Celeste. 2016. *Accidental Activists: Victim Movements and Government Accountability in Japan and South Korea*. Ithaca, NY: Cornell University Press.

Arthur, Brian. 1994. *Increasing Returns and Path Dependence in the Economy*. Ann Arbor, MI: University of Michigan Press.

Avril, Lola. 2019. "Le Costume Sous la Robe: Les avocats en professionnels multi-cartes de l'État régulateur européen." PhD dissertation, Université Paris 1 Panthéon-Sorbonne, Paris.

Baetens, Freya. 2019. *Legitimacy of Unseen Actors in International Adjudication*. New York, NY: Cambridge University Press.

Bailleux, Julie. 2012. "Penser l'Europe par le droit." PhD dissertation, Université Paris 1 Panthéon-Sorbonne, Paris.

Bailleux, Julie. 2013. "Michel Gaudet, a Law Entrepreneur." *Common Market Law Review*, 50: 359–368.

Baldwin, David. 2015. "Misinterpreting Dahl on Power." *Journal of Political Power*, 8(2): 209–227.

Banfield, Edward. 1958. *The Moral Basis of a Backward Society*. New York, NY: Free Press.

Barbiche, Bernard. 2010. "Les attributions judiciaires du Conseil du roi." *Histoire, Economie, & Société*, 29(3): 9–17.

Bartolini, Antonio, and Angela Guerrieri. 2017. "The Pyrrhic Victory of Mr. Francovich and the Principle of State Liability in the Italian Context." In *EU Law Stories: Contextual and Critical Histories of European Jurisprudence*. Fernanda Nicola and Bill Davies, eds., New York, NY: Cambridge University Press.

Beach, Derek, and Rasmus Pedersen. 2019. *Process-Tracing Methods*. Ann Arbor, MI: University of Michigan Press.

Bebr, Gerhard. 1982. "The Possible Implications of *Foglia* v. *Novello II*." *Common Market Law Review*, 19(3): 421–441.

1987. "The Preliminary Proceedings of Article 177 EEC: Problems and Suggestions for Improvement." In *Article 177 EEC: Experiences and Problems*. Henry Schermers, Christiaan Timmermans, Alfred Kellermann, and J. Stewart Watson, eds., New York, NY: Elsevier.

Bednar, Jenna, and Scott E. Page. 2018. "When Order Affects Performance: Culture, Behavioral Spillovers, and Institutional Path Dependence." *The American Political Science Review*, 112(1): 8–98.

Beissinger, Mark. 2002. *Nationalist Mobilization and the Collapse of the Soviet State*. New York, NY: Cambridge University Press.

Bell, John. 2001. *French Legal Cultures*. New York, NY: Cambridge University Press.

2006. *Judiciaries within Europe*. New York, NY: Cambridge University Press.

Benna, Alessandro, and Lucia Compagnino. 2005. *30 Giugno 1960*. Genoa: Frilli.

Bennett, Andrew, and Jeffrey Checkel. 2015. *Process Tracing: From Metaphor to Analytic Tool*. New York, NY: Cambridge University Press.

Bernier, Alexandre. 2012. "Constructing and Legitimating: Transnational Jurist Networks and the Making of a Constitutional Practice of European Law, 1950–70." *Contemporary European History*, 21(3): 399–415.

2018. "La France et le Droit Communautaire 1958–1981." PhD dissertation, University of Copenhagen, Copenhagen.

Berry, Jeffrey M. 2002. "Validity and Reliability Issues in Elite Interviewing." *PS: Political Science & Politics*, 35(4): 679–682.

Bessy, Christian. 2016. "Organisation des cabinets d'avocats et marchés des services juridiques." *Revue d'économie industrielle*, 155(3): 41–69.

Biland, Émilie, and Hélène Steinmetz. 2017. "Are Judges Street-Level Bureaucrats? Evidence from French and Canadian Family Courts." *Law and Social Inquiry*, 42(2): 298–324.

Biland, Émilie, and Rachel Vanneuville. 2012. "Government Lawyers and the Training of Senior Civil Servants." *International Journal of the Legal Profession*, 9(1): 29–54.

Blauberger, Michael, and Dorte Martinsen. 2020. "The Court of Justice in Times of Politicisation: 'Law as a Mask and Shield' Revisited." *Journal of European Public Policy*, 27(3): 382–399.

Blauberger, Michael, and Susanne Schmidt. 2017. "Free Movement, the Welfare State, and the European Union's Over-Constitutionalization." *Public Administration*, 95: 437–449.

Boerger, Anne, and Morten Rasmussen. 2014. "Transforming European Law." *European Constitutional Law Review*, 10(2): 199–225.

Boerger de Smedt, Anne. 2012. "Negotiating the Foundations of European Law, 1950–57." *Contemporary European History*, 21(3): 339–356.

Börzel, Tanja. 2006. "Participation through Law Enforcement." *Comparative Political Studies*, 39(1): 128–152.

Bourdieu, Pierre. 1986. "The Force of Law." *Hastings Law Journal*, 38: 805–853.
1990. *The Logic of Practice*. Stanford, CA: Stanford University Press.

Boyarsky, Saul. 1991. "'Let's Kill All the Lawyers'." *Journal of Legal Medicine*, 12: 571–574.

Brubacker, Rogers. 1994. "Rethinking Nationhood." *Contention*, 4: 3–14.

Bull, Martin. 2018. "In the Eye of the Storm: The Italian Economy and the Eurozone Crisis." *South European Society and Politics*, 23(1): 13–28.

Burkhart, Simone. 2008. "Reforming Federalism in Germany." *Publius: The Journal of Federalism*, 39(2): 341–365.

Burley, Anne-Marie, and Walter Mattli. 1993. "Europe before the Court: A Political Theory of Legal Integration." *International Organization*, 47(1): 41–76.

Butz, David, and John Eyles. 1997. "Reconceptualizing Senses of Place: Social Relations, Ideology and Ecology." *Geografiska Annaler: Series B, Human Geography*, 79(1): 1–25.

Buzogany, Aron. 2017. "Illiberal Democracy in Hungary." *Democratization*, 24(7): 1307–1325.

Byberg, Rebecca. 2017. "A Miscellaneous Network: The History of FIDE 1961–94." *American Journal of Legal History*, 57: 142–165.

Call, Samantha, and Seth Jolly. 2020. "Euroscepticism in the Populism Era." *The Journal of Politics*, 82(1): e7–e12.

Calon, Jean-Paul. 1978. "La Cour de Cassation et le Conseil d'État: Une comparaison." *Revue internationale de droit comparé*, 1: 229–245.

Calvino, Italo. 2017. *The Baron in the Trees*. New York, NY: Houghton Mifflin Harcourt.

Capelli, Fausto. 1979. *Scritti di Diritto Comunitario*, vol. II. Broni: Tipolito Fraschini di G. Peroni.
1987. "The Experiences of the Parties in Italy." In *Article 177 EEC: Experiences and Problems*. Henry Schermers, Christiaan Timmermans, Alfred Kellermann, and J. Stewart Watson, eds., New York, NY: Elsevier.
2005. "Giovanni Maria Ubertazzi (1919–2005)." *Diritto Comunitario e degli Scambi Internazionali*, 4: 623–624.
2020. *Un Percorso tra Etica e Trasparenza per Riformare la Democrazia in Italia*. Soveria Mannelli: Rubettino.

Capoccia, Giovanni, and R. Daniel Kelemen. 2007. "The Study of Critical Junctures: Theory, Narrative, and Counterfactuals in Historical Institutionalism." *World Politics*, 59(3): 341–369.

Carbone, Sergio, and Francesco Munari. 1994. "La legge italiana di riforma dei porti ed il diritto comunitario." *Il Foro Italiano*, 114(4): 367–392.

Cariddi, Corrado, Maria Saponari, Donato Boscia, Angelo de Stradis, Giuliana Loconsole, Franco Nigro, Francesco Porcelli, O. Potere, and Giovanni Martelli. 2014. "Isolation of a *Xylella fastidiosa* Strain Infecting Olive and Oleander in Apulia, Italy." *Journal of Plant Pathology*, 96: 425–429.

Carpenter, Daniel. 2001. *The Forging of Bureaucratic Autonomy: Reputation, Networks, and Policy Innovation in Executive Agencies, 1862–1928*. Princeton, NJ: Princeton University Press.

Carrère, Emmanuel. 2011. *Lives Other than My Own: A Memoir*. New York, NY: Metropolitan Books.

Case, Rhonda Evans. 2011. "Eurolegalism and the Case of the Missing Agents: Should We Call Off the Search?" *Tulsa Law Review*, 47(1): 195–204.

Caserta, Salvatore. 2020. *International Courts in Latin America and the Caribbean: Foundations and Authority*. New York, NY: Oxford University Press.

Castells, Manuel. 1997. "An Introduction to the Information Age." *City*, 6: 2–16.

Catalano, Nicola. 1964. "Annotation by M. Nicola Catalano." *Common Market Law Review*, 2: 225–235.

1965a. "Lo stile delle sentenze della Corte di giustizia delle Comunità europee." *Il Foro Italiano*, 92(10): 141–148.

1965b. *Zehn Jahre Rechtsprechung des Gerichtshofs der Europaischen Gemeinschaften*. Cologne: Institut für das Recht europaischen Gemeinschaften.

Chalmers, Adam. 2013. "Trading Information for Access: Lobbying Strategies and Interest Group Access to the European Union." *Journal of European Public Policy*, 20(1): 39–58.

Cichowski, Rachel. 2004. "Women's Rights, the European Court, and Supranational Constitutionalism." *Law and Society Review*, 38(3): 489–512.

2006. "Courts, Rights, and Democratic Participation." *Comparative Political Studies*, 39(1): 50–75.

2007. *The European Court and Civil Society: Litigation, Mobilization, and Governance*. New York, NY: Cambridge University Press.

Cohen, Jonathan. 2002. *Inside Appellate Courts: The Impact of Court Organization on Judicial Decision Making in the United States Courts of Appeals*. Ann Arbor, MI: University of Michigan Press.

Colella, Christian, Roberto Carradore, and Andrea Cerroni. 2019. "Problem Setting and Problem Solving in the Case of Olive Quick Decline Syndrome in Apulia, Italy." *Phytopathology Review*, 109(2): 187–199.

Comune di Genova. 2003. *I Numeri e La Storia del Porto di Genova*. Genoa: Sistema Statistico Nazionale.

Conant, Lisa. 2001. "Europeanization and the Courts: Variable Patterns of Adaptation among National Judiciaries." In *Transforming Europe*. Maria Green Cowles, James Caporaso, and Thomas Risse, eds., Ithaca, NY: Cornell University Press.

2002. *Justice Contained: Law and Politics in the European Union*. Ithaca, NY: Cornell University Press.

2021. "Failing Backward? EU Citizenship, the Court of Justice, and Brexit." *Journal of European Public Policy*, 28(10): 1592–1610.

Conant, Lisa, Andreas Hofmann, Dagmar Soennecken, and Lisa Vanhala. 2018. "Mobilizing European Law." *Journal of European Public Policy*, 25(9): 1376–1389.

Corrales, Javier. 2015. "The Authoritarian Resurgence: Autocratic Legalism in Venezuela." *Journal of Democracy*, 26(2): 37–51.

Costamagia, Giorgio. 1965. *Gli Statuti della Compagnia dei Caravana del Porto di Genova, 1340–1600*. Turin: Accademia della Scienza.

Cramer, Katherine. 2016. *The Politics of Resentment: Rural Consciousness and the Rise of Scott Walker*. Chicago, IL: University of Chicago Press.

Cramer-Walsh, Katherine. 2012. "Putting Inequality in Its Place: Rural Consciousness and the Power of Perspective." *American Political Science Review*, 106(3): 517–532.

Dahl, Robert. 1957. "The Concept of Power." *Behavioral Science*, 2(3): 201–215.

Daly, Tom Gerald. 2019. "Democratic Decay: Conceptualising an Emerging Research Field." *Hague Journal on the Rule of Law*, 11: 9–36.

Davies, Bill. 2013. *Resisting the European Court of Justice*. New York, NY: Cambridge University Press.

De Wilde, Pieter, and Michael Zürn. 2012. "Can the Politicization of European Integration Be Reversed?" *Journal of Common Market Studies*, 50(1): 137–153.

Deringer, Arved. 1987. "Some Comments by a German Advocate on Problems Concerning the Application of Article 177 EEC." In *Article 177 EEC: Experiences and Problems*. Henry Schermers, Christiaan Timmermans, Alfred Kellermann, and J. Stewart Watson, eds., New York, NY: Elsevier.

Desmazières de Séchelles, Alain. 1987. "Experiences and Problems in Applying the Preliminary Proceedings of Article 177 of the Treaty of Rome, as Seen by a French Advocate." In *Article 177 EEC: Experiences and Problems*. Henry Schermers, Christiaan Timmermans, Alfred Kellermann, and J. Stewart Watson, eds., New York, NY: Elsevier.

Dezelay, Yves, and Bryant Garth. 1995. "Merchants of Law as Moral Entrepreneurs." *Law & Society Review*, 29(1): 27–64.

1996. *Dealing in Virtue: International Commercial Arbitration and the Construction of a Transnational Legal Order*. Chicago, IL: University of Chicago Press.

1997. "Law, Lawyers, and Social Capital." *Social & Legal Studies*, 6(1): 109–141.

2011. *Lawyers and the Rule of Law in an Era of Globalization*. New York, NY: Routledge.

2012. "Corporate Law Firms, NGOs, and Issues of Legitimacy for a Global Legal Order." *Fordham Law Review*, 80(6): 2309–2345.

Dezelay, Yves, and Mikael Rask Madsen. 2012. "The Force of Law and Lawyers." *Annual Review of Law & Social Science*, 8: 433–452.

Diamond, Larry. 2021. "Democratic Regression in Comparative Perspective." *Democratization*, 28(1): 22–42.

DiMaggio, Paul, and Walter Powell. 1983. "The Iron Cage Revisited: Institutional Isomorphism and Collective Rationality in Organizational Fields." *American Sociological Review*, 48(2): 147–160.

Dinan, Desmond. 2005. *Ever Closer Union: An Introduction to European Integration*, 3rd ed. Boulder, CO: Lynne Rienner.

Dunoff, Jeffrey, and Mark Pollack. 2018. "A Typology of International Judicial Practices." In *The Judicialization of International Law*. Andreas Follesdal and Geir Ulfstein, eds., New York, NY: Oxford University Press.

Dyevre, Arthur, and Nicolas Lampach. 2018. "The Origins of Regional Integration: Untangling the Effect of Trade on Judicial Cooperation." *International Review of Law and Economics*, 56: 122–133.

2021. "Subnational Disparities in EU Law Use: Exploring the GEOCOURT Dataset." *Journal of European Public Policy*, 28(4): 615–631.

Earshaw, David, and David Judge. 2002. "No Simple Dichotomies: Lobbyists and the European Parliament." *Journal of Legislative Studies*, 8(4): 61–79.

EFSA. 2013. "Statement of EFSA on Host Plants, Entry and Spread Pathways and Risk Reduction Options for *Xylella fastidiosa* Wells et al." *EFSA Journal*, 11(11): 3468.

2015. "Scientific Opinion on the Risk to Plant Health Posed by *Xylella fastidiosa* in the EU Territory, with the Identification and Evaluation of Risk Reduction Options." *EFSA Journal*, 13(1): 3989.

2015. "Response to Scientific and Technical Information Provided by an NGO on *Xylella fastidiosa*." *EFSA Journal*, 13(4): 4082.

Ehle, Dietrich. 1964-12-10. "Comment on *Costa v. ENEL*." *New Juristische Wochenschrif*, 2331–2333.

Emmons, Cassandra, and Tommaso Pavone. 2021. "The Rhetoric of Inaction: Failing to Fail Forward in the EU Rule of Law Crisis." *Journal of European Public Policy*, 28(10): 611–629.

Epp, Charles. 1998. *The Rights Revolution: Lawyers, Activists, and Supreme Courts in Comparative Perspective*. Chicago, IL: University of Chicago Press.

Ewick, Patricia, and Susan Silbey. 1998. *The Common Place of Law: Stories from Everyday Life*. Chicago, IL: University of Chicago Press.

Falleti, Tulia, and James Mahoney. 2015. "The Comparative Sequential Method." In *Advances in Comparative Historical Analysis*. James Mahoney and Kathleen Thelen, eds., New York, NY: Cambridge University Press.

Faulconbridge, James, and Daniel Muzio. 2015. "Transnational Corporations Shaping Institutional Change." *Journal of Economic Geography*, 15(6): 1195–1226.

Fenno, Richard. 1978. *Home Style: Congressmen in Their Districts*. New York, NY: Little, Brown, & Company.

Fine, Gary Alan. 2009. *Authors of the Storm: Meteorologists and the Culture of Prediction*. Chicago, IL: University of Chicago Press.

Finer, Samuel. 1966. *The Man on Horseback*. London: Pall Mall Press.

Fisher, Frank. 2000. *Citizens, Experts, and the Environment*. Durham, NC: Duke University Press.

Fligstein, Neil, and Alec Stone Sweet. 2002. "Constructing Polities and Markets: An Institutionalist Account of European Integration." *American Journal of Sociology*, 107(5): 1206–1243.

Fraenkel, Ernst. 2017. *The Dual State: A Contribution to the Theory of Dictatorship*. New York, NY: Oxford University Press.

Freedman, David. 2011. "Ecological Fallacy." In *The SAGE Encyclopedia of Social Science Research*. Michael Lewis-Beck, Alan Bryman, and Tim Futing Liao, eds., Thousand Oaks, CA: SAGE.

Frymer, Paul. 2003. "Acting When Elected Officials Won't: Federal Courts and Civil Rights Enforcement in U.S. Labor Unions, 1935–85." *American Political Science Review*, 97(3): 483–499.

    2008. *Black and Blue: African Americans, the Labor Movement, and the Decline of the Democratic Party*. Princeton, NJ: Princeton University Press.

Fukuyama, Francis. 2006. *The End of History and the Last Man*. New York, NY: Free Press.

Galanter, Marc. 1974. "Why the 'Haves' Come out Ahead: Speculations on the Limits of Legal Change." *Law & Society Review*, 9(1): 95–160.

    1983. "The Radiating Effects of Courts." In *Empirical Theories about Courts*. Keith Boyum and Lynn Mather, eds., New York, NY: Longman.

Gallagher, Mary. 2013. "Capturing Meaning and Confronting Measurement." In *Interview Research in Political Science*. Layna Mosley, ed., Ithaca, NY: Cornell University Press.

Garoupa, Nunu, and Tom Ginsburg. 2015. *Judicial Reputation*. Chicago, IL: University of Chicago Press.

George, Alexander L., and Andrew Bennett. 2005. *Case Studies and Theory Development in the Social Sciences*. Cambridge, MA: MIT Press.

Gerring, John. 2007. "Is There a (Viable) Crucial-Case Method?" *Comparative Political Studies*, 40(3): 231–253.

Getis, Arthur, and J. K. Ord. 1992. "The Analysis of Spatial Association by Use of Distance Statistics." *Geographical Analysis*, 24(3): 189–206.

Gilbert, Mark. 1996. "The Oak Tree and the Olive Tree." *Italian Politics*, 111: 101–117.

Ginsborg, Paul. 2003. *A History of Contemporary Italy*. New York, NY: Palgrave Macmillan.

Ginsburg, Tom. 2003. *Judicial Review in New Democracies: Constitutional Courts in Asian Cases*. New York, NY: Cambridge University Press.

Ginsburg, Tom, and Tamir Moustafa. 2008. *Rule by Law: The Politics of Courts in Authoritarian Regimes*. New York, NY: Cambridge University Press.

Glavina, Monika. 2020. "To Refer or Not to Refer – That Is the (Preliminary) Question." *Croatian Yearbook of European Law*, 16: 25–60.

González-Ocantos, Ezequiel. 2016. *Shifting Legal Visions: Judicial Change and Human Rights Trials in Latin America*. Chicago, IL: Cambridge University Press.

Gray, Julia, R. Daniel Kelemen, and Terence Teo. 2019. "Pecunia Non Olet: The Political Economy of Financial Flows into Illiberal European Countries." 11th Annual EU Workshop, Princeton, NJ, April.

Gray, Paul. 2007. *The Research Imagination*. New York, NY: Cambridge University Press.

Gündisch, Jürgen. 1994. *Rechtsschutz in der Europäischen Gemeinschaft: ein Leitfaden für die Praxis*. Stuttgart: R. Boorberg Verlag.

Gündisch, Jürgen, and Petrus Mathijsen. 1999. *Rechtsetzung und Interessen-vertretung in der Europäischen Union*. Stuttgart: R. Boorberg Verlag.

Haas, Ernst. 1958. *The Uniting of Europe: Political, Social, and Economic Forces, 1950–1957*. Stanford, CA: Stanford University Press.

Haire, Susan, Roger Brodie, and Stefanie Lindquist. 1999. "Attorney Expertise, Litigant Success, and Judicial Decisionmaking in the US Courts of Appeals." *Law and Society Review*, 33(3): 667–686.

Hall, Peter, and Rosemary Taylor. 1996. "Political Science and the Three New Institutionalisms." *Political Studies*, 44(5): 936–957.

Halliday, Terence. 1987. *Beyond Monopoly: Lawyers, State Crises, and Professional Empowerment*. Chicago, IL: University of Chicago Press.

Halliday, Terence, and Lucien Karpik. 1988. "Political Lawyering." In *International Encyclopedia of Social and Behavioral Sciences*. Neil J. Smelser and Paul B. Baltes, eds., New York, NY: Elsevier.

Halliday, Terence, and Lucien Karpik. 1997. *Lawyers and the Rise of Western Political Liberalism*. New York, NY: Oxford University Press.

Halliday, Terence, Lucien Karpik, and Malcolm Feeley. 2007. *Fighting for Political Freedom*. New York, NY: Bloomsbury.

Halliday, Terence, and Sida Liu. 2007. "Birth of a Liberal Moment? Looking through a One-Way Mirror at Lawyers' Defence of Criminal Defendants in China." In *Fighting for Political Freedom: Comparative Studies of the Legal Complex and Political Liberalism*. Terence Halliday, Lucien Karpik, and Malcolm Feeley, eds., New York, NY: Hart.

Halliday, Terence, and Gregory Shaffer. 2015. *Transnational Legal Orders*. New York, NY: Cambridge University Press.

Hamilton, Alexander. 1961. "The Federalist No. 78." In *The Federalist*. Jacob Cooke, Middletown, CT: Wesleyan University Press.

Hamlin, Rebecca. 2016. "'Foreign Criminals,' the Human Rights Act, and the New Constitutional Politics of the United Kingdom." *Journal of Law & Courts*, 4: 437–461.

Hand, Learned. 1958. *The Bill of Rights*. Cambridge, MA: Harvard University Press.

Hein, Paul, and James Piereson. 1975. "Lawyers and Politics Revisited." *American Journal of Political Science*, 19(1): 41–51.

Heinz, John, and Edward Laumann. 1982. *Chicago Lawyers: The Social Structure of the Bar*. New York, NY: Russell Sage.

Heinz, John, Robert Nelson, and Ethan Michelson. 1998. "The Changing Character of Lawyers' Work." *Law & Society Review*, 32(4): 751–776.

Helmke, Gretchen, and Steven Levitsky. 2004. "Informal Institutions and Comparative Politics." *Perspectives on Politics*, 2(4): 725–740.

Hill, Louise L. 1995. "Lawyer Publicity in the European Union." *The George Washington Journal of International law and Economics*, 29(2): 381–451.

Hilson, Chris. 2002. "New Social Movements: The Role of Legal Opportunity." *Journal of European Public Policy*, 9: 238–255.

Hirschl, Ran. 2007. *Towards Juristocracy: The Origins and Consequences of the New Constitutionalism*. Cambridge, MA: Harvard University Press.

Hirschman, Albert. 1971. "Political Economics and Possibilism." In *A Bias for Hope*. New Haven, CT: Yale University Press, 1–34.

1991. *The Rhetoric of Reaction: Perversity, Futility, Jeopardy*. Cambridge, MA: Harvard University Press.

Hoevenaars, Jos. 2018. *A People's Court? A Bottom-Up Approach to Litigation before the European Court of Justice*. The Hague: Eleven International.

Hoffmann, Stanley. 1966. "Obstinate or Obsolete? The Fate of the Nation-State and the Case of Western Europe." *Daedalus*, 95: 862–915.

Hofmann, Andreas. 2018. "Resistance against the Court of Justice of the European Union." *International Journal of Law in Context*, 14: 258–274.

Hooghe, Liesbet, and Gary Marks. 2009. "A Postfunctionalist Theory of European Integration: From Permissive Consensus to Constraining Dissensus." *British Journal of Political Science*, 39(1): 11–23.

Hooghe, Liesbet, Gary Marks, Arjan H. Schakel, Sandra Chapman Osterkatz, Sara Niedzwiecki, and Sarah Shair-Rosenfield. 2016. *Measuring Regional Authority*. New York, NY: Oxford University.

Hooghe, Liesbet, and Gary Marks. 2013. "Politicization." In *The Oxford Handbook of the European Union*. Erik Jones, Anand Menon, and Stephen Weatherill, eds., New York, NY: Oxford University Press.

Hula, Kevin. 1999. *Lobbying Together: Interest Group Coalitions in Legislative Politics*. Washington, DC: Georgetown University Press.

Imig, Doug, and Sidney Tarrow. 2000. "Political Contention in a Europeanising Polity." *West European Politics*, 23(4): 73–93.

Jaremba, Urszula. 2020. "Defending the Rule of Law or Reality-Based Self-Defence?" *European Papers*, 5(2): 851–869.

Kagan, Robert. 1997. "Should Europe Worry about Adversarial Legalism?" *Oxford Journal of Legal Studies*, 17: 165–184.

Kagan, Robert. 2003. *Adversarial Legalism: The American Way of Law*. Cambridge, MA: Harvard University Press.

Karpik, Lucien. 1999. *French Lawyers: A Study in Collective Action, 1274–1994*. New York, NY: Oxford University Press.

2007. "Political Lawyers." In *Fighting for Political Freedom: Comparative Studies of the Legal Complex and Political Liberalism*. Terence Halliday, Lucien Karpik, and Malcolm Feeley, eds., Portland, OR: Hart.

Kelemen, R. Daniel. 2003. "The EU Rights Revolution: Adversarial Legalism and European Integration." In *The State of the European Union, 6: Law, Politics, and Society*. Tanja Borzel and Rachel Cichowski, eds., New York, NY: Oxford University Press.

2006. "Suing for Europe." *Comparative Political Studies*, 39(1): 101–127.

2011. *Eurolegalism: The Transformation of Law and Regulation in the European Union*. Cambridge, MA: Harvard University Press.

2017. "Europe's Other Democratic Deficit: National Authoritarianism in Europe's Democratic Union." *Government and Opposition*, 52(2): 211–238.

2019. "Is Differentiation Possible in Rule of Law?" *Comparative European Politics*, 17(2): 246–260.

Kelemen, R. Daniel, and Kathleen McNamara. 2021. "State-building and the European Union: Markets, War, and Europe's Uneven Political Development." *Comparative Political Studies* (ahead of print): 1–29.

Kelemen, R. Daniel, and Tommaso Pavone. 2016. "Mapping European Law." *Journal of European Public Policy*, 23(8): 1118–1138.

2018. "The Political Geography of Legal Integration: Visualizing Institutional Change in the European Union." *World Politics*, 70(3): 358–360.

Kelemen, R. Daniel, and Eric Sibbitt. 2004. "The Globalization of American Law." *International Organization*, 58(1): 103–136.

Kelemen, R. Daniel, and Alec Stone Sweet. 2017. "Assessing the Transformation of Europe." In *The Transformation of Europe*. Marlene Wind and Miguel Poiares Maduro, eds., New York, NY: Oxford University Press.

King, Gary, Robert Keohane, and Sidney Verba. 1994. *Designing Social Inquiry*. Princeton, NJ: Princeton University Press.

Koopmans, Thijmen. 1987. "The Technique of the Preliminary Question – A View from the Court of Justice." In *Article 177 EEC: Experiences and Problems*. Henry Schermers, Christiaan Timmermans, Alfred Kellermann, and J. Stewart Watson, eds., New York, NY: Elsevier.

Kritzer, Herbert. 1998. *Legal Advocacy: Lawyers and Nonlawyers at Work*. Ann Arbor, MI: University of Michigan Press.

Laguette, Serge-Pierre. 1987. *Lawyers in the European Community*. Luxembourg: Office for Official Publications of the European Communities.

Lampedusa, Giuseppe Tomasi di. 1964. *The Leopard*. London: Fontana.

Latour, Bruno. 2010. *The Making of Law: An Ethnography of the Conseil d'État*. Malden, MA: Polity Press.

Li Vigni, Ilaria. 2015. *Avvocate Negli Studi Associati e Giuriste D'Impresa*. Milan: Franco Angeli.

Lindseth, Peter. 2010. *Power and Legitimacy: Reconciling Europe and the Nation-State*. New York, NY: Oxford University Press.

Lipsky, Michael. 2010. *Street-Level Bureaucracy*, 30th ed. New York, NY: Russell Sage.

Liu, Sida. 2008. "Globalization as Boundary-Blurring: International and Local Law Firms in China's Corporate Law Market." *Law & Society Review*, 42(4): 771–804.

    2013. "The Legal Profession as a Social Process." *Law & Social Inquiry*, 38(3): 670–693.

Liu, Sida, and Terrence Halliday. 2016. *Criminal Defense in China: The Politics of Lawyers at Work*. New York, NY: Cambridge University Press.

Luivisi, Andrea, Francesca Nicolì, and Luigi de Bellis. 2017. "Sustainable Management of Plant Quarantine Pests: The Case of Olive Quick Decline Syndrome." *Sustainability*, 9: 659–678.

Lukes, Steven. 2015. "Robert Dahl on Power." *Journal of Political Power*, 8(2): 261–271.

Lustick, Ian. 1996. "History, Historiography, and Political Science: Multiple Historical Records and the Problem of Selection Bias." *American Political Science Review*, 90(3): 605–618.

Madsen, Mikael Rask, Henrik Palmer Olsen, and Urška Šadl. 2017. "Competing Supremacies and Clashing Institutional Rationalities: the Danish Supreme Court's Decision in the *Ajos* Case and the National Limits of Judicial Cooperation." *European Law Journal*, 23: 140–150.

Madsen, Mikael Rask, Pola Cebulak, and Micha Weibusch. 2018. "Backlash against International Courts: Explaining the Forms and Patterns of Resistance to International Courts." *International Journal of Law in Context*, 14(2): 197–220.

Maduro, Miguel Poiares. 1998. *We the Court: The European Court of Justice and the European Economic Constitution*. New York, NY: Hart.

Maestripieri, Cesare. 1972. "The Application of Community Law in Italy in 1972." *Common Market Law Review*, 10: 340–351.

Mahoney, James. 2000. "Path Dependence in Historical Sociology." *Theory and Society*, 29: 507–538.

Mahoney, James, and Kathleen Thelen. 2010. "A Theory of Gradual Institutional Change." In *Explaining Institutional Change: Ambiguity, Agency, and Power*. James Mahoney and Kathleen Thelen, eds., New York, NY: Cambridge University Press.

Majone, Giandomenico. 2005. *Dilemmas of European Integration*. New York, NY: Oxford University Press.

Malatesta, Maria. 1995. "The Italian Professions from a Comparative Perspective." In *Society and the Professions in Italy, 1860–1914*. Maria Malatesta, ed., New York, NY: Cambridge University Press.

Mamadouh, Virginie, and Anne van Wageningen. eds. 2016. *Urban Europe: Fifty Tales of the City*. Amsterdam: Amsterdam University Press.

Marchesiello, Michele. 2017. *La Città Portuale*. Rome: Aracane Editrice.

Markovits, Andrei, and Lars Rensmann. 2013. *Gaming the World*. Princeton, NJ: Princeton University Press.

Martinsen, Dorte Sindbjerg, Michael Blauberger, Anita Heindlmaier, and Jessica Sampson Thierry. 2019. "Implementing European Case Law at the Bureaucratic Frontline: How Domestic Signaling Influences the Outcomes of EU Law." *Public Administration*, 97(4): 814–828.

Massot, Jean. 2009. "Les pouvoirs et les devoirs du juge administratif dans l'examen des requêtes." Troisièmes journées juridiques et administratives franco-croates, Split, October.

Massoud, Mark. 2021. *Shari'a, Inshallah: Finding God in Somali Legal Politics*. New York, NY: Cambridge University Press.

Mastrogiovanni, Marialù. 2015. *Xylella Report: Uccidete quella foresta. Attacco agli ulivi secolari del Salento*. Bari: Il Tacco d'Italia.

Mattli, Walter, and Anne-Marie Slaughter. 1998. "The Role of National Courts in the Process of European Integration." In *The European Court and National Courts*. Alec Stone Sweet Anne-Marie Slaughter, and Joseph Weiler, eds., New York, NY: Hart.

Mayoral, Juan. 2017. "In the CJEU Judges Trust: A New Approach in the Judicial Construction of Europe." *Journal of Common Market Studies*, 55(3): 551–568.

Mayoral, Juan, Ursuzula Jaremba, and Tobias Nowak. 2014. "Creating EU Law Judges: The Role of Generational Differences, Legal Education and Judicial Career Paths in National Judges' Assessment Regarding EU Law Knowledge." *Journal of European Public Policy*, 21(8): 1120–1141.

McCann, Michael. 1994. *Rights at Work: Pay Equity Reform and the Politics of Legal Mobilization*. Chicago, IL: University of Chicago Press.

2008. "Litigation and Legal Mobilization." In *The Oxford Handbook of Law and Politics*. Gregory Caldeira, R. Daniel Kelemen, and Keith Whittington, eds., New York, NY: Oxford University Press.

McGuire, Kevin. 1995. "Repeat Players in the Supreme Court." *Journal of Politics*, 57(1): 187–196.

McKee, J. Y. 2007. "Le recruitement et l'avancement des juges français." Tribunal de Grande Instance de Rennes, Rennes, March.

McNamara, Kathleen. 2015. *The Politics of Everyday Europe: Constructing Authority in the European Union*. New York, NY: Oxford University Press.

Meilicke, Wienand. 1989. *Die 'verschleierte' Sacheinlage*. Stuttgart: Schärfer Verlag.

Merry, Sally Engle. 1990. *Getting Justice and Getting Even: Legal Consciousness Among Working-Class Americans*. Chicago, IL: University of Chicago Press.

2009. *Human Rights and Gender Violence: Translating International Law into Local Justice*. Chicago, IL: University of Chicago Press.

Merryman, John Henry, and Rogelio Perez-Perdomo. 2007. *The Civil Law Tradition*, 3rd ed. Stanford, CA: Stanford University Press.

Miller, Clark. 2004. "Resisting Empire: Globalism, Relocalization, and the Politics of Knowledge." In *Earthly Politics*. Sheila Jasanoff and Marybeth Martello, eds., Cambridge, MA: MIT Press.

Moeschel, Mathias. 2019. "How 'Liberal' Democracies Attack(ed) Judicial Independence." In *Judicial Power in a Globalized World*. Paulo Pinto de Albuquerque and Krzysztof Wojtyczek, eds., Cham: Springer.

Montesquieu. 1951. *De l'ésprit des lois*. Paris: Gallimard.

Moravcsik, Andrew. 2013. "Did Power Politics Cause European Integration? Realist Theory Meets Qualitative Methods." *Security Studies*, 22(4): 773–790.

2014a. "Transparency: The Revolution in Qualitative Research." *PS: Political Science & Politics*, 47(1): 48–53.

2014b. "Trust but Verify." *Security Studies*, 23(4): 663–688.

Morgan, Glenn, and Sigrid Quack. 2005. "Institutional Legacies and Firm Dynamics." *Organizational Studies*, 26(12): 1765–1785.

Müller, Jan-Werner. 2019. "The Problem with Illiberal Democracy." *Project Syndicate*, January 21.

2019. "Populism and the People." *London Review of Books*, 41(10): 35–37.

Musso, Bruno. 2008. *Il Porto di Genova*. Turin: Celid.

Musso, Bruno. 2017. *Il Cuore in Porto*. Milan: Mursia Editore.

Neville-Brown, Lionel, John Bell, and Jean-Michel Galabert. 1998. *French Administrative Law*, 5th ed. Oxford: Clarendon Press.

Nicola, Fernanda, and Bill Davies. 2017. *EU Law Stories: Contextual and Critical Histories of European Jurisprudence*. New York, NY: Cambridge University Press.

Nicolaysen, Gert. 1988. "Difficile Est Satiram Non Scribere." *Europarecht*, 23: 409–412.

Nielsen, Laura Beth. 2000. "Situating Legal Consciousness." *Law & Society Review*, 34(4): 1055–1090.

Nowak, Tobias. 2019. "Using Mixed Methods to Explore the Legal Consciousness of Judges." *SAGE Research Methods Cases*, 1–11, https://methods.sagepub.com/case/using-mixed-methods-explore-the-legal-consciousness-of-judges.

Noy, Chaim. 2008. "Sampling Knowledge." *International Research of Social Research Methodology*, 11(4): 327–344.

Oberdorfer, Conrad, and Alfred Gleiss. 1963. *Common Market Cartel Law*. New York, NY: Commerce Clearing House.

O'Donnell, Guillermo. 2004. "Why the Rule of Law Matters." *Journal of Democracy*, 15(4): 32–46.

O'Donnell, Guillermo, and Philippe Schmitter. 1986. *Transitions from Authoritarian Rule, Vol. 4: Tentative Conclusions about Uncertain Democracies*. Baltimore, MD: Johns Hopkins University Press.

Olgiati, Vittorio, and Valerio Pocar. 1988. "The Italian Legal Profession: An Institutional Dilemma." In *Lawyers in Society, Volume II: The Civil Law World*. Richard Abel and Philip Lewis, eds., Berkeley and Los Angeles, CA: University of California Press.

Orren, Karen, and Stephen Skowronek. 2004. *The Search for American Political Development*. New York, NY: Cambridge University Press.

O'Toole, Fintan. 2019. "The Ham of Fate." *New York Review of Books*, 66(13): 29.

Pachirat, Timothy. 2018. *Among Wolves: Ethnography and the Immersive Study of Power*. New York, NY: Routledge.

Pagano, Mario. 2019. "Who Will Save the Olive Tree? C-443/18, Commission v Italy." *European Journal of Risk Regulation*, 10(4): 811–820.

Parsons, Craig. 2003. *A Certain Idea of Europe*. Ithaca, NY: Cornell University Press.

Pauwelyn, Joost, and Krzysztof Pelc. 2019. "Who Writes the Rulings of the World Trade Organization?" *Social Science Research Network (SSRN)*, URL: https://papers.ssrn.com/sol3/papers.cfm?abstract_id=3458872.

Pavone, Tommaso. 2016. "Democracy by Lawsuit: Or, Can Litigation Alleviate the EU's 'Democratic Deficit?'" *Constitutional Studies*, 2: 59–80.

2018. "Revisiting Judicial Empowerment in the European Union: Limits of Empowerment, Logics of Resistance." *Journal of Law & Courts*, 6(2): 303–331.

2019. "From Marx to Market: Lawyers, European Law, and the Contentious Transformation of the Port of Genoa." *Law & Society Review*, 53(3): 1–38.

2020a. "Lawyers, Judges, and the Obstinate State: The French Case and an Agenda for Comparative Politics." *French Politics*, 18(4): 416–432.

2020b. "Putting European Constitutionalism in Its Place: The Spatial Foundations of the Judicial Construction of Europe." *European Constitutional Law Review*, 16(4): 669–60.

2022. "Selecting Cases for Comparative Sequential Analysis: Novel Uses for Old Methods." In *The Case For Case Studies*. Michael Woolcock, Jennifer Widner, and Daniel Ortega-Nieto, eds., New York, NY: Cambridge University Press.

Pavone, Tommaso, and R. Daniel Kelemen. 2019. "The Evolving Judicial Politics of European Integration: The European Court of Justice and National Courts Revisited." *European Law Journal*, 25(3): 352–373.

Pech, Laurent, and Kim Lane Scheppele. 2017. "Illiberalism Within: Rule of Law Backsliding in the EU." *Cambridge Yearbook of European Legal Studies*, 19: 3–47.

Pedersen, Jonas Langeland. 2016. "Constructive Defiance? Denmark and the Effects of European Law, 1973–1993." PhD dissertation, Aarhus University.

Pellet, Alain, and Alina Miron. 2015. *Les Grandes Decisions de la Jurisprudence Française de Droit International Public*. Paris: Dalloz.

Perry, H. W. 1994. *Deciding to Decide*. Cambridge, MA: Harvard University Press.

Pescatore, Pierre. 1981. "Les Travaux du 'Groupe Juridique' dans la Negociation des Traités de Rome." *Studia Diplomatica*, 34: 159–92.

Pierson, Paul. 1996a. *Dismantling the Welfare State?* New York, NY: Cambridge University Press.

1996b. "The Path to European Integration." *Comparative Political Studies*, 29(2): 123–163.

2000. "Increasing Returns, Path Dependence, and the Study of Politics." *American Political Science Review*, 94(2): 251–267.

2003. "Big, Slow-Moving, and … Invisible: Macrosocial Processes in the Study of Comparative Politics." In *Comparative Historical Analysis in the Social Sciences*. James Mahoney and Dietrich Rueschemeyer, eds., New York, NY: Cambridge University Press.

2004. *Politics in Time: History, Institutions, and Social Analysis*. Princeton, NJ: Princeton University Press.

Poli, Raffaele, Löic Ravanel, and Roger Besson. 2016. "Foreign Players in Football Teams." *CIES Football Observatory Monthly Report*, 12(4): 1–9.

Pollack, Mark. 2013. "The New EU Legal History." *American University International Law Review*, 28(5): 1257–1310.

Pouliot, Vincent. 2015. "Practice Tracing." In *Process Tracing: From Metaphor to Analytic Tool*. Andrew Bennett and Jeffrey Checkel, eds., New York, NY: Cambridge University Press.

Pouliot, Vincent, and Jérémie Cornut. 2015. "Practice Theory and the Study of Diplomacy: A Research Agenda." *Cooperation and Conflict*, 50(3): 297–315.

Ramsay, Ian. 2017. *Personal Insolvency in the 21st Century: A Comparative Analysis of the US and Europe*. Oxford: Hart.

Ramseyer, J. Mark. 1994. "The Puzzling (In)Dependence of Courts: A Comparative Approach." *The Journal of Legal Studies*, 23(2): 721–747.

Rasmussen, Hjalte. 1986. *On Law and Policy in the European Court of Justice*. Boston, MA: Martinus Nijhoff.

    2007. "Present and Future European Judicial Problems after Enlargement and the Post-2005 Ideological Revolt." *Common Market Law Review*, 44(1): 1661–1687.

Rasmussen, Morten. 2012. "Rewriting the History of European Public Law." *American University International Law Review*, 28: 1187–1222.

    2013. "Establishing a Constitutional Practice." In *Societal Actors in European Integration*. Jan-Henrik Meyer and W. Kaiser, eds., Basingstoke: Palgrave Macmillan.

    2014. "Revolutionizing European Law." *International Journal of Constitutional Law*, 12: 136–163.

Relph, Edward. 1985. "Geographical Experiences and Being-in-the-World: The Phenomenological Origins of Geography." In *Dwelling, Place, and Environment*. David Seamon and Robert Mugerauer, eds., Dordrecht: Nijhoff.

Richards, Diana. 2016. "Current Models of Judicial Training." *Judicial Education and Training*, 6: 41–52.

Romzek, Barbara, and Jennifer Utter. 1997. "Congressional Legislative Staff: Political Professionals or Clerks?" *American Journal of Political Science*, 41(4): 1251–1279.

Rosenbluth, Frances, and J. Mark Ramseyer. 1993. *Japan's Political Marketplace*. Cambridge, MA: Harvard University Press.

Rosenthal, Jeffrey, and Albert Yoon. 2010. "Judicial Ghostwriting: Authorship on the U.S. Supreme Court." *Cornell Law Review*, 96(6): 1307–1344.

Sadurski, Wojciech. 2019. *Poland's Constitutional Breakdown*. New York, NY: Oxford University Press.

Sanjek, Roger. 1990. *Fieldnotes*. Ithaca, NY: Cornell University Press.

Saponari, Maria, Donato Boscia, Franco Nigro, and Giovanni Martelli. 2013. "Identification of DNA Sequences Related to *Xylella fastidiosa* in Oleander, Almond and Olive Trees Exhibiting Leaf Scorch Symptoms in Apulia (Southern Italy)." *Journal of Plant Pathology*, 95: 668.

Sarat, Austin, and William Felstiner. 1989. "Lawyers and Legal Consciousness." *Yale Law Journal*, 98(8): 1663–1688.

Sarat, Austin, and Thomas Kearns. 1995. *Law in Everyday Life*. Ann Arbor, MI: University of Michigan Press.

Sarat, Austin, and Stuart Scheingold. 2006. *Cause Lawyers and Social Movements*. Stanford, CA: Stanford University Press.

Sartori, Giovanni. 1970. "Concept Misformation in Comparative Politics." *American Political Science Review*, 64(4): 1033–1053.

Sassen, Saskia. 1994. *Cities in a World Economy*. Thousand Oaks, CA: Pine Forge Press.

2004. "The Global City: Introducing a Concept." *Brown Journal of World Affairs*, 11(4): 27–44.

Schatz, Edward. 2009. "Ethnographic Immersion and the Study of Politics." In *Political Ethnography*. Edward Schatz, ed., Chicago, IL: University of Chicago Press.

Scheingold, Stuart. 1965. *The Rule of Law in European Integration*. New Haven, CT: Yale University Press.

Scheppele, Kim Lane. 2018. "Autocratic Legalism." *University of Chicago Law Review*, 85: 545–584.

2019a. "Autocracy under the Cover of the Transnational Legal Order." In *Constitution-Making and Transnational Legal Order*. Gregory Shaffer, Tom Ginsburg, and Terence Halliday, eds., New York, NY: Cambridge University Press.

2019b. "The Legal Complex and Lawyers-in-Chief." In *The Legal Process and the Promise of Justice: Studies Inspired by the Work of Malcolm Feeley*. Rosann Greenspan, Hadar Aviram, and Jonathan Simon, eds., New York, NY: Cambridge University Press.

Scheppele, Kim Lane, Dimitry Kochenov, and Barbara Grabowska-Moroz. 2021. "EU Values Are Law, After All: Enforcing EU Values through Systemic Infringement Actions by the European Commission and the Member States of the European Union." *Yearbook of European Law*, 39: 3–121.

Schermers, Henry. 1974. "The Law as It Stands against Treaty Violations by States." In *Legal Issues of European Integration*. D. Gijlstra, Henry Schermers, and E. Völker, eds., Dordrecht: Springer.

Schermers, Henry. 1987. "Introduction." In *Article 177 EEC: Experiences and Problems*. Henry Schermers, Christiaan Timmermans, Alfred Kellermann, and J. Stewart Watson, eds., New York, NY: Elsevier.

Schmidt, Susanne K. 2018. *The European Court of Justice and the Policy Process: The Shadow of Case Law*. New York, NY: Oxford University Press.

Schmitter, Philippe. 2009. "On the Way to a Post-functionalist Theory of European Integration." *British Journal of Political Science*, 39(1): 211–215.

Schneider, Kevin, Wopke van der Werf, Martina Candoya, Monique Mourits, Juan Navas-Cortés, Antonio Vincent, and Alfons Oude Lansink. 2020. "Impact of *Xylella fastidiosa* Subspecies *Pauca* in European Olives." *PNAS*, 117(17): 9250–9259.

Schwartz-Shea, Peregrine, and Dvora Yanow. 2012. *Interpretive Research Design: Concepts and Processes*. New York, NY: Routledge.

Scott, James C. 1990. *Domination and the Arts of Resistance: Hidden Transcripts*. New Haven, CT: Yale University Press.

Sewell, William. 1996. "Historical Events as Transformations of Structures: Inventing Revolution at the Bastille." *Theory and Society*, 25(6): 841–881.

2016. *Logics of History: Social Theory and Social Transformation*. Chicago, IL: University of Chicago Press.

Shapiro, Martin. 1991. "The European Court of Justice." In *Euro-Politics: Institutions and Policymaking in the New European Community*. Alberta Sbragia, ed., Washington, DC: Brookings Institution.

1993. "The Globalization of Law." *Indiana Journal of Global Legal Studies*, 1(1): 37–64.

Shapiro, Martin, and Alec Stone Sweet. 2002. *On Law, Politics, and Judicialization*. New York, NY: Oxford University Press.

Silbey, Susan. 2005. "After Legal Consciousness." *Annual Review of Law & Social Science*, 1: 323–368.

Simion, Kristina. 2021. *Rule of Law Intermediaries: Brokering Influence in Myanmar*. New York, NY: Cambridge University Press.

Skowronek, Stephen. 1992. *Building a New American State: The Expansion of National Administrative Capacities, 1877–1920*. New York, NY: Cambridge University Press.

Slater, Dan, and Erica Simmons. 2009. "Informative Regress: Critical Antecedents in Comparative Politics." *Comparative Political Studies*, 43(7): 886–917.

Slaughter, Anne-Marie. 1997. "The Real New World Order." *Foreign Affairs*, 76(5): 183–197.

2004. *A New World Order*. Princeton, NJ: Princeton University Press.

Slaughter, Anne-Marie, and Walter Mattli. 1998. "The Role of National Courts in the Process of European Integration." In *The European Court and National Courts*. Alec Stone Sweet, Anne-Marie Slaughter, and Joseph Weiler, eds., New York, NY: Hart.

Smith, Dorothy. 2005. *Institutional Ethnography: A Sociology for People*. Ithaca, NY: Rowman & Littlefield.

Smith, Miriam. 2005. "Social Movements and Judicial Empowerment: Courts, Public Policy, and Lesbian and Gay Organizing in Canada." *Politics & Society*, 33(2): 327–353.

Snow, David, and Robert Benford. 1988. "Ideology, Frame Resonance, and Participant Mobilization." *International Social Movement Research*, 1: 197–217.

Snyder, Richard. 2001. "Scaling Down: The Subnational Comparative Method." *Studies in Comparative International Development*, 36(1): 93–110.

Soifer, Hillel. 2012. "The Causal Logic of Critical Junctures." *Comparative Political Studies*, 45(12): 1572–1597.

2015. "Shadow Cases in Comparative Research." IQMR Author's Workshop, Syracuse, NY, June.

Songer, Donald, Reginald Sheehan, and Susan Haire. 1999. "Do the Haves Come Out Ahead Over Time? Applying Galanter's Framework to Decisions of the U.S. Courts of Appeals, 1925–1988." *Law and Society Review*, 33(4): 811–832.

St. John, Taylor. 2018. *The Rise of Investor-State Arbitration: Politics, Law, and Unintended Consequences.* New York, NY: Oxford University Press.

Stein, Eric. 1981. "Lawyers, Judges, and the Making of a Transnational Constitution." *American Journal of International Law,* 75(1): 1–27.

Steiner, Eva. 2010. *French Law: A Comparative Approach.* New York, NY: Oxford University Press.

Stern, Rachel. 2013. *Environmental Litigation in China: A Study in Political Ambivalence.* New York, NY: Cambridge University Press.

Stinebrickner, Bruce. 2015. "Robert A. Dahl and the Essentials of Modern Political Analysis: Politics, Influence, Power, and Polyarchy." *Journal of Political Power,* 8(2): 189–207.

Stokes, Susan. 1999. "Political Parties and Democracy." *Annual Reviews of Political Science,* 2: 243–267.

Stone, Alec. 1992. *The Birth of Judicial Politics in France: The Constitutional Council in Comparative Perspective.* New York, NY: Oxford University Press.

Stone Sweet, Alec. 1995. "Constitutional Dialogues in the European Community." *EUI Working Paper Series,* 95(38): 1–28.

2000. *Governing with Judges.* New York, NY: Oxford University Press.

2004. *The Judicial Construction of Europe.* New York, NY: Oxford University Press.

Stone Sweet, Alec, and Thomas Brunell. 1998. "The European Court and National Courts." *Journal of European Public Policy,* 5(1): 66–97.

Strayer, Joseph. 1970. *On the Medieval Origins of the Modern State.* Princeton, NJ: Princeton University Press.

Streeck, Wolfgang, and Kathleen Thelen. 2005. *Beyond Continuity.* New York, NY: Oxford University Press.

Strona, Giovanni, Corrie Jacobien Carstens, and Pieter Beck. 2017. "Network Analysis Reveals Why *Xylella fastidiosa* Will Persist in Europe." *Scientific Reports,* 7(71): 1–8.

Szente, Zoltan, and Konrad Lachmayer. 2017. *The Principle of Effective Legal Protection in Administrative Law: A European Comparison.* New York, NY: Routledge.

Szmer, John, Susan Johnson, and Tammy Sarver. 2007. "Does the Lawyer Matter? Influencing outcomes on the Supreme Court of Canada." *Law and Society Review,* 41(2): 279–304.

Szmer, John, Donald Songer, and Jennifer Bowie. 2016. "Party Capability and the US Courts of Appeals: Understanding Why the Haves Win." *Journal of Law and Courts,* 4(1): 65–102.

Tacchi, Francesca. 2002. *Gli Avvocati Italiani dall'Unità alla Repubblica.* Bologna: Il Mulino.

Tam, Waikeung. 2012. *Legal Mobilization under Authoritarianism: The Case of Post-Colonial Hong Kong.* New York, NY: Cambridge University Press.

Tansey, Oisin. 2007. "Process Tracing and Elite Interviewing: A Case for Non-probability Sampling." *PS: Political Science and Politics*, 40(4): 765–773.

Tarrow, Sidney. 1989. *Democracy and Disorder: Protest and Politics in Italy, 1965–1975*. New York, NY: Oxford University Press.

1993. "Modular Collective Action and the Rise of the Social Movement." *Politics & Society*, 21: 647–670.

2013. *The Language of Contention: Revolutions in Words, 1688–2012*. New York, NY: Cambridge University Press.

Thaler, Richard, and Cass Sunstein. 2009. *Nudge: Improving Decisions about Health, Wealth, and Outcomes*. New York, NY: Penguin Books.

Thierry, Jessica Sampson, and Dorte Martinsen. 2018. "Lost in Translation: How Street-Level Bureaucrats Condition Union Solidarity." *Journal of European Integration*, 40(6): 819–834.

Tilly, Charles. 1993. *Coercion, Capital, and European States, A.D. 990–1992*. New York, NY: Wiley-Blackwell.

1995. *Popular Contention in Great Britain 1758–1834*. Cambridge, MA: Harvard University Press.

de Tocqueville, Alexis. 2003. *Democracy in America*, vols. I & II. New York, NY: Barnes & Noble Books.

Toeller, Annette E. 2010. "Measuring and Comparing the Europeanization of National Legislation." *Journal of Common Market Studies*, 48(2): 417–444.

Touffait, Adolphe. 1983. "Réflexions d'un magistrat français sur son expèrience à la Cour de justice des Communautés europèennes." *Revue internationale de droit comparé*, 2: 283–299.

Tsebelis, George. 2002. *Veto Players: How Political Institutions Work*. Princeton, NJ: Princeton University Press.

Turnbull-Dugarte, Stuart, and Daniel Devine. 2021. "Can EU Judicial Intervention Increase Polity Scepticism? Quasi-experimental Evidence from Spain." *Journal of European Public Policy*, online first: 1–26.

Valverde, Mariana. 2015. *Chronotopes of Law*. New York, NY: Routledge.

Vanhala, Lisa. 2009. "Anti-discrimination Policy Actors and Their Use of Litigation Strategies." *Journal of European Public Policy*, 16(5): 738–754.

2011. *Making Rights a Reality?: Disability Rights Activists and Legal Mobilization*. New York, NY: Cambridge University Press.

2012. "Legal Opportunity Structures and the Paradox of Legal Mobilization by the Environmental Movement in the UK." *Law & Society Review*, 46(3): 523–556.

Vauchez, Antoine. 2008. "The Force of a Weak Field: Law and Lawyers in the Government of Europe." *International Political Sociology*, 2(2): 128–144.

2014. "Communities of International Litigators." In *The Oxford Handbook of International Adjudication*. Cesare Romano, Karen Alter, and Yuval Shany, eds., New York, NY: Oxford University Press.

2015. *Brokering Europe: Euro-Lawyers and the Making of a Transnational Polity*. New York, NY: Cambridge University Press.

2017. "EU Law Classics in the Making: Methodological Notes on Grands Arrêts at the European Court of Justice." In *EU Law Stories: Contextual and Critical Histories of European Jurisprudence*. Fernanda Nicola and Bill Davies, eds., New York, NY: Cambridge University Press.

Vauchez, Antoine, and Pierre France. 2021. *The Neoliberal Republic: Corporate Lawyers, Statecraft, and the Making of Public-Private France*. Ithaca, NY: Cornell University Press.

Vauchez, Antoine, and Bruno de Witte. 2013. *Lawyering Europe: European Law as a Transnational Social Field*. New York, NY: Hart.

Voeten, Erik. 2020. "Populism and Backlashes against International Courts." *Perspectives on Politics*, 18(2): 407–422.

Volcansek, Mary. 2007. "Appointing Judges the European Way." *Fordham Urban Law Journal*, 34(1): 363–385.

Voss, Reimer. 1986. "Erfahrungen und Probleme bei der Andwendung des Vorabentscheidungsverfahrens nacht Art. 177 EWGV." *Europarecht*, 1: 95–111.

1987. "Experiences and Problems in Applying Article 177 of the EEC Treaty – From the Point of View of a German Judge." In *Article 177 EEC: Experiences and Problems*. Henry Schermers, Christiaan Timmermans, Alfred Kellermann, and J. Stewart Watson, eds., New York, NY: Elsevier.

1993. "The National Perception of the Court of First Instance and the European Court of Justice." *Common Market Law Review*, 6: 1119–1134.

Wada, Takeshi. 2012. "Modularity and Transferability of Repertoires of Contention." *Social Problems*, 59(4): 544–571.

Weber, Max. 2013. *Economy and Society*, vol. II. Berkeley and Los Angeles, CA: University of California Press.

Weiler, Joseph H. H. 1987. "The European Court, National Courts and References for Preliminary Rulings- the Paradox of Success: A Revisionist View of Article 177 EEC." In *Article 177 EEC: Experiences and Problems*. Henry Schermers, Christiaan Timmermans, Alfred Kellermann, and J. Stewart Watson, eds., New York, NY: Elsevier.

1991. "The Transformation of Europe." *The Yale Law Journal*, 100: 2403–2483.

1993. "Journey to an Unknown Destination: A Retrospective and Prospective of the European Court of Justice in the Arena of Political Integration." *Journal of Common Market Studies*, 31(4): 417–446.

1994. "A Quiet Revolution: The European Court of Justice and Its Interlocutors." *Comparative Political Studies*, 26(4): 510–534.

2012. "In the Face of Crisis: Input Legitimacy, Output Legitimacy and the Political Messianism of European Integration." *Journal of European Integration*, 34(7): 825–841.

Wells, John, Bligala Raju, Hsueh-Yun Hung, William Weisburg, Linda Mandelco-Paul, and Don Brenner. 1987. "*Xylella fastidiosa* gen. nov., sp. nov: Gram-Negative, Xylem-Limited, Fastidious Plant Bacteria Related to *Xanthomonas* spp." *International Journal of Systematic Bacteriology*, 37(2): 136–143.

White, Steven, James Bullock, Danny Hooftman, and Daniel Chapman. 2017. "Modelling the Spread and Control of *Xylella fastidiosa* in the Early Stages of Invasion in Apulia, Italy." *Biological Invasions*, 19(6): 1825–1837.

Wind, Marlene. 2010. "The Nordics, the EU and the Reluctance towards Supranational Judicial Review." *Journal of Common Market Studies*, 48(4): 1039–1063.

Yom, Sean. 2015. "From Methodology to Practice: Inductive Iteration in Comparative Research." *Comparative Political Studies*, 48(5): 616–644.

Zakaria, Fareed. 1997. "The Rise of Illiberal Democracy." *Foreign Affairs*, 76(6): 22–43.

Zan, Stefano. 2003. *Fascicoli e Tribunali*. Bologna: Il Mulino.

Ziblatt, Daniel. 2006. *Structuring the State: The Formation of Italy and Germany and the Puzzle of Federalism*. Princeton, NJ: Princeton University Press.

Zürn, Michael. 2014. "The Politicization of World Politics and Its Effects." *European Political Science Review*, 6: 47–71.

2016. "Opening up Europe: Next Steps in Politicisation Research." *West European Politics*, 39(1): 164–182.

# INDEX

and ecological fallacies, 44
and judicial rebellions, 12, 13, 32, 88–95, 115–124
as "motor" of European integration, 12, 42, 124
as a "copernican revolution", 44
as inter-court competition, 88–95
as unintended consequence, 42
geneology, 40–42
resistance to, 13, 32, 57, 125
judicialization of politics, 3–4, 13, 39
and backlash to courts, 20–21, 34, 242–247, 268–272, 281, 296–298, 301–303
and compliance constituencies, 21, 245, 247, 268, 311
and dejudicialization, 20, 245
and judicial activism, 3–4, 6, 13–14, 24, 33, 39–40, 57, 91, 136, 312
and populism, 242, 244
and the politics of (non-)compliance, 34, 42, 242–250, 271–273, 277–278, 281–282, 295–299, 303
and the radiating effects of courts, 21, 247
as "juristocracy", 310
as a feedback loop, 18, 198, 299
as self-reinforcing, 6, 18, 20
as teleology, 21, 245
cold spots, 25, 201, 209–222, 281
hot spots, 25, 201, 205–211, 222–237, 247
Justice of the Peace of Milan, 162
Justice of the Peace of Rovigo, 134–139

Kaczyński, Jarosław, 315
Karl Prantl (case 16/83, 1984), 80
Karpik, Lucien, 200
Kelemen, R. Daniel, 27
Koopmans, Thijmen, 183

La Gazzetta del Mezzogiorno (newspaper), 248, 289, 296
La Mattina, Andrea, 274
La Repubblica (newspaper), 248, 251, 265, 296
Lahaille (joined cases 10/75 to 14/75, 1975), 193
Landgerichte (German lower regional courts), 69
Landry, Klaus, 132, 144–145, 151, 157–159, 164
Latour, Bruno, 99, 101
Law and Justice (PiS; political party), 315
lawyer capability, see legal mobilization
Le Monde (newspaper), 39, 148–149
Le Sportif (Belgian magazine), 134
Legal 500, 203, 205–207, 211, 222, 222–230
legal complex, 6, 131, 309
legal consciousness, 15, 17–18, 20, 132, 193, 200–201, 211, 218, 227, 233, 237, 247, 261, 273–276, 281, 311–312, 312

as a logic of integration, 201, 233–237
as a logic of partition, 200–201, 211–222
as defiance, 281, 300
legal mobilization
and access to justice, 5, 17, 33, 201, 237–238, 313
and cause lawyering, 9, 312
and civil disobedience, 243, 250, 291
and contentious politics, 21–22, 34, 241–247
and lawyer capability, 7, 132
and legal aid, 213
and modularity, 139–140, 155–156, 165, 189, 312
and party capability, 19–20
and political liberalism, 10, 317–319
and repertoires of strategic litigation, 5, 15–17, 20, 30, 33, 132, 139–141, 152, 155, 165, 189, 212, 231, 312
and resource deprivation, 211–217
and resource mobilization, 18–20, 199–201, 212–213, 228
and rights-consciousness, 4, 14, 33, 132, 136, 156, 309–312
and social movements, 7, 19–20, 302–303
and the "resurrection of civil society", 317–319
and the US civil rights movement, 277, 312
as a feedback loop, 18, 198, 275, 299
cold spots, 25, 201, 209–222, 281
ecologies of, 17, 201, 233, 235
hot spots, 25, 201, 205–211, 222–237, 247
jurist advocacy movements, 131
legal opportunity structures, 195–196, 247, 260
litigation support structure, 19, 131
one-shotters, 116, 212–216
repeat lawyers, 153
repeat players, 116, 229
legal opportunity structures, see legal mobilization
legal science, 10
Leonesio (case 93/71, 1972), 169, 192
Les Verts v. European Parliament (case 294/83, 1986), 9, 317
liberalism, political
struggles for, 10, 142, 308, 317
Linklaters, 224
litigation, see legal mobilization
lobbyists, 307
local knowledge, politics of, 246–247, 267, 280, 291, 299
Lodi, Silvano, 164
logic of integration, see legal consciousness
logic of partition, see legal consciousness
Long, Marceau, 99
Lord Denning, 198
Luisi and Carbone (case 286/82, 1982), 257

CAMBRIDGE STUDIES IN LAW AND SOCIETY

*Judicial Review and Bureaucratic Impact: International and Interdisciplinary Perspectives*
Edited by Marc Hertogh and Simon Halliday

*Immigrants at the Margins: Law, Race, and Exclusion in Southern Europe*
Kitty Calavita

*Lawyers and Regulation: The Politics of the Administrative Process*
Patrick Schmidt

*Law and Globalization from Below: Towards a Cosmopolitan Legality*
Edited by Boaventura de Sousa Santos and César A.
Rodríguez-Garavito

*Public Accountability: Designs, Dilemmas and Experiences*
Edited by Michael W. Dowdle

*Law, Violence and Sovereignty among West Bank Palestinians*
Tobias Kelly

*Legal Reform and Administrative Detention Powers in China*
Sarah Biddulph

*The Practice of Human Rights: Tracking Law between the Global and the Local*
Edited by Mark Goodale and Sally Engle Merry

*Judges beyond Politics in Democracy and Dictatorship: Lessons from Chile*
Lisa Hilbink

*Paths to International Justice: Social and Legal Perspectives*
Edited by Marie-Bénédicte Dembour and Tobias Kelly

*Law and Society in Vietnam: The Transition from Socialism in Comparative Perspective*
Mark Sidel

*Constitutionalizing Economic Globalization: Investment Rules and Democracy's Promise*
David Schneiderman

*The New World Trade Organization Knowledge Agreements: Second Edition*
Christopher Arup

*Justice and Reconciliation in Post-Apartheid South Africa*
Edited by François du Bois and Antje du Bois-Pedain

*Militarization and Violence against Women in Conflict Zones in the Middle East: A Palestinian Case-Study*
Nadera Shalhoub-Kevorkian

*Child Pornography and Sexual Grooming: Legal and Societal Responses*
Suzanne Ost

*Darfur and the Crime of Genocide*
John Hagan and Wenona Rymond-Richmond

*Fictions of Justice: The International Criminal Court and the Challenge of Legal Pluralism in Sub-Saharan Africa*
Kamari Maxine Clarke

*Conducting Law and Society Research: Reflections on Methods and Practices*
Simon Halliday and Patrick Schmidt

*Planted Flags: Trees, Land, and Law in Israel/Palestine*
Irus Braverman

*Culture under Cross-Examination: International Justice and the Special Court for Sierra Leone*
Tim Kelsall

*Cultures of Legality: Judicialization and Political Activism in Latin America*
Javier Couso, Alexandra Huneeus, and Rachel Sieder

*Courting Democracy in Bosnia and Herzegovina: The Hague Tribunal's Impact in a Postwar State*
Lara J. Nettelfield

*The Gacaca Courts, Post-Genocide Justice and Reconciliation in Rwanda: Justice without Lawyers*
Phil Clark

*Law, Society, and History: Themes in the Legal Sociology and Legal History of Lawrence M. Friedman*
Edited by Robert W. Gordon and Morton J. Horwitz

*After Abu Ghraib: Exploring Human Rights in America and the Middle East*
Shadi Mokhtari

*Adjudication in Religious Family Laws: Cultural Accommodation, Legal Pluralism, and Gender Equality in India*
Gopika Solanki

*Water on Tap: Rights and Regulation in the Transnational Governance of Urban Water Services*
Bronwen Morgan

*Elements of Moral Cognition: Rawls' Linguistic Analogy and the Cognitive Science of Moral and Legal Judgment*
John Mikhail

*Mitigation and Aggravation at Sentencing*
Edited by Julian V. Roberts

Edited by John R. Bowen, Christophe Bertossi, Jan Willem Duyvendak, and Mona Lena Krook

*Environmental Litigation in China: A Study in Political Ambivalence*
Rachel E. Stern

*Indigeneity and Legal Pluralism in India: Claims, Histories, Meanings*
Pooja Parmar

*Paper Tiger: Law, Bureaucracy and the Developmental State in Himalayan India*
Nayanika Mathur

*Religion, Law and Society*
Russell Sandberg

*The Experiences of Face Veil Wearers in Europe and the Law*
Edited by Eva Brems

*The Contentious History of the International Bill of Human Rights*
Christopher N. J. Roberts

*Transnational Legal Orders*
Edited by Terence C. Halliday and Gregory Shaffer

*Lost in China? Law, Culture and Society in Post-1997 Hong Kong*
Carol A. G. Jones

*Security Theology, Surveillance and the Politics of Fear*
Nadera Shalhoub-Kevorkian?

*Opposing the Rule of Law: How Myanmar's Courts Make Law and Order*
Nick Cheesman

*Ironies of Colonial Governance: Law, Custom and Justice in Colonial India*
James Jaffe

*The Clinic and the Court: Law, Medicine and Anthropology*
Edited by Ian Harper, Tobias Kelly, and Akshay Khanna

*The World of Indicators: The Making of Government Knowledge through Quantification*
Edited by Richard Rottenburg, Sally E. Merry, Sung-Joon Park, and Johanna Mugler

*Contesting Immigration Policy in Court: Legal Activism and Its Radiating Effects in the United States and France*
Leila Kawar

*The Quiet Power of Indicators: Measuring Governance, Corruption, and Rule of Law*
Edited by Sally Engle Merry, Kevin E. Davis, and Benedict Kingsbury

*Buried in the Heart: Women, Complex Victimhood and the War in Northern Uganda*
Erin Baines

*Palaces of Hope: The Anthropology of Global Organizations*
Edited by Ronald Niezen and Maria Sapignoli

*The Politics of Bureaucratic Corruption in Post-Transitional Eastern Europe*
Marina Zaloznaya

*Revisiting the Law and Governance of Trafficking, Forced Labor and Modern Slavery*
Edited by Prabha Kotiswaran

*Incitement on Trial: Prosecuting International Speech Crimes*
Richard Ashby Wilson

*Criminalizing Children: Welfare and the State in Australia*
David McCallum

*Global Lawmakers: International Organizations in the Crafting of World Markets*
Susan Block-Lieb and Terence C. Halliday

*Duties to Care: Dementia, Relationality and Law*
Rosie Harding

*Insiders, Outsiders, Injuries, and Law: Revisiting "The Oven Bird's Song"*
Edited by Mary Nell Trautner

*Hunting Justice: Displacement, Law, and Activism in the Kalahari*
Maria Sapignoli

*Injury and Injustice: The Cultural Politics of Harm and Redress*
Edited by Anne Bloom, David M. Engel, and Michael McCann

*Ruling Before the Law: The Politics of Legal Regimes in China and Indonesia*
William Hurst

*The Powers of Law: A Comparative Analysis of Sociopolitical Legal Studies*
Mauricio García-Villegas

*A Sociology of Justice in Russia*
Edited by Marina Kurkchiyan and Agnieszka Kubal

*Constituting Religion: Islam, Liberal Rights, and the Malaysian State*
Tamir Moustafa

*The Invention of the Passport: Surveillance, Citizenship and the State, Second Edition*
John C. Torpey

*Law's Trials: The Performance of Legal Institutions in the US "War on Terror"*
Richard L. Abel

*Law's Wars: The Fate of the Rule of Law in the US "War on Terror"*
Richard L. Abel

*Transforming Gender Citizenship: The Irresistible Rise of Gender Quotas in Europe*
Edited by Eléonore Lépinard and Ruth Rubio-Marín

*Muslim Women's Quest for Justice: Gender, Law and Activism in India*
Mengia Hong Tschalaer

*Children as 'Risk': Sexual Exploitation and Abuse by Children and Young People*
Anne-Marie McAlinden

*The Legal Process and the Promise of Justice: Studies Inspired by the Work of Malcolm Feeley*
Jonathan Simon, Rosann Greenspan, Hadar Aviram

*Gift Exchanges: The Transnational History of a Political Idea*
Grégoire Mallard

*Measuring Justice: Quantitative Accountability and the National Prosecuting Authority in South Africa*
Johanna Mugler

*Negotiating the Power of NGOs: Women's Legal Rights in South Africa*
Reem Wael

*Indigenous Water Rights in Law and Regulation: Lessons from Comparative Experience*
Elizabeth Jane Macpherson

*The Edge of Law: Legal Geographies of a War Crimes Court*
Alex Jeffrey

*Everyday Justice: Law, Ethnography, and Injustice*
Sandra Brunnegger

*The Uncounted: Politics of Data in Global Health*
Sara L. M. Davis

*Transnational Legal Ordering of Criminal Justice*
Gregory Shaffer and Ely Aaronson

*Five Republics and One Tradition*
Pablo Ruiz-Tagle

*The Law Multiple: Judgment and Knowledge in Practice*
Irene van Oorschot

*Health as a Human Right: The Politics and Judicialisation of Health in Brazil*
Octávio Luiz Motta Ferraz

*Shari'a, Inshallah: Finding God in Somali Legal Politics*
Mark Fathi Massoud

*Policing for Peace: Institutions, Expectations, and Security in Divided Societies*
Matthew Nanes

*Rule of Law Intermediaries: Brokering Influence in Myanmar*
Kristina Simion

*Lactation at Work: Expressed Milk, Expressing Beliefs, and the Expressive Value of Law*
Elizabeth A. Hoffmann

*The Archival Politics of International Courts*
Henry Redwood

*Global Pro Bono: Causes, Context, and Contestation*
Edited by Scott L. Cummings, Fabio de Sa e Silva and Louise G. Trubek

*The Practice and Problems of Transnational Counter-Terrorism*
Fiona de Londras

*Decoupling: Gender Injustice in China's Divorce Courts*
Ethan Michelson

*Anti-Constitutional Populism*
Martin Krygier, Adam Czarnota and Wojciech Sadurski

*The Ghostwriters: Lawyers and the Politics behind the Judicial Construction of Europe*
Tommaso Pavone

CPSIA information can be obtained
at www.ICGtesting.com
Printed in the USA
LVHW020924081122
732630LV00008B/339

9 781009 074988